The Institute of Chartered Accountants in England and Wales

TAX COMPLIANCE
FA2014

For exams from 2015

Study Manual

ICAEW

www.icaew.com

Tax Compliance
The Institute of Chartered Accountants in England and Wales

ISBN: 978-0-85760-998-4
Previous ISBN: 978-0-85760-860-4

First edition 2013
Third edition 2014

British Library Cataloguing-in-Publication Data
A catalogue record for this book is available from the British Library

Printed in the United Kingdom by Polestar Wheatons

Polestar Wheatons
Hennock Road
Marsh Barton
Exeter
EX2 8RP

Your learning materials are printed on paper obtained from traceable,
sustainable sources.

Welcome to ICAEW

I am delighted that you have chosen ICAEW to progress your journey towards joining the chartered accountancy profession. It is one of the best decisions I also made.

The role of the accountancy profession in the world's economies has never been more important. People making financial decisions need knowledge and guidance based on the highest technical and ethical standards. ICAEW Chartered Accountants provide this better than anyone. They challenge people and organisations to think and act differently, to provide clarity and rigour, and so help create and sustain prosperity all over the world.

As a world leader of the accountancy and finance profession, we are proud to promote, develop and support over 142,000 chartered accountants worldwide. Our members have the knowledge, skills and commitment to maintain the highest professional standards and integrity. They are part of something special, and now, so are you. It's with our support and dedication that our members and hopefully yourself, will realise career ambitions, maintain a professional edge and contribute to the profession.

You are now on your journey towards joining the accountancy profession, a profession that offers a highly rewarding career with endless opportunities. By choosing to study for our world-leading chartered accountancy qualification, the ACA, you too have made the first of many great decisions in your career.

You are in good company, with a network of over 20,000 students around the world made up of like-minded people, you are all supported by ICAEW. We are here to support you as you progress through your studies and career, we will be with you every step of the way, visit page x to review the key resources available as you study.

I wish you the best of luck with your studies and look forward to welcoming you to the profession in the future.

Michael Izza
Chief Executive
ICAEW

Contents

- Introduction vii
- Tax Compliance ix
- Key Resources x

1. Ethics	1
2. Income tax computation	23
3. Property income	49
4. Pensions	65
5. Employment income	87
6. Trading income	113
7. Capital allowances – plant and machinery	141
8. Partnerships	167
9. Cash basis of accounting	183
10. Income tax for trusts	197
11. Chargeable gains for individuals and trustees	213
12. Shares and securities	239
13. Leases	253
14. Overseas aspects of income tax and capital gains tax	267
15. National insurance and further administrative matters	289
16. Inheritance tax – basic principles	307
17. Inheritance tax – death estate and valuation	333
18. Inheritance tax – other aspects	357
19. Corporation tax	375
20. Chargeable gains for companies	399
21. Additional aspects of corporation tax	423
22. Value added tax	451
23. Stamp taxes	485
Index	503

ICAEW

1   Introduction

ACA Overview

The ICAEW chartered accountancy qualification, the ACA, is one of the most advanced learning and professional development programmes available. Its integrated components provide you with an in-depth understanding across accountancy, finance and business. Combined, they help build the technical knowledge, professional skills and practical experience needed to become an ICAEW Chartered Accountant.

Each component is designed to complement each other, which means that you can put theory into practice and can understand and apply what you learn to your day-to-day work. The components are:

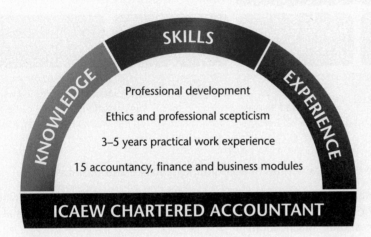

Professional development

ICAEW Chartered Accountants are known for their professionalism and expertise. Professional development prepares you to successfully handle a variety of different situations that you encounter throughout your career.

The ACA qualification improves your ability and performance in seven key areas:

*   Adding value
*   Communication
*   Consideration
*   Decision making
*   Problem solving
*   Team working
*   Technical competence

Ethics and professional scepticism

Ethics is more than just knowing the rules around confidentiality, integrity, objectivity and independence.

It's about identifying ethical dilemmas, understanding the implications and behaving appropriately. We integrate ethics throughout the ACA qualification to develop your ethical capabilities – so you will always know how to make the right decisions and justify them.

3-5 years practical work experience

Practical work experience is done as part of a training agreement with one of our 2,850 authorised training employers or authorised training principals around the world. You need to complete 450 days, which normally takes between three and five years. The knowledge, skills and experience you gain as part of your training agreement are invaluable, giving you the opportunity to put what you're learning into practice.

15 accountancy, finance and business modules

You will gain in-depth knowledge across a broad range of topics in accountancy, finance and business.

There are 15 modules over three levels. These can be taken in any order with the exception of the Case Study which has to be attempted last. You must pass every exam (or receive credit) – there are no options. This ensures that once qualified, all ICAEW Chartered Accountants have a consistent level of knowledge, skills and experience.

Certificate Level

There are six modules that introduce the fundamentals of accountancy, finance and business.

Each module is examined by a 1.5 hour computer-based assessment which can be sat at any time. You may be eligible for credit for some modules if you have studied accounting, finance, law or business at degree level or through another professional qualification.

These six modules also provide a stand-alone certificate, the ICAEW Certificate in Finance, Accounting and Business (ICAEW CFAB). Once you have completed all six Certificate Level assessments, you can apply for the ICAEW CFAB certificate of completion, visit icaew.com/cfab for more information.

The aim of the Principles of Taxation module was to enable students to understand the general objectives of tax and to calculate income tax, national insurance contributions, capital gains tax, corporation tax and VAT in straightforward scenarios.

Professional Level

The next six modules build on the fundamentals and test your understanding and ability to use technical knowledge in real-life scenarios. Each module has a 2.5-3 hour exam, which are available to sit four times per year. These modules are flexible and can be taken in any order. The Business Planning: Taxation and Business Strategy modules in particular will help you to progress to the Advanced Level.

The knowledge base that was put into place in the Principles of Taxation module is developed further in the Tax Compliance module, which enables students to prepare tax computations for individuals and companies, again in straightforward scenarios and recognise the ethical issues which can arise in the course of performing tax work.

The Business Planning: Taxation module requires students to apply technical knowledge and professional skills to identify and resolve tax issues that arise in the context of preparing tax computations and to advise on tax-efficient strategies for businesses and individuals.

Advanced Level

The Corporate Reporting and Strategic Business Management modules test understanding and strategic decision making at a senior level. They present real-life scenarios, with increased complexity and wider implications from the Professional Level modules.

The Case Study presents a complex business issue which challenges your ability to problem solve, identify the ethical implications and provide an effective solution. The Case Study tests through contextualisation the ability to apply your knowledge, skills and experience.

The Advanced Level exams are fully open book, so they replicate a real-life scenario where all the resources are at your fingertips. The Corporate Reporting and Strategic Business Management exams are 3.5 hours and the Case Study is 4 hours. The Strategic Business Management exam will consist of two scenario-based questions, forming a stepping stone to the Case Study.

Access further exam resources and support at icaew.com/dashboard

2   Tax Compliance

The full syllabus and technical knowledge grids can be found within the module study guide. Visit icaew.com/dashboard for this and more resources.

2.1   Module aim

To enable students to prepare tax computations for individuals and companies in straightforward scenarios.

On completion of this module, students will be able to:

- Recognise the ethical issues arising in the course of performing tax work and identify the obligations the UK system of tax imposes on taxpayers and the implications for taxpayers of non-compliance

- Calculate the capital gains tax payable by individuals and trustees

- Calculate the amounts of inheritance tax due on lifetime transfers and transfers on death by individuals, personal representatives and trustees

- Calculate the amounts of income tax owed by or owed to individuals and trustees

- Calculate the amounts of national insurance payable by individuals, businesses and companies

- Calculate the corporation tax liabilities of companies

- Calculate the amount of VAT owed by or owed to businesses

- Calculate the amount of stamp taxes due in straightforward transactions.

Taxes covered in this module

- Capital gains tax
- Corporation tax
- Income tax
- Inheritance tax
- National insurance
- Stamp taxes
- VAT

Method of assessment

The Tax Compliance module will be examined using traditional paper based assessments. The paper based exam will be 2.5 hours in length. The exam will test each of the taxes on the syllabus as a discrete topic. Candidates may use the appropriate tax tables.

The exam will consist of four questions. Ethics and law may be tested in any of the questions.

2.2   Specification grid

This grid shows the relative weightings of subjects within this module and should guide the relative study time spent on each. Over time the marks available in the assessment will equate to the weightings below, while slight variations may occur in individual assessments to enable suitably rigorous questions to be set.

		Weighting (%)
1	Ethics and law	5-10
2	Capital taxes	15-25
3	Income tax	30-40
4	National insurance contributions	2-10
5	Corporation tax	10-20
6	VAT & stamp taxes	10-20

This grid provides guidance on the relative weighting between knowledge and skills:

	Weighting (%)
Knowledge	65-75
Skills	25-35

3 Key Resources

Student support team

Our student support team are here to help you as much as possible, providing full support throughout your studies.

T +44 (0)1908 248 250
F +44 (0)1908 248 069
E studentsupport@icaew.com

Student website

The student area of our website provides you with information on exam applications, deadlines, results and regulations as well as applying for credit for prior learning (CPL). The study resources section includes advice from the examiners, module syllabi, past papers and sample papers, webinars and study guides. The study guides are designed to help put the learning for each module into context and highlight the practical significance of what you'll learn. They also include the syllabus, technical knowledge grids and learning outcomes for each module, enabling you to gain an overview of how your learning links to the qualification. Visit icaew.com/dashboard for these resources and more.

If you are studying for the ICAEW CFAB qualification, you can access exam resources and support at icaew.com/cfab

Online student community

The online student community is a forum to ask questions, gain study and exam advice from fellow ACA and ICAEW CFAB students and access our free webinars. There are also regular Ask a Tutor sessions to help you with key technical topics and exam papers. Access the community at icaew.com/studentcommunity

Tuition

The ICAEW Partner in Learning scheme recognises tuition providers who comply with our core principles of quality course delivery. If you are receiving structured tuition with an ICAEW Partner in Learning, make sure you know how and when you can contact your tutors for extra help. If you are not receiving structured tuition and are interested in classroom, online or distance learning tuition, take a look at our recognised Partner in Learning tuition providers in your area, on our website icaew.com/dashboard

Faculties and Special Interest Groups

Faculties and special interest groups support and develop members and students in areas of work and industry sectors that are of particular interest.

Our seven faculties provide knowledge, events and essential technical resources. They cover Audit and Assurance, Corporate Finance, Finance and Management, Financial Reporting, Financial Services, Information Technology and Tax. As an ACA or ICAEW CFAB student, you are entitled to register to receive either complimentary factsheets from the Financial Reporting Faculty or an e-newsletter from one faculty of your choice each year throughout your studies.

Our 12 special interest groups provide practical support, information and representation within a range of industry sectors including Charity and Voluntary, Entertainment and Media, Farming and Rural Business, Forensic and Expert Witness, Healthcare, Insolvency and Restructuring, Interim Management, Solicitors, Tourism and Hospitality, Public Sector, Valuation and Non-Executive Directors. As an ACA student you can receive free provisional membership of one group each year throughout your studies, apart from the Public Sector group, where a subscription charge is required.

Find out more about faculties and special interest groups at icaew.com/facultiesandsigs

Library & Information Service

The Library & Information Service is ICAEW's world-leading accountancy and business library. You have access to online and print facilities which include company information, country and sector resources, economic forecasts and eBooks, with services that include book loans, document delivery and help with research queries. Visit icaew.com/library for more information.

CHAPTER 1

Ethics

Introduction

Learning objectives

- Identify the five fundamental principles and guidance given in the IESBA Code of Ethics for Professional Accountants and the ICAEW Code of Ethics in relation to a tax practice with regard to:
  - The threats and safeguards framework
  - Disclosure of information
  - Conflicts of interest
  - Confidentiality

- Identify the law and the guidance in the ICAEW Code of Ethics with regard to:
  - New client procedures
  - HM Revenue & Customs errors
  - Money laundering
  - Tax avoidance and tax evasion

- Identify legal and ethical issues arising from tax work undertaken and explain the significance of these issues

Specific syllabus references for this chapter are 1a, 1b and 1c.

Syllabus links

In the ethics chapter of your Principles of Taxation study manual, which you should now review, you learned about ethical issues in relation to tax work. This specifically included elements of the IESBA Code of Ethics for Professional Accountants and ICAEW Code of Ethics.

In this chapter we extend this knowledge by giving greater consideration to practical scenarios, including guidance drawn from Professional Conduct in Relation to Taxation.

Examination context

In the examination candidates may be required to:

- Identify the recommended course of action to be taken in response to an ethical issue within the ethical conflict resolution framework

- Demonstrate knowledge of appropriate guidance relating to new clients, conflicts of interest, HMRC errors and disclosure of information

- Determine whether action taken by a client amounts to tax avoidance or tax evasion and explain the consequences

- Demonstrate knowledge of anti-money laundering regulations and procedures to be followed by professional accountants

1 Fundamental principles, threats and safeguards

Section overview

- The International Ethics Standards Board for Accountants (IESBA) is an independent standard-setting body which aims to serve the public interest by setting robust, internationally appropriate ethics standards for professional accountants worldwide.

- The ICAEW Code of Ethics is derived in part from the IESBA 'Code of Ethics for Professional Accountants'. In particular, the five fundamental principles of professional ethics for accountants appear in both.

- The ICAEW Code of Ethics ('the Code') also contains additional requirements and discussion.

- 'Professional Conduct in Relation to Taxation' has been produced by various accountancy and taxation bodies including the ICAEW. It includes practical advice about ethical and legal issues arising in the course of tax work and considers the relationship with both clients and HMRC.

1.1 Identifying fundamental principles

The Codes require professional accountants to comply with the five fundamental principles. Identifying instances where threats arise to the fundamental principles is necessary if the professional accountant is to handle ethical issues appropriately.

Definition

Professional accountant: A member of the ICAEW.

Professional accountants have a responsibility to act in the public interest as well as considering their client or employer. The Codes require professional accountants to comply with the following five fundamental principles:

- Integrity
- Objectivity
- Professional competence and due care
- Confidentiality
- Professional behaviour

Worked example: Identifying the most relevant principles

You have recently completed your first tax return for Mrs Jennings. Her son, whom you have not met before, arrives at your office and starts shouting at your colleagues. He demands to see the workings for his mother's tax return, saying that her enormous tax bill cannot possibly be correct and that this is causing his mother anxiety.

Requirement

Identify which of the five fundamental principles is most threatened here and the nature of the threat.

Solution

Confidentiality is threatened here. Mrs Jennings' son has asked for information about his mother's tax return. You owe a duty of confidentiality to Mrs Jennings, so you are not free to disclose any information, nor to discuss her return with anyone else. There is no legal or professional right or duty to disclose the information you have been asked for.

The threat here is an intimidation threat (see below) from the son's aggressive behaviour.

1.2 Identifying threats

Compliance with these fundamental principles may be threatened by:

- Self-interest threats
- Self-review threats
- Advocacy threats
- Familiarity threats
- Intimidation threats

Interactive question 1: Identifying threats and principles affected

[Difficulty level: Exam standard]

Having drafted Whizzco Ltd's corporation tax computation, you have emailed the FD with a few questions, commenting that certain allowable expenses are very high compared to last year. The FD replies 'I decided to double all the real amounts as I didn't want the company to have to pay tax this year. I know we shouldn't really claim the extra, so the return won't be quite correct, but nobody's likely to check, are they? So please use the figures I've given you. If you do, I promise I'll pass you some nice tax work that's coming up for one of Whizzco's subsidiaries.'

Requirement

Identify which type of threat to fundamental principles arises here and explain which three of the five fundamental principles are most threatened.

See **Answer** at the end of this chapter.

1.3 Safeguards

Certain safeguards may increase the likelihood of identifying or deterring unethical behaviour. Such safeguards may be created by the accounting profession, legislation, regulation or an employing organisation and the nature of the safeguards to be applied will vary depending on the circumstances.

Worked example: Appropriate safeguards

Mr Shah is a successful new entrepreneur who is considering engaging a professional accountant for the first time to help with his tax and your name as an ICAEW member working in tax has been recommended to him.

Mr Shah's brother had a bad experience with a previous accountant who apparently was not competent. Mr Shah is keen to know what standards apply to your work and to check that if he has any problem, he can make a complaint.

Requirement

List four safeguards which it may reassure Mr Shah to know of.

Solution

- The educational, training and experience requirements for entry into the profession
- The continuing professional development requirements
- The ICAEW Code
- The complaints procedures available, within your firm and/or to the ICAEW

2 Ethical conflict resolution

Section overview

- To ensure compliance with the fundamental principles a professional accountant may need to resolve a conflict in applying the principles.

- Having considered the six recommended factors, steps to resolve the conflict are to be followed. If the conflict cannot be resolved the professional accountant should, where possible, refuse to remain associated with the matter creating the conflict.

2.1 Conflict resolution process

When initiating either a formal or informal conflict resolution process, a professional accountant should consider the following six factors:

- Relevant facts
- Relevant parties
- Ethical issues involved
- Fundamental principles related to the matter in question
- Established internal procedures
- Alternative courses of action

Having considered these issues, the appropriate course of action can be determined which resolves the conflict with all or some of the five fundamental principles. If the matter remains unresolved, the professional accountant should consult with other appropriate persons within the firm for help in obtaining resolution.

Where a matter involves a conflict with, or within, an organisation, a professional accountant should also consider consulting with those charged with governance of the organisation such as the board of directors.

If a significant conflict cannot be resolved, a professional accountant may wish to obtain professional advice from the relevant professional body or legal advisors, and thereby obtain guidance on ethical and legal issues without breaching confidentiality. The ICAEW runs a confidential ethics helpline service.

It is advisable for the professional accountant to document the issue and details of any discussions held or decisions taken concerning that issue.

It is possible that, after exhausting all relevant possibilities, the ethical conflict remains unresolved. A professional accountant should, where possible, refuse to remain associated with the matter creating the conflict. The professional accountant may determine that, in the circumstances, it is appropriate to withdraw from the engagement team or specific assignment, or to resign altogether from the engagement or the firm.

Interactive question 2: Ethical conflict resolution   [Difficulty level: Exam standard]

Jasmine is a professional accountant working in the tax department of a large ICAEW firm. An ethical issue has arisen in regard to one particular client, an ongoing personal disagreement which Jasmine considers threatens her objectivity and possibly her professional behaviour.

Jasmine has followed the suggested procedure for conflict resolution including speaking to her line manager. She has been advised to see how the relationship with the client goes over the next few months, a particularly busy time for the firm, and take care to be polite to the client. Jasmine is concerned that the conflict remains.

Requirement

Outline five options open to Jasmine in this situation.

See **Answer** at the end of this chapter.

3 Confidentiality & disclosure of information

Section overview

- A professional accountant has a duty to respect the confidentiality of information acquired as a result of professional and business relationships.

- In limited circumstances, a professional accountant may disclose client information to third parties without the client's permission.

3.1 Confidentiality

The fundamental principle of confidentiality requires professional accountants

'To respect the confidentiality of information acquired as a result of professional and business relationships and, therefore, not disclose any such information to third parties without proper and specific authority, unless there is a legal or professional right or duty to disclose, nor use the information for the personal advantage of the member or third parties.'

3.2 When to disclose

Client information may not be disclosed without the client's consent unless there is an express legal or professional right or duty to disclose.

A professional accountant may disclose confidential information if:

- Disclosure is authorised by the client or the employer.

- Disclosure is required by law, for example:

    - Production of documents or other provision of evidence in the course of legal proceedings, or

    - Disclosure to the appropriate public authorities of infringements of the law, eg under anti-money laundering legislation.

- There is a professional duty or right to disclose, when not prohibited by law:

    - To comply with the quality review of a member body or professional body
    - To respond to an inquiry or investigation by a member body or regulatory body
    - To protect the professional interests of a professional accountant in legal proceedings
    - To comply with technical standards and ethics requirements

Worked example: Disclosure of information

You have prepared tax returns for Grimco Ltd for that last two years. HMRC makes an informal request for certain information you hold about your client, over and above what was in the last tax return. You ask Grimco Ltd's directors for permission to forward this information to HMRC but they refuse. A few weeks later, HMRC issues a statutory demand for the information. You inform Grimco Ltd's directors and again they ask you not to disclose the information.

Requirement

Explain how confidentiality applies at each stage in this scenario.

Solution

Information relating to Grimco Ltd may not be disclosed without the directors' consent unless there is an express legal or professional right or duty to disclose.

An informal request from HMRC does not give rise to a legal right to disclose. You must therefore respect the directors' instructions to keep the information confidential.

The statutory demand, assuming it is validly issued, does impose a legal obligation. The information must be disclosed to HMRC despite your client's request that it be withheld.

It is possible to include in client engagement letters authorisation to disclose information in this type of situation.

4 Conflicts of interest

Section overview

- The Code requires a professional accountant to take reasonable steps to avoid, identify and resolve conflicts of interest.
- Both actual and perceived conflicts must be considered.
- The Code and Professional Conduct in Relation to Taxation give examples of situations in which a conflict may arise.

4.1 The threat of a conflict of interest

The fundamental principle of objectivity requires professional accountants to ensure that bias, conflict of interest or undue influence of others do not override professional or business judgements. A professional accountant must take reasonable steps to identify circumstances that could pose a conflict of interest.

A conflict may arise between the firm and the client or between two conflicting clients being managed by the same firm, for example where a firm acts for:

- A client which has specific interests which conflict with those of the firm
- Financial involvements between the client and the firm eg where a loan is made by or to a client
- Both a husband and wife in a divorce settlement
- A company and for its directors in their personal capacity
- A partnership and for its partners in their personal capacity
- Two competing businesses

Professional Conduct in Relation to Taxation mentions also the potential for conflict where a professional accountant is seconded to HMRC. See section 4.3 below.

Evaluation of threats includes consideration as to whether the professional accountant has any business interests or relationships with the client or a third party that could give rise to threats. If threats are other than clearly insignificant, safeguards should be considered and applied as necessary.

4.2 Safeguards

Depending upon the circumstances giving rise to the conflict, safeguards should ordinarily include the professional accountant in public practice:

- Notifying the client of the firm's business interest or activities that may represent a conflict of interest.
- Notifying all known relevant parties that the professional accountant is acting for two or more parties in respect of a matter where their respective interests are in conflict.
- Notifying the client that the professional accountant does not act exclusively for any one client in the provision of proposed services (for example, in a particular market sector or with respect to a specific service).

In each case the professional accountant should obtain the consent of the relevant parties to act.

Where a professional accountant has requested consent from a client to act for another party (which may or may not be an existing client) and that consent has been refused, then he must not continue to act for one of the parties in the matter giving rise to the conflict of interest.

The following additional safeguards should also be considered:

- The use of separate engagement teams.
- Procedures to prevent access to information (eg strict physical separation of such teams, confidential and secure data filing).
- Clear guidelines for members of the engagement team on issues of security and confidentiality.
- The use of actual and perceived confidentiality agreements signed by employees and partners of the firm; to ensure actual and perceived confidentiality.

- Regular review of the application of safeguards by a senior individual not involved with relevant client engagements.

Where a conflict of interest poses a threat to one or more of the fundamental principles that cannot be eliminated or reduced to an acceptable level through the application of safeguards, the professional accountant should conclude that it is not appropriate to accept a specific engagement or that resignation from one or more conflicting engagements is required.

4.3 Secondment to HMRC

From time to time professionals outside HMRC may be seconded to HMRC. A professional accountant might be seconded, for example, to assist in drafting new tax legislation. Any potential conflict of interest, actual or perceived, needs to be carefully managed.

The secondee should serve the interests of HMRC whilst on secondment and steps should be taken to remove them from any situation where there is scope for a conflict of interest between HMRC and the seconding organisation. In particular:

- The secondee should not be involved in matters relating to the seconding organisation or the clients it is representing while working for HMRC.

- Following the end of the secondment, the secondee should not be involved in the affairs of any taxpayer he was involved with at HMRC for a significant period.

Interactive question 3: Conflict of interest   [Difficulty level: Intermediate]

A professional accountant in public practice has had two partners, Eric and Ernie, as clients for many years. Eric is intending to sell his share of the partnership to Ernie so that Ernie can continue as a sole trader. Both have asked if you will be their adviser.

Requirement

Outline the accountant's position with regard to the potential conflict of interest.

See **Answer** at the end of this chapter.

5 New client procedures

Section overview

- Particular procedures are needed when taking on new clients.
- The ICAEW requires practising members to hold professional indemnity insurance.
- Professional accountants are subject to the Data Protection Act.

5.1 Client and engagement acceptance

Before accepting a new client, a professional accountant in public practice shall determine whether acceptance would create any threats to compliance with the fundamental principles. Potential threats to integrity or professional behaviour may be created from, for example, questionable issues associated with the client (its owners, management or activities). A professional accountant in public practice shall evaluate the significance of any threats and apply safeguards when necessary to eliminate them or reduce them to an acceptable level.

The fundamental principle of professional competence and due care imposes an obligation on a professional accountant in public practice to provide only those services that the professional accountant in public practice is competent to perform. Before accepting a specific client engagement, a professional accountant in public practice shall determine whether acceptance would create any threats to compliance with the fundamental principles. For example, a self-interest threat to professional competence and due care is created if the engagement team does not possess, and cannot acquire, the competencies necessary to properly carry out the engagement.

5.2 Engagement letter

The contractual relationship should be governed by an appropriate letter of engagement in order that the scope of both the client's and the professional accountant's responsibilities are made clear.

An explanation as to whether an accountant is acting as agent or principal should be given in the engagement letter. The letter should also explain the scope of the client's and the accountant's responsibilities in each case.

Every contractual relationship should be covered; if the member acts for a partnership and also for one or more of the partners, then the partnership and each partner acted for are separate clients for the purposes of these guidelines. Likewise, if the member acts for a husband and wife, each is a separate client.

Authority to disclose information in certain circumstances should be considered for inclusion in the engagement letter. See sections 3.2 and 6.1.

5.3 Agent or principal

It is very important that it is understood when an accountant is acting as an agent on behalf of a client and when he is acting as the principal. The two different capacities carry different degrees of risk and potential liability.

5.3.1 Agent

An accountant acts as agent when he merely prepares documents on behalf of a client. The client retains responsibility for the accuracy of the document itself. The accountant is thus an agent when performing tax compliance work such as preparing and submitting a tax return on behalf of a client. The client is required to sign the return prior to its submission.

The accountant takes no responsibility for any information which he passes on to the tax authorities when acting as an agent. The accountant is not normally liable to HMRC if any of the information proves to be incorrect. An accountant who prepares a return on behalf of a client is however still responsible to the client for the accuracy of the return based on the information provided.

Acting as an agent as opposed to a principal is considered to be a low-risk activity.

Note that agent in this legal context is not to be confused with HMRC's use of the word agent to refer to any professional authorised to deal with them on a taxpayer's behalf.

5.3.2 Principal

An accountant acts as principal when he provides advice to the client as to the taxation consequences of different courses of action. The accountant takes full responsibility for the advice given and may be liable to the taxpayer in the event the advice turns out to be incorrect or inappropriate.

Acting as a principal as opposed to an agent is considered to be a high-risk activity.

Where an accountant does not have the professional skill required to act as a principal in a particular case, it may still be appropriate to accept the engagement if the opinion of a suitably qualified accountant is sought.

5.4 Professional indemnity insurance

Every qualified member of the ICAEW who is in public practice and resident in the United Kingdom or Republic of Ireland is required to have professional indemnity insurance (PII).

The ICAEW's PII Regulations sets the minimum amount of indemnity as follows:

- If the gross fee income of a firm is less than £600,000, the minimum limit of indemnity must be equal to two and a half times its gross fee income, with a minimum of £100,000.

- Otherwise, the minimum is £1.5 million.

Employed members will normally be covered by their employer's insurance policy. The PII regulations apply to individual members but in practical terms professional indemnity insurance usually covers their practising entity, for example their partnership or their sole practice.

A member ceasing to be in public practice should ensure that cover remains in place for at least two years. It is recommended that members consider maintaining cover for six years after they cease to practise.

 Interactive question 4: Professional indemnity insurance [Difficulty level: Intermediate]

Dewi and Dilys are professional accountants who are resigning as employees of a large accountancy firm to set up their own tax practice in partnership. They know they need professional indemnity insurance (PII) cover but do not know the level required. They only expect turnover of around £60,000 in their first year of trading and wonder whether it would be acceptable to wait a year before taking out a PII policy.

Requirement

Answer the questions raised by Dewi and Dilys with regard to PII cover.

See **Answer** at the end of this chapter.

5.5 Data protection

Anyone who handles personal information has a number of legal obligations to protect that information under the Data Protection Act 1998.

Every organisation that processes personal information must notify the Information Commissioner's Office (ICO) unless it is exempt, and be entered onto the ICO's register of data controllers. The only exemption at all applicable to practising firms of accountants would be where computers are not used in any way to process or store any client information, records or correspondence.

Failure to notify is a strict liability criminal offence.

The eight data protection principles include requirements to ensure that data held is accurate, up to date, securely stored, and used for a specified, lawful purpose.

6 HM Revenue & Customs errors

 Section overview

- Professional Conduct in Relation to Taxation gives guidance to professional accountants on various issues specific to tax, including HM Revenue & Customs (HMRC) errors.

- Certain steps must be followed in the event that an HMRC error results in a client paying too little tax, or receiving an excessive repayment.

6.1 HMRC errors in client's favour

It may be apparent to the professional accountant that a mistake has been made by HMRC, such as:

- The raising of an inadequate assessment
- An under collection of tax or interest
- An excessive repayment of tax or interest

The mistake may be

- One of law
- A calculation or clerical error
- A misunderstanding on the part of HMRC of the facts as presented

Professional accountants are advised to include in their letters of engagement authority to advise HMRC of errors, so that further consent from the client is not needed. Where no such authority has been obtained, the procedure set out below must be followed.

6.2 Disclosure of HMRC errors

Where a professional accountant becomes aware that HMRC, in full possession of the facts, has made a material error in dealing with the affairs of a client, then unless the tax at stake is considered trivial, the professional accountant should refer the matter to the client.

The client should be:

- Asked to authorise the professional accountant to advise HMRC of the error.

- Warned of the possible legal consequences of refusal to give the authority sought, including interest and penalties and possible criminal prosecution.

- Advised that if consent is not given, the professional accountant will cease to act for the client.

The professional accountant should ensure that a written record is kept of all advice given to clients in connection with HMRC errors.

Professional accountants, if specifically asked by HMRC to agree a figure, must agree what they believe to be the correct figure; this may be a figure negotiated in the course of discussions following full disclosure of the facts and circumstances. Professional accountants may not accept a figure they know to be incorrect, and they do not need to seek the client's authority to disclose to HMRC its errors in that case.

A deliberate attempt to benefit from an error made by HMRC may constitute a criminal offence under UK law. For example, the client may face a prosecution under the Theft Act 1968. If a crime is committed it brings the non-disclosure of the error into the scope of anti-money laundering legislation. This would then require the professional accountant to report the matter in accordance with this legislation.

In principle, every such error should be disclosed and there is no official de minimis. However, Professional Conduct in Relation to Taxation suggests that errors resulting in a loss of tax of less than £200 might be considered to be de minimis.

Worked example: Disclosure of information

HMRC have issued a repayment of £2,000 in error to your client Mr Nott. You have asked Mr Nott's permission to alert HMRC to this and advised him to return the repayment, but Mr Nott is determined to keep the payment and will not authorise you to contact HMRC regarding it. Unfortunately the engagement letter is silent on the matter of HMRC errors. Mr Nott is keen to forget about the repayment and would like you to begin work on his next tax return.

Requirement

Outline the steps you would take next as a professional accountant.

Solution

It would be necessary to cease to act for Mr Nott. He should be given written notice of this. HMRC should also be notified that you are ceasing to act, but not informed of the reason.

Full records should be kept of your contact regarding the repayment and your decision to terminated the engagement.

It may be necessary to consider making a report under anti-money laundering regulations. See section 7.

7 Anti-money laundering

Section overview

- ICAEW members in practice must comply with their obligations in relation to the prevention, recognition and reporting of money laundering.

- Failure to take account of the guidance could have serious legal, regulatory or professional disciplinary consequences.

7.1 Money-laundering offences and penalties

The term money laundering is used for a number of offences involving the proceeds of crime or terrorist funds. It now includes possessing, or in any way dealing with, or concealing, the proceeds of any crime.

The proceeds or monetary advantage arising from tax offences are treated no differently from the proceeds of theft, drug trafficking or other criminal conduct. Tax evasion can therefore have money-laundering consequences.

Accountants are required to comply with the Proceeds of Crime Act 2002 (POCA) as amended by the Serious Organised Crime and Police Act 2005 (SOCPA) and the Money Laundering Regulations 2007 (the Regulations) which came into force on 15 December 2007. The ICAEW Members' Regulations and guidance includes guidance issued by the Consultative Committee of Accountancy Bodies (CCAB) in December 2007.

Where a professional accountant suspects that a client is involved in money laundering he should report this to his Money Laundering Reporting Officer (MLRO) on an internal report or directly to the National Crime Agency (NCA) in the form of a suspicious activity report (SAR) (see section 7.2).

Penalties for money-laundering offences include an unlimited fine and/or

- Up to fourteen years for the main money laundering offences
- Up to five years for failure to disclose or for tipping off
- Up to two years for contravention of the systems requirements of the Regulations

7.2 Reporting

The money laundering legislation requires an accountant to disclose confidential information without client consent in certain circumstances. In order to disclose confidential information, the accountant must have knowledge or suspicion, or reasonable grounds for knowledge or suspicion, that a person has committed a money-laundering offence. Disclosure without reasonable grounds for knowledge or suspicion will increase the risk of a business or an individual being open to an action for breach of confidentiality.

A professional accountant with knowledge or suspicion of money laundering must make a report. If the accountant works for a firm with a Money Laundering Reporting Officer (MLRO), then an internal report must be made direct to the MLRO.

The MLRO is then responsible for deciding whether the information contained in an internal report needs to be relayed to the NCA in the form of an external report, a SAR, and if so, for compiling and despatching the SAR. There are specific offences applying to MLROs failing to make a report where one is needed.

An accountant in sole practice needing to make a report would be required to submit a SAR direct to NCA.

7.3 Defences

There are several possible defences against a charge of failure to report:

- The individual does not actually know or suspect money laundering has occurred and has not been provided by his employer with the training required, although this is then an offence on the part of the employer.

- The privilege reporting exemption: An accountant who suspects or has reasonable grounds for knowing or suspecting that another person is engaged in money laundering is exempted from making a money laundering report where his knowledge or suspicion comes to him in privileged circumstances (the privilege reporting exemption).

- There is reasonable excuse for not making a report (note that there is no money laundering case law on this issue and it is anticipated that only relatively extreme circumstances, such as duress and threats to safety, might be accepted).

- It is known, or reasonably believed that the money laundering is occurring outside the UK, and is not unlawful under the criminal law of the country where it is occurring.

7.4 Anti-money laundering procedures

All 'relevant' businesses, including those providing accounting and tax services, need to maintain the following procedures:

- Register with an appropriate supervisory authority (see 7.5).

- Appoint a Money Laundering Reporting Officer (MLRO) and implement internal reporting procedures.

- Train staff to ensure that they are aware of the relevant legislation, know how to recognise and deal with potential money laundering, how to report suspicions to the MLRO, and how to identify clients.

- Establish appropriate internal procedures relating to risk assessment and management to deter and prevent money laundering, and make relevant individuals aware of the procedures.

- Carry out customer due diligence on any new client and monitor existing clients to ensure the client is known and establish areas of risk.

- Verify the identity of new clients and maintain evidence of identification and records of any transactions undertaken for or with the client.

- Report suspicions of money laundering to the National Crime Agency (NCA), using a suspicious activity report (SAR).

Records of client identification need to be maintained for five years after the termination of a client relationship by any part of the firm providing relevant business. Records of transactions also need to be maintained for five years from the date when all activities in relation to the transaction were completed.

 Interactive question 5: Failure to report [Difficulty level: Exam standard]

Peter is a junior accountant working at Figg & Co. He joined last year and underwent anti-money laundering training when he started his job, a one-day course organised for him by the Money Laundering Reporting Officer, Milo, and run by a tuition provider in partnership with the ICAEW. Despite this, Peter failed to notice a significant money-laundering cash transaction carried out by a client whose tax he was working on. Peter therefore made no report.

Requirement

Explain whether Peter and/or Milo have committed an offence here and if so, whether there is any defence available.

See **Answer** at the end of this chapter.

7.5 Supervisory bodies

The 2007 Regulations require all businesses to be supervised by an appropriate anti-money laundering supervisory authority.

Accountancy firms must determine the extent of customer due diligence measures which is appropriate on a risk-sensitive basis depending on the type of client, business relationship, and services. Firms must be able to demonstrate to their anti-money laundering supervisory authorities that the extent of their customer due diligence measures is appropriate in view of the risks of money laundering.

Firms are required to take a risk-based approach in establishing their procedures.

The ICAEW is one of the approved supervisory authorities for the accountancy sector. Accountants not regulated by one of the approved bodies will be supervised by HMRC.

The ICAEW conducts monitoring visits to firms overseen. This is typically once every eight years for small firms or annually for large or high-risk firms.

After the first monitoring visit to a firm, and provided the ICAEW are satisfied that the firm has addressed any matters identified as unsatisfactory, the firm will receive written confirmation that it may use the legend 'A member of the ICAEW Practice Assurance scheme'.

8 Tax evasion v tax avoidance

Section overview

- Tax evasion is illegal and could lead to prosecution for both taxpayer and accountant.

- Tax avoidance is legal, but may nevertheless be unacceptable to HMRC.

8.1 Tax evasion

Tax evasion consists of seeking to mislead HMRC by either:

- Suppressing information to which HMRC is entitled, for example by:

    – Failing to notify HMRC of a liability to tax
    – Understating income or gains
    – Omitting to disclose a relevant fact (eg duality of a business expense)

    or

- Providing HMRC with deliberately false information, for example by:

    – Deducting expenses that have not been incurred, or
    – Claiming capital allowances on plant that has not been purchased.

Minor cases of tax evasion are generally settled out of court via the payment of penalties. However, there is a statutory offence of evading income tax that can be dealt with in a magistrates court.

Serious cases of tax evasion, particularly those involving fraud, continue to be the subject of criminal prosecutions which may lead to fines and/or imprisonment on conviction.

Furthermore, tax evasion offences will fall within the definition of money laundering and in certain cases individuals may be prosecuted under one of the money laundering offences. This includes both the under declaring of income and the over claiming of expenses.

Where an accountant is aware of or suspects that a client has committed tax evasion, he himself may commit an offence under money laundering legislation if he has in any way facilitated the evasion. Even if the accountant was not involved in the tax evasion itself, failure to report such a suspicion is also an offence.

8.2 Tax avoidance

Tax avoidance is not defined, but is broadly any legal method of reducing the tax burden. Such methods might include a higher-rate taxpayer choosing to operate a business through a company so that profits are taxed at a lower rate than they would otherwise be. However, it also includes taking advantage of unintended loopholes in the legislation.

In the past HMRC has responded to major tax avoidance schemes by changing legislation as the scheme has come to its attention. However there is a general presumption that the effect of the changes cannot be backdated.

In recent years there has been a requirement for promoters of certain tax avoidance schemes to disclose their schemes to HMRC, and for taxpayers to disclose details of which schemes they have used. This may enable HMRC to take action more rapidly to close the loopholes.

8.3 Case law on avoidance

The courts have also struck down some planning schemes, by effectively ignoring elements of transactions which have no commercial purpose or effect. They have done so by applying purposive construction to the relevant statutory provisions, which means that the courts will look to the original purpose of the legislation when they attempt to apply it to the facts of the case.

In a tax context, this approach is often referred to as the 'Ramsay doctrine', after *Ramsay v IRC (1982)* which was one of the first tax cases to which it was applied.

In *Ramsay* the taxpayers had a tax avoidance scheme consisting of a circular series of pre-planned transactions, designed to create two debts due to the taxpayer. The scheme ensured that one debt produced a gain for the taxpayer and the other an equivalent loss. This would leave the taxpayer in a neutral financial position. The aim of the scheme was to create the gain as a tax exempt gain, but the loss as tax deductible. If the scheme had been successful the taxpayer could have set off this loss against other 'real' gains. The House of Lords refused to allow the loss, with one of the judges commenting that capital gains tax was 'a tax on gains [...] not a tax on arithmetical differences'.

In *Ramsay* and some of the other early cases, this approach was expressed as only applying to tax avoidance schemes. However, later cases have now developed the approach so that it is clear that it can also apply in other cases. It is still most often applied to tax avoidance schemes, but this is because they often involve transactions or terms which have little or no commercial purpose or effect.

Later cases have also demonstrated that the *Ramsay* doctrine cannot be applied to counteract all tax avoidance even when it includes transactions or terms which have no commercial effect. In particular, there have been several cases where the courts have concluded that the planning which had been undertaken was consistent with the purpose of the legislation. There have also been cases where the courts have decided that the legislation was formulated in such a way that it was not possible to discern its purpose. This has been primarily in areas where there are complicated statutory rules to determine the amounts which are taxed, which do not relate to commercial ideas of profits or losses.

The different conclusions can be seen from considering some of the decided cases.

In *Furniss v Dawson* (1984), the taxpayer arranged for shares in a company which he wished to sell to be transferred to an Isle of Man company by way of share for share exchange, with the Isle of Man company selling the shares to the intended buyer on the same day. Under the law at the time, this was intended to defer the gain until the taxpayer sold the shares in the Isle of Man company. However, the House of Lords concluded that the transaction was in substance a sale directly from the taxpayer to the buyer, and it was taxed on that basis.

In *Craven v White* (1988), there was also a share for share exchange of shares which were later on-sold. However, in that case there were two possible buyers, and the negotiations with the one who eventually bought the shares had been broken off at the time of the share for share exchange. In that case a majority of the House of Lords concluded that the commercial uncertainty which meant that it was possible that the foreign holding company would have been left holding the shares, meant that they could not ignore the share for share exchange. The taxpayer therefore succeeded.

In *Barclays Mercantile Business Finance Ltd (BMBF) v* Mawson (2004), the arrangements were very complex, but the cash went round in a circle. The House of Lords concluded that the taxpayer (a bank leasing company) did in fact incur expenditure on the provision of plant and machinery as a result of which the plant and machinery belonged to it. The Capital Allowances Act made no provision about the funding of the expenditure, and considered only the position of the taxpayer claiming the allowances, so the claim for capital allowances succeeded.

This contrasts with the conclusion in *HMRC v Tower McCashback LLP* (2011), in which the Supreme Court concluded that a claim for first year allowances on software was excessive. The software was acquired by partnerships in which individuals had provided 25% of the funds, with 75% provided by way of interest free loan from a company related to the company which had developed the software. Looking at the transactions as a whole, the court concluded that only 25% of the amounts which the partnership had paid were in fact paid for the software rights. One of the key differences between the two cases was that in BMBF there was no suggestion that the assets which had been acquired were worth less than the amount paid.

In *Mayes v HMRC* (2010), the Court of Appeal concluded that it could not strike out a planning scheme which used life assurance policies because the statute set out a formula which did not try to approximate to the actual economic profit or loss which an individual taxpayer made. A similar conclusion was reached by the *Special Commissioners in Campbell v IRC* (2004) in relation to a claim for a loss under the Relevant Discounted Securities rules.

The *Ramsay* doctrine therefore means that there will often be uncertainty as to whether more aggressive tax avoidance transactions will be successful.

8.4 Distinguishing tax evasion from tax avoidance

The distinction between tax evasion and avoidance should be obvious, as a taxpayer engaged in avoidance has no intention of misleading HMRC. However, the distinction between acceptable avoidance, unacceptable avoidance and evasion has become rather blurred in recent years.

The accountant should take particular care in situations where a client believes that a tax avoidance measure has been successful and so does not submit a tax return, or does submit a return but without disclosing a particular transaction.

Note that the fact that a taxpayer is not acting illegally does not mean that steps taken to minimise tax will necessarily be acceptable to HMRC.

8.5 General anti-abuse rule (GAAR)

The GAAR has been introduced to provide additional means for HMRC to 'counteract' tax advantages arising from abusive 'tax arrangements', ie arrangements that involve obtaining a tax advantage as (one of) their main purpose(s).

Summary and Self-test

Summary

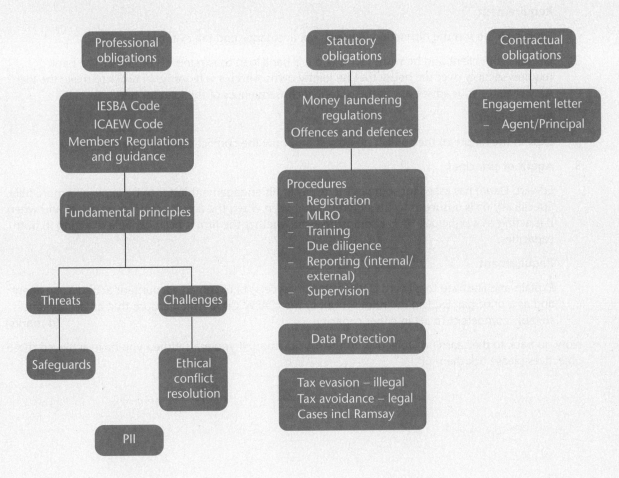

Self-test

Answer the following questions.

1   On further discussion with the son of a client it seems that valuable assets have been deliberately excluded from the death estate of the client. The claim is that the assets were gifted to the son several years ago, however there is no evidence to support this claim.

   Requirement

   Explain to the son the distinction between tax avoidance and tax evasion.

2   James is your client and he wishes to take out a bank loan to expand his business. The bank requires security over the house that he jointly owns with his wife, Amy, in order to make the loan. Amy requires your advice about the potential consequences of the loan for her.

   Requirement

   Explain the nature of the conflict of interest and how the conflict can be managed.

3   **Agent or principal**

   Edward Dante has asked for some of the terms in his engagement letter to be explained more fully. Specifically he is unsure as to the difference between when the firm is acting as an agent and when it is acting as a principal. He is also unsure as to whether the firm is even capable of acting in both capacities.

   Requirement

   Explain and illustrate to Edward Dante the difference(s) between an accountant acting as an agent and as a principal. Explain the rules set out in the ICAEW Code which ensure that an accountant is suitably competent to act in either capacity.   **(4 marks)**

Now go back to the Learning Objectives in the Introduction. If you are satisfied you have achieved these objectives please tick them off.

Legislation

IESBA Code of Ethics for Professional Accountants

ICAEW Members My Guide to Regulations: Code of Ethics

ICAEW Members My Guide to Regulations: Professional Conduct in Relation to Taxation

ICAEW Members My Guide to Regulations: Anti-money laundering guidance for the accountancy sector

ICAEW Professional indemnity insurance regulations and guidance 2014

Serious Organised Crime and Police Act 2005

Money Laundering Regulations 2007

GAAR ss.203-212 FA2013

HMRC manual references

The main source of guidance from HMRC on dealing with errors is given in a 'Complaints' factsheet. This is found at http://www.hmrc.gov.uk/factsheets/complaints-factsheet.pdf Information Commissioner's Office http://www.ico.gov.uk/

ICAEW Ethics helpline service +44 (0)1908 248 250 http://www.icaew.com/members/advisory-helplines-and-services

> This technical reference section is designed to assist you. It should help you to know where to look for further information on the topics covered in this chapter.

Answer to Interactive question 1

The threat here is a self-interest threat. There is a promise of future work in return for including false information in a tax return.

The fundamental principles most threatened by this are:

- Objectivity, if the professional accountant allows the FD and the promise of work to influence their judgement here

- Integrity, which would be breached by submitting false information to HMRC

- Professional behaviour, part of which is complying with relevant laws. Assisting a client in any way with misleading HMRC would be against the law

Answer to Interactive question 2

Jasmine's options include:

- Waiting a while as her line manager suggests
- Speaking to someone else in her firm
- Contacting the ICAEW's confidential ethics helpline service
- Asking to withdraw from acting for the client in question
- Resigning her employment altogether

Answer to Interactive question 3

Both Eric and Ernie must be notified of the situation. The accountant's options are then:

- Obtaining consent from both Eric and Ernie to continue to act for them both
- Acting for one client only
- Ceasing to act for both Eric and Ernie

Depending on the size of the firm, it may be possible to use two separate engagement teams.

Answer to Interactive question 4

Dewi and Dilys must have PII cover as soon as they are trading in partnership, even if fee income is low at first.

Where fee income is less than £600,000, the minimum PII required is the higher of 2.5 times the fee income and £100,000. Fee income of £60,000 would mean that 2.5 x £60,000 = £150,000 of cover (higher than the £100,000 minimum) would be required.

Answer to Interactive question 5

The relevant offence here is failure to report.

Peter failed to make an internal report when he should reasonably have suspected money laundering. He has therefore committed the offence of failure to report. There is a defence where there has been insufficient training to enable the person to spot actual or suspected money laundering. The course taken within the last two years is likely to have been sufficient to enable Peter to recognise the money laundering activities.

Milo will not have committed any offence in regard to the transaction as he had no knowledge of this from any internal report. If Figg & Co's anti-money laundering procedures were found to be inadequate, then Milo as MLRO could potentially be charged.

1   Tax avoidance is the legal method of reducing tax liabilities, for example the use of a deed of variation in this case. There is no intention to mislead HMRC.

Tax evasion is the illegal suppression of information or deliberate provision of false information.

2   If your firm acts for both James and Amy they are two separate clients and the principle of confidentiality must be maintained for each client.

The firm has three options:

- To act for both

  Both parties should be advised of the conflict, and given the opportunity to seek alternative advice

  The two clients should be advised by different partners

  The advice should be overseen by a more senior partner

- To act for one

  Advise Amy that the firm cannot act and just act for James

- To act for neither

  If there is any major doubt this is the most appropriate action

3   **Agent or principal**

The purpose of this note is to set out the difference between when a firm is acting as an agent and when it is acting as a principal.

Agent

An accountant acts as a client's agent when preparing tax compliance work such as income tax returns or calculating tax returns.

Acting as an agent is a low risk activity. As such, no specialist assistance is required.

Principal

An accountant acts as a client's principal when giving tax advice eg inheritance tax planning, or tax avoidance schemes.

Acting as a principal is a high risk activity. As such, specialist assistance should be obtained if the accountant is not personally competent in that subject area.

The firm is capable of acting both in the capacity of an agent and in the capacity of a principal.

Engagement letter

The engagement letter should specify which activities fall under each heading.

Even if the accountant is not personally competent to act as a principal in all areas, the client may still be accepted. However, specialist advice must be sought as required.

The accountant must keep detailed working papers to provide evidence of when acting as an agent and when as a principal.

CHAPTER 2

Income tax computation

Introduction

Examination context

Topic List

Summary and Self-test

Technical reference

Answer to Interactive question

Answers to Self-test

Introduction

Learning objectives

- Calculate taxable savings, income from property, dividend income, taxed income and investment income ☐

- Calculate total taxable income and the income tax payable or repayable for trustees, beneficiaries, employees, company directors, partners and self employed individuals ☐

Specific syllabus references for this chapter are 3j and 3n.

Syllabus links

In Chapter 3 of your Principles of Taxation study manual, you learnt about the basics of the Income Tax Computation. This included chargeable and exempt income, the computation of taxable income, the personal allowance, computing a tax liability, Gift Aid and allowances for older taxpayers.

In this chapter, we review this knowledge and then extend it in relation to gifts to charity, income from jointly owned assets and more details about the allowances for taxpayers born before 6 April 1948.

Examination context

In the examination candidates may be required to:

- Prepare an income tax computation for an individual
- Identify whether income is taxable or exempt
- Determine whether income is received net or gross
- Understand the treatment of gifts/payments to charities
- Identify which interest payments are deductible from total income
- Allocate income from jointly held assets between spouses/civil partners
- Calculate the allowances available for individuals born before 6 April 1948

A methodical approach is required to prepare an income tax computation. Historically candidates have scored well on income tax computations if they know the pro forma computation and have worked their way down the question one step at a time.

Open book – CCH Hardman's Tax Rates & Tables

Hardman's is an invaluable source of information during the exam. Remember that in addition to the summary index on the back cover, there is a full index at the back of the text itself. Most points of administration including claim deadlines and much of the detail regarding VAT can be accessed direct from your open book if you know where to look, ie by using the full index.

Throughout this study manual you will find the relevant page in Hardman's cross referenced for you. As you work through this study manual use the page references to become familiar with the information you can look up and the information you will need to remember.

The information you require for your exam will either be given to you in the exam paper itself (eg recent RPI figures), or will be available to you in Hardman's. However, if you cannot find the information you need in Hardman's do not waste time; simply state your assumption and move on.

Further exam guidance

'HMRC' will be used in your exam to refer to HM Revenue & Customs.

In the examination, you will generally be expected to assume that any beneficial election, claim or deduction has been made, for example when calculating the assessable property income when rent-a-room is in question (see Chapter 3). However, this general assumption does not apply if a question either directs you to consider two different treatments, or specifically tells you which treatment applies.

1 Charge to income tax

Section overview

- Taxable persons are individuals, trustees and personal representatives.
- Some income is exempt from income tax, eg income from ISAs and Premium Bond prizes.
- Income received net must be shown gross in the income tax computation.
- There are three types of income: non-savings income, savings income and dividend income, each with its own rate of tax.
- There are seven steps to calculating a person's income tax liability.
- Taxable income is net income less the personal allowance.
- Tax payable or repayable is a person's tax liability less tax deducted at source.

1.1 Taxable persons

Income tax is chargeable each tax year on:

- Individuals – every individual is treated as a separate taxable person (including children) and is liable to income tax on his own income
- Trustees – liable to income tax on income of the trust
- Personal representatives (executors or administrators) – liable to income tax on income from the estate of a deceased person

Children who are under 18 are taxable persons in their own right in the same way as adults. However, the income of most children is covered by their personal allowance and so no income tax is actually payable on it.

However, if the income is generated from a gift by a parent, this income is treated as the income of the parent, not the child, if it exceeds £100 per year. Transfers of income generating assets by a parent into the child's name are therefore ineffective for utilising the child's personal allowance. However, transfers by other relatives to a child are tax effective.

1.2 Chargeable income and exempt income

The main types of chargeable income are:

- Income from employment (**employment income**)
- Income from trades and professions (**trading income**)
- Income from renting out property (**property income**)
- Income from investments such as interest on loans and bank and building society accounts (**savings income**)
- Income from investments such as dividends (**dividend income**)
- Income from other sources (eg income from casual work) (**miscellaneous income**)

The main types of exempt income are:

- Interest on National Savings Certificates
- Income from Individual Savings Accounts (ISAs)
- Betting, lottery and Premium Bond winnings
- Some social security benefits such as housing benefit and child benefit (but see later in this chapter for a possible child benefit tax charge)
- First £4,250 of gross annual rents from letting under the **rent-a-room** scheme (see later in this text)
- Scholarships
- Income tax repayment interest
- Universal Credit

1.3 Income taxed at source and income received gross

Income received net must be grossed up and shown gross in the income tax computation. Income which is received net includes:

- Interest on investments such as building society interest, most bank interest, debenture and other loan interest paid by UK companies and interest on PPI compensation payments (received net of 20% tax, gross up by 100/80)

- Patent royalties received (received net of 20% tax, gross up by 100/80)

- Employment income (taxed under PAYE, normally stated gross in the examination. Income tax deducted via PAYE will be given as a separate figure)

Dividends from UK companies are received with a deemed 10% tax credit. The dividend must be grossed up by 100/90. The tax credit is not repayable, but can reduce income tax payable.

Income received gross includes:

- Property income

- Trading income

- Miscellaneous income

- National Savings and Investments (NS&I) Direct Saver Account and Investment Account interest

- Interest on government securities (gilt-edged securities/gilts) such as Exchequer Stock and Treasury Stock

- Interest received gross by an individual who has signed a declaration of non-taxpayer status and supplied a certificate to the bank/building society (self-certification); mainly used by children and pensioners

- Interest on non-commercial investments such as a loan between friends

1.4 Types of income

The three types of income are:

- **Non-savings income** (employment income, pension income, taxable social security benefits, trading income, property income, miscellaneous income)

- **Savings income** (interest from investments)

- **Dividend income** (dividends from UK companies)

Note that income received from a pension (pension income) and taxable social security benefits such as jobseeker's allowance (social security income) are taxed in the same way as employment income, except that, pension income and social security income is taxable in a tax year if the individual is entitled to the income in that tax year, regardless of whether payment is received in the tax year.

Income that is not categorised as from a specific source is taxed as miscellaneous income.

1.5 Steps to calculating the income tax liability

To calculate a taxpayer's income tax liability the following steps must be performed:

Step 1   Add together all types of chargeable income to give '**total income**'.

Step 2   Deduct reliefs, such as gifts of assets to charities (see below), qualifying interest payments (see below) and property losses (see Chapter 3) from the relevant component of 'total income' to give '**net income**'. There is a cap on various income tax reliefs that can be claimed by an individual. This cap applies to qualifying interest payments. Relief is capped at the higher of £50,000 and 25% of adjusted total income. Adjusted total income is total income plus any payroll giving less gross personal pension contributions.

Step 3 Deduct the personal allowance from the relevant components of 'net income' to give '**taxable income**'.

The basic personal allowance for 2014/15 is £10,000. [Hp6]

The personal allowance is deducted from the different components of income in the following order:

- Non-savings income
- Savings income
- Dividend income

The full personal allowance of £10,000 is not available for individuals with an adjusted net income of more than £100,000. The personal allowance is reduced by £1 for every £2 that the individual's adjusted net income exceeds £100,000.

The personal allowance will be withdrawn completely for adjusted net income of £120,000 and above.

The restriction on the personal allowance has given rise to an effective marginal income tax rate of 60% on the adjusted net income between £100,000 and £120,000.

Once you earn more than £100,000 you continue to pay tax at 40% but for each extra £2 that you earn you lose £1 of personal allowance – so you pay 40% on the extra £2 earned and you lose the nil rate of tax on £1. So you have to pay £0.80 in tax on the £2 and £0.40 in tax on the £1 which no longer receives a personal allowance. This gives total extra tax of £1.20 on £2 of additional income which as a percentage is 60%.

In addition, if the income which takes a taxpayer over £100,000 is earned income, then national insurance at 2% will also be payable making the marginal rate of tax 62%.

Adjusted net income is a person's net income after **deducting** grossed up amounts of any Gift Aid donations and pension contributions.

Therefore any taxpayer subject to the additional rate of tax (see Step 4) will not be entitled to a personal allowance.

Step 4 Calculate tax at the applicable rates on the 'taxable income'.

Tax on the three types of income is calculated in the following order:

- Non-savings income
- Savings income
- Dividend income

The rates of tax for 2014/15 are: [Hp2]

	Non-savings income	Savings income	Dividend income
Starting rate for savings	N/A	10%	N/A
Basic rate	20%	20%	10%
Higher rate	40%	40%	32.5%
Additional rate	45%	45%	37.5%

Non-savings income up to the basic rate limit of £31,865 is taxable at 20%.

There is a starting rate for savings income of 10%, with a rate limit of £2,880 (see example Nancy later in the chapter). Thereafter any savings income within the basic rate limit of £31,865 is taxable at 20%.

Non-savings and savings income between the basic rate limit of £31,865 and the higher rate limit of £150,000 is taxable at 40%. For income above £150,000 the additional rate of tax of 45% applies.

The dividend ordinary rate is 10% and the upper rate is 32.5%. An additional rate of 37.5% applies for dividend income above the higher rate limit of £150,000.

Step 5 Add together all amounts of tax at Step 4.

Step 6 From the Step 5 figure, deduct tax reductions such as married couple's allowance (see below).

Step 7 To the Step 6 figure, add certain other amounts of tax, such as the pensions annual allowance charge (Chapter 4) and child benefit charge (see Section 1.6).

The resulting figure is the '**income tax liability**'.

'**Tax payable or repayable**' is the amount of income tax payable by a taxpayer (or repayable to him) under self-assessment after reducing the 'income tax liability' by tax deducted at source, and increasing it by income tax retained, for example, on patent royalties paid (Chapter 6, Section 5.1).

1.6 Child benefit tax charge

The child benefit rate for 2014/15 is £1,066 per year for the eldest (or only) child and £705 per year for each other child.

An income tax charge applies if a taxpayer in receipt of Child Benefit (or whose partner is in receipt of Child Benefit) has adjusted net income over £50,000 in a tax year. The charge is 1% of the Child Benefit amount for each £100 of income between £50,000 and £60,000. The charge is the full Child Benefit amount if the taxpayer has income over £60,000.

If both partners have income over £50,000, the partner with the higher income is liable for the charge. There is an option for claimants to choose not to receive Child Benefit at all in order to avoid the charge.

The tax charge is added in at arriving at income tax liability at Step 7 of the calculation (see above).

Worked example: Child benefit tax charge

Sara and Terry Evans have two children and receive Child Benefit. Sara is a stay at home mum with minimal income, while Terry runs his own business. His net income during 2014/15 was £57,500, and he made gross Gift Aid donations of £400 in the year.

Requirement

What is the Child Benefit tax charge on Terry?

Solution

2014/15	£	£
Child benefit: £1,066 + £705	1,771	
Adjusted net income (£57,500 – £400)	57,100	
Less threshold	(50,000)	
Excess	7,100	
÷ £100	71	
Charge: 1% × £1,771 × 71		1,257

1.7 Pro forma income tax computation

The pro forma income tax computation is as follows:

A Taxpayer

Income tax computation

2014/15

	Non-savings income £	Savings income £	Dividend income £	Total £
Income				
Employment income	X			
Interest		X		
Dividends			X	
Property income	X			
Total income	X	X	X	X
Less reliefs:				
Gifts of assets to charity/qualifying interest payments	(X)			(X)
Net income	X	X	X	X
Personal allowance	(10,000)			(10,000)
Taxable income	X	X	X	X

Tax £

£	
	X
Less tax reductions (for example, married couple's allowance)	(X)
Add child benefit tax charge and pension annual allowance charge	X
Income tax liability	X
Less tax deducted at source	(X)
Plus tax retained on patent royalties paid	X
Income tax payable/repayable	X/(X)

The pro forma will gradually be built up over the following chapters of the Study Manual.

Interactive question: Computation of tax payable [Difficulty level: Intermediate]

In the tax year 2014/15, Michael had the following income:

Gross salary	£23,695
Income tax deducted via PAYE	£3,788
Property income	£6,000
National Savings Certificates interest received on cashing in certificates	£1,100
Betting winnings	£500
Building society interest received	£320
Bank deposit interest received	£400
Dividends from UK companies	£1,890

Requirement

Using the standard format below, compute the income tax payable by Michael for 2014/15.

Michael
Tax payable

	Non-savings income £	Savings income £	Dividend income £	Total £
Net income				
Less PA				
Taxable income				
Tax				£

£

Tax liability

Less tax deducted at source

Tax payable

See **Answer** at the end of this chapter.

Worked example: Anita

Anita has a part-time cleaning job and earns £9,125 in 2014/15. She also received the following income:

	£
National Lottery scratch card winnings	250
Bank interest	800
Dividends from UK company	549

Anita was born in 1971.

Requirement

Calculate Anita's income tax payable/repayable.

Solution

Anita
Income tax repayable

	Non-savings income £	Savings income £	Dividend income £	Total £
Employment income	9,125			
BI £800 × 100/80		1,000		
Dividends £549 × 100/90			610	
Net income	9,125	1,000	610	10,735
Less PA	(9,125)	(875)		(10,000)
Taxable income	NIL	125	610	735

Tax

	£
£125 × 10% (the starting rate band for SI below £2,880 applies)	13
£610 × 10%	61
	74
Less: Tax credit on dividend	(61)
Interest £1,000 × 20%	(200)
Repayable	(187)

Note that as the dividend tax credit is not repayable, the tax credit on dividends is always set off first to ensure that the full amount of the tax credit is recoverable.

Worked example: Mavis

Mavis' only source of income in 2014/15 was dividends of £48,600. Mavis was born in 1971.

Requirement

Calculate Mavis' income tax payable/repayable.

Solution

Mavis
Income tax repayable

	Dividend income £	Total £
Dividends £48,600 × 100/90	54,000	54,000
Net income	54,000	54,000
Less PA	(10,000)	(10,000)
Taxable income	44,000	44,000

Tax

	£
£31,865 × 10%	3,187
£12,135 × 32.5%	3,944
£44,000	7,131
Less tax credit on taxable dividend (£44,000 × 10%)	(4,400)
Income tax payable	2,731

Note that the tax credit on dividends is restricted to the tax credit on the taxable dividend only.

Worked example: Nancy

Nancy, who is aged 23, has earnings from employment of £10,495. She also receives bank interest of £2,800 during 2014/15.

Requirement

Calculate the income tax liability for Nancy for 2014/15.

Solution
Nancy
Income tax liability

	Non-savings income £	Savings income £	Total £
Employment income	10,495		10,495
BI £2,800 × 100/80		3,500	3,500
Net income	10,495	3,500	13,995
Less PA	(10,000)		(10,000)
Taxable income	495	3,500	3,995

Tax

	£
£495 × 20%	99
£2,385 × 10% (savings)	239
£2,880	
£1,115 × 20% (savings)	223
£3,995	
Income tax liability	561

Worked example: Elise

Elise receives the following income in 2014/15:

- Employment income £95,875
- Property income £31,700

- Bank interest £21,140
- Dividends from UK companies £15,300

Requirement

What is Elise's income tax liability for 2014/15?

Solution

Elise
Income tax liability

	Non-savings income £	Savings income £	Dividend income £	Total £
Employment income	95,875			
Property income	31,700			
Bank interest £21,140 × 100/80		26,425		
Dividends £15,300 × 100/90			17,000	
Net income	127,575	26,425	17,000	171,000
Personal allowance	–			
Taxable income	127,575	26,425	17,000	171,000

Tax

	£
£31,865 × 20%	6,373
£95,710 × 40%	38,284
£127,575	
£22,425 × 40% (savings)	8,970
£150,000	
£4,000 × 45% (savings)	1,800
£17,000 × 37.5% (dividends)	6,375
£171,000	
Income tax liability	61,802

Worked example: Julia

Julia had net income of £118,000 in 2014/15. She had made gross pension contributions of £7,000 during the year.

Requirement

What is Julia's taxable income for 2014/15?

Solution

Julia
Taxable income

	£	£	Total £
Net income			118,000
Less personal allowance		10,000	
Net income	118,000		
Gross pension contributions	(7,000)		
Adjusted net income	111,000		
(£111,000 – £100,000) = £11,000 × ½		(5,500)	
			(4,500)
Taxable income			113,500

2 Gifts to charity

Section overview

- Gift Aid gives tax relief for cash donations to charity.
- The payroll giving scheme allows employees to obtain tax relief on gifts to charity out of employment income.
- Gifts of certain shares and land to charity are deductible in computing net income.

2.1 Gift Aid

The Gift Aid Scheme gives tax relief for cash donations to charity. A Gift Aid declaration must be made.

Basic rate tax relief is given by deeming the Gift Aid donation to be made net of basic rate tax. Higher rate and additional rate tax relief is given by extending the basic rate band and increasing the higher rate limit by the amount of the grossed up Gift Aid donation, at Step 4.

Gift Aid donations are grossed up by 100/80 and the basic rate band is extended, and higher rate limit is increased, by this amount in order for a taxpayer to claim the further tax relief due. A higher rate tax payer will receive further tax relief of 20% of the gross Gift Aid donation whereas an additional rate tax payer will receive further tax relief of 25% of the gross Gift Aid donation.

Worked example: Luca

Luca had assessable business profits of £170,000 in 2014/15. On 20 May 2014 Luca made a £1,600 donation under Gift Aid to a local charity.

Requirement

What is Luca's income tax liability for 2014/15?

Solution

Luca

Taxable income

	£	£	Total £
Net income			170,000
Less personal allowance			(nil)
Taxable income			170,000
Tax			
			£
£33,865 × 20% (W1)			6,773
£118,135 × 40%			47,254
£152,000 (W1)			
£18,000 × 45%			8,100
£170,000			
Income tax liability			62,127

W1 – Increased basic rate and higher rate limits

Basic rate threshold	31,865
Add extension due to Gift Aid (£1,600 × 100/80)	2,000
	33,865
Higher rate threshold	150,000
Add extension due to Gift Aid	2,000
	152,000

Note. If Luca had not made the Gift Aid donation his income tax liability would have been £62,627 (£500 higher). The Gift Aid donation has therefore received further tax relief of 25% of the gross donation of £2,000 (£500).

An election can be made to carry back a Gift Aid donation to the previous tax year. This election must be made to HMRC no later than the date when the taxpayer files his tax return for the previous year and, in any event, no later than 31 January following the end of the previous tax year.

2.2 Payroll Giving Scheme

Employees can make donations to charity under an **approved payroll giving scheme**.

The employer deducts the amount of the donation from the employee's employment income. Income tax is then calculated on employment income after the deduction of the charitable donation. This gives income tax relief at the individual's highest rate of tax. [Hp83]

2.3 Gifts of assets to charity

A deduction is given against total income at Step 2, if the whole of any beneficial interest in qualifying shares or securities is given, or sold at an undervalue, to a charity.

The amount that an individual can deduct in calculating his net income is:

- The market value of the shares or securities at the date of disposal; plus

- Any incidental costs of disposing of the shares (broker's fees, etc); less

- Any consideration given in return for disposing of the shares; and less

- The value of any other benefits received by the donor, or a person connected with the donor, in consequence of disposing of the shares.

The following are qualifying shares and securities for these purposes: [Hp11]

- Shares or securities listed on a recognised stock exchange (UK or otherwise)

- Shares or securities dealt with on a recognised stock exchange (UK or otherwise) (this definition appears to include Alternative Investment Market shares)

- Units in an authorised unit trust

- Shares in an open-ended investment company

- Holdings in certain foreign collective investment schemes

Individuals can also claim a deduction in calculating net income, equal to the market value of any freehold or leasehold land or buildings given to a charity. Where land is sold at an undervalue, relief is given for the difference between market value and the price paid by the charity.

The deduction is given when calculating net income and is made from income in the following order:

- Non-savings income
- Savings income
- Dividend income

3 Interest payments

Section overview

- Interest payments are deductible from total income if they are for certain qualifying purposes.

- The interest paid during the tax year is the amount that is deductible.

3.1 Interest payments

Interest payments are deductible from total income when a loan is used for the following purposes.

(a) **To buy plant or machinery for use in a partnership**. Interest qualifies for three years from the end of the tax year in which the loan was taken out. If the plant is used partly for private purposes, only a proportion of the interest is eligible for relief.

(b) **To buy plant or machinery for employment purposes**. Interest qualifies for three years from the end of the tax year in which the loan was taken out. If the plant is used partly for private purposes, only a proportion of the interest is eligible for relief.

(c) **To buy an interest in a close company (ordinary shares)** (other than a close investment holding company) or lending money to such a company for the purpose of its business. When the interest is paid the borrower must either hold some shares and work full time as a manager or director of the company or have a material interest in the close company (ie hold more than 5% of the shares).

A close company is a UK resident company controlled by its shareholder-directors or by five or fewer shareholders. From 6 April 2014, interest payments are also deductible if the company invested in is resident in an EEA state other than the UK, and the company would be close if it were resident in the UK.

(d) **To buy shares in an employee-controlled company**. The company must be an unquoted trading company resident in the UK (or, from 6 April 2014, another EEA state) with at least 50% of the voting shares held by employees.

(e) **To invest in a partnership**, or contribute capital or make a loan. The borrower must be a partner (other than a limited partner), note that relief ceases when he ceases to be a partner.

(f) **To buy shares in or lend money to a co-operative**. The borrower must work for the greater part of his time in the co-operative or a subsidiary.

(g) **To pay inheritance tax**. Interest paid by the personal representatives qualifies for 12 months.

(h) The replacement with other loans qualifying under (c) to (f) above.

The amount of interest paid during the tax year is the amount that can be deducted from total income. These interest payments are made gross.

If the interest is paid wholly and exclusively for business purposes the taxpayer can instead deduct the interest when computing his trade profits, rather than from total income. The interest need not fall into any of the categories outlined above (see Chapter 6).

Interest on a loan taken out to buy a letting property will qualify as an expense when computing property income (see Chapter 3).

Where interest is allowable in the computation of trade profits or property income, the amount *payable* (on an accruals basis) is deducted rather than interest *paid* in the tax year.

Worked example: Interest payments

Arthur was aged 42 during 2014/15. He had the following income and payments for 2014/15:

	£
Salary	48,200
Dividends received	675
Gift Aid paid	912
Interest paid	3,500

The interest paid of £3,500 is made up of £3,000 on the loan to purchase Arthur's house, and £500 to purchase shares in Marco Ltd, an employee controlled company.

Requirement

Compute Arthur's income tax liability for 2014/15.

Solution

Arthur
Tax liability

	Non-savings income £	Dividend income £	Total £
Employment income	48,200		
Dividends £675 × 100/90		750	
Total income	48,200	750	48,950
Qualifying interest payment on loan to purchase shares in an employee controlled company (N1)	(500)		(500)
Net income	47,700	750	48,450
Less PA	(10,000)		(10,000)
Taxable income	37,700	750	38,450

Note:

(1) Interest on a loan to purchase a house is not a qualifying purpose and the interest payment of £3,000 is not deductible.

Tax

	£
£33,005 × 20% (W1)	6,601
£ 4,695 × 40%	1,878
£37,700	
£ 750 × 32.5%	244
£38,450	
Tax liability	8,723

WORKINGS

(1) The basic rate band is extended by the amount of the gross Gift Aid payments.

	£
Basic rate band	31,865
Gift aid paid (£912 × 100/80)	1,140
Revised basic rate band	33,005

4 Independent taxation and jointly owned assets

Section overview

- Each individual is a separate taxable person.

- Income from assets owned by spouses/civil partners is usually split equally.

- A declaration of ownership in unequal proportions can be made.

- Income from jointly held shares in family companies is always split in accordance with actual ownership.

4.1 Independent taxation

Every individual is treated as a separate taxable person who is liable to income tax on his own income.

An income tax computation must be prepared for each spouse/civil partner, showing his or her own taxable income.

4.2 Jointly owned assets

A potential problem arises in deciding how spouses/civil partners are entitled to income received from a jointly held asset.

Special rules apply to allocate income where spouses/civil partners living together hold property jointly (eg a joint holding of shares, land or bank account).

The basic rule is that spouses/civil partners are deemed to own the property in equal proportions, irrespective of actual ownership. Therefore, joint income is normally divided equally between them (ie a 50/50 split).

If spouses/civil partners actually own the property in unequal proportions, they can make a declaration to HM Revenue & Customs (HMRC). This declaration is optional but, if made, each spouse/civil partner will be taxed on the income to which he or she is actually entitled.

Notice of the declaration must be sent to HMRC within 60 days of the declaration. A declaration cannot be made in respect of a jointly owned bank or building society account.

The declaration cannot be made for an unequal split unless it is consistent with the owners' actual entitlements. Therefore, if property is actually held jointly in equal proportions, it is not possible to make a declaration for any other split in order to save tax.

Income distributions (ie dividends) from shares in a family company which are jointly owned by spouses/civil partners will be taxed according to actual ownership. This income will not be automatically split equally between them.

5 Allowances for taxpayers born before 6 April 1948

Section overview

- Personal Age Allowance (PAA) is available to taxpayers born before 6 April 1948 instead of the basic Personal Allowance. The PAA is reduced if the taxpayer's income exceeds a certain limit.

- Gift Aid donations and personal pension contributions need to be taken into account when working out any reduction in PAA.

- Married Couple's Allowance (MCA) is reduced in the same way as PAA if the taxpayer's income exceeds a certain limit.

- MCA can be transferred from one spouse/civil partner to the other.

5.1 Personal Age Allowance (PAA)

The Personal Age Allowance is available to older taxpayers instead of the basic Personal Allowance, at Step 3.

A taxpayer who was born between 6 April 1938 and 5 April 1948 is entitled to a personal age allowance of £10,500.

A taxpayer who is was born before 6 April 1938 is entitled to a personal age allowance of £10,660.[Hp6]

Where the taxpayer's net income exceeds £27,000 in 2014/15, the Personal Age Allowance is reduced by £1 for every £2 that the net income exceeds £27,000. The PAA cannot fall below £10,000 unless adjusted net income exceeds £100,000, in which case it can be reduced to £nil – see above. This ensures that high income individuals, whatever their age, do not escape the restriction to the personal allowance.

The taxpayer's net income for this purpose is reduced by the gross amount of any Gift Aid donation and any personal pension contributions – ie in the same way as the personal allowance is tapered for individuals with adjusted net income in excess of £100,000.

Worked example: Personal Age Allowance

Emily was born on 29 March 1940. Her net income for 2014/15 is £27,800 which is all non-savings income.

Emily made a Gift Aid donation of £400 in December 2014.

Requirement

Compute Emily's taxable income.

Solution

Emily is born between 6 April 1938 and 5 April 1948.

The grossed up Gift Aid donation is £400 × 100/80	£500

	£
Personal Age Allowance	10,500
Less ([£27,800 – £500] – £27,000) = £300 × $^1/_2$	(150)
Reduced Personal Age Allowance	10,350

Taxable income:	£
Net income	27,800
Less Personal Age Allowance	(10,350)
Taxable income	17,450

5.2 Married Couple's Allowance (MCA)

There is an additional allowance available for older married couples and civil partners in the form of a tax reducer at a fixed rate of 10%, at Step 6 of the income tax computation. This is called the Married Couple's Allowance (MCA).

A married man who married before 5 December 2005, whose wife is living with him during all or part of 2014/15, is entitled to the MCA. The amount he is entitled to depends on the husband's net income.

For civil partners and couples who married on or after 5 December 2005, the MCA is claimed by the spouse or civil partner who has the higher net income. The amount depends on the net income of the spouse or civil partner with the higher income.

A taxpayer is entitled to make a claim for MCA if he or his spouse or civil partner was born before 6 April 1935 (ie aged 80 by 5 April 2015).

The amount of the MCA is £8,165.

When the relevant taxpayer's net income exceeds £27,000 and the Personal Age Allowance has been reduced to £10,000, any excess income reduces the MCA in the same way as for the PAA. However, the MCA cannot be reduced below the minimum amount of £3,140.

Worked example: Married Couple's Age Allowance

Simon was born on 19 July 1938. His net income for 2014/15 is £32,770. He married Jean, who was born on 22 August 1932, in January 2007. Jean has net income for 2014/15 of £12,380.

Requirement

Compute Simon's Personal Age Allowance and Married Couple's Allowance.

Solution

Simon is aged 76 and Jean aged 82 on 5 April 2015. The MCA is therefore based on Jean's age. However, Simon is the taxpayer entitled to claim the MCA since he has the higher net income in 2014/15 and the couple were married on or after 5 December 2005.

	£
Personal Age Allowance	10,500
Less (£32,770 – £27,000) = £5,770 × ½ = £2,885 restricted to	(500)
Reduced Personal Age Allowance	10,000

	£
Married Couple's Allowance	8,165
Less remainder of excess (£2,885 – £500)	(2,385)
Reduced Married Couple's Allowance	5,780

The spouse/civil partner who would not be entitled to claim the MCA may unilaterally (ie alone) make a claim for half of the minimum amount of the MCA to be transferred to him or her (ie £3,140 × 50% = £1,570). The claim must be made by the start of the tax year.

Alternatively, the couple may jointly elect, again by the start of the tax year, to transfer the whole of the minimum amount of the MCA to the spouse/civil partner who would not normally be entitled to it (ie £3,140). For the year of marriage/civil partnership, an election can be made during the year.

A MCA which turns out to be wasted (because either spouse or partner has insufficient tax to reduce) may then be transferred to the other spouse or partner.

In the year of marriage/civil partnership, the MCA is reduced by 1/12 for each complete tax month (running from the 6th of one month to the 5th of the following month) which has passed before the marriage/registration of the civil partnership.

Summary

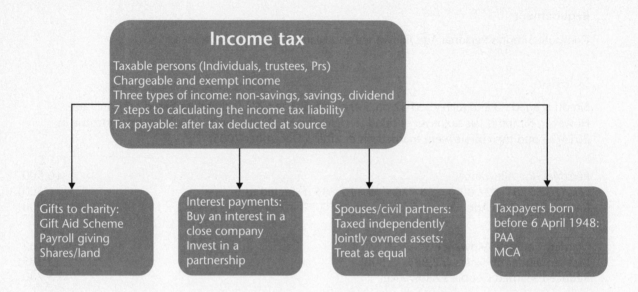

Self-test

Answer the following questions.

1   Marjorie is aged 22 and is a full-time student. In 2014/15, she received the following income:

Scholarship from university	£350
Earnings from vacation work (gross, IT deducted via PAYE deducted £910)	£9,950
Dividends from UK company shares	£450

How much tax is repayable to Marjorie?

A   £915
B   £910
C   £850
D   £960

2   Jerry is aged 40. His only source of income in 2014/15 was trading income of £30,000.

In July 2014, Jerry gave some shares quoted on the London Stock Exchange worth £5,000 to a charity.

What is Jerry's taxable income?

A   £30,000
B   £25,000
C   £20,000
D   £15,000

3   Paul and Oliver are civil partners. They own a house which they let out. The house is owned 40% by Paul and 60% by Oliver.

Which **one** of the following statements is true?

A   The property income must be taxed equally on Paul and Oliver

B   Paul and Oliver are taxed together on the property income because they are civil partners

C   Paul and Oliver can elect for the property income to be taxed 40% on Paul and 60% on Oliver

D   Paul and Oliver can elect for the property income to be taxed 60% on Paul and 40% on Oliver

4   Albert was born on 10 April 1937. During 2014/15, he received gross pension income of £23,100 and bank interest of £3,200. He paid £600 under the Gift Aid Scheme in September 2014.

What Personal Age Allowance is available to Albert?

A   £10,450
B   £10,500
C   £10,610
D   £10,660

5   Richard was born on 22 August 1933. His net income for 2014/15 is £31,660. Richard has been married to Lucy for many years. Lucy, who was born on 30 April 1938, has net income for 2014/15 of £33,400.

What Married Couple's Allowance is available and to whom is it given, assuming no election to transfer it has been made?

A   Lucy £5,465
B   Lucy £5,625
C   Richard £6,495
D   Richard £5,835

6   Jennie received a gross salary of £112,000 in 2014/15. She paid personal pension contributions of £7,000 during 2014/15.

What is Jennie's personal allowance for 2014/15?

A   £10,000
B   £8,375
C   £6,750
D   £7,500

7   Dave, aged 42, has earnings from employment in 2014/15 of £133,000. He also received bank interest of £22,080 and dividends of £13,500 during 2014/15.

What is Dave's income tax liability for 2014/15?

A   £66,522
B   £62,742
C   £59,522
D   £64,022

8   **Toby and Jane**

Toby and Jane have been married for 40 years.

Toby was born on 13 November 1938 and Jane was born on 19 June 1933.

In the tax year 2014/15, Toby and Jane had the following income:

	Toby £	Jane £
Pension (gross)	24,800	13,000
(tax deducted)	(2,540)	(970)
Building society interest received	1,200	240
Dividends from UK companies	1,800	2,700
ISA dividends	1,500	
Premium bond winnings		200
Property income	5,600	2,400

The property income is derived from a house which Toby and Jane own together in the proportions 70:30.

In December 2014, Toby made a Gift Aid donation of £1,200. In March 2015, Jane gave quoted shares worth £2,500 to a charity.

No elections have been made.

Requirement

Calculate the tax payable by Toby and Jane.   **(15 marks)**

Now go back to the Learning Objectives in the Introduction. If you are satisfied you have achieved these objectives please tick them off.

Technical reference

Legislation

References are to Income and Tax Act 2007 (*ITA 2007*) unless otherwise stated

Payroll Giving Scheme	Income Tax (Earnings and Pensions) Act 2003 ss.713 – 715
Gifts of shares/land to charity	s.431
Jointly owned assets	ss.836 – 837
Personal allowances	ss.35 – 37
Married couple's allowance	ss.45 – 46
Interest payments	ss.388 – 403
Child benefit tax charge	Income Tax (Earnings and Pensions) Act 2003 ss.681B – 681H

HMRC manual references

Relief Instructions Manual (Found at http://www.hmrc.gov.uk/manuals/remanual/index.htm)

Gift Aid relief: outline of the relief	RE1830

This technical reference section is designed to assist you. It should help you know where to look for further information on the topics covered in this chapter.

Answer to Interactive question

Answer to Interactive question 1

Michael

Tax payable

	Non-savings income £	Savings income £	Dividend income £	Total £
Employment income	23,695			
Property income	6,000			
BSI £320 × 100/80		400		
Bank interest £400 × 100/80		500		
Dividends £1,890 × 100/90			2,100	
Net income	29,695	900	2,100	32,695
Less PA	(10,000)			(10,000)
Taxable income	19,695	900	2,100	22,695

Tax

	£
£19,695 × 20%	3,939
£900 × 20%	180
£2,100 × 10%	210
£22,695	
Tax liability	4,329
Less tax deducted at source	
£2,100 × 10%	(210)
IT on salary via PAYE	(3,788)
£900 × 20%	(180)
Tax payable	151

Interest on National Savings Certificates and betting winnings are exempt from income tax.

1   B – £910

Marjorie
Income tax repayable

	Non-savings income £	Dividend income £	Total £
Employment income	9,950		
Dividends £450 × 100/90		500	
Net income	9,950	500	10,450
Less PA	(9,950)	(50)	(10,000)
Taxable income	NIL	450	450

Scholarship is exempt from income tax.

Tax

	£
£450 × 10%	45
Less: tax credit on taxable dividend	(45)
IT on salary via PAYE	(910)
Repayable	(910)

Note that the tax credit on dividends is set off first to ensure that the full amount is recoverable. However, the excess tax credit of £5 (£50 – £45) is not recoverable.

2   D – £15,000

Jerry
Taxable income

	Non-savings income £
Trading income	30,000
Less gift of quoted shares to charity	(5,000)
Net income	25,000
Less PA	(10,000)
Taxable income	15,000

3   C – Paul and Oliver can elect for the property income to be taxed 40% by Paul and 60% by Oliver

Statement A is incorrect because, although the property income will usually be taxed equally on Paul and Oliver, they can make an election for them to be taxed in accordance with their actual shares.

Statement B is incorrect because all individuals are independent taxpayers liable for tax on their own income.

Statement D is incorrect because the election for unequal shares can only be made to reflect the actual shares in which the property is held.

4   D – £10,660

Albert is born before 6 April 1938.

Net income adjusted for Gift Aid is:

	£
Pension	23,100
Bank interest £3,200 × 100/80	4,000
Net income	27,100
Less Gift Aid £600 × 100/80	(750)
Adjusted net income	26,350

Since the adjusted net income does not exceed the limit of £27,000, there is no adjustment in the Personal Age Allowance.

PAA (born before 6 April 1938)	£10,660

5   C – Richard £6,495

Since Richard and Lucy were married before 5 December 2005, Richard as the married man is entitled to the MCA. The allowance is awarded because Richard was born prior to 6 April 1935.

Richard is aged 81 on 5 April 2015.

	£
Personal Age Allowance	10,660
Less (£31,660 – £27,000) = £4,660 × ½ = £2,330 restricted to	(660)
Reduced Personal Age Allowance	10,000

	£
Married Couple's Allowance	8,165
Less remainder of excess (£2,330 – £660)	(1,670)
Reduced Married Couple's Allowance	6,495

6   B – £8,375

Adjusted net income = £112,000 – (£7,000 × 100/80) = £103,250

	£
Personal Allowance	10,000
Less (£103,250 – £100,000) = £3,250 × ½	(1,625)
Reduced Personal Age Allowance	8,375

7   D – £64,022

Dave
Income tax liability

	Non-savings income £	Savings income £	Dividend income £	Total £
Employment income	133,000			
Bank interest (£22,080 × 100/80)		27,600		
Dividends (£13,500 × 100/90)			15,000	
Net income	133,000	27,600	15,000	175,600
Less PA (Note)				–
Taxable income	133,000	27,600	15,000	175,600

Note: As an additional rate taxpayer Dave's personal allowance will have been fully abated to nil.

Tax

	£
£31,865 × 20%	6,373
£101,135 × 40%	40,454
£133,000	
£17,000 × 40%	6,800
£150,000	
£10,600 × 45%	4,770
£15,000 × 37.5%	5,625
£175,600	
Income tax liability	64,022

8 Toby

Tax payable

	Non-savings income £	Savings income £	Dividend Income £	Total £
Pension income	24,800			
Property income (N2)	4,000			
BSI £1,200 × 100/80		1,500		
Dividends £1,800 × 100/90			2,000	
Net income	28,800	1,500	2,000	32,300
Less PAA (W1)	(10,000)			(10,000)
Taxable income	18,800	1,500	2,000	22,300

Notes

(1)   ISA investment income is exempt from income tax.

(2)   Property income from jointly owned property is taxed equally on a married couple unless an election is made to reflect actual ownership. Therefore each owner is taxed on

(£5,600 + £2,400) = £8,000/2 = £4,000.

Tax

	£
£18,800× 20%	3,760
£1,500 × 20%	300
£2,000 × 10%	200
£22,300	
	4,260
Less MCA £6,765 × 10% (W2)	(677)
Tax liability	3,583
Less tax deducted at source	
£2,000 × 10%	(200)
Pension tax	(2,540)
£1,500 × 20%	(300)
Tax payable	543

WORKINGS

(1)   Toby was born after 5 April 1938 but before 6 April 1948.

	£
Personal Age Allowance	10,500
Less: (£[32,300 – 1,500] – £27,000) = £3,800 × $^1/_2$ = £1,900 restricted to	(500)
Reduced Personal Age Allowance	10,000

Note: Gift Aid is £1,500 (£1,200 × 100/80)

(2) Toby will be entitled to the MCA because Toby and Jane were married before 5 December 2005 and Toby is the married man.

The allowance is awarded because Jane was born before 6 April 1935.

	£
Married Couple's Allowance	8,165
Less remainder of excess (£1,900 – £500)	(1,400)
Reduced Married Couple's Allowance	6,765

Jane
Tax payable

	Non-savings income £	Savings income £	Dividend income £	Total £
Pension Income	13,000			
Property Income	4,000			
BSI £240 × 100/80		300		
Dividends £2,700 × 100/90			3,000	
Total income	17,000	300	3,000	20,300
Less reliefs: gift to charity	(2,500)			
Net income	14,500	300	3,000	17,800
Less PAA	(10,660)			(10,660)
Taxable income	3,840	300	3,000	7,140

Tax

	£
£3,840 × 20%	768
£300 × 20%	60
£3,000 × 10%	300
£7,140	
Tax liability	1,128
Less tax deducted at source	
£3,000 × 10%	(300)
Pension tax	(970)
£300 × 20%	(60)
Tax repayable	(202)

Premium bond winnings are exempt from income tax.

CHAPTER 3

Property income

Introduction

Examination context

Topic List

Summary and Self-test

Technical reference

Answer to Interactive question

Answers to Self-test

Introduction

Learning objective

Tick off

- Describe and calculate the principal aspects of the taxation of property income, including rent a room relief and premiums on short leases

Specific syllabus references for this chapter are 3k.

Syllabus links

None of the topics in this chapter were covered in the Principles of Taxation study manual in any detail.

Examination context

In the examination candidates may be required to:

- Calculate the total property income assessment of an individual, including dealing with 'rent a room' and lease premiums.

In past examinations candidates have found lease premium calculations difficult. It is essential that time is spent understanding the methods for calculating lease premiums.

1 Property income

Section overview

- Property income is taxed on the amount accrued in a tax year.

- Allowable expenses are deductible, including a wear and tear allowance for furnished property.

- Losses are carried forward and set against the first available property income.

- Rent a room relief applies to lettings in the taxpayer's own home.

- Real Estate Investment Trusts (REITs) allow a taxpayer to spread his investment in property.

1.1 Property income

The main type of property income is rental income from the letting of unfurnished or furnished property. Rental income specifically includes any amounts receivable for the use of furniture if the property is furnished property.

Rental income is taxed on the amount accrued in a tax year. Therefore, for 2014/15 the rental income taxable is the amount accrued between 6 April 2014 and 5 April 2015, after allowable expenses. Expenses are also allowable on an accruals basis.

Worked example: Property income – accruals basis

Susan rents out an unfurnished house. Until 30 June 2014, rent is £1,250 per calendar month, payable in arrears on the last day of each month. Thereafter the rent is increased to £1,500 per month. The rent is usually paid promptly, but the payment due on 31 March 2015 was not received until 10 April 2015.

Susan paid an insurance premium of £1,600 on 1 January 2014 for the year to 31 December 2014 and an insurance premium of £1,800 on 1 January 2015 for the year to 31 December 2015.

Susan had other allowable expenses of £6,020 accrued in 2014/15.

Requirement

Calculate Susan's taxable property income for 2014/15.

Solution

Susan
Property income

	£	£
Rent accrued		
April – June 2014 £1,250 × 3		3,750
July 2014 – March 2015 £1,500 × 9		13,500
		17,250
Less: insurance premium		
April – December 2014		
£1,600 × 9/12	1,200	
January – March 2015		
£1,800 × 3/12	450	
other expenses	6,020	(7,670)
Taxable property income		9,580

Note that the fact that the March 2015 rental payment is not received until 2015/16 is not relevant – the amount due is accrued in 2014/15 and is therefore taxable in that year.

If more than one property is let, all income and expenditure is pooled to calculate a single amount of taxable property income.

However if one or more properties satisfy the conditions to be treated as furnished holiday accommodation, the income from such lettings is taxed separately (see later in this section).

1.2 Allowable expenses

Allowable expenses include the following:

- Legal, professional and administrative costs

- Interest paid eg on loans to buy property, overdraft interest relating to property letting

- Rates and taxes paid by the landlord eg council tax, water rates

- Ancillary services provided by the landlord eg cleaning, gardening

- Insurance for the property (in all cases)

- Furnishings (if let furnished) see below

- Repairs and maintenance eg painting, redecoration

- Landlord energy saving allowance up to £1,500 per dwelling house for installing loft/cavity wall/floor insulation, draught proofing and hot water system insulation. If a building contains more than one dwelling, the £1,500 applies per dwelling

If a property is partly owner-occupied and partly let, expenses relating to periods of owner-occupation are not allowable.

1.3 Bad debt relief

Rental income is taxed on an accruals basis. If a tenant does not pay the rent, the income is still taxable.

However, if the debt remains unpaid and the debt is written off by the landlord, relief is given for the amount written off.

1.4 Capital expenditure

Capital allowances are only available on the cost of plant and machinery used for the repair or maintenance of the property.

Capital allowances are therefore not available for most items of plant and machinery, furniture and other equipment provided for use in a furnished property.

Instead, where a property is let furnished, the landlord can **claim** a **wear and tear allowance**.

The wear and tear allowance is calculated as 10% of rents accrued less any amounts paid by the landlord which are legally the responsibility of the tenant (eg water rates and council tax). The allowance is given for the period when the property is available for letting.

Interactive question: Taxable property income [Difficulty level: Exam standard]

Lee owns a flat which he lets out furnished at a weekly rental of £125.

During 2014/15, the flat was let out for 34 weeks, occupied by Lee for 9 weeks and then let out for the remaining 9 weeks to a new tenant.

Lee had the following expenditure during the year:

	£
Repairs	460
Council tax	680
Water rates	255
Redecoration	500
Insurance	240
Gardening and cleaning (during tenanted period only)	440
Advertising for new tenant	25

Requirement

Using the standard format below, compute the taxable property income for Lee.

£   £   £

Income

Expenses
Allowable in full:

_____

Allowable for let period:

_____

Total allowable for let period   .... × ..../52
Wear and tear allowance:
10% × [.................... − ((...........................) × ..../52)]   _____

          (............)

Taxable property income

See **Answer** at the end of this chapter.

1.5 Losses

In each tax year, all property letting income and expenditure is pooled. As a result, a single overall profit (or loss) figure is calculated for that tax year.

If a loss arises, there is no taxable property income in that tax year.

The loss is carried forward and set, as far as possible, against the first available future property income. The deduction is made at Step 2 of the income tax liability computation (Chapter 2) in arriving at net income.

1.6 Rent a room relief

If an individual lets out part of his home, he will receive taxable property income. However, **rent a room relief** may apply.

To be eligible for the relief, the accommodation let to the tenant must be furnished and part of the individual taxpayer's only or main domestic residence (ie house or flat).

The tax treatment of rental income depends on the level of gross annual rents.

Where gross rental income is not more than £4,250 per tax year: [Hp7]

- The income and expenses arising in relation to the letting are ignored for income tax

- Similarly, no property losses arise unless the taxpayer elects to set aside the rent a room rules for a particular tax year and so claim a property loss

Where gross rental income is more than £4,250 per tax year:

- The normal property income rules usually apply

- Alternatively, the taxpayer can elect to be assessed under the rent a room rules on the gross rents in excess of the rent a room limit of £4,250. However, in this case, there is no relief for expenses. This election applies for subsequent tax years until the election is withdrawn or the gross rents do not exceed the rent a room limit

Where two or more people, including husband and wife/civil partners, share a home each has rent a room relief of £2,125 (£4,250/2). The limit is always halved like this for each co-owner, even if there are three or more co-owners.

Worked example: Rent a room relief

Gina let out a room in her house at a rent of £120 a week throughout 2014/15. Her allowable expenses for the year were £5,100 (including a wear and tear allowance).

Requirement

Show the tax position for Gina if:

(a) The normal property income rules apply; or
(b) She has previously made an election in 2013/14 to use the rent a room rules.

Based on your computations, what advice would you give to Gina?

Solution

(a) Normal property income rules

	£
Rent received £120 × 52	6,240
Less expenses	(5,100)
Taxable property income	1,140

(b) Rent a room rules

	£
Gross rents	6,240
Less rent a room limit	(4,250)
Taxable property income	1,990

Gina should withdraw her election to use the rent a room rules, as the normal property income rules give a lower taxable amount of property income.

In this question you are specifically asked to look at both possible tax treatments, but remember that in the examination, if you are not directed to do this, you should assume the more beneficial treatment applies.

1.7 Real Estate Investment Trusts (REITs)

A company can, if it fulfils certain conditions, be treated as a Real Estate Investment Trust (REIT). Investing in a REIT rather than an individual property enables the investor to spread his investment over a number of properties. The shares should be more marketable than a property would be, but the investor is still exposed to fluctuations in the property market. Some income generated by a REIT is tax-exempt, other income may not be tax-exempt.

REITs are exempt from corporation tax on their property income and gains. Amounts paid out of tax-exempt property income or gains to a shareholder of a REIT are taxable on the shareholder as property income and are paid net of basic rate tax at 20%.

Amounts paid out of non tax-exempt property income or gains to a shareholder of a REIT are taxable as normal dividends and are grossed up by $\frac{100}{90}$.

Gains on disposals of shares are subject to capital gains tax in the normal way (see later in this study manual).

1.8 Property Authorised Investment Funds (AIFs)

Authorised Investment funds (AIFs) with an investment portfolio which consists mainly of real property or shares in UK-REITs will be able to elect to use the AIF tax rules.

The AIF is exempt from tax on rental profits and certain other property related income. The AIF makes payments to its shareholders as either a property or interest distribution; or as a dividend.

The property and interest distributions are taxable on the shareholder as property and interest income and are paid net of basic rate tax at 20%. The dividend distribution is taxable as normal dividends and grossed up by $\frac{100}{90}$.

2 Furnished holiday accommodation

Section overview

- Income from commercial lettings of furnished holiday accommodation in the UK and other parts of the European Economic Area (EEA) is taxed as property income but, provided certain conditions are satisfied, is treated for most tax purposes as if it were trading income.

- Accommodation is only furnished holiday accommodation if it satisfies three conditions: the availability test; the occupancy test; and the pattern of availability test.

- Where the conditions are satisfied the income qualifies as relevant income for pension purposes; capital allowances are available; and special reliefs are available (outside the scope of your syllabus).

2.1 Introduction

Income from commercial lettings of furnished holiday accommodation in the UK and other parts of the European Economic Area (EEA) is taxed as property income but, provided certain conditions are satisfied, is treated for most tax purposes as if it were trading income.

A commercial letting of furnished holiday accommodation requires the letting to be on a commercial basis with a view to the realisation of profits, with the tenant being entitled to the use of the furniture.

Where the taxpayer also has other letting income, he is treated as running a 'business of letting' and a 'business of furnished holiday letting' and the two are computed separately.

Where the taxpayer owns properties in both the UK and the EEA, these are treated as two separate furnished holiday letting (FHL) businesses.

Accommodation is only furnished holiday accommodation if it satisfies three conditions:

(a)   The availability test
(b)   The occupancy test
(c)   The pattern of occupancy test

2.2   Conditions

2.2.1   The availability condition

The property must be available for commercial letting to the public for at least 210 days in a tax year.

2.2.2   The occupancy condition

The property must be let for at least 105 days in the year.

If a landlord has two or more properties and each passes the 210 day test separately, then he can elect to average the days so they need only pass the 105 day test on average.

This averaging election must be made by the anniversary of the self assessment filing date for the tax year in question, ie by 31 January 2017 for FHL income reported on a 2014/15 tax return.

A landlord may choose to leave particular properties out of the averaging computation if they would pull the average down to below 105 days.

Where the actual letting condition (ie 105 days in 2014/15) is the only one not met for that tax year by a previously qualifying FHL, a grace period of two years will be available so the property can continue to qualify. The landlord will need to submit an election for each year of the grace period on or before the first anniversary of the self assessment filing date for the relevant tax year. An election can only be made for the second year if one has been made for the first year.

2.2.3   The pattern of occupancy condition

If the property is let out to the same person for periods longer than 31 days, ie a period of 'longer term occupation', in one stretch, none of the days counts towards the occupation threshold (unless there are exceptional and unforeseen circumstances, such as where a holidaymaker falls ills and cannot leave the accommodation in time).

If the total of all or any longer term occupation lettings exceeds 155 days in the year, the property cannot qualify as a FHL for that period.

The property can be let to the same person more than once as long as each let is less than 31 days. All of these lettings together to the same person can total more than 31 days and still count towards the occupation threshold.

2.3   Tax treatment

The key income tax advantages are:

- Profits are relevant earnings for pension scheme purposes, so pension contributions may be made in respect of such profits

- Capital allowances are available on all plant and machinery including furniture (instead of the wear and tear allowance)

The main capital gains tax advantage is that the property is treated as a business asset. This entitles the individual to the associated capital gains tax reliefs (the details are outside the scope of your syllabus).

For inheritance tax business property relief may be available (outside the scope of your syllabus).

Losses on FHL can only be offset against income from the same FHL business (outside the scope of your syllabus).

3 Premiums on leases

Section overview

- A lease is the right to use an asset for a specified period of time.
- Part of the premium received by a landlord on the grant of a short lease is taxable property income.

3.1 Basic principle

A 'lease' is a right to use an asset (in this case a property) for a specified period of time. Any amount paid up front by the lessee (the tenant) to the lessor (landlord) for the use of a property is referred to as a 'premium' and is treated as a capital receipt. There are usually therefore no income tax implications for a premium as it is a capital sum.

However, when a premium is received on the grant (that is, by a landlord to a tenant) of a short lease (50 years or less), part of the premium is treated as rent and is taxed as property income in the year of grant.

3.2 Amount taxed as property income

If a lease is granted by a landlord to a tenant, the landlord may receive a capital payment from the tenant. This is called a **premium**. If the lease is a short lease (50 years or less), part of the premium is taxable as property income.

The amount of the premium taxable as property income is: [Hp40]

$$P \times \frac{50 - Y}{50}$$

Where:

P = total premium paid
Y = complete number of years of the lease minus one

Worked example: Grant of short lease

Sasha grants a 30 year lease to Greg for a premium of £45,000.

Requirement

Compute the amount of the premium which is taxable as property income.

Solution

$$P \times \frac{50-Y}{50} = £45,000 \times \frac{50-(30-1)}{50} = \qquad \underline{£18,900}$$

3.3 Deemed additional rent

Where a trader pays a premium for a lease, he can deduct an amount from his trading profits in each year of the lease. The deduction is the amount of the premium taxed on the landlord as property income divided by the number of years of the lease. Where the lease starts or ends during the trader's accounting period the deduction is pro rated. [Hp41]

Worked example: Lease deduction for trader

Sean grants a 25 year lease of a workshop to Fred, who carries on a trade in the workshop. The premium paid by Fred on the grant of the lease is £15,000.

Requirement

Compute the amount that Fred can deduct each year from his trading profits.

Solution

Amount taxable on Sean

Taxable property income

$$£15,000 \times \frac{50-(25-1)}{50} = \qquad £7,800$$

Amount deductible each year by Fred

$$\frac{£7,800}{25} \qquad £312$$

3.4 Premiums for granting subleases

If a tenant grants a sublease of the property to a sub-tenant, any premium he receives will also be subject to these rules. If the tenant paid a premium on the grant of the lease to him, he can deduct the appropriate part of the amount taxed on the landlord on the original grant, from the part of the premium he receives which is taxable as property income.

Worked example: Grant of sub lease

Misha granted a lease to Eleanor on 1 December 2005 for 40 years. Eleanor paid a premium of £80,000.

On 1 December 2014, Eleanor granted a 10 year sub-lease to Wayne. Wayne paid a premium of £16,000.

Requirement

Compute the amount of the premium paid by Wayne to Eleanor which will be taxed on Eleanor as property income.

Solution

Amount taxed on Misha

Taxable property income

$$£80,000 \times \frac{50-(40-1)}{50} = \qquad £17,600$$

Amount taxed on Eleanor

	£
Taxable property income	
$£16,000 \times \dfrac{50-(10-1)}{50} =$	13,120
Less $£17,600 \times \dfrac{10}{40}$	(4,400)
Taxable property income	8,720

Summary

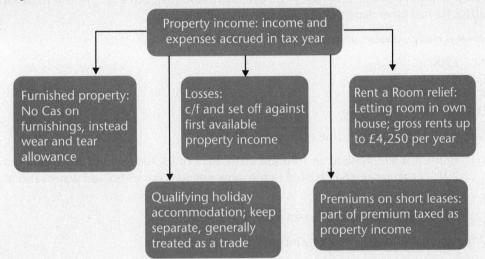

Property income: income and expenses accrued in tax year

Furnished property: No Cas on furnishings, instead wear and tear allowance

Losses: c/f and set off against first available property income

Rent a Room relief: Letting room in own house; gross rents up to £4,250 per year

Qualifying holiday accommodation; keep separate, generally treated as a trade

Premiums on short leases: part of premium taxed as property income

Self-test

Answer the following questions.

1 Harry owns a property which he lets for the first time on 1 November 2014 at a rent of £6,000 a year, payable in four equal instalments on 1 November, 1 February, 1 May and 1 August.

Harry paid an insurance premium of £1,200 on 1 November 2014 for the year to 31 October 2015. He had other expenses of £900 relating to the letting.

What is Harry's taxable property income for 2014/15?

A £900
B £1,100
C £1,600
D £3,900

2 Jane received property income as follows in 2014/15.

(1) House first let furnished on 1 August 2014. Rent of £4,200 accrued in the period to 5 April 2015. Expenses of £649 related to the same period. Council tax and water rates are paid by the tenant.

(2) £4,000 from letting a furnished room in her home.

What amount of taxable property income does Jane have?

A £3,131
B £7,131
C £3,551
D £7,551

3 **Jonas**

Jonas is aged 35. In 2014/15 he had the following income and expenses:

Trading income	£13,750
Building society interest received:	
Deposit account	£485
Cash ISA	£120
UK dividends:	
Quoted company	£1,098
Property income (letting of furnished flat):	
Rent received	£10,720
Redecoration	£700
Insurance	£600
Agent's fees	£500
Water rates	£360
Interest on loan to buy flat	£6,000

Requirement

Calculate the tax payable by Jonas.   **(10 marks)**

Now go back to the Learning Objectives in the Introduction. If you are satisfied you have achieved these objectives please tick them off.

Technical reference

Legislation

References are to Income Tax (Trading and Other Income) Act 2005 (*ITTOIA 2005*)

Charge to tax	ss.268 – 271
Calculation of profits	s.272
Furnished lettings	s.308
Rent a room relief	s.309
Furnished holiday accommodation	ss. 323 – 328
Premiums on short leases	s.277

HMRC manual references

Property Income Manual (Found at http://www.hmrc.gov.uk/manuals/pimmanual/index.htm)

Income chargeable: overview	PIM 1051
Deductions: general rules: introduction	PIM 2005

> This technical reference section is designed to assist you. It should help you know where to look for further information on the topics covered in this chapter.

CHAPTER

3

Answer to Interactive question

	£	£	£
Income			
Rent received			
(34 + 9) = 43 × £125			5,375
Expenses			
Allowable in full:			
Gardening and cleaning	440		
Advertising for new tenant	25	465	
Allowable for let period:			
Repairs	460		
Council tax	680		
Water rates	255		
Redecoration	500		
Insurance	240		
Total allowable for let period	2,135 × 43/52	1,765	
Wear and tear allowance:			
10% × [£5,375 – ((£680 + £255) × 43/52)]		460	(2,690)
Taxable property income			2,685

Remember that in the examination, you should assume any beneficial claims, elections or deductions are made ie here that the wear and tear allowance applies.

Answers to Self-test

1 B – £1,100

	£	£
Rent accrued		
November 2014 – March 2015		
£6,000 × 5/12		2,500
Less: insurance premium		
November 2014 – March 2015		
£1,200 × 5/12	500	
other expenses	900	(1,400)
Taxable property income		1,100

2 A – £3,131

House

	£	£
Rent		4,200
Less: expenses	649	
wear and tear – claim assumed as beneficial		
10% × £4,200	420	(1,069)
Property income		3,131

Room in own house

Exempt under rent a room (gross rent less than £4,250)

3 **Jonas**
   Tax payable

	Non-savings income £	Savings income £	Dividend income £	Total £
Trading income	13,750			
Property income (W)	1,524			
BSI £485 × 100/80		606		
Dividends £1,098 × 100/90			1,220	
Net income	15,274	606	1,220	17,100
Less PA	(10,000)			(10,000)
Taxable income	5,274	606	1,220	7,100

Tax

	£
£5,274 × 20%	1,055
£606 × 20%	121
£1,220 × 10%	122
£7,100	
Tax liability	1,298
Less tax deducted at source	
£1,220 × 10%	(122)
£606 × 20%	(121)
Tax payable	1,055

Interest on ISA is exempt from income tax.

WORKING

	£	£
Income		
Rent received		10,720
Expenses		
Redecoration	700	
Insurance	600	
Agent's fees	500	
Water rates	360	
Interest	6,000	
Wear and tear allowance:		
10% × [£10,720 − £360]	1,036	(9,196)
Taxable property income		1,524

CHAPTER 4

Pensions

Introduction

Examination context

Topic List

    1   Pension schemes

    2   Contributing to a pension scheme

    3   Receiving benefits from a pension scheme

Summary and Self-test

Technical reference

Answer to Interactive question

Answers to Self-test

Learning objective

- Explain the alternative ways in which an individual can provide for retirement and calculate the tax relief available

Specific syllabus references for this chapter are 3l.

Syllabus links

Pension schemes were not covered in your Principles of Taxation study manual.

Examination context

In the examination candidates may be required to:

- Calculate and include relief for pension contributions within an income tax computation

- Calculate the charge on excess contributions, and the lifetime allowance charge

- Explain to individuals the types of pension scheme available and the benefits obtained from investments in pensions

1 Pension schemes

Section overview

- Employees may join an occupational pension scheme and/or a personal pension scheme.

- Self-employed individuals may join a personal pension scheme.

- If an individual has more than one pension arrangement, all of them will be looked at together for tax purposes.

- Pension schemes are not liable to tax.

1.1 Occupational pension scheme

Definition

Occupational pension scheme: A pension scheme run by an employer or group of employers for employees.

An employee may join an occupational pension scheme. Occupational pension schemes may either require contributions from employees or be non-contributory. The employer may use the services of an insurance company (an insured scheme) or may set up a totally self administered pension fund.

An employee cannot be forced to join an occupational pension scheme; instead he may make personal pension provision.

Occupational pension schemes may be earnings-related or investment-related. In an earnings-related scheme, the benefits are defined by the level of earnings of the employee. They are therefore called **defined benefits schemes**. For defined benefits schemes the level of compulsory employee contributions will be fixed by the employer.

Alternatively, the scheme may be investment-related so that the value of the pension benefits that will be provided depends on the performance of the pension fund investments. These are called **money purchase schemes**.

1.2 Personal pension scheme

Definition

Personal pension scheme: A pension scheme run by a financial institution such as an insurance company or a bank.

Any individual (whether employed or self-employed) may join a personal pension scheme.

Personal pension schemes are usually money purchase schemes.

1.3 Multiple pension schemes

An individual may join a number of different pension schemes depending on his circumstances.

For example, he may be a member of an occupational pension scheme and also join a personal pension scheme.

If the individual joins more than one pension scheme, the rules we will look at in detail later apply to **all** the pension schemes that he joins. For example, there is a limit on the amount of contributions that the individual can make in a tax year. This limit will apply to all the pension schemes that he joins, not each scheme separately.

1.4 Taxation of pension schemes

Pension schemes registered with HMRC are not liable to tax on income or gains. They are therefore a tax-efficient form of investment.

1.5 Comparison of pension provision for employees/self employed

Employees	Self employed
Can be a member of an occupational pension scheme and/or personal pension scheme	Can only be a member of a personal pension scheme
Can make own contributions and employer can also make contributions (exempt benefit for employee, tax deductible for employer)	Can make own contributions
Occupational pension schemes may be defined benefit (eg final salary) or money purchase	Personal pension schemes are usually only money purchase so pension depends on growth in underlying investments

2 Contributing to a pension scheme

Section overview

- Individuals can contribute to a pension scheme up to the age of 75.

- The maximum contributions on which tax relief can be given is the higher of the taxpayer's relevant earnings and the basic amount.

- Tax relief can be given at source or under net pay arrangements.

- There is a tax charge on tax relievable contributions above the annual allowance.

2.1 Who can make contributions attracting tax relief?

An individual, who is an active member of a pension scheme registered with HMRC and under the age of 75, is entitled to tax relief on his contributions to the scheme.

An active member of a pension scheme is an individual for whom there are presently arrangements being made (such as contributions) under the pension scheme for accrual of benefits to that person or in respect of him (eg benefits for his dependants).

2.2 Annual limit for relief

The maximum amount of contributions made by an individual in a tax year attracting tax relief is the higher of: [Hp27]

- The individual's relevant earnings chargeable to income tax in the year; and
- The basic amount (£3,600 for 2014/15).

Relevant earnings are employment income, trading income, patent income in respect of inventions and income from qualifying holiday accommodation.

This means that if the individual does not have any earnings in a tax year, he can make a maximum gross contribution of £3,600 in that year.

Where an individual contributes to more than one pension scheme, the aggregate of his contributions will be used to determine the total amount of tax relief.

There is an interaction between this provision and the annual allowance, which will be discussed later in this chapter.

2.3 Tax relief given at source

Relief given at source is used where an individual makes a contribution to a pension scheme run by a personal pension provider such as an insurance company.

Relief is given at source by the contributions being deemed to be made net of basic rate tax, in the same way as relief is given for Gift Aid donations. For example, an individual with no earnings can make a payment of £2,880 (80% × £3,600). This applies whether the individual is an employee, self-employed or not employed at all and even if he has no taxable income. HMRC then pays an equivalent amount of basic rate tax to the pension provider.

Further tax relief is given for contributions to personal pension schemes if the individual is a higher rate or additional rate taxpayer. As with Gift Aid donations, the relief is given by increasing the basic rate limit and the higher rate limit for the year by the gross amount of contributions for which he is entitled to relief, at Step 4 of the income tax liability computation (Chapter 2).

 ### Worked example: Tax relief at source

Tabitha has earnings of £60,000 in 2014/15. She pays a personal pension contribution of £7,200 (net). She has no other chargeable income.

Requirement

Calculate Tabitha's tax liability for 2014/15.

Solution

Tabitha
Tax liability

	£
Earnings/net income	60,000
Less: Personal Allowance	(10,000)
Taxable income	50,000

Tax

	£
£31,865 × 20%	6,373
£9,000 (7,200 × 100/80) × 20%	1,800
£9,135 × 40%	3,654
£50,000	
Tax liability	11,827

If Tabitha had earned £180,000 then her basic rate band would have been extended to £40,865 (as above) and her higher rate limit would have been increased to £159,000 (ie £150,000 + £9,000). The additional rate would then only have applied to the income in excess of this increased higher rate limit: ie to £21,000 of income (£180,000 – £159,000). Remember that her income would then be in excess of £120,000 so she would not be entitled to a personal allowance.

2.4 Tax relief given under net pay arrangements

An occupational scheme will normally operate net pay arrangements.

In this case, the employer will deduct gross pension contributions from the individual's employment income before operating PAYE. The individual therefore obtains tax relief without having to make any claim. A contribution to an occupational pension scheme therefore has no effect on either the basic rate band or the higher rate band.

For the purposes of the exam assume all occupational pension schemes operate net pay arrangements.

Interactive question: Net pay arrangements [Difficulty level: Easy]

James has taxable employment income of £60,000 in 2014/15. His employer deducts a pension contribution of £9,000 from these earnings before operating PAYE. He has no other taxable income.

Requirement

Using the standard format below, calculate James' tax liability for 2014/15.

James
Tax liability

	£
Earnings/net income	
Less Personal Allowance	( )
Taxable income	
Tax	£
£_____	_____
Tax liability	

See **Answer** at the end of this chapter.

2.5 Contributions by active scheme member not attracting tax relief

An active scheme member can also make contributions to his pension scheme which do not attract tax relief, for example out of capital.

The member must notify the scheme administrator if he makes contributions in excess of the higher of his relevant earnings and the basic amount.

Such contributions do not count towards the annual allowance limit (discussed later in this section) but will affect the value of the pension fund for the lifetime allowance.

2.6 Contributions by employer

Where the active scheme member is an employee, his employer will often make contributions to his pension scheme as part of his employment benefits package. Such contributions are exempt benefits for the employee.

There is no limit on the amount of the contributions that may be made by an employer but they always count towards the annual allowance and will also affect the value of the pension fund for the lifetime allowance (see later in this chapter).

All contributions made by an employer are made gross and the employer will usually obtain tax relief for the contribution by deducting it as an expense in calculating trading profits for the period of account in which the payment is made.

Where the employer contribution is to a personal pension scheme remember that as it is a contribution made gross by the employer it does not need any further tax relief. Therefore it has no effect on either the basic rate band or the higher rate band.

2.7 Annual allowance

Definition

Annual allowance: The overriding limit for total pension input to the active member's pension fund for each tax year.

2.7.1 Overview

The amount of the annual allowance is as follows: [Hp27]

Tax year	Annual allowance £
2011/12	50,000
2012/13	50,000
2013/14	50,000
2014/15	40,000

2.7.2 Pension input period

The annual allowance is tested against the pension input amount for the pension input period which ends in the tax year. The pension input period is normally a period of 12 months chosen by the scheme member or the scheme. There must be one pension input period ending in every tax year.

The pension input period aligns with the tax year for new scheme members from 6 April 2011, unless they nominate a different period (existing members have to write to their pension provider to change their period to the tax year).

2.7.3 Pension input amount

The calculation of the pension input amount depends on the type of pension scheme involved.

Where the pension scheme is a money purchase arrangement, the pension input amount is the aggregate of:

- Any tax relievable pension contributions paid by the individual under the arrangement

- Contributions paid in respect of the individual under the arrangement by an employer of the individual

Only tax relieved contributions made by or on behalf of an individual count towards the limit. Contributions on which tax relief is not obtained (eg capital contributions) will not affect the position. On the other hand, all contributions by an employer will count towards the annual allowance. No account is taken of any increase in the value of the investments held in the scheme during the pension input period.

Where the pension scheme is a defined benefits arrangement, the pension input amount is the increase in value of the individual's rights under the arrangement during the pension input period, including the effect of any increase in salary. The value of the individual's rights at any time is calculated as 16 times the pension that would be paid if the individual became entitled to payment, plus the lump sum that would also be due.

2.7.4 Carry forward of unused annual allowance

Unused annual allowance can be carried forward for three years, so even where pension savings exceed the annual allowance in a pension input period, there may not be a charge if the individual has not used all of his annual allowance in the previous three tax years. In this case, the current year's allowance is set off first, then any unused allowance from the earliest of the three tax years in priority to later years.

An unused annual allowance can only be carried forward from a year in which the individual was a member of a registered pension scheme (even if he did not make a contribution in that year).

Prior to 2011/12, a notional annual allowance applied, but questions in your exam will not require knowledge of the notional annual allowance.

Worked example: Carry forward of unused annual allowance

Karen is a member of a money purchase personal pension scheme. She has gross pension contributions to the scheme of £67,000 for 2011/12, £54,000 for 2012/13, £42,000 for 2013/14 and £42,000 for 2014/15.

Requirement

Explain the amount of any unused annual allowance brought forward to 2014/15 and how it will be relieved.

Solution

Unused allowance brought forward

In both 2011/12 and 2012/13, Karen's gross pension contributions exceeded the annual allowance (£50,000 in each year) and so she has no unused allowance brought forward from these years. In 2013/14 she makes pension contributions below the annual allowance and will generate unused annual allowance of £8,000 to carry forward.

Allowance utilised in 2014/15

In 2014/15 Karen will have unused allowance of £8,000 from 2013/14, £2,000 of which will be used in 2014/15 as the pension input is £2,000 above the annual allowance for 2014/15, which is £40,000. The remaining balance of £6,000 can be carried forward to 2015/16:

	Allowance unused as at 6 April 2014 £	Allowance utilised in 2014/15 £	Allowance remaining to c/f to 2015/16 £
2011/12 c/f	0	0	0
2012/13 c/f	0	0	0
2013/14 c/f	8,000	2,000	6,000
2014/15	40,000	40,000	0
		42,000	6,000

Worked example: Carry forward of unused annual allowance

Maurice makes the following gross contributions into his personal pension scheme.

2011/12	£35,000
2012/13	£25,000
2013/14	£30,000

In 2014/15 Maurice makes a contribution to his pension fund of £78,000.

Requirement

Calculate the amount of any unused annual allowance remaining at 5 April 2015 for each of the tax years 2011/12 to 2014/15 showing how the gross payment of £97,500 by Maurice in 2014/15 is allocated.

Solution

	Unused allowance £	Allowance utilised in 2014/15 £	Allowance remaining as at 5 April 2015 £
2011/12	15,000	15,000	0
2012/13	25,000	25,000	0
2013/14	20,000	17,500	2,500
2014/15	40,000	40,000	0
		97,500	2,500

2.7.5 Annual allowance charge

If the pension input amount exceeds the annual allowance there is a charge to income tax on the individual. This might happen where the individual makes tax relievable contributions in excess of the annual allowance where his earnings exceed the amount of allowance or where the employer makes excess contributions. [Hp27]

The annual allowance charge will remove the tax relief received on the pension input in excess of the annual allowance. This could be in whole or part at 45%, 40% or 20% depending on the taxable income of the individual.

The tax charge is added to an individual's income tax computation at Step 7 (Chapter 2) in arriving at his income tax liability for the year.

Employer contributions are not treated as earnings or taxable benefits for NIC purposes. Therefore, there is a slight advantage to the employer making contributions directly to a pension scheme instead of paying the individual the money for that individual to make contributions, even if the charge applies.

2.7.6 Calculating the annual allowance charge (AAC)

The income tax charge is calculated by treating the excess contributions as the taxpayer's top slice of income (above all other sources, including termination payments – see later in this study manual). For example, if the taxpayer has part of the basic rate band remaining, after taking account of his taxable income, the amount of excess contributions equal to the basic rate band remaining is taxed at 20%. Any remaining excess contributions are then taxed at the higher rate and additional rates as appropriate. Remember that the basic rate and higher rate limits are extended for personal pension contributions and, if appropriate, Gift Aid donations.

The tax is added to the taxpayer's income tax liability at Step 7 in the income tax calculation (see Chapter 2).

Worked example: Annual allowance charge

Simon is a member of a money purchase personal pension scheme. In the tax year 2014/15, he has taxable earnings of £95,500. During that year, he makes a contribution of £48,000 to the pension scheme and his employer makes further contributions of £30,000 to the scheme. Simon has no other taxable income in the year. Simon made a donation of £480 to charity under Gift Aid during 2014/15.

Simon has £10,000 unused annual allowance bought forward.

Requirement

Calculate Simon's income tax liability for 2014/15.

Solution

Simon has made a net contribution of £48,000 to the pension scheme which grosses up to (£48,000 × 100/80) = £60,000.

This is all tax-relievable since it is lower than the greater of:

- His relevant earnings of £95,500; and
- The basic amount of £3,600.

However, the excess pension contributions are:

	£
Individual contribution subject to tax relief	60,000
Employer contributions	30,000
Total tax relievable contributions	90,000
Less: annual allowance 2014/15	(40,000)
Less: unused annual allowance b/f	(10,000)
Excess contributions	40,000

His basic and higher rate limits are increased by £60,600 to take account of both the gross Gift Aid (£480 × 100/80) and gross pension contribution, as follows:

- Basic rate band: £92,465 (£31,865 + £600 + £60,000)
- Higher rate limit: £210,600 (£150,000 + £600 + £60,000)

	£
Earnings/net income	95,500
Less: Personal allowance	(10,000)
Taxable income	85,500

Tax

	£
£85,500 × 20%	17,100
£85,500	

	£
Annual allowance charge	
(£92,465 – £85,500) £6,965 × 20%	1,393
(£40,000 – £6,965) £33,035 × 40%	13,214
Tax liability	31,707

Worked example: Excess contributions

Julia is a member of a money purchase personal pension scheme. In the tax year 2014/15, she has taxable earnings of £275,000. During that year, she makes a contribution of £120,000 to her pension scheme and her employer makes a further contribution of £120,000 to the scheme. Julia has no other taxable income in the year and has no unused pension annual allowance brought forward.

Requirement

Calculate Julia's income tax liability for 2014/15.

Solution

Julia has made a net contribution of £120,000 to the pension scheme which grosses up to (£120,000 × 100/80) = £150,000.

This is all tax-relievable since it is lower than the greater of:

- Her relevant earnings of £275,000; and
- The basic amount of £3,600.

Julia's pension contributions in excess of the annual allowance are:

	£
Individual contribution subject to tax relief	150,000
Employer contributions	120,000
Total tax relievable contributions	270,000
Less annual allowance	(40,000)
Excess contributions	230,000

Her basic and higher rate limits are increased by £150,000, as follows:

- Basic rate band: £181,865 (£31,865 + £150,000)
- Higher rate limit: £300,000 (£150,000 + £150,000)

	£
Earnings/net income	275,000
Less Personal Allowance (Note 1)	(nil)
Taxable income	275,000

Tax

£181,865 × 20%	36,373
£93,135 × 40%	37,254
£275,000	

Annual allowance charge

(£300,000 – £275,000) £25,000 × 40%	10,000
(£230,000 – £25,000) £205,000 × 45%	92,250
Tax liability	175,877

Note 1 – Julia's adjusted net income is £275,000 – £150,000 = £125,000 and therefore her personal allowance is nil.

3 Receiving benefits from a pension scheme

Section overview

- When an individual reaches the minimum retirement age he may draw a pension. This may include a tax free lump sum as well as the purchase of an annuity. All pension income is taxable as non-savings income.

- There is a maximum value of a pension fund called the lifetime allowance.

- Pension benefits may be taken in the lifetime of the member or by his dependants on his death.

- The lifetime allowance charge arises on a benefit crystallisation event if the lifetime allowance has been exceeded.

3.1 Drawing a pension – pension age

The minimum age that an individual can receive a pension (including a tax free lump sum, see below) from either an occupational or a personal pension scheme is 55.

Employees can draw part of their pension from a company occupational pension scheme whilst they are still working full or part time for the same employer so long as they have reached the requisite age.

3.2 Drawing a pension – tax free lump sum

Individuals can usually take a tax free lump sum of as much as 25% of their pension fund, subject to a maximum of 25% × the lifetime allowance.

There is no maximum age for taking the tax free lump sum.

3.3 Drawing a pension – balance of the pension fund

There are a number of alternative ways of taking the balance of the pension fund:

(a) Take a scheme pension – secure for life

(b) Buy an annuity – providing a secure, regular (usually monthly) income for life

(c) Receive a single cash lump sum at age 60 or over where the pension is small, or 'trivial' (ie valued at up to £30,000), 25% of which will be tax free (see above)

(d) Draw a capped amount of income (150% of the equivalent annuity that could have been bought) directly from the pension (a drawdown pension)

(e)   Draw an unlimited amount of income directly from the pension so long as the equivalent annuity is at least £12,000 a year (a flexible drawdown pension)

Drawing income means that regular income may be withdrawn from the pension fund while the fund remains invested. Although the fund may continue to grow, it could also fall, so a drawdown pension is a riskier choice.

3.4   Drawing a pension – taxation of pension income

Apart from the tax free lump sum (above) all other income taken from a pension (including the state pension) is taxed as non savings income.

3.5   Lifetime allowance

Definition

Lifetime allowance: The maximum value for a pension fund (for money purchase schemes) or for the value of benefits (for defined benefits schemes).

The amount of the lifetime allowance is as follows: [Hp27]

Tax year	Lifetime allowance £
2008/09	1,650,000
2009/10	1,750,000
2010/11	1,800,000
2011/12	1,800,000
2012/13	1,500,000
2013/14	1,500,000
2014/15	1,250,000

The lifetime allowance was reduced to £1,250,000 for the tax year 2014/15 onwards. However, transitional provisions have been introduced to protect individuals who have pension funds valued at higher than £1,250,000 on 5 April 2014. In such a case, provided the individual has applied to HMRC for individual pension protection, the lifetime allowance for that individual will be the higher of the value of their pension fund at 5 April 2014 (subject to a maximum of £1,500,000) and the actual lifetime allowance.

Where the pension scheme is a money purchase scheme, the value of the fund for the lifetime allowance will be the value of the investments in the fund.

Where the pension scheme is a defined benefits scheme, the income benefits are usually valued on a 20:1 ratio, so that, for example, a pension of £10,000 will be valued at £200,000 for this purpose and lump sum benefits are valued at face value.

The individual does not have to keep a running total of the value of his pension scheme. Instead, the lifetime allowance limit is tested only when a benefit crystallisation event occurs.

The most common benefit crystallisation events are:

*   When a member becomes entitled to a scheme pension

*   Where a scheme pension already being paid is increased by more than the greater of 5% or the increase in the RPI

*   Where a member becomes entitled to a lifetime annuity under a money purchase scheme

*   Where a member reaches the age of 75 under a defined benefit scheme without having vested all or part of his entitlement to a pension and/or lump sum

*   When a member becomes entitled to a lump sum, for example a tax-free lump sum when the entitlement to pension income arises

*   Where a lump sum is paid on the death of a member

3.6 When does a lifetime allowance charge arise?

When a member takes a benefit from a pension scheme, there is a **benefit crystallisation event**. The value of the pension fund has to be tested against the lifetime allowance for the year in which the event occurs.

In many cases, the lifetime allowance will not have been exceeded and there will be no income tax charge.

However, the lifetime allowance to be used for future benefit crystallisation events will be reduced by the value of the benefits that have crystallised in the current event.

In some cases, the pension fund will exceed the lifetime allowance and this will give rise to an income tax charge on the excess value of the fund which has been vested to provide either a lump sum or a pension income. The rate of the charge depends on the type of benefit that will be taken from the excess funds.

3.7 Calculation of lifetime allowance charge

Where funds are vested to provide a lump sum, there will be a charge to tax at 55% on the value of the lump sum. [Hp27]

Where the excess funds are vested to provide pension income, the rate of charge is 25%. In this case, it is necessary to look at the value of the vested funds to work out the tax charge, not the annual value of the pension income that will be provided.

The different rates apply because the pension income is taxable in the hands of the individual whereas the lump sum is not.

Where the charge arises in the lifetime of the member, the tax charge primarily falls on him, but the pension scheme administrator has joint liability for the tax charge and will withhold sufficient sums to cover the charge.

Where the charge arises on the payment of a lump sum following the death of a member, the tax charge is payable by the recipient of the lump sum and in this case there will be no withholding tax retained by the scheme administrator.

Worked example: Lifetime allowance charge

Andrew was 60 years old on 1 July 2014 and decided to vest his pension benefits on that date. He had a money purchase fund which was valued at £1,900,000 on 1 July 2014.

Andrew took the maximum tax-free lump sum of £1,250,000 × 25% = £312,500. The balance of the fund up to the lifetime allowance [(£1,250,000 − £312,500) = £937,500] was vested to provide pension income benefits.

Andrew also took the excess of the fund over the lifetime allowance [(£1,900,000 − £1,250,000) = £650,000] as a lump sum.

Requirement

Compute the lifetime allowance charge and the amount that the scheme administrator will pay to Andrew, in addition to the tax-free lump sum.

How would your answer be different if Andrew had applied for individual protection, and the value of his pension fund on 5 April 2014 was £1,850,000?

Solution

Lifetime allowance charge is £650,000 × 55%	£357,500

The scheme administrator will pay Andrew:

(£650,000 − £357,500)	£292,500

If Andrew had applied for individual protection, his personalised lifetime allowance would be the higher of his fund at 5 April 2014 up to a maximum of £1,500,000, and £1,250,000 ie £1,500,000.

The excess of the fund over the lifetime allowance would then be [(£1,900,000 − £1,500,000) = £400,000] taken as a lump sum.

Lifetime allowance charge is £400,000 × 55%	£220,000

The scheme administrator will pay Andrew:

(£400,000 – £220,000)	£180,000

In the examination, such a question will state if individual protection applies.

The pension member may decide to vest benefits over a number of years.

In this case, the lifetime allowance must be adjusted for the value of benefits already vested.

If there has been a change in the value of the lifetime allowance, the benefits vested earlier must be increased or decreased by multiplying the benefits by the lifetime allowance in force at the date of the later event and dividing it by the lifetime allowance in force at the date of the earlier event.

Worked example: Vesting pension rights in different tax years

Shona vests pension rights of £600,000 in 2011/12 and a further £1,200,000 in 2014/15.

All pension rights are vested to produce pension income. Individual protection has not been claimed.

Requirement

Compute the lifetime allowance charge on the second vesting.

Solution

The lifetime allowance in 2011/12 was £1,800,000.

The lifetime allowance in 2014/15 is £1,250,000.

The vesting of rights in 2011/12 must be adjusted for comparison in 2014/15 to:

$\dfrac{1.25}{1.8} \times £600,000$	£416,667

Lifetime allowance for 2014/15 is:

(£1,250,000 – £416,667)	£833,333
Excess is (£1,200,000 – £833,333)	£366,667
Lifetime allowance charge £366,667 × 25%	£91,667

Summary

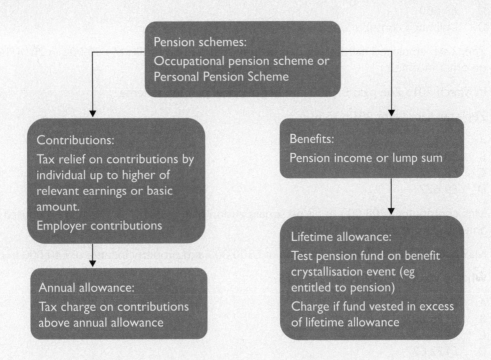

Pension schemes:
Occupational pension scheme or Personal Pension Scheme

Contributions:
Tax relief on contributions by individual up to higher of relevant earnings or basic amount.
Employer contributions

Annual allowance:
Tax charge on contributions above annual allowance

Benefits:
Pension income or lump sum

Lifetime allowance:
Test pension fund on benefit crystallisation event (eg entitled to pension)
Charge if fund vested in excess of lifetime allowance

C
H
A
P
T
E
R

4

Self-test

Answer the following questions.

1   Mark earns £2,500 from part time work in 2014/15.

   What is the maximum gross pension contribution that Mark may make on which there is tax relief?

   A   Nil
   B   £2,500
   C   £3,600
   D   Unlimited contribution

2   Zoe, a self-employed hairdresser, had tax adjusted trading profits of £50,000 in 2014/15. She had no other income.

   In March 2015 Zoe paid £3,600 into her personal pension scheme.

   Zoe's tax liability for 2014/15 is:

   A   £7,827
   B   £8,907
   C   £8,727
   D   £9,627

3   Max contributes £208,000 to his personal pension plan in 2014/15. He had no unused pension annual allowance brought forward.

   Max had tax adjusted trading income of £300,000 and property income of £40,000 in the year.

   What is Max's tax liability for 2014/15?

   A   £73,627
   B   £168,627
   C   £173,127
   D   £172,627

4   Neil has gross pension input to his personal pension scheme of £50,000 in 2014/15.

   Neil had gross pension input of £60,000 in 2011/12, £30,000 in 2012/13 and £35,000 in 2013/14.

   What amount of unused annual allowance, if any, is carried forward to 2015/16?

   A   £15,000
   B   £25,000
   C   £35,000
   D   £45,000

5   Nathan vests pension rights of £1,900,000 in 2014/15. Nathan first takes £300,000 as a tax free lump sum.

   The remainder of the vested amount is used to provide income benefits. Assume Nathan has not applied for individual pension protection.

   What tax charge arises?

   A   £162,500
   B   £357,500
   C   £300,000
   D   £880,000

6   Mr Lee

You have received the following email from a client, Mr Lee:

I have just started a new job and thought that I ought to start making some pension provision now that I am in my mid-30s.

My initial salary is £100,000 a year, but I am hoping that, with bonuses, it may increase in the next few years to around £500,000.

My employer operates an occupational pension scheme and I have been given a booklet about it. The booklet says that the scheme is a 'money purchase' scheme. If I join the scheme, my employer will make contributions to the scheme in addition to the amount that I pay into it.

Could you answer the following questions:

(1)   Do I have to join my employer's pension scheme or can I make other pension arrangements?

(2)   What is a 'money purchase' scheme?

(3)   If I join my employer's pension scheme, how much can I contribute to the scheme and how much can my employer contribute?

(4)   I have heard that there is tax relief on my contributions to a pension scheme. How does that work if I join my employer's pension scheme?

Requirement

Draft an email in response.   **(8 marks)**

Now go back to the Learning Objectives in the Introduction. If you are satisfied you have achieved these objectives please tick them off.

Technical reference

Legislation

References are to Finance Act 2004 (*FA 2004*)

Types of pension scheme	s.150
Tax relief for contributions by member	s.188
Annual limit for relief	s.190
Tax relief at source	s.192
Net pay arrangements	s.193
Contributions by employer	s.196
Annual allowance charge	ss.227 – 238
Pension rules during life of member	s.165
Lump sum rules during life of member	s.166
Lifetime allowance	ss.214 – 226

HMRC manual references

Registered Pensions Schemes Manual (Found at
http://www.hmrc.gov.uk/manuals/rpsmmanual/Index.htm)

This is a highly technical and complex area and the content of this manual reflects this.

> This technical reference section is designed to assist you. It should help you know where to look for
> further information on the topics covered in this chapter.

Answer to Interactive question

James

Tax liability

	£
Earnings/net income (£60,000 – £9,000)	51,000
Less Personal Allowance	(10,000)
Taxable income	41,000

Tax

	£
£31,865 × 20%	6,373
£9,135 × 40%	3,654
£41,000	
Tax liability	10,027

Note that this is the same net result as for Tabitha in the previous example. Although Tabitha obtained relief for £9,000 of pension contributions in her income tax computation she actually only paid £7,200 thus saving £1,800. Tabitha had received basic rate tax relief at source of (£9,000 – £7,200) = £1,800 so her overall tax liability was (£11,827 – £1,800) = £10,027.

In other words the after tax cost for both types of scheme is the same:

	PPS £	OPS £
Earnings/net income	60,000	60,000
Less: Pension contribution in cash	(7,200)	(9,000)
tax liability	(11,827)	(10,027)
Net income after pension and tax	40,973	40,973

1 C – £3,600

The maximum amount of contributions made by an individual in a tax year attracting tax relief is the higher of:

- The individual's relevant earnings chargeable to income tax in the year; and
- The basic amount (£3,600 for 2014/15).

2 C – £8,727

	£
Earnings/net income	50,000
Less personal allowance	(10,000)
Taxable income	40,000

Tax

	£
£31,865 × 20%	6,373
£4,500 (£3,600 × 100/80) × 20%	900
£3,635 × 40%	1,454
£40,000	
Tax liability	8,727

3 B – £168,627

	£
Trading income	300,000
Property income	40,000
Net income	340,000
Less personal allowance (W1)	(10,000)
Taxable income	330,000

Tax

	£
£31,865 × 20%	6,373
£260,000 (£208,000 × 100/80) × 20%	52,000
£38,135 × 40%	15,254
£330,000	
Annual allowance charge (W2)	
(£410,000 – £330,000) £80,000 × 40%	32,000
(£220,000 – £80,000) £140,000 × 45%	63,000
Tax liability	168,627

As Max's higher rate limit is increased by £260,000 to £410,000 Max is a higher rate tax payer for 2014/15 not an additional rate tax payer, before calculating the annual allowance charge.

WORKINGS

1 The personal allowance is tapered where adjusted net income exceeds £100,000 and reduces to nil when adjusted net income exceeds £120,000. Adjusted net income is total income less gross Gift Aid donations and gross personal pension contributions made by the individual. Employer contributions, if any, do not affect the adjusted net income working.

Max's adjusted net income for the purposes of the tapering of the personal allowance is:

	£
Net income	340,000
Less gross personal pension contribution	(260,000)
Taxable income	80,000

Max is therefore entitled to the full personal allowance as his adjusted net income is less than £100,000.

2   The excess contributions are:

	£
Individual gross pension contribution	260,000
Less annual allowance	(40,000)
Excess contributions	220,000

4   B – £25,000

The input in 2011/12 exceeds the annual allowance of £50,000 so there is no unused amount to carry forward. There is unused allowance of £20,000 in 2012/13 and £15,000 in 2013/14 to carry forward to 2014/15.

In 2014/15 pension input exceeds the annual allowance of £40,000 by £10,000 and so £10,000 of the £35,000 unused allowance brought forward will be used leaving £25,000 to carry forward to 2015/16. This is made up of £10,000 from 2012/13 and £15,000 from 2013/14.

5   A – £162,500

	£
Amount vested	1,900,000
Less lifetime allowance in 2014/15	(1,250,000)
Excess amount	650,000

Vested to provide pension income

Lifetime allowance charge
£650,000 × 25%   £162,500

6   To: Mr Lee@red.co.uk
      From: An Advisor@taxadvice.co.uk
      Date: [   ]
      Re: Pension advice

Thank you for your e-mail about pension advice. My answers to your questions are as follows:

(1)   You do not have to join your new employer's pension scheme. Instead you could start a pension with a financial institution such as a bank or insurance company. However, your employer may not want to contribute to a private pension scheme so you need to bear this in mind when considering whether to join your employer's scheme.

(2)   A money purchase scheme is one where the value of your pension benefits depends on the value of the investments in the pension scheme at the date that you set aside (ie vest) funds to produce those benefits.

      This is distinct from a defined benefits scheme where the benefits are defined from the outset. If you decide to use a private pension scheme, this is also likely to be a money purchase scheme.

(3)   You can contribute an amount up to all of your UK earnings into the pension scheme and obtain tax-relief on those contributions.

      You can also make any amount of further contributions, for example out of capital, but these will not obtain initial tax relief. However, since there is no income tax nor capital gains tax payable by a pension scheme, it may still be beneficial for such extra contributions to be made into this tax-exempt fund.

      In addition, your employer can make any amount of contributions and the employer will usually obtain tax relief for contributions by deducting it as an expense in calculating trading profits for the period of account that the payment is made.

      However, there are two limits that you need to be aware of.

      First, there is an annual allowance which limits the inputs that can be put into the pension fund. For 2014/15, this limit is £40,000. The amounts that you contribute and gain tax relief on, plus any contributions made by your employer, will count towards the annual allowance.

      If those contributions exceed the annual allowance, there will be a tax charge which claws back the tax relief received on the amount of any contributions in excess of the annual allowance. This annual allowance charge is payable by you.

As you have not been a member of a registered pension scheme in the past you will not have any unused annual allowance brought forward. If however you do not pay in the full £40,000 possible into your pension fund in 2014/15 then the amount by which your gross contributions is less than £40,000 can be carried forward as unused annual allowance. This enables you to make contributions in excess of the annual allowance in a future year without incurring the annual allowance charge.

The second limit is the lifetime allowance limit. This is the maximum value of the pension fund that you are allowed to build up to provide pension benefits without incurring adverse tax consequences.

The lifetime allowance is £1,250,000 in 2014/15. This limit is tested against the value of your pension fund when you vest pension benefits. If your fund exceeds the lifetime allowance at that time, there will be a tax charge of 55% on excess funds vested to provide a lump sum and 25% on excess funds vested to provide a pension income.

Although there are no adverse tax consequences if your pension fund exceeds the lifetime allowance other than at the time that pension benefits are vested, it would be wise to adjust your contributions if necessary so as to keep within the lifetime allowance.

(4) The usual method for giving tax relief in occupational pension schemes is called net pay arrangements.

Your employer deducts your pension contributions gross from your pay before applying income tax. This means that tax relief is given automatically at your highest rate of tax and no adjustment is needed in your tax return.

As an example, if you contribute £1,000 to your pension and that amount of income would have been taxed at 40%, your pay will be reduced by £1,000 but the amount of tax that would be deducted from your pay would be reduced by £400, so that the net cost of the contribution payable by you would be £600.

Obviously I can only outline the basics of pension provision in this e-mail as this is very complex area, so I suggest that we meet once you have decided how to proceed.

CHAPTER 5

Employment income

Introduction

Examination context

Topic List

Introduction

Learning objective

Tick off

- Calculate assessable employment income for an employee or director, taking into account expenses, allowable deductions and assessable benefits

Specific syllabus references for this chapter are 3i.

Syllabus links

You met the basics of employment income in Chapter 4 of your Principles of Taxation study manual: the receipts basis and the main taxable and exempt benefits.

In this chapter, we review these basic topics and extend your knowledge to include the special receipts rules for directors, further rules on car and fuel benefits, employment related loans, private use of assets and transfers of assets. You will also learn about allowable deductions from employment income and the statutory mileage rate scheme.

Examination context

In the examination candidates may be required to:

- Identify when employment income is treated as received, especially for directors

- Identify whether expenses of employment are allowable, with specific reference to travel expenses, mileage allowances and entertainment expenses

- Determine how benefits are taxable on P11D employees

Candidates need to take great care when calculating the value of a benefit, as one important piece of information is often missed when working this out.

1 Charge to tax on employment income

Section overview

- Employment income is received by an employee or director.

- General earnings is money and non-monetary benefits received as a result of the employment.

- General earnings are taxed on a receipts basis.

- There are special rules for the receipt of general earnings by directors.

- Benefits and termination payments are taxed when received by the employee.

1.1 General earnings

Employment income includes income arising from an employment and the income of an officer holder such as a director. We will use the term employee to cover anyone who receives employment income.

Definition

General earnings: Any salary, wages or fee, any gratuity or other profit or incidental benefit of any kind obtained by an employee consisting of money or money's worth, and anything else constituting an emolument of the employment, together with anything treated under any statutory provision as earnings (eg benefits).

General earnings therefore includes bonuses, commissions, reimbursed expenses, expense allowances, inducements, tips and gratuities (even if received voluntarily from third parties).

1.2 Receipt of employment income

The basis of assessment of general earnings is the receipts basis ie actual amounts received between 6 April 2014 and 5 April 2015 are taxable in 2014/15.

General earnings consisting of money are treated as received on the earlier of:

- The time when payment is made; and
- The time when a person becomes entitled to payment.

If the recipient is a director, general earnings consisting of money are treated as received on the earliest of:

- The time when payment is made

- The time when a person becomes entitled to payment

- The date the earnings are credited in the company's records or accounts

- The end of a period of account if earnings for that period are determined before the period ends

- The date earnings are determined if the amount is not determined until after the end of the period of account

Earnings are treated as credited in the company's records or accounts even if the director cannot draw the money at that time.

If an amount is set aside for payment to directors pending approval at the company's AGM, normally the earnings will be determined on the date of the AGM. However, if the directors are also controlling shareholders, HMRC considers that the earnings are received on the date of the directors' meeting to determine the amount of the earnings, not on the date of the formal ratification at the AGM.

Worked example: Receipt of general earnings by director

Jordan became a director of Y Ltd on 1 November 2014. He does not own any shares in the company. He is entitled to a salary of £36,000 per year payable in equal instalments on the last day of each month.

Jordan is also entitled to a bonus related to Y Ltd's profits for its period of account. Y Ltd prepared accounts to 31 March 2015 and Jordan's bonus for this period of account is £6,000. This was determined on 1 April 2015, credited in the company's accounts on 10 April 2015 and paid with his April salary on 30 April 2015.

Y Ltd changed its accounting date and made up its next set of accounts to 31 July 2016. It decided to pay an interim bonus to its directors for this period of account. Jordan's bonus was £5,000. This was determined on 1 April 2016, credited in the company's accounts on 10 April 2016 and paid with his April salary on 30 April 2016. Due to adverse trading conditions, no further bonus was paid for this period of account nor for the following period of account.

Requirement

Calculate Jordan's general earnings for 2014/15, 2015/16 and 2016/17 giving brief explanations.

Solution

2014/15

	£
November 2014 – March 2015 £36,000 × 5/12	15,000
Bonus received 1 April 2015 (W1)	6,000
Total general earnings	21,000

2015/16

	£
April 2015 – March 2016	£36,000

2016/17

	£
April 2016 – March 2017	36,000
Bonus received 10 April 2016 (W2)	5,000
Total general earnings	41,000

WORKINGS

(1) Bonus for y/e 31 March 2015

Received on the earliest of:

- Date of payment — 30 April 2015
- Date credited in accounts — 10 April 2015
- Date of determination if after end of period of account — 1 April 2015

(2) Bonus for p/e 31 July 2016

Received on the earliest of:

- Date of payment — 30 April 2016
- Date credited in accounts — 10 April 2016
- End of period of account if determined before end of period of account — 31 July 2016

General earnings not in the form of money (ie benefits) are received when the benefit is received by the employee.

2 Allowable deductions

Section overview

- Net taxable earnings are total taxable earnings less total allowable deductions.

- Allowable deductions against general earnings are employee expenses and reimbursed expenses.

- Employee expenses must generally be incurred in the employment and be wholly, exclusively and necessarily in the performance of that employment.

- There are special rules for qualifying travel expenses.

- Entertainment expenses can be deducted from a specific entertainment allowance but not from a general round sum allowance.

- Professional subscriptions are deductible.

- HMRC may agree a dispensation for benefits matched by allowable deductions.

2.1 Net taxable earnings

The total taxable earnings less total allowable deductions are the net taxable earnings of a tax year taxed on an employee.

Allowable deductions are not permitted to exceed the earnings against which they are set off (ie they cannot create a loss). If there is more than one employment in the year, separate calculations are required for each employment.

There are two main groups of allowable deduction:

- Against general earnings – employee expenses and reimbursed expenses

- Against employment income (both general earnings and specific employment income) – pension contributions under net pay arrangements and donations under an approved payroll giving scheme. Both of these deductions were considered earlier in this study manual

A deduction against general earnings is allowable for an employee's expenses if the amount is:

- Paid by the employee; or
- Paid on an employee's behalf by someone else and is included in earnings.

If an amount paid by the employee is reimbursed by the employer, a deduction is allowed for certain types of expenditure if the reimbursement is included in earnings.

2.2 General rule for employee expenses

The general rule for deduction of an expense has two conditions:

- The employee is obliged to incur and pay the expense as a holder of the employment; and

- The amount is incurred wholly, exclusively and necessarily in the performance of the duties of the employment.

Interpretation of this rule has been applied in the courts very strictly. The inclusion of the requirement for expenses to be incurred **necessarily** and **in the performance of the duties** makes this rule particularly restrictive.

Worked example: General rule for employee expenses

The following expenses are incurred by employees:

(a) A solicitor joins a golf club as a social member. He uses the club solely to meet clients.

(b) A doctor incurs examination fees to obtain a further qualification in a specialist area of medicine.

(c) The Welsh representative of a company (with offices only in Scotland) is required to work at home. He incurs additional household expenses for heating, lighting, metered water use and business telephone calls. No reimbursement is made by his employer.

Requirement

Explain whether these expenses are deductible against general earnings.

Solution

(a) The expense of a club is not deductible.

Even if the club was used wholly and exclusively for meeting clients in the performance of the solicitor's duties, it is not necessary for him to meet them at the golf club in order to perform his duties.

(b) The examination fees are not deductible.

The examination may improve the ability of the employee to do his or her job but the fee is not incurred in performing the duties of the employment.

(c) The additional household expenses are deductible.

The employee is not working from home by choice but by necessity and therefore the additional expenses are incurred wholly, exclusively and necessarily in performing the duties of the employment.

(Note however, that HMRC does not allow a deduction for council tax, water rates (as opposed to metered water), mortgage interest or insurance as these are not incurred exclusively in the performance of the duties.)

Some taxpayers are specifically allowed to deduct the cost of necessary tools, protective clothing and uniforms against general earnings. In certain cases HMRC has agreed a flat rate tax deduction.

2.3 Qualifying travel expenses

Special rules apply to travel and subsistence expenses.

An employee may deduct travelling and subsistence expenses from general earnings if:

- The expenses were necessarily incurred in the performance of the duties of the office or employment (the duties do not usually begin until the employee arrives at the permanent workplace and they finish when he leaves the permanent workplace)

- The expenses are not expenses of ordinary commuting (defined as home or other non-workplace to permanent workplace) or private travel

Therefore, in general, travelling between home and work is not allowable. However, there are some exceptions to this rule, as follows:

- Where an employee has no normal place of work ('site-based' employee), travel from home to work will be allowable

- Where it can be shown that a taxpayer's home is his work location, travel from one work location (home) to another work location will be allowable

- Where an employee works at a temporary workplace for no more than 24 months, travel from home to the temporary workplace during that period will be allowable

2.4 Entertaining expenses

Special rules apply in relation to the deduction of business entertaining expenses incurred by an employee.

Deduction of entertainment expenses is subject to the general rule that they must have been incurred wholly, exclusively and necessarily in the performance of the duties of the employment.

If the employee is reimbursed for the actual expenses or is given a special entertaining allowance, the employee can deduct the actual expenses from the reimbursement or specific allowance. Any excess will be taxable on the employee as general earnings. In this case, the employer cannot deduct the entertainment expenses in its own tax computation.

If the employee is given an increase in salary or a general round sum allowance, the employee is taxed on that amount and no deduction is allowed against his general earnings for actual entertaining expenses. However, the employer can deduct the whole amount (including any sums spent on entertaining expenses in its own tax computation).

2.5 Subscriptions to professional bodies

An annual subscription paid by an employee to a professional body is deductible if it is relevant to the duties of the employment.

The professional body must be on the HMRC's list of such bodies. The list includes most UK professional bodies (eg ICAEW) and some overseas and international bodies.

2.6 Dispensations

HMRC will issue a **notice of nil liability** (or dispensation) if:

- An employer notifies HMRC with a statement of the cases where particular types of benefits provided by the employer are covered by allowable deductions; and

- An Officer of Revenue and Customs agrees that there is no tax liability arising.

It is effective for both income tax and national insurance contributions.

The effect of the dispensation is that:

- The employer can exclude information about the benefits in future on the employee's PAYE forms; and

- The employee does not have to make a claim for the allowable deduction to prove nil liability.

Provided that the circumstances under which the dispensation was issued remain unchanged, the dispensation will remain effective until revoked by HMRC.

A dispensation is not available for round sum expense allowances (see earlier in this section).

State if, and to what extent, the following expenses incurred by an employee are allowable deductions:

Expense	Fill in your answer here
£10 train ticket from home to normal place of work	
£50 a month subscription to health club (many clients also use club)	
£500 for smart clothes suitable for office work	
£320 subscription by doctor to British Medical Association	
£50 a month specific entertainment allowance of which £45 used on actual entertaining	
£25 train ticket from home to temporary work place for six month secondment	
£500 general round sum allowance of which £300 used on actual entertaining	
£100 for weekend computer course to improve skills of office manager	

See **Answer** at the end of this chapter.

3 Statutory mileage rate scheme

Section overview

- The statutory mileage rate scheme sets out rates for using cars and other vehicles for business travel.

- If the employer reimburses the employee more than the statutory amount, a taxable benefit arises.

- If the employer reimburses the employee less than the statutory amount, the employee can claim an allowable deduction.

3.1 Statutory rates

The statutory mileage rate scheme applies to:

- Mileage allowance payments for a qualifying vehicle (privately owned car, van, motorcycle or bicycle)

- Passenger payments made to an employee for a car or van (if received in addition to mileage allowance payments)

The mileage allowance payments are amounts paid to an employee or volunteer driver in respect of using a private vehicle for business travel or as part of his voluntary work. For 2014/15 the rates are: [Hp53]

Kind of vehicle	Rate per mile
Car or van	45p for first 10,000 miles, 25p thereafter
Motorcycle	24p
Cycle	20p

The passenger payments are amounts paid to an employee or volunteer who, while using a car or van for business travel or in his voluntary work, carries one or more fellow employees or passengers making the same trip. The rate is 5p per passenger per mile.

3.2 Taxable benefit or allowable deduction

If the payments received from the employer exceed the statutory rate amount, a benefit arises on the excess.

If the payments received (if any) from the employer are less than the statutory rate amount, an allowable deduction is available on the shortfall. However the allowable deduction is not available in respect of passenger payments where the employer rate is less than 5p per mile.

Worked example: Statutory mileage rate scheme

Graham, Hetty and Irene are employees of J plc. In 2014/15, they receive the following payments:

	Vehicle	Mileage allowance	Business miles
Graham	Motorcycle	35p	5,000
Hetty	Car	28p	4,000
Irene	Van	48p	12,000

Hetty took a fellow employee with her to a business meeting and received an additional £32 for the 320 mile journey.

Requirement

Explain the employment income consequences for each employee.

Solution

Graham

	£
Amount reimbursed 5,000 × 35p	1,750
Less statutory allowance 5,000 × 24p	(1,200)
Taxable benefit	550

Hetty

Car

	£
Amount reimbursed 4,000 × 28p	1,120
Less statutory allowance 4,000 × 45p	(1,800)
Allowable deduction	(680)

Passenger

	£
Amount reimbursed	32
Less statutory allowance 320 × 5p	(16)
Taxable benefit	16

Irene

	£
Amount reimbursed 12,000 × 48p	5,760
Less: statutory allowance	
10,000 × 45p	(4,500)
2,000 × 25p	(500)
Taxable benefit	760

4 Taxable and exempt benefits

Section overview

- The Benefits Code deals with taxable benefits and applies in full to most employees.

- Certain parts of the Benefits Code do not apply to employees in excluded employment (**P9D employees**; ie earning less than £8,500 per year and not directors).

- All employees are taxable on vouchers and living accommodation.

- Employees not in excluded employment (**P11D employees**) are also taxable on other benefits such as cars, fuel, vans, loans, private use of assets and assets transferred.

- There are a number of benefits which are exempt from the charge to tax on employment income.

4.1 Taxable benefits

Taxable benefits are set down in legislation called the Benefits Code.

The Benefits Code generally applies to all employees. However, only certain parts of it apply to employees in **excluded employment** (in general employees earnings less than £8,500 per tax year who are not directors).

Employees in excluded employment (also known as **P9D employees**) are only taxable on:

- Benefits convertible into cash. The value of such benefits can be thought of as the '**second-hand value**'

- Vouchers

- Living accommodation (but not expenses associated with the living accommodation)

Most employees are not in excluded employment. Such employees are sometimes called **P11D employees**. Employees not in excluded employment are subject to tax on all the benefits in the Benefits Code.

You are already familiar with the following benefits:

Benefit	Amount of benefit
Vouchers	Cash voucher – cash obtainable, others (eg credit card) cost to employer less amount paid by employee.
Living accommodation	No benefit if job related. Otherwise taxable on basic rental benefit (annual value or rent paid) and additional yearly rent (for accommodation costing over £75,000) less amount paid by employee.
Expenses connected with provision of living accommodation	Generally taxable on cost to employer less amount paid by employee. Discussed in more detail below.
Cars and fuel for private use	Based on CO_2 emissions of car. Discussed in more detail below.
Vans and fuel for private use	Flat rate benefit of £3,090 for private use of the van, less any contributions paid in that tax year by the employee for private use.
	Flat rate benefit of £581 for provision of private fuel, not reduced by employee contributions unless covering the full cost of all private fuel.
Assets made available for private use	Generally, 20% of market value of asset when first provided for employee use less any amount payable by employee. Discussed in more detail below.

Benefit	Amount of benefit
Any other non-monetary benefit provided by reason of the employment	Cost to employer of provision less any amount paid by employee. Where benefits provided in-house, marginal cost to employer less any amount paid by employee.

4.2 Expenses connected with the provision of living accommodation

In addition to the living accommodation benefits, P11D employees are also taxed on related expenses paid by the employer such as heating, lighting, cleaning, repairs, maintenance and decoration.

The provision of furniture in the property is also taxable under the rules on assets made available for private use (20% of market value of the asset when first provided for employee use).

If the accommodation is job related, all of these additional expenses are limited to 10% of the employee's net earnings. Net earnings are all earnings from the employment (excluding these additional expenses) less allowable deductions from general earnings, statutory mileage allowance relief and occupational pension scheme contributions (but not personal pension scheme contributions).

Any payment made by the employee in respect of additional expenses is deducted. This applies regardless of whether the accommodation is job-related.

Worked example: Expenses connected with the provision of living accommodation

Wilson is a caretaker and is provided with job related living accommodation.

In 2014/15, his employer pays electricity bills of £300, gas bills of £400 and redecoration costs of £1,000. Wilson is also provided with furniture which had a market value of £3,000 when first provided.

Wilson is paid an annual salary of £12,000. He pays 5% into his employer's occupational pension scheme which operates net pay arrangements. He also has qualifying travelling expenses of £240 during the year.

Requirement

Calculate the net taxable earnings for Wilson.

Solution

	£	£
Salary		12,000
Less: occupational pension scheme		
£12,000 × 5%	600	
qualifying travel expenses	240	(840)
Net earnings		11,160
Expenses connected with living accommodation:		
Electricity	300	
Gas	400	
Redecoration	1,000	
Furniture £3,000 × 20%	600	
Total	2,300	
Restricted to £11,160 × 10%		1,116
Net taxable earnings		12,276

4.3 Cars and fuel for private use

There is a taxable benefit for P11D employees on the provision of a car available for private use by the employee (including home to work travel).

The basis of the charge is the list price of the car plus any optional accessories originally provided with the car and any further accessories costing £100 or more which are provided at a later date.

If the employee makes a capital contribution towards the cost of the car, this is deducted from the list price up to a maximum deduction of £5,000.

The benefit is calculated by applying a percentage to that list price. The percentage depends on the carbon dioxide (CO_2) emissions of the car expressed in grams per kilometre (g/km). This figure will be given to you in the question.

The emissions thresholds are as follows:

- For cars with zero emissions there will be no taxable benefit.

- For cars classed as 'ultra- low emission cars', the percentage will be 5% for cars with emissions between one g/km and 75g/km inclusive (8% for diesel cars). [Hp43]

- For cars with CO_2 emissions above 75g/km but less than 95g/km, the percentage will be 11% (14% for diesel cars). [Hp43]

- For cars with CO_2 emissions of 95g/km, the relevant threshold for the year, the percentage will be 12%. [Hp43]

- For every 5g/km over the 95g/km threshold (rounded down to the nearest 5g/km), an additional 1% is added up to a maximum of 35%.

Where the car uses diesel instead of petrol, the percentage is increased by 3%, subject to the overall maximum of 35%.

If the employee makes a contribution to the employer for the use of the car, this contribution reduces the taxable benefit but only if the contribution is actually paid within the tax year of the private use.

Worked example: Car benefit

Matt is employed at a salary of £25,000. He is provided with a car available for private use during the whole of 2014/15. The car has a petrol engine and CO_2 emissions of 126g/km. The car has a list price of £18,395, but the employer only paid £14,395 for it after discounts.

Matt contributed £5,395 towards the capital cost of the car and contributes £50 per month for its private use.

Requirement

Calculate Matt's taxable benefit in respect of the car.

Solution

CO_2 emissions are 126g/km, round down to 125g/km

Appropriate percentage: (125 – 95) = 30g/km in excess of threshold

30/5 = 6% + 12% = 18%

	£
List price £(18,395 – 5,000 (max) contribution) = £13,395 × 18%	2,411
Less contribution for use £50 × 12	(600)
Taxable benefit	1,811

If a car is not available for private use for a full tax year, the benefit is time apportioned (for exam purposes on a monthly basis). However, periods where the car is not available for private use of less than 30 days (eg due to repairs) are not taken into account for time apportionment.

Interactive question 2: Car benefit for part of tax year [Difficulty level: Intermediate]

Dawn is employed at a salary of £40,000. She is provided with a car for private use from 6 July 2014. The car had a list price of £16,800 and CO_2 emissions of 167g/km. It runs on diesel.

The car was unavailable from 1 October 2014 to 25 October 2014 whilst it was being repaired.

Following her disqualification from driving, the car was withdrawn from Dawn by her employer on 6 February 2015.

Dawn makes no contributions towards the cost or running of the car.

Requirement

Using the standard format below, calculate Dawn's taxable benefit in respect of the car.

CO_2 emissions .... g/km, round down to .... g/km

Appropriate percentage: (..................... – ....) = ... g/km in excess of threshold

...................../5 = ...% + ...% + ...% (diesel) = ...%

£........................ × ....% =   £_____

Available .... to ....

Time apportionment: £........................ × ....   £_____

See **Answer** at the end of this chapter.

There is a separate charge for the provision by the employer of fuel for private use for a car provided by the employer with private use. The private fuel benefit uses the same percentage used for the car benefit. This is then applied to a fixed amount which is £21,700 in 2014/15. [Hp50]

There is no reduction in the benefit if the employee makes a partial contribution to the cost of private fuel. There will be a taxable benefit unless the employee reimburses the employer with the full cost of private fuel.

If the car for which the fuel is provided is not available for part of the tax year, the fuel benefit is time apportioned on the same basis as the car benefit.

If private fuel is not available for part of a tax year (eg the employee opts out of an arrangement to be provided with fuel for private use), the fuel benefit is also time-apportioned. However, this does not apply if private fuel again becomes available to the employee later in the tax year.

Worked example: Fuel benefit

Frank is a P11D employee who is provided by his employer with a car for private use. The CO_2 emissions of the car are 222g/km and the car uses petrol.

Frank is provided with fuel for private use under an arrangement with his employer from 6 April 2014 to 5 October 2014. He then decided to opt out of this arrangement and pay for his own private fuel. However, on 6 February 2015, he rejoined the arrangement.

Frank is required to pay a nominal amount of £30 per month towards the cost of private fuel for the months when he is in the arrangement with his employer.

Requirement

Calculate Frank's fuel benefit.

Solution

CO_2 emissions are 222g/km, round down to 220g/km

Appropriate percentage (220 – 95) = 125g/km in excess of threshold

125/5 = 25% + 12% = 35% (maximum)

£21,700 × 35%   £7,595

No reduction for partial contribution for private fuel nor for non-availability for part of tax year where private fuel becomes available to the employee again later in the same tax year.

4.4 Employment related loans

An employment related loan to a P11D employee or his relatives gives rise to a taxable benefit to the extent that all or part of the loan is written off (unless the employee has died).

A taxable benefit also arises on taxable cheap loans where no interest is paid by the employee on the loan or the interest paid is less than the official rate of interest.

There is no taxable benefit if the loan is made on commercial terms in the course of the employer's money lending business if such loans are made on the same terms to non-employees.

There is also no taxable benefit if the total amount on all loans made by the employer to the employee does not exceed £10,000.

There are two methods of calculating the loan benefit: the average method and the strict method. The average method applies unless either the employee or HMRC elects to use the strict method. HMRC will not make the election unless there is a significant difference between the methods.

Under the average method, the average of the balance of the loan at the start and end of the tax year is used. If the loan is outstanding for the whole year, this amount is then multiplied by the official rate of interest. If the official rate of interest changes during the tax year, an average official interest rate for the year is used. [Hp57]

If the loan is made and/or repaid during the year the amount of the loan made or repaid is used instead and only the months for which the loan is outstanding are taken into account.

Under the strict method, interest is computed at the official rate in force on the outstanding balance of the loan. For examination purposes, this should be done on a monthly basis. The strict method election should be made by the taxpayer, for example, if he repays a substantial amount of the loan early in the tax year. The strict method election will be made by HMRC, for example, if there is a substantial repayment of the loan late in the tax year.

For the purposes of the examination, you should usually assume that the more beneficial (for the taxpayer) of any two alternative tax treatments applies. However, in the case of beneficial loans because HMRC may demand the strict method, if the amount of a beneficial loan changes over the course of the tax year, you should perform workings for both the average method and the strict method and choose the appropriate method which benefits the taxpayer.

Any interest actually paid by the employee is deductible in calculating the taxable loan benefit. This applies to both methods.

Worked example: Employment related loans

Fennella is a P11D employee. She has the following employment related loans:

(1) Interest free loan of £1,300
(2) Loan of £50,000 on which interest is payable at 3% by Fennella
(3) Interest free loan of £100,000

All of the loans were granted before 6 April 2014. Fennella repaid £200 of the first loan on 6 March 2015 and £70,000 of the third loan on 5 July 2014. The official rate of interest throughout 2014/15 is 3.25%.

Requirement

Compute the taxable benefits arising to Fennella in respect of the loans.

Solution

Since the total of all the loans exceeds £10,000, all three loans give rise to taxable benefits.

Loan 1

Average method

Balance at start of year £1,300
Balance at end of year (£1,300 – £200) = £1,100

$$\frac{£1,300 + £1,100}{2} = £1,200 \times 3.25\% \qquad\qquad £39$$

Strict method

	£
6 April 2014 – 5 March 2015 11/12 × £1,300 × 3.25%	39
6 March 2015 – 5 April 2015 1/12 × £1,100 × 3.25%	3
Total interest	42

Fennella would use the average method. In practice, the strict method is not different enough to be worth election by HMRC.

Loan 2

Average method

Balance at start of year £50,000
Balance at end of year £50,000

	£
$\dfrac{£50,000 + £50,000}{2} = £50,000 \times 3.25\%$	1,625
Less interest paid £50,000 × 3%	(1,500)
Taxable benefit	125

Strict method would give the same benefit as the average method.

Loan 3

Average method

Balance at start of year £100,000
Balance at end of year £30,000

$\dfrac{£100,000 + £30,000}{2} = £65,000 \times 3.25\%$	£2,113

Strict method

	£
6 April 2014 – 5 July 2014 3/12 × £100,000 × 3.25%	813
6 July 2014 – 5 April 2015 9/12 × £30,000 × 3.25%	731
Total interest	1,544

Fennella should elect for the strict basis on this loan.

4.5 Assets available for private use

A taxable benefit arises to a P11D employee who is provided by his employer with an asset available for private use by him or his family.

The amount of the taxable benefit is the higher of the annual value of the asset or any rent or hire charge payable by the employer. In both cases, any expenses relating to the provision of the asset are also added.

The annual value is 20% of the market value of the asset when first provided for private use to any employee.

If the asset is only provided for part of the year, the benefit is time-apportioned (on a monthly basis for exam purposes).

The taxable benefit is reduced by any contribution made by the employee for private use.

4.5.1 Computers

There will be no taxable benefit on the provision of a computer to an employee to carry out his employment duties where the private use of the computer by the employee is not significant.

Where the private use of the computer is significant the benefit is calculated as under the general rule above, but then reduced by the percentage of actual business use. HMRC guidance suggests 40% private use would be deemed to be significant.

Worked example: Assets with private use

Connie is provided with the following assets which are available for private use:

- DVD recorder (provided on 6 October 2014) costing £1,200.

- Computer (provided on 6 July 2012) costing £2,900. The computer was returned to her employer on 5 February 2015. Connie's private use of the computer was insignificant.

Connie makes a contribution of £15 a month for private use of the DVD recorder.

Requirements

(i) Compute the taxable benefits on Connie for 2014/15 for private use of these assets.

(ii) Recalculate the taxable benefit on the provision of the computer assuming Connie's private use of the computer was agreed as 55%.

Solution

(i) **DVD recorder**

Annual value

20% × £1,200	£240

Available for 6 months in tax year

	£
£240 × 6/12	120
Less employee contribution £15 × 6	(90)
Taxable benefit	30

Computer

No taxable benefit	£nil

(ii) **Computer**

	£
Annual value	
20% × £2,900 × 10/12	483
Less business use 45% × £483	(217)
Taxable benefit	266

4.6 Assets transferred to employee

A taxable benefit arises to a P11D employee where an asset is transferred to him. This often (but not always) occurs where an asset has previously been provided to the employee with private use.

The taxable benefit on the transfer is the greater of:

- The current market value

- The market value of the asset when first provided less any amounts already taxed under the private use rules (ignoring any contributions made by the employee)

In either case, the taxable benefit is reduced by any amount paid by the employee for the transfer.

Worked example: Asset transferred to employee

Naomi is a P11D employee. On 6 April 2013, she was provided with furniture available for her private use at a cost of £4,000. She made no contribution to her employer for use of the furniture.

On 5 January 2015, Naomi bought the furniture from her employer for £700 when its market value was £1,000.

Requirement

Compute the taxable benefits for Naomi for 2014/15 in respect of the furniture.

Solution

First, work out the amounts taxable under the private use rules:

2013/14	£4,000 × 20%	£800
2014/15	£4,000 × 20% × 9/12	£600

Then work out the taxable benefit on the transfer of the asset:

Greater of:

Current market value	£1,000
Market value at provision less amounts taxed	
£(4,000 – 800 – 600)	£2,600

ie £2,600 less price paid £700 = £1,900

Total taxable benefits for 2014/15 in respect of furniture	
(£600 + £1,900)	£2,500

If the asset transferred is a car, a van or a bicycle, a special rule applies. In these cases the taxable benefit on the transfer is the current market value less any price paid by the employee.

4.7 Exempt childcare payments

There is an exemption for childcare payments made under a contract between the employer and an approved child carer or by childcare vouchers, provided that childcare payments are available to all employees, with some exclusions for those earning close to the national minimum wage. [Hp70]

For employees already in a scheme at 5 April 2011 childcare payments of up to £55 per week are exempt. For employees joining a scheme from 6 April 2011 the amount of the childcare payment that is exempt depends on the level of the individual's basic earnings assessment.

The basic earnings assessment is the individual's expected earnings for the current tax year. It is calculated by adding together the employee's basic earnings and taxable benefits and then deducting excluded income which includes occupational pension contributions, allowable expense payments and the personal allowance.

	Exempt weekly payment £
Basic rate taxpayer (on earnings)	55
Higher rate taxpayer (on earnings)	28
Additional rate taxpayer (on earnings)	25

4.8 Exempt benefits

There are a number of benefits which are specifically exempt from the charge on employment income. Exempt benefits include:

- Contributions by an employer to a registered pension scheme

- Pension advice available to all employees up to £150 per tax year

- Counselling and outplacement services and retraining courses on termination of employment

- Childcare facilities run by or on behalf of an employer eg workplace nurseries

- One mobile telephone (which can be a smartphone) available for private use by an employee [Hp70]

- Free or subsidised meals in a canteen where such meals are available to all staff. However, the exemption does not apply where the employee has a contractual entitlement to receive canteen meals instead of cash salary (ie salary sacrifice arrangements)

- Total loans not exceeding £10,000 outstanding per tax year

- Social events paid for by the employer up to £150 per head per tax year. If one event costs more than £150, the total cost of the event is taxable. If there is more than one event in a tax year and the total costs exceed £150, the events totalling up to £150 are exempt and the cost of the other events are taxed in full

- Entertainment provided by a third party (eg seats at sporting/cultural events)

- Non-cash gifts from third parties up to £250 per tax year from the same donor

- Provision of a parking space at or near the employee's place of work

- Awards of up to £5,000 made under a staff suggestion scheme

- Work-related training courses

- Sports and recreation facilities available to employees generally but not to the general public

- Payments towards the additional costs of an employee working from home (up to £4 per week without supporting evidence, payments in excess of £4 per week require documentary evidence that the payment is wholly in respect of such additional costs)

- Personal incidental expenses (eg cost of telephone calls home) whilst the employee is required to stay away overnight on business up to £5 per night in the UK, £10 abroad [Hp58]

- Overseas medical treatment and insurance when employee is working abroad

- Payment of travel expenses where public transport is disrupted, late night journeys and where car sharing arrangements break down

- Use of bicycles or cyclist's safety equipment if made available to all employees

- Works buses and subsidies to public bus services [Hp55]

- Reimbursement for use of own vehicle for business journeys under the statutory mileage rate scheme (see earlier in this chapter) [Hp53]

- Reasonable removal expenses (maximum £8,000) paid for by an employer for a new employment position or on relocation [Hp71]

- Non-cash long service awards in respect of at least 20 years' service, not exceeding £50 per year of service

- Cost of eye tests and prescription glasses for an employee required to use visual display unit (VDU) equipment (eg computers)

- Health screening assessment or medical check up provided for an employee, by the employer (maximum of one of each per tax year)

- Cost of officially recommended medical treatment (up to £500 per employee per year) to help the employee return to work after a period of absence due to ill-health or injury

Summary

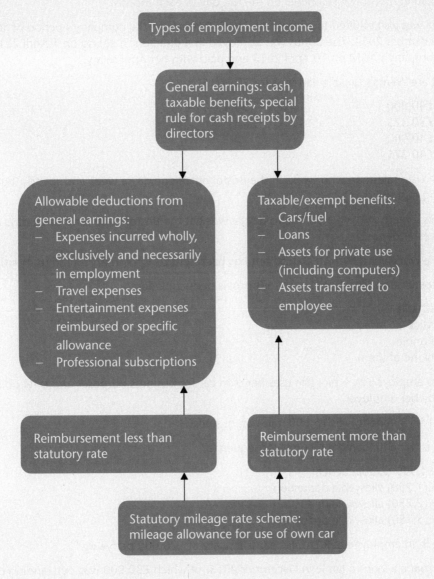

Types of employment income

↓

General earnings: cash, taxable benefits, special rule for cash receipts by directors

Allowable deductions from general earnings:
– Expenses incurred wholly, exclusively and necessarily in employment
– Travel expenses
– Entertainment expenses reimbursed or specific allowance
– Professional subscriptions

Taxable/exempt benefits:
– Cars/fuel
– Loans
– Assets for private use (including computers)
– Assets transferred to employee

Reimbursement less than statutory rate

Reimbursement more than statutory rate

Statutory mileage rate scheme: mileage allowance for use of own car

Self-test

Answer the following questions.

1   Wilma is a director of D Ltd. She owns 30% of the shares of the company and the other 70% are owned by the other director of the company.

   Wilma is entitled to an annual salary of £30,000 which was increased by 5% from 1 January 2015. It is paid in monthly instalments on the last day of each month.

   Wilma was also entitled to a bonus of £10,000 based on the company's period of account to 31 December 2014. The bonus was approved in a directors' meeting on 1 April 2015, ratified by the company's AGM on 10 April 2015 and paid with her April salary.

   What are Wilma's taxable earnings for 2014/15?

   A   £30,000
   B   £30,375
   C   £40,000
   D   £40,375

2   Charlie is a salesman who works in the Bristol office one day a week and spends the rest of his time visiting customers.

   Mick is a mechanic who works two days a week at the Bristol depot and three days a week at the Gloucester depot.

   Ronnie works for a bank in Oxford but has been sent to work in Bristol for 18 months.

   The cost of travelling from home to Bristol is deductible for:

   A   Charlie
   B   Mick
   C   Ronnie
   D   None of them

3   June is employed by E plc. She uses her own car for business purposes and is reimbursed 30p per mile by her employer.

   In 2014/15, June travels 15,000 miles on business.

   What is the employment income consequence?

   A   £4,500 taxable benefit
   B   £(1,250) allowable deduction
   C   £(2,250) allowable deduction
   D   £(5,750) allowable deduction

4   Jamie is an employee of R Ltd. He earns a salary of £20,000 per year.

   R Ltd made a loan to Jamie in December 2013, of which £30,000 was outstanding on 6 April 2014. Jamie repaid a further £20,000 on 6 January 2015.

   Jamie paid interest of 2% on the loan. The official rate of interest throughout the year was 3.25%.

   What is the taxable benefit for 2014/15?

   A   £650
   B   £812
   C   £312
   D   £150

5 **Edward Dante**

Edward Dante is both a director and a shareholder of Inferno Ltd. He has yet to complete his self-assessment return for the tax year ended 5 April 2015. The file provides the following details as to his income for 2014/15.

- His salary was £435,000 from which income tax of £121,800 was deducted via PAYE.

- He is provided with a fully expensed petrol company car which has CO_2 emissions of 137g/km and a list price of £68,200. He uses the car 20% for business purposes and makes no reimbursement for private petrol. Inferno Ltd paid for insurance and repairs to the car, which totalled £4,600 during 2014/15.

- Edward received a round sum allowance of £5,790 during 2014/15, all of which he spent on entertaining clients.

- A note from Inferno Ltd apologising for the delay in payment of a bonus of £38,272. Edward Dante's contract states that the bonus should have been paid on 31 March 2015 but, due to a payroll error, it was not paid until 6 April 2015.

- Edward paid contributions of £3,625 per month into Inferno Ltd's occupational pension scheme.

- Dividends from Inferno Ltd of £55,250.

- Building society interest received of £20,350.

- Buy to let property income of £35,000. The mortgage interest on the buy to let property is £5,600 per annum and the letting agents annual fee is £2,750. The property is let unfurnished.

Edward, who was 56 on 6 July 2014, is a member of a personal pension scheme although he has not made any contributions into this pension scheme since he joined Inferno Ltd many years ago. Edward has decided to take retirement from his personal pension scheme on 6 December 2015 even though he intends to carry on working. He will firstly take the maximum possible tax free lump sum, then use £1,400,000 of the personal pension fund to purchase an annuity on 6 December 2015 when the fund will be valued at £1,850,000. The rest of the fund will be taken as a further lump sum payment.

Edward has made no claim for individual pension protection.

Requirements

(a) Calculate Edward Dante's income tax liability for 2014/15. **(9 marks)**

(b) Advise Edward of the tax implications of his retirement from his personal pension scheme. Assume that the tax rates and allowances for 2014/15 apply in the future. **(3 marks)**

Now go back to the Learning Objectives in the Introduction. If you are satisfied you have achieved these objectives please tick them off.

Technical reference

This gives an overview of the benefits code and provides links to further guidance on individual types of benefit.

This gives links to more unusual types of benefit from employment, including those which are not taxable.

This technical reference section is designed to assist you when you are working in the office. It should help you know where to look for further information on the topics covered in this chapter. **You will not be examined on the contents of this section in your examination**.

Answers to Interactive questions

Answer to Interactive question 1

Expense	Fill in your answer here
£10 train ticket from home to normal place of work	No deduction. Normal commuting is not a qualifying travel expense.
£50 a month subscription to health club (many clients also use club)	No deduction. Not necessarily for performance of duties of employment, even if wholly and exclusively conditions satisfied.
£500 for smart clothes suitable for office work	No deduction. Not wholly, exclusively or necessarily for performance of duties of employment.
£320 annual subscription by doctor to British Medical Association	Deduction £320. Professional subscription.
£50 a month specific entertainment allowance of which £45 used on actual entertaining	£45 deductible. The balance (£50 – £45) will be taxable on the employee.
£25 train ticket from home to temporary work place for six month secondment	£25 for each journey. Where an employee works at a temporary workplace for no more than 24 months, travel from home to the temporary workplace during that period will be deductible.
£500 general round sum allowance of which £300 used on actual entertaining	No deduction. Full £500 will be taxable on employee.
£100 for weekend computer course to improve skills of office manager	No deduction. Even though the course improves the manager's skills, attending the course is not in the performance of his duties.

Answer to Interactive question 2

CO_2 emissions are 167g/km, round down to 165g/km

Appropriate percentage: (165 – 95) = 70g/km in excess of threshold

70/5 = 14% + 12% + 3% (diesel) = 29%

£16,800 × 29% =   £4,872

Available 6 July 2014 to 5 February 2015 (ignore period of repair as less than 30 days)

Time apportionment: £4,872 × 7/12   £2,842

1   D – £40,375

		£
Salary:	£30,000 × 9/12	22,500
	£30,000 × 105% = £31,500 × 3/12	7,875
Bonus:	received on date of directors' meeting (directors have control of company)	
	1 April 2015	10,000
Total taxable earnings		40,375

2   C – Ronnie

Charlie – Bristol is permanent workplace – not deductible

Mick – Both Bristol and Gloucester are permanent workplaces – not deductible

Ronnie – Bristol is temporary workplace for less than 24 months – deductible

3   B – £(1,250) allowable deduction

	£
Amount reimbursed 15,000 × 30p	4,500
Less: statutory allowance	
10,000 × 45p	(4,500)
5,000 × 25p	(1,250)
Allowable deduction	(1,250)

4   D – £150

Average method

Balance at start of year £30,000
Balance at end of year £10,000

$$\frac{£30,000 + £10,000}{2} = £20,000 × 3.25\%$$ £650

Strict method

	£
6 April 2014 – 5 January 2015 9/12 × £30,000 × 3.25%	731
6 January 2015 – 5 April 2015 3/12 × £10,000 × 3.25%	81
Total interest	812

Therefore Jamie would use the average method. Given the small difference between the two calculations (especially once tax is applied), it is unlikely that HMRC would elect for the strict basis.

Interest paid

	£
6 April 2014 – 5 January 2015 9/12 × £30,000 × 2%	450
6 January 2015 – 5 April 2015 3/12 × £10,000 × 2%	50
Total interest	500

Net benefit (£650 – £500)   £150

5   (a)   **Edward Dante income tax liability for 2014/15**

	Non-savings income £	Savings income £	Dividend income £	Total £
Employment income (W1)	453,542			
Dividends £55,250 × 100/90			61,389	
Interest £20,350 × 100/80		25,438		
Property income (W2)	26,650			
Net income	480,192	25,438	61,389	567,019
Less PA	NIL			NIL
Taxable income	480,192	25,438	61,389	567,019

Tax

	£
£31,865 × 20%	6,373
£118,135 × 40%	47,254
£330,192 × 45%	148,586
£25,438 × 45%	11,447
£61,389 × 37½%	23,021
£567,019	
Tax liability	236,681

WORKINGS

(1)   Employment income

	£
Salary	435,000
Car (135 – 95) = 40/5 = 8% + 12% = 20% × £68,200	13,640
Fuel 20% × £21,700	4,340
Round sum allowance (no deduction for client entertaining from a round sum allowance)	5,790
Bonus – deemed to be received on the date Edward Dante became entitled to it, ie 31 March 2015	38,272
	497,042
Less occupational pension contributions 12 × £3,625	(43,500)
Net taxable earnings	453,542

(2)   Property income

	£
Rent	35,000
Less: mortgage interest	(5,600)
agent's fees	(2,750)
Taxable property income	26,650

(b) Mr Dante has chosen to purchase an annuity with £1.4m of his personal pension fund. This will generate pension income for him which will be taxable as non-savings income.

Mr Dante is entitled to take a lump sum on retirement. However, the maximum which may be taken as a tax free lump sum (TFLS) is 25% of the lifetime allowance at that time ie £1,250,000 × 25% = £312,500.

Where the pension fund exceeds the lifetime allowance a tax charge is payable. If the excess is used to buy an annuity the charge is 25%. However, if the excess is taken as a lump sum it will be subject to a charge of 55%. Mr Dante's fund exceeds the lifetime allowance by £600,000.

The excess of £600,000 will be taxed as follows:

- After the TFLS is taken, the remaining lifetime allowance is £937,500. Therefore of the amount used to purchase the annuity £462,500 is in excess of the lifetime allowance and will be taxed at 25%:

  £462,500 × 25% = £115,625

- The remaining fund is taken as a lump sum and will be taxable at 55%:

  £137,500 × 55% = £75,625

The total tax liability from the vesting of retirement benefits is therefore £191,250.

Mr Dante should note that this retirement will use up 100% of his lifetime allowance meaning that all future pension benefits will be subject to a tax charge at either 25% or 55%.

CHAPTER 6

Trading income

Introduction

Examination context

Topic List

Summary and Self-test

Technical reference

Answers to Interactive questions

Answers to Self-test

Learning objectives

- Explain the relevance of the distinction between revenue and capital for both receipts and expenses and apply the distinction in a given scenario ☐

- Recognise the effect on trading profits for the treatment of:

    - Provisions ☐
    - Capitalised revenue expenditure ☐
    - Intangible assets ☐

- Calculate trading profits or losses after adjustments and allowable deductions (including capital allowances on plant and machinery) ☐

- Calculate the assessable trading profits or losses for a new unincorporated business and identify the overlap profits on the commencement of trade ☐

- Calculate the assessable trading profits or losses for a continuing business ☐

- Calculate the final assessable trading profits or losses for an unincorporated business ceasing to trade ☐

- Calculate the assessable trading profits or losses of a continuing business following a change in accounting date ☐

- Calculate total taxable income for self-employed individuals ☐

Specific syllabus references for this chapter are 3a-c, 3e-h and 3n and 5a-c.

Syllabus links

You have already met the basics of trading income in Chapter 5 of your Principles of Taxation study manual: badges of trade, adjustment to profits and allowable/disallowable expenditure. Chapter 7 covered the basis periods.

In this chapter, we will review these basic topics and extend your knowledge to enable you to make a full adjustment of profit calculation for a sole trader. You will also learn about change of accounting date and the income tax treatment of royalties.

Examination context

In the examination candidates are required to:

- Integrate knowledge acquired previously in the Principles of Taxation examination to compute adjusted profits computations for a trader

- Identify the adjustments required and determine whether pre trading expenditure is an allowable expense

    Calculate the assessments on a change of accounting date

    income is an important part of the syllabus. Candidates often struggle with the calculation of
    ading profits in the opening years of a business or on a change of accounting date.

1 Badges of trade

Section overview

- Badges of trade are key factors which indicate whether a trade is being carried on.
- However, all the circumstances need to be taken into account to decide whether a taxpayer is carrying on a trade.

1.1 What are the badges of trade?

A trade is defined in the tax legislation as **every trade, manufacture, adventure or concern in the nature of trade**. The courts have interpreted this definition in a number of cases which have identified a number of key factors in deciding whether an activity constitutes a trade (**badges of trade**).

You will be expected to know the badges of trade and the facts of the cases described below. The case names are not examinable.

No one factor is decisive. The badges of trade merely provide guidance to be used in conjunction with all the facts surrounding the transaction and with common sense.

1.2 Outline of the badges of trade

- **Profit seeking motive** eg purchase (rather than gift or inheritance) with intention of reselling at profit. An example was the purchase and resale of £20,000 of silver bullion as protection against the devaluation of sterling being treated as a trading activity (*Wisdom v Chamberlain 1968*).

- **The number of transactions** eg a number of similar transactions may indicate trading. An example was the purchase of a mill-owning company and the subsequent stripping of its assets. (*Pickford v Quirke 1927*). Since this was the fourth such transaction by this taxpayer, the transaction was a trading activity.

- **Nature of the asset** eg not for personal use or investment, but for resale at profit. Example include 34,000,000 yards of aircraft linen (*Martin v Lowry 1927*) and 1,000,000 rolls of toilet paper (*Rutledge v Commissioners of Inland Revenue 1929*).

- **Existence of similar trading transactions or interests** eg where a builder sells a property which he claims has been held as an investment it is more likely to be considered a trading transaction than if it were sold by a person not in the building trade.

- **Changes to the asset** eg if an asset is purchased and then subjected to a process before resale to enhance its marketability, the sale is more likely to be regarded as a trading activity. An example was the purchase of a quantity of brandy which was blended and recasked before sale. The sale was treated as a trading activity (*Cape Brandy Syndicate 1921*). Active marketing and advertising is also likely to lead to the conclusion that there is a trading activity.

- **The way the sale was carried out** eg a woodcutter who bought a consignment of whisky in bond and sold it through an agent was held to be trading. Where a sale is carried out in a way that is typical of a trading organisation (eg through an agent), it is more likely to be considered as trading.

- **Source of finance** eg a person (not a bullion trader) who acquired silver bullion financed by loans on terms such that he had to sell the bullion to repay the loan was held to be trading. Where a loan is required to acquire an asset which will be repaid through the sale of the asset it is likely to indicate trading.

- **Interval of time between purchase and sale** eg asset bought and resold shortly afterwards may indicate a trading activity.

- **Method of acquisition** eg where goods are not acquired by purchase (eg by gift or inheritance) it is difficult to impute a trading motive. Where an asset is purchased specific circumstances at the date of acquisition may indicate that it was bought for resale (trading) or as an investment (capital). However a change in intention after the acquisition may also be taken into account.

2 Adjustment of profits

2.1 Allowable and disallowable expenditure and other adjustments to profit

Definition

Allowable expenditure: Expenditure incurred wholly and exclusively for the purposes of the trade, which is not specifically disallowed by legislation.

Expenditure allowable for accounting purposes, but not for tax purposes is **disallowable** and must be added back to the accounting profit or loss.

In practice HMRC will allow a reasonable apportionment between business (allowable) and private (disallowable) use.

Expenditure will also be disallowable if it is too remote from the purposes of the trade.

Rules prohibiting and allowing certain expenses sometimes conflict, in which case the rule allowing the expense usually takes priority. However, a targeted anti-avoidance rule (TAAR) has been introduced. The TAAR applies where the expense arises due to tax avoidance arrangements, in which case the prohibiting rule takes precedence and the deduction of an otherwise allowable expenses is prohibited.

You are already familiar with the following adjustments to profit:

Item	Treatment
Capital expenditure	Disallowable – add back.
	Distinguish between repairs (allowable as revenue expenditure) and improvements (disallowable as capital).
Depreciation	Disallowable – add back.
Appropriation of profit	Disallowable – add back.
	Examples include payment of 'salary' to sole trader or payment of his pension contributions, payment of his tax liabilities and payment of excessive salary to family member.
General provision eg for stock or debts	Disallowable – add back.
	Distinguish from a specific provision which is allowable.
Non-trade bad debts – specific provision or written off	Disallowable – add back.
	Distinguish from trade debts which are allowable.
Non-staff entertaining	Disallowable – add back.
	Distinguish from staff entertaining which is allowable.

Item	Treatment
Gifts	Disallowable – add back except: • Gifts to employees • Gifts of trade samples (not for resale) • Gifts to customers if they incorporate a conspicuous advertisement for the business, are not food, drink, tobacco or vouchers exchangeable for goods, and the total cost per customer is no more than £50
Donations and subscriptions	Disallowable – add back except: • Small donations to local charities • Trading stock or plant gifted to charities or UK educational establishments • Subscriptions to trade and professional associations
Fines and penalties	Disallowable – add back except: • Employee parking fines
Interest on late payment of tax	Disallowable – add back.
Legal and professional fees relating to capital	Disallowable – add back except: • Legal costs relating to renewal of short lease (up to 50 years) • Costs of registration of patent or copyright for trade use • Incidental costs of raising long-term finance
Irrecoverable VAT	If relates to disallowable expenditure: disallowable – add back.
Employment payments and pensions	Generally allowable. However, on cessation of trade, payments in addition to redundancy payments are only allowable up to 3 × statutory redundancy pay.
Leased cars	If the leased car (not motorcycle) has CO_2 emissions: • In excess of 130g/km for leases commencing on or after 6 April 2013 (160g/km for lease commencing prior to 6 April 2013) the disallowance is 15% × hire charge • No more than 130g/km for leases commencing on or after 6 April 2013 (160g/km for leases commencing prior to 6 April 2013) the hire charge is fully allowable
Trading income not shown in accounts	Eg goods are taken from the business by the owner for personal use without reimbursing the business with the full value. If nothing recorded in accounts: add back selling price. If entered at cost: add back profit.
Non trading income in accounts	Eg rental income, profit on disposal of fixed assets. Deduct.
Expenditure not shown in accounts	Eg business expenditure paid personally by the owner. Allowable and so make deduction.
Lease premium paid by trader on grant of short lease	Allowable deduction: premium taxed on the landlord as property income divided by the number of years of the lease (see Chapter 3).
Trade related patent royalties	Allowable deduction: the gross amount after grossing up for basic rate tax (see later in this chapter).

Worked example: Adjustment of profit

Dean is a sole trader, carrying on a manufacturing trade. His profit and loss account for the year ended 30 June 2014 shows the following:

	Note	£	£
Gross profit for year	1		168,000
Add: interest receivable			3,000
			171,000
Less: wages and NICs	2	61,355	
rent and rates		29,460	
repairs and renewals	3	3,490	
miscellaneous expenses	4	1,025	
Dean's income tax		15,590	
bad debts	5	820	
legal/professional expenses	6	2,310	
Depreciation		630	
lease rental on car	7	2,400	
charitable donations	8	80	
transport costs		3,250	
interest	9	990	
Dean's car expenses	10	5,600	
lighting and heating		1,250	
sundry expenses	11	3,750	(132,000)
Net profit			39,000

Notes

1 Sales include £500 reimbursed by Dean for stock taken for personal use representing cost price. The selling price of the stock would have been £625.

2 Included in wages are Dean's drawings of £50 per week, his Class 2 NICs of £143, wages and NICs of £11,750 for his wife's part-time employment in the business (similar to wages which would have been paid to any employee doing that work) and wages of £1,000 for his son who did not in fact perform any work.

3 Repairs and renewals are:

	£
Decoration of premises	400
New heating system	3,000
Boiler maintenance fee	90
	3,490

4 Miscellaneous expenses are:

	£
Political donation to Green Party	260
Gifts to customers of 20 T-shirts with Dean's logo	201
Dean's private medical insurance premium	564
	1,025

5 Bad debts are:

	£	£
Trade debt written off		420
Loan to employee written off		250
General provision for bad debts	600	
Less opening provision	(450)	150
		820

6   Legal and professional expenses are:

	£
Defending action for alleged faulty goods	330
Fees relating to renewal of short lease	250
Fees relating to acquisition of machinery	200
Fees on defence against Dean's motoring offence	190
Debt collection and accountancy fees	1,340
	2,310

7   Lease car rental relates to the car provided to an employee which has a retail price of £30,000 and CO_2 emissions of 145g/km. The lease contract was taken out on 1 May 2014.

8   Two charitable donations made: one of £50 to a local charity and one of £30 to Oxfam.

9   Interest consists of £860 bank overdraft interest and £130 interest on overdue tax.

10   Dean's motor car expenses are:

	£
Servicing and repairs	1,560
Fuel	3,255
Vehicle excise duty	160
Motoring offence: speeding fine	625
	5,600

The speeding fine was incurred when Dean was late for a business meeting. One third of Dean's mileage was for private purposes.

11   Sundry expenses are:

	£
Entertaining customers	850
Staff party	120
Gift to employee on exam success	100
Subscription to trade association	310
Other expenses (all allowable)	2,370
	3,750

Requirement

Prepare a statement of taxable trading income (before capital allowances).

Solution

Dean
Taxable trading income (before capital allowances)
y/e 30 June 2014

	£
Net profit per accounts	39,000
Add: **Disallowable expenditure**	
Drawings £50 × 52	2,600
Dean's NICs	143
Wages to son	1,000
New heating system	3,000
Political donation	260
Private medical insurance for Dean	564
Dean's income tax	15,590
Non-trade debt written off	250
Increase in general bad debt provision	150
Fees on acquisition of machinery (capital asset)	200
Fees relating to motoring offence	190
Depreciation	630
Lease rental on car disallowed – (15% × £2,400)	360
Oxfam donation	30
Interest on overdue tax	130
Dean's speeding fine	625
Private motoring 1/3 × (£1,560 + £3,255 + £160)	1,658
Entertaining customers	850
	67,230
Trading income not shown in accounts	
Goods for own consumption (£625 – £500)	125
	67,355
Less: **Non-trading income**	
Interest receivable	(3,000)
Taxable trading income (before capital allowances)	64,355

2.2 Pre-trading expenditure

Expenditure incurred before a trade starts is not deductible under the general wholly and exclusively rule. This is because it will not have been incurred for the purposes of the trade. Special rules exist to allow a deduction for pre-trading expenditure.

Pre-trading expenditure is deductible and deemed to have been incurred on the first day of trading, if:

* It was incurred within seven years of the starting date of trade; and
* The expenditure would have been deductible if it had been incurred in the trade.

Similar rules exist for capital allowances in respect of capital expenditure incurred before the commencement of trade (see later in this Manual).

2.3 Fixed rate expenses

Any unincorporated business, including partnerships (and those using the cash basis, see later in this Manual) may, for tax purposes, deduct certain business expenses at a fixed rate rather than on the usual basis of actual expenditure incurred.

The fixed rate deductions are optional but are intended to simplify the process for claiming a tax deduction for certain types of expenditure, where the calculation of allowable expenditure can be quite complex eg business use of home premises.

You will be told in an exam question whether the business makes deductions on a fixed rate basis. Otherwise, you should assume that these do not apply, and you should make the usual deductions for the actual expenditure incurred.

Fixed rate deductions can be claimed in respect of:

- Expenditure on motor vehicles
- Use of home for business purposes
- Business premises partly used as trader's home

2.3.1 Motor vehicles

A sole trader who incurs expenditure on the acquisition, lease, hire or use of a car, motor cycle or goods vehicle (such as a van) used in his trade, may make a deduction in respect of the expenditure incurred using approved mileage allowances.

The allowable rates per business mile travelled in a period are 45p for the first 10,000 miles (25p thereafter) for a car or goods vehicle and 24p per mile for a motor cycle. [Hp53] These are the same rates we saw in relation to employment income for an employee using his own vehicle for business purposes.

The fixed rate deduction cannot be made if the trader has previously claimed capital allowances in respect of that vehicle. Nor can it be claimed if it is a goods vehicle or motor cycle and the trader made a deduction under the cash basis when acquiring the vehicle (see later in this Manual).

If such a fixed rate deduction is made, then no other deduction can be made in respect of the expenditure on the vehicle in that period (for example capital allowances or actual running or maintenance costs). In addition, once adopted, the fixed rate method must be used in every future period that that vehicle is used for business purposes. However, a trader does not have to use the same basis for each vehicle used in the business.

Worked example: Fixed rate method for vehicles

Delia has been a sole trader for many years. During the year ended 31 March 2015 Delia leased a car with CO_2 emissions of 145g/km and lease rental payments for the year of £4,700. In addition, the cost of fuel for the year (for private and business purposes) was £1,800. Delia did 16,000 business miles and 4,000 private miles in the car in the year.

Delia's trading profit for the year to 31 March 2015, after charging the costs relating to the car of £6,500, was £39,000.

Requirement

Calculate the tax adjusted trading profit for Delia for the year ended 31 March 2015 assuming:

(1) Delia claims for the actual costs incurred in respect of the vehicle
(2) Delia claims a fixed rate mileage deduction in respect of the vehicle.

Solution

(1) *Deduction for actual costs incurred*

	£
Profit per accounts	39,000
Disallowed lease payments (£4,700 × 20%) + (£4,700 × 80% × 15%)	1,504
Private fuel (£1,800 × 20%)	360
Tax adjusted trading profit	40,864

Delia travelled 4,000 private miles out of 20,000 miles ie 20% of the costs relate to private usage.

(2) *Fixed rate mileage deduction claimed*

	£	£
Profit per accounts		39,000
Add actual costs incurred (£4,700 + £1,800)		6,500
Less Fixed rate mileage deduction		
10,000 business miles at 45p per mile	4,500	
6,000 business miles at 25p per mile	1,500	
		(6,000)
Tax adjusted trading profit		39,500

2.3.2 Use of home for business purposes

A fixed rate monthly deduction can be claimed where a trader or his employee(s) uses part of the trader's home for business purposes.

This is significantly simpler than the normal deduction rules whereby an apportionment of actual household costs eg heating, lighting, rent, repairs etc between business and private use must be performed. However, the trader still has the option to use the apportionment method if it is beneficial.

The fixed rate deduction can only be used if the trader (or his employee(s)) works at least 25 hours per month from the trader's home.

The monthly deduction rates are as follows:

Number of hours worked	Monthly adjustment
25 to 50 per month	£10
51 to 100 per month	£18
101 or more per month	£26

The hours worked must be wholly and exclusively for the purposes of the trade either by the sole trader or his employee(s).

Worked example: Business use of home

Jamie runs a retail business as a sole trader. He uses one of the rooms in his house for business purposes. During the year to 31 March 2015 he spent 35 hours a month working from home apart from two months when he spent 55 hours a month.

Requirement

Calculate the fixed rate monthly deduction Jamie can claim for use of his home for business purposes.

Solution

Jamie can claim a fixed rate deduction for the year ended 31 March 2015 of:

	£
10 months × £10	100
2 months × £18	36
	136

2.3.3 Business premises partly used as trader's home

A fixed rate monthly adjustment can be made where a trader uses part of his business premises as his home eg where a trader owns a property from which he runs a guesthouse and also resides at the property as his main residence. The adjustment is deducted from the actual allowable business premises costs to reflect the private portion of the costs.

Again, this is a much simpler method of adjusting for private expenditure than the usual apportionment of actual costs for business and private use. However, this apportionment method may still be used if beneficial.

The monthly adjustment is based on the number of occupants using the business premises as a home each month. Remember that this is the amount by which the allowable costs are reduced, so if all costs relating to the business premises have been deducted in the accounts, the monthly adjustment must be added back when calculating the tax adjusted trading profits of the business.

Number of occupants	Monthly adjustment
1	£350
2	£500
3 or more	£650

3 Basis periods

Section overview

- Current year basis applies to a continuing business.

- There are special rules in the opening and closing years of a business.

- Overlap profits may be created where there is double counting in the opening years.

- Relief for overlap profits can be given on cessation.

3.1 Introduction

Having calculated the adjusted profit or loss for a period of account, it then needs to be determined when those profits are to be taxed. The basis period rules allocate the tax adjusted profits or losses to a tax year.

Note that where there is a tax adjusted trading loss, the income tax computation will use a trading income figure of nil. The options available for relieving a loss are not examinable.

3.2 Current year basis

The basic rule is called the current year basis (CYB). The basis period for the tax year is the 12-month period of account ending in that tax year.

3.3 Opening year rules

Special rules are needed for the opening years of a business because there will not usually be a 12-month period of account ending in the tax year in which the business starts.

The basis of assessment in the first tax year that a business operates is the **actual basis**. The taxable trading income for the first tax year is the taxable trading income of the business from the date of commencement to the following 5 April.

It will usually be necessary to time-apportion the taxable trading income in the first (and sometimes the second) period of account to find this amount. For examination purposes, time-apportionment should be made to the nearest month. In practice, apportionment is made on a daily basis.

The basis of assessment in the second tax year depends on the length of the period of account ending in the second tax year. There are four possibilities:

Period of account ending in tax year	Basis period
12 months	That 12-month period of account
Less than 12 months	First 12 months trading ie from commencement
More than 12 months	12 months to the end of the period of account which ends in the second tax year
No such period of account	Actual basis (6 April to 5 April)

Usually, the current year basis applies to the third tax year of trading because there will be a 12-month period of account ending in that year.

Occasionally, there will not be a 12-month period of account ending in the third tax year. In this case the basis period will be the 12 months to the end of the period of account ending in the third tax year.

In the opening years, some taxable trading income may be taxed in more than one tax year. Choosing a period of account which ends on a date other than on 5 April will result in this double counting. Any taxable trading income taxed more than once is called **overlap profits**.

Relief will be given for overlap profits either when there is a change of accounting date or when the trade ceases, as we will see later in this chapter.

Interactive question 1: Opening years and overlap profits   [Difficulty level: Intermediate]

Jerome started trading on 1 January 2013. He decided to make up his accounts to 30 April each year.

His taxable trading income is:

	£
4 months ended 30 April 2013	8,000
y/e 30 April 2014	15,000

Requirement

Using the standard format below, compute the amounts of taxable trading income taxed in the first three tax years of trading and the amount of overlap profits.

First tax year (.........................../...........)
.... basis
Basis period .... to ....
.... × £.......................   £ _____

Second tax year (.........................../...........)
Basis period .... to ....
                                                                                    £
                                                                          _____   £ _____

Third tax year (.........................../...........)
Basis period   £ _____

Overlap profits
                                                                                    £

.... to ....

.... to ....   _____   £ _____

See **Answer** at the end of this chapter.

3.4 Closing year rules

The last tax year for a business is the tax year in which the business ceases to trade.

The basis period for the last tax year is one of the following three possibilities:

Business ends	Basis period for last tax year
Not in the first tax year nor in the second tax year	From end of basis period for the penultimate tax year to date of cessation
In the first tax year	Period for which business traded
In the second tax year	6 April to date of cessation

Usually, the current year basis will apply to the penultimate tax year (ie 12-month period of account ending in the penultimate tax year).

If the final period of account exceeds 12 months, there may be no period of account ending in the penultimate tax year. In this case, the basis period for the penultimate tax year will be the 12 months to the normal year end falling in that tax year.

3.5 Relief for overlap profits on cessation

Overlap profits, which have not already been relieved on a change of accounting date (see next section), are deducted from the taxable trading income in the last tax year.

Worked example: Closing year rules and overlap profit

Muriel started trading in 1985, making up accounts to 31 March each year. Muriel has overlap profits of £3,000.

Muriel ceased trading on 30 June 2014 and made up her final set of accounts for the 15 month period to that date. Those accounts showed taxable trading income of £21,000.

Requirement

Calculate the taxable trading income for the last two tax years of trading, showing relief for overlap profits.

Solution

Penultimate tax year (2013/14)

No 12-month period of account

12 months to normal year end

1 April 2013 to 31 March 2014

12/15 × £21,000   £16,800

Last tax year (2014/15)

End of previous basis period to cessation

1 April 2014 to 30 June 2014

	£	
3/15 × £21,000	4,200	
Less: overlap relief	(3,000)	£1,200

4 Change of accounting date

Section overview

- A trader may change his accounting date.

- A change in accounting date may result in the creation of overlap profits where there is a short period of account or no period of account ending in the tax year.

- Overlap relief may be available to reduce taxable profits to 12 months where there is a long period of account or two periods of account ending in the tax year.

- Where the change is not in the first three years of trading, there are conditions which need to be satisfied before the change is effective.

4.1 Introduction

A trader may wish to change his accounting date, for example to mirror seasonal variations in his trade.

This will result in a period of account which is not 12 months in length in the tax year of the change.

There are special rules which match the new period of account to the relevant tax year or years.

There are four possible situations in the tax year of the change:

- One short period of account for less than 12 months
- One long period of account for more than 12 months
- No period of account
- Two periods of account

We will consider each of these situations in turn.

4.2 One short period of account

The basis period for the tax year in which there is a short period of account is the 12 months to the new accounting date.

As in opening years, this will mean that overlap profits will be created. These overlap profits are relieved on a further change of accounting date or on cessation.

Worked example: One short period of account

Beattie is a sole trader making up accounts to 31 March each year. She decides to change her accounting date to 31 August and makes up a five month set of accounts to 31 August 2014.

Her taxable trading income is:

	£
y/e 31 March 2014	18,000
p/e 31 August 2014	10,000

Requirement

Calculate the taxable trading income for 2013/14 and 2014/15 and the amount of overlap profits.

Solution

2013/14

CYB

y/e 31 March 2014		£18,000

2014/15 (Tax year of change of accounting date)

Short period of account ending in year

12 months to new accounting date

1 September 2013 to 31 August 2014

	£	
7/12 × £18,000	10,500	
p/e 31 August 2014	10,000	£20,500

Overlap profits

1 September 2013 to 31 March 2014

7/12 × £18,000		£10,500

4.3 One long period of account

If there is a long period of account ending in the tax year, the basis period for that year starts immediately after the basis period for the previous year and ends on the new accounting date.

This will result in a basis period in excess of 12 months. If there are opening years' overlap profits, overlap relief can be used to bring down the number of months of profits which are taxable to 12.

Worked example: One long period of account

Karim started in business as a sole trader on 1 January 2012 making up accounts to 31 December each year.

He decides to change his accounting date to 31 January and makes up a 13 month set of accounts to 31 January 2015.

His taxable trading income is:

	£
y/e 31 December 2012	18,000
y/e 31 December 2013	24,000
p/e 31 January 2015	22,100

Requirement

Calculate the taxable trading income for 2011/12, 2012/13, 2013/14 and 2014/15.

Solution

2011/12 (First tax year)

Actual basis

Basis period 1 January 2012 to 5 April 2012

3/12 × £18,000   £4,500

2012/13 (Second tax year)

12-month period of account ending in 2nd tax year

1 January 2012 to 31 December 2012

y/e 31 December 2012   £18,000

Overlap profits

1 January 2012 to 5 April 2012 (3 months)

3/12 × £18,000   £4,500

2013/14 (Third tax year)

CYB

y/e 31 December 2013   £24,000

2014/15 (Tax year of change of accounting date)

Basis period 1 January 2014 to 31 January 2015

	£	
13 month period to 31 January 2015	22,100	
Less overlap 1/3 × £4,500	(1,500)	£20,600

Note that one month overlap relief (out of three months overlap profits arising in the opening years) is relievable on the change of accounting date. The remaining (£4,500 – £1,500) = £3,000 will be carried forward and relieved on another change of accounting date or on cessation.

4.4 No period of account ending in tax year

If there is no period of account ending in the tax year, a notional period of account must be created.

This is a 12-month period ending 12 months before the actual new accounting date.

This will result in overlap profits being created on the change of accounting date. Again, these will be carried forward for relief on a further change of accounting date or on cessation.

The basis period for the year following the change of accounting date will be the 12 months to the new accounting date.

Interactive question 2: No period of accounting ending in tax year

[Difficulty level: Exam standard]

Joanne has been trading as a sole trader for many years, making up accounts to 31 December.

She decides to change her accounting date to 31 May and makes up a 17 month set of accounts to 31 May 2014.

Her taxable trading income is:

	£
y/e 31 December 2012	15,000
p/e 31 May 2014	25,500

Requirement

Using the standard format below, calculate the taxable trading income for 2012/13, 2013/14 and 2014/15 and the amount of any overlap profits.

Solution

2012/13

	£
	___

2013/14 (Tax year of change of accounting date)

Basis period

	£	
.... × £...................		
.... × £...................	_____	£ ___

Overlap profits

.... to ....

		£
.... × £...................		___

2014/15

		£
.... × £...................		___

See **Answer** at the end of this chapter.

4.5 Two periods of account ending in tax year

If there are two periods of account ending in the tax year, the basis period starts immediately after the end of the previous basis period and ends on the new accounting date.

This will result in a basis period in excess of 12 months. If there are opening years' overlap profits, overlap relief can be used to bring down the number of months of profits which are taxable to 12.

Worked example: Two periods of account

Fergus is a sole trader making up accounts to 31 July 2014. He changes his accounting date to 31 December and makes up a five month set of accounts to 31 December 2014. His taxable trading income is:

	£
y/e 31 July 2013	6,000
y/e 31 July 2014	9,000
p/e 31 December 2014	4,800

He has eight months of unrelieved overlap profits totalling £2,400.

Requirement

Calculate the taxable trading income for 2013/14 and 2014/15.

Solution

2013/14 – CYB

y/e 31 July 2013 £6,000

2014/15 (Tax year of change of accounting date)

Two periods of account ending in year

1 August 2013 to 31 December 2014

	£	
y/e 31 July 2014	9,000	
p/e 31 December 2014	4,800	
	13,800	
Less overlap 5/8 × £2,400	(1,500)	£12,300

4.6 Conditions for change of accounting date

A change of accounting date within the first three tax years of a business will be automatically accepted by HMRC.

In any other case, certain conditions must be satisfied:

- The trader must notify HMRC of the change of accounting date by the 31 January following the end of the tax year of the change

- The period of account resulting from the change must not exceed 18 months

- Usually, there must have been no previous change of accounting date in the last five tax years. However, a second change can be made within this period provided that there are genuine commercial grounds for the change

5 Patent royalties

Section overview

- Patent royalties are deductible in computing trade income.

- Patent royalties are paid net of basic rate tax which must be brought into account in computing the tax payable by the taxpayer.

5.1 Dealing with patent royalties in the income tax computation

A trader may pay a patent royalty relating to his trade. It is deductible in the computation of taxable trading income. In general no adjustment will be required in the adjustment of profits.

A patent royalty is paid net of basic rate tax (20%). The gross amount of the patent royalty must be deducted. Therefore where the net amount paid has been deducted from the accounting profit an adjustment must be made for tax purposes to reflect the gross amount of the patent.

Worked example: Gross amount deductible

Able is a sole trader. His draft taxable trading income for 2014/15 is £13,210. This figure includes a deduction of £660 for patent royalties paid in March 2015. Able has no other sources of income.

Requirement

Compute Able's taxable income, after making any necessary adjustments.

Solution

Able

Income tax computation

	£
Trading income (W1)	13,045
Less PA	(10,000)
Taxable income	3,045

WORKING 1

	£
Draft trading income	13,210
Tax deducted at source on patent royalties (£660 × $\frac{20}{80}$)	(165)
Adjusted trading income	13,045

Note: The net payment of patent royalties has already been deducted. Only the additional tax element needs to be deducted.

The taxpayer will have already obtained basic tax relief by making the payment net of 20%. This amount must be taken into account to avoid double relief.

Worked example: Avoiding double relief

Iris is a sole trader. Her taxable trading income for 2014/15 is £45,000. This figure includes a deduction for a gross patent royalty of £1,200.

Iris has no other sources of income.

Requirement

Compute the income tax payable by Iris.

Solution

Iris
Income tax payable

	Non-savings Income £
Trading income	45,000
Less PA	(10,000)
Taxable income	35,000

Tax

	£
£31,865 × 20%	6,373
£3,135 × 40%	1,254
Tax liability	7,627
Add tax retained on patent royalty £1,200 × 20%	240
Tax payable	7,867

If the taxpayer has no taxable income, he must pay the basic rate tax retained on the charge to HMRC. If he were allowed to retain this tax, he would be given tax relief to which he is not entitled. The tax is paid via self-assessment.

Worked example: No taxable income

Ray is a sole trader. His taxable trading income for 2014/15 is £5,000. This figure includes a deduction for a gross patent royalty of £800.

Ray has no other sources of income.

Requirement

Compute the income tax payable by Ray.

Solution

Ray
Income tax payable

	Non-savings income £
Trading income	5,000
Less PA	(10,000)
Taxable income	NIL
	£
Income tax liability	–
Tax on patent royalty £800 × 20%	160
Income tax payable	160

Summary

Badges of trade:
- Profits seeking motive
- Number of transactions
- Nature of the asset
- Existence of similar transactions
- Changes to the asset
- The way the sale was carried out
- Source of finance
- Interval of time between puschase and sale
- Method of acquisition

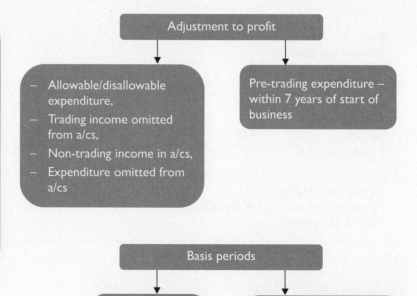

Adjustment to profit

- Allowable/disallowable expenditure,
- Trading income omitted from a/cs,
- Non-trading income in a/cs,
- Expenditure omitted from a/cs

Pre-trading expenditure – within 7 years of start of business

Basis periods

CYB, special rules in opening and closing years

Change of accounting date:
- Short period of account
- Long period of account
- No period of account
- 2 periods of account

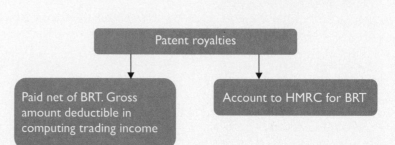

Patent royalties

Paid net of BRT. Gross amount deductible in computing trading income

Account to HMRC for BRT

Self-test

Answer the following questions.

1   Thompson's accounts for the year ended 31 May 2014 include a deduction for sundry expenses of £5,700. These were:

	£
Christmas turkeys with an advertisement for Thompson's business, given to customers (£25 each)	3,250
Seminar for customers to launch new product	1,650
Christmas party for staff	800
	5,700

What is the amount of sundry expenses allowable for tax purposes?

    A   £4,050
    B   £2,450
    C   £800
    D   £5,700

2   Petra is a sole trader, making up accounts to 31 December.

She takes goods for her own use costing £480 during the accounting period for the year ended 31 December 2014. She calculates that goods taken for the year to 5 April 2015 cost £560. Her normal mark-up is 40%. No record has been made in the accounts for such goods.

What amount will be included in her 2014/15 taxable trading income for goods taken for own use?

    A   £784
    B   £560
    C   £672
    D   £480

3   A trader commenced business on 1 September 2014. He made his first set of accounts to 30 April 2015 and to 30 April thereafter.

His taxable trading income is:

	£
Period ended 30 April 2015	8,000
Year ended 30 April 2016	15,000

What is his taxable trading income for 2014/15?

    A   £6,000
    B   £4,667
    C   £7,000
    D   £8,000

4   Roy, a sole trader who has been trading for many years, has always made up accounts to 31 December. He wishes to change his accounting date to 30 September. His last set of accounts was made up to 31 December 2013.

Which **one** of the following statements is **false**?

    A   Roy can make up accounts for a long period of account to 30 September 2015

    B   Roy must make a claim to change his accounting date by 31 January 2016

    C   Roy can make up accounts for a short period of account to 30 September 2014

    D   Roy cannot change his accounting date again until 2020/21 unless he has a genuine commercial reason

5   Owen is a sole trader. His taxable trading income for 2014/15 was £46,000. Owen also paid a patent royalty of £600 during the accounting period which has not been accounted for. Owen has no other sources of income.

What is the tax payable by Owen?

A   £7,727
B   £7,787
C   £7,877
D   £8,027

6   **Eleanor and Colin**

(a)   Eleanor is a sole trader. Her profit and loss account for the year to 31 December 2014 is as follows:

Expenses	£	Income	£
Cost of sales	52,364	Sales	96,060
Rent, rates, heat, light	2,900	Bank interest received	170
Depreciation	1,050	Rents receivable	1,400
Office salaries	8,250	Profit on sale of fixed asset	390
Advertising	2,500		
Bank charges	70		
Interest on bank loan	680		
Professional charges (N1)	1,030		
Bad debts (N2)	240		
Delivery van expenses	939		
Eleanor's car expenses (N3)	1,930		
Telephone calls (N3)	857		
Sundry expenses (N4)	690		
Salary – Eleanor	5,500		
Net profit	19,020		
	98,020		98,020

Notes

1   Professional charges are:

	£
Costs of registering patent	200
Stocktaking fees	150
Accountancy	680
	1,030

2   Bad debts account is:

	£		£
Loan to customer written off	180	Specific provision b/f	170
Trade debts written off	290	General provision b/f	200
Specific provision c/f	100	Trade debt recovered	80
General provision c/f	120	Profit and loss account	240
	690		690

3   It has been agreed that 75% of the telephone calls and 60% of motor expenses are for business purposes.

4   Sundry expenses are:

	£
Subscription to trade association	75
Subscription to political party	82
Donation to national charity	48
Entertaining customers	100
Staff business travel	160
Wine as gifts to customers	225
	690

Requirement

Compute the taxable trading income.   (8 marks)

(b) Colin started in business as a sole trader on 1 August 2009, making up accounts to 31 July for the first two years of the business.

He decided to change his accounting date and prepared accounts for the 15-month period to 31 October 2012.

Colin ceased trading on 31 December 2014 and made up his final accounts for the two-month period to that date.

His taxable income was:

	£
y/e 31 July 2010	24,000
y/e 31 July 2011	32,000
p/e 31 October 2012	40,000
y/e 31 October 2013	20,000
y/e 31 October 2014	16,000
p/e 31 December 2014	5,000

Requirement

Compute the taxable trading income for all tax years.   **(5 marks)**

Now go back to the Learning Objectives in the Introduction. If you are satisfied you have achieved these objectives please tick them off.

Technical reference

> This technical reference section is designed to assist you. It should help you know where to look for further information on the topics covered in this chapter.

Answer to Interactive question 1

First tax year (2012/13)

Actual basis

Basis period 1 January 2013 to 5 April 2013

3/4 × £8,000   **£6,000**

Second tax year (2013/14)

Period of account ending in 2nd tax year is less than 12 months long

First 12 months trading

Basis period 1 January 2013 to 31 December 2013

	£	
p/e 30 April 2013	8,000	
8/12 × £15,000	10,000	**£18,000**

Third tax year (2014/15)

CYB

Basis period y/e 30 April 2014   **£15,000**

Overlap profits

	£	
1 January 2013 to 5 April 2013	6,000	
1 May 2013 to 31 December 2013	10,000	**£16,000**

Answer to Interactive question 2

2012/13

CYB

y/e 31 December 2012   **£15,000**

2013/14 (Tax year of change of accounting date)

No period of account ending in tax year

Basis period 1 June 2012 to 31 May 2013

	£	
7/12 × £15,000	8,750	
5/17 × £25,500	7,500	**£16,250**

Overlap profits

1 June 2012 to 31 December 2012

7/12 × £15,000   **£8,750**

2014/15

12 months to new accounting date

1 June 2013 to 31 May 2014

12/17 × £25,500   **£18,000**

1   B – £2,450

Gift of food is not allowable.

Seminar is not customer entertaining so is allowable.

Staff entertaining is allowable.

2   C – £672

£480 × 140/100   <u>£672</u>

3   C – £7,000

2014/15 (First tax year)

Actual basis

Basis period 1 September 2014 to 5 April 2015

7/8 × £8,000   <u>£7,000</u>

4   A – Roy can make up accounts for a long period of account to 30 September 2015 is **false**.

This would produce a period of account in excess of eighteen months which is not permissible.

5   C – £7,877

	Non-savings Income £
Trading income	46,000
Less patent royalty paid £600 × 100/80	(750)
Adjusted trading income	45,250
Less PA	(10,000)
Taxable income	35,250

Tax

	£
£31,865 × 20%	6,373
£3,385 × 40%	1,354
£35,250	7,727
Add tax on patent royalty £750 × 20%	150
Tax payable	7,877

6 (a) **Eleanor**

Taxable trading income
y/e 31 December 2014

		£
Net profit per accounts		19,020
Add:	**Disallowable expenditure**	
	Depreciation	1,050
	Non-trade debt written off	180
	Private car expenses 40% × £1,930	772
	Private telephone 25% × £857	214
	Political donation	82
	Donation to national charity	48
	Entertaining customers	100
	Wine for customers	225
	Eleanor's salary	5,500
		27,191
Less:	**Non-trading income**	
	Interest receivable	(170)
	Rents receivable	(1,400)
	Profit on sale of fixed asset	(390)
	Decrease in general bad debt provision (£200 – £120)	(80)
Taxable trading income		25,151

(b) **Colin**

Taxable trading income

2009/10 (First tax year)

Actual basis

Basis period 1 August 2009 to 5 April 2010

8/12 × £24,000 .... £16,000

2010/11 (Second tax year)

12-month period of account ending in 2nd tax year

1 August 2009 to 31 July 2010

y/e 31 July 2010 .... £24,000

Overlap profits

1 August 2009 to 5 April 2010

8/12 × £24,000 .... £16,000

2011/12 (Third tax year)

CYB

y/e 31 July 2011 .... £32,000

2012/13 (Tax year of change of accounting date)

Long period of account

Basis period 1 August 2011 to 31 October 2012

	£	
p/e 31 October 2012	40,000	
Less overlap relief 3/8 × £16,000	(6,000)	£34,000

2013/14 (Penultimate tax year)

CYB

y/e 31 October 2013 .... £20,000

2014/15 (Last tax year)

End of previous basis period to cessation

1 November 2013 to 31 December 2014

	£
y/e 31 October 2014	16,000
p/e 31 December 2014	5,000
	21,000
Less overlap relief £(16,000 – 6,000)	(10,000)
	£11,000

CHAPTER 7

Capital allowances – plant and machinery

Introduction

Examination context

Topic

Summary and Self-test

Technical reference

Answer to Interactive question

Answers to Self-test

Introduction

Learning objective

Tick off

- Calculate trading profits or losses after adjustments and allowable deductions (including capital allowances on plant and machinery)

The specific syllabus references for this chapter are 3c and 5c.

Syllabus links

In Chapter 6 of your Principles of Taxation study manual, you studied capital allowances on plant and machinery. In this chapter, we extend your knowledge of this topic by covering aspects such as the special rate pool, short life assets, hire purchase, business cessations and interaction with VAT.

Examination context

In the examination candidates may be required to:

- Identify whether items of expenditure qualify as plant and machinery

- Understand the effect of VAT in the calculation of capital allowances

- Calculate plant and machinery capital allowances with particular emphasis on the special rate pool, short life assets and pre-trading expenditure

Candidates have often not taken the time to ensure they are aware of which assets can be treated as plant and machinery for capital allowance purposes, therefore throwing away easy marks.

1 Introduction to capital allowances

Section overview

- Plant includes assets which perform an active function in a business and some expenditure specified in legislation.

- Sole traders, partners and companies qualify for capital allowances on assets used in their businesses.

- The acquisition cost of an asset is usually the net cost of the asset to the business. The disposal value of an asset cannot exceed original cost.

- If fixtures are purchased the seller and purchaser must make an election to agree the value to be attributed to the fixtures in order that the purchaser can claim capital allowances on the expenditure.

1.1 What is plant and machinery?

Plant includes such things as office furniture and equipment.

Difficulties sometimes arise with expenditure related to buildings such as lighting and partitions. There are a number of decided cases in this area. You will be expected to know the facts of the cases described below. The case names are not examinable.

In general, if the assets perform an active function in the business they are considered to be plant. The following cases are examples of this test where the items were held to be plant (these items are now specifically defined as plant by statute):

- Moveable office partitioning designed to be as flexible as possible to meet the changing demands of the trade *(Jarrold v John Good and Sons Ltd 1963)*

- Free standing decorative screens in the windows of a building society designed to attract local custom *(Leeds Permanent Building Society v Procter 1982)*

- Dry dock which acted as a hydraulic chamber in which a variable amount of water could be used to raise and lower a ship. It was deemed to be not merely a shelter but an essential part in the operation of the business *(IRC v Barclay Curle & Co. Ltd 1969)*

- Swimming pool at a caravan park which performed the function of giving buoyancy and enjoyment to the persons using the pool *(Cooke v Beach Station Caravans Ltd 1974)*

- Light fittings, décor and murals in a hotel which created atmosphere conducive to the comfort and well being of the customers *(IRC v Scottish and Newcastle Breweries 1982)*

- Special display lighting *(Cole Brothers Ltd v Phillips 1982)*

If, however, the assets are merely part of the setting in which the business is carried on, they do not qualify as plant. The following cases are examples of this test where the items were **not** held to be plant:

- Ship used as floating restaurant was a structure in which the business was carried on rather than apparatus employed in the business *(Benson v Yard Arm Club 1978)*

- Stand at football ground was the setting or place where the trade was carried on, rather than the means by which the trade was carried on *(Brown v Burnley Football and Athletic Club 1980)*

- False ceilings containing conduits, ducts and lighting apparatus in a motorway service station did not perform a function in the business but were merely part of the setting *(Hampton v Fortes Autogrill Ltd 1979)*

- Shopfronts, tiles, water-tanks, staircases and raised floors in chain of restaurants were part of the premises or setting in which the trade was carried on *(Wimpy International Ltd v Warland 1988)*

- Canopy at petrol station merely provided shelter and was not part of the means by which the operation of supplying petrol was performed *(Dixon v Fitch's Garage Ltd 1975)*

- A building housing car wash machinery functioned as premises in which the business was carried on rather than apparatus functioning as plant *(Attwood v Anduff Car Wash Ltd 1997)*

Machinery is easier to define and includes all machines, motor vehicles and computers.

There are some types of expenditure which are specified in legislation as qualifying for capital allowances on plant and machinery. These include:

- Building alterations incidental to the installation of plant and machinery
- Licence to use computer software

Plant and machinery capital allowances are not available for expenditure incurred to comply with legal fire safety regulations for business premises made in response to a notice from a Fire Authority. However relief is available for expenditure on fire safety equipment such as fire alarms and sprinkler systems.

1.2 Claiming capital allowances

Capital allowances are available to a taxable person (sole trader, partner or company) who incurs capital expenditure on assets to be used for the purposes of a trade carried on by that person.

Capital allowances must be claimed by the taxpayer. The taxpayer may claim less than the full amount of the capital allowances, for example if trading profits are not sufficient to absorb the full allowances. This will mean that larger allowances will be available in future periods of account.

Capital allowances for a sole trader or a partnership are calculated for each period of account, not for each tax year. In other words calculate the tax adjusted trading profits less the capital allowances being claimed for the sole trader or partnership and then apply the basis period rules. Capital allowances for a company are calculated for each accounting period (companies are covered in detail later in this study manual).

1.3 Acquisition cost and disposal value

If the business is VAT registered and the VAT input tax on the asset is recoverable by the business, the cost of the asset for capital allowance purposes is the VAT exclusive price. If the VAT input tax is not recoverable (because the asset is a car or the business is not VAT registered), the cost of the asset for capital allowance purposes is the VAT inclusive price. This is because this amount is the net cost of the asset to the business.

The asset may be acquired in a part exchange transaction. This particularly applies to motor vehicles. The acquisition cost of the new asset is the total of the part-exchange value and the cash amount paid.

The owner may bring personally-owned assets into the business. The acquisition cost is the market value of the asset when it is brought into the business.

Assets bought on hire purchase are treated as if bought for the cash price (excluding interest) at the date of the hire-purchase agreement. The dates when the instalments are payable are not relevant.

The disposal value is usually the sale proceeds of the asset. However, this cannot exceed the original cost of the asset.

If the asset is given away or sold for less than market value, the disposal value will be the market value on the date of disposal.

If the asset is scrapped or destroyed, the disposal value is the scrap value or the compensation received, as appropriate.

1.4 Purchase of fixtures

The availability of capital allowances on the purchase of fixtures from a seller who has previously used them in his trade will be conditional on the following:

- The seller of the fixtures must have either claimed first year allowances on the fixtures or have allocated them to a capital allowance pool prior to the date of sale.

- The value of the fixtures must be formally fixed, in most cases by a joint election by the seller and the purchaser which specifies the amount of the sale proceeds to be allocated to the fixtures. This election must be made within two years of the transfer. The value allocated to the fixtures cannot exceed the seller's original cost.

If these conditions are not satisfied then no capital allowances will be available to the purchaser.

A typical scenario where these conditions are required is when the fixtures are purchased as part of a second-hand building.

Even if the purchaser does not make the necessary election and so has a nil cost for the fixtures the seller must still bring a disposal value into their capital allowances computation on their sale.

2 The allowances available

Section overview

- Expenditure on most assets is pooled in the main pool.
- A writing down allowance (WDA) is given on the balance of the main pool at the end of the period of account. The WDA is 18% for a 12-month period.
- The tax written down value (TWDV) is carried forward to the start of the next period of account.
- First Year Allowances (FYAs) may be given in the period of account in which expenditure is incurred.
- FYAs of 100% are available for expenditure on low emission cars; zero emission goods vehicles; certain energy saving and water technologies; and research and development capital expenditure.
- FYAs of 100% are available for companies only for expenditure in an enterprise zone.
- A special rate pool exists to include expenditure on integral features, thermal insulation and long life assets. This pool has a WDA of 8% for a 12-month period.
- An annual investment allowance (AIA) of £500,000 for a 12-month period, for expenditure incurred from 6 April 2014 (1 April for companies), is available to all sized businesses. From 1 January 2013 to 6 April 2014 (1 April for companies) the AIA was £250,000 for a 12-month period. The AIA can be allocated to any pool of expenditure the business chooses.
- Any small balances, up to the small pool limit of £1,000, remaining at the end of the period of account on the main or special rate pool are eligible for a WDA of up to the amount remaining.

2.1 Pro forma computation for capital allowances on plant and machinery

The pro forma as set out below is considered in detail throughout this section.

	FYA £	Main pool £	Special rate pool £	Private use asset £	Allowances £
Period of accounts					
TWDV b/f		X	X		
Acquisitions – FYA	X				
FYA @ 100%	(X)				X
	—				
Acquisitions (AIA)		X	X		
AIA		(X)	(X)		X
Acquisitions (no AIA or FYA) – cars		X	X	X	
Disposals		(X)	(X)		
		X	X	X	
WDA @ 18%		(X)			X
@ 8%			(X)		
@ 18% or 8% (Note)				(X) × bus%	X
TWDV c/f		X	X	X	
Total allowances					X

Note: The rate of WDA is dependent on the type of asset (for example, the CO$_2$ emissions of a car).

2.2 Cars – an overview

The treatment of cars depends on their emissions, with the rules from April 2013 being as follows: [Hp145]

- Cars with emissions of not more than 130g/km are 'main pool cars' and are added to the main pool and written down at 18% pa. (Although note that new cars with low emissions (≤95g/km) currently qualify for a first year allowance of 100%.)

- Cars with emissions of more than 130g/km are added to the special rate pool (see later in this chapter) and written down at 8% pa.

The definition of a car does not include a motorcycle.

For the purposes of the examination, you do not need to know the treatment of cars bought prior to April 2009.

2.3 Main pool: writing down allowances

Expenditure on assets which are in the main pool includes:

- All machinery, fixtures and fittings and equipment

- Vans, forklift trucks, lorries

- Second-hand low emission cars (CO_2 emissions 95g/km or less from 6 April 2013 (1 April for companies) or 110g/km or less prior to 6 April 2013) regardless of cost unless they are partly used privately by the sole trader or partner

- Cars with CO_2 emissions of 130g/km or less from 6 April 2013 (1 April for companies) (160g/km or less between 6 April 2009 and 5 April 2013), unless they are partly used privately by the sole trader or partner

A writing down allowance (WDA) is given on the balance of the main pool at the end of the period of account.

The WDA is 18% per annum. If the period of account is greater than or shorter than 12 months long, the WDA is increased or decreased accordingly. [Hp140]

Once the WDA has been deducted from the pool balance, the remainder of the value of the pool is then carried forward to the start of the next period of account as the **tax written down value** (TWDV).

2.4 100% first year allowances

A 100% FYA is available for all business for expenditure on:

- Designated energy saving and water technologies such as combination heat and power equipment. A FYA on this type of expenditure is also known as an enhanced capital allowance (ECA).

- Technologically-efficient hand dryers.

- Qualifying research and development capital expenditure (see Chapter 21).

- New (ie not second-hand) low emission cars where expenditure is incurred prior to 31 March 2018. To qualify as a low emission car it must emit not more than 95g/km of CO_2 (was 110 g/km for expenditure before 6 April 2013 or 1 April for companies) or it must be electrically propelled.

- New and unused (ie not second-hand) zero emission goods vehicles where expenditure is incurred on or after 6 April 2010 (1 April 2010 for companies). This measure will have effect for eight years.

- A 100% FYA is available for expenditure by a **company** on the provision of new (ie not second-hand) plant and machinery in an area which at the date the expenditure is incurred is a designated assisted area within an enterprise zone. It will apply for expenditure incurred in the eight years commencing on 1 April 2012, for use in expanding or new activities of the company.

If the full 100% FYA is claimed, there will be no further WDAs on such expenditure.

2.5 Annual Investment Allowance (AIA)

An Annual Investment Allowance (AIA) is available to all businesses/companies irrespective of size. [Hp137]

It can be used against qualifying expenditure, which includes plant and machinery, integral features, long life assets, and private use assets, but not cars.

The maximum allowance is £500,000 per annum for expenditure incurred on or after 6 April 2014 (1 April for companies) and £250,000 per annum for expenditure incurred from 1 January 2013. It must be set against expenditure in the accounting period in which it is incurred.

For periods of account which are not 12 months long, the AIA is pro-rated up or down accordingly.

For accounting periods that straddle 6 April 2014 (1 April 2014 for companies), the maximum AIA for the accounting period will need to be calculated on a pro rata basis. It is necessary to apply the portion of the accounting period prior to April 2014 to the £250,000 AIA and then apply the portion of the accounting period from April 2014 to the £500,000 AIA, in order to calculate the maximum entitlement. However in the part of the accounting period falling after 1 January 2013 and before 6 April 2014 (1 April for companies), the maximum expenditure that can be covered by the AIA is £250,000 (for a 12-month period).

If a business had an accounting period for the year ended 31 December 2014, the maximum AIA would be calculated as [(3/12 × £250,000) + (9/12 × £500,000)] which is (£62,500 + £375,000) = £437,500. However the maximum expenditure incurred in the period before 6 (or 1) April 2014, which can be covered by the AIA, is £250,000. There is no such restriction on expenditure incurred from April 2014. Therefore in this example, expenditure of up to the maximum of £437,500 incurred between 6 (or 1) April 2014 and 31 December 2014 could be covered by the AIA.

Within a period the AIA will be applied to qualifying expenditure and the balance of expenditure on which AIA is not given will then receive the relevant WDA at the end of the chargeable period.

Worked example: Nina

Nina is a sole trader and makes up accounts to 30 September each year.

At 30 September 2013, the tax written down value on her main pool was £40,000. During the year ended 30 September 2014 Nina made the following acquisitions:

1.12.13	Machinery at a cost of £300,000
10.5.14	Computer and office equipment costing £95,000

Requirement

Calculate the maximum capital allowances available to Nina for the year ended 30 September 2014. Ignore VAT.

Solution

	Main pool £	Allowances £
Year ended 30 September 2014		
TWDV b/f	40,000	
Acquisitions (AIA)		
1.12.13 Machinery	300,000	
AIA (note)	(250,000)	250,000
10.5.14 Equipment	95,000	
AIA (Note)	(95,000)	95,000
	90,000	
WDA @ 18%	(16,200)	16,200
TWDV c/f	73,800	
Total allowances		361,200

Note:

The maximum AIA for the year ended 30 September 2014 is:

$((6/12 \times £250,000) + (6/12 \times £500,000)) = £125,000 + £250,000 = £375,000.$

However expenditure prior to 6 April 2014 can utilise a maximum AIA of £250,000. Therefore only £250,000 AIA can be claimed against the expenditure in December 2013 of £300,000.

There is no restriction on expenditure in the period from 6 April 2014 other than being subject to an overall maximum AIA for the period of £375,000. Therefore the expenditure in May 2014 is fully relieved by the AIA.

The AIA can be allocated against any qualifying expenditure. Therefore it is sensible to allocate it against that expenditure which will attract the lowest rate of WDA, for example any assets in the special rate pool that will only attract a WDA at 8% rather than those in the main pool where the WDA is 18%.

A company will receive only one AIA irrespective of the number of qualifying activities it undertakes.

Interactive question: Main pool allowances [Difficulty level: Intermediate]

Percy is in business as a sole trader. He makes up accounts to 31 December each year.

At 31 December 2013, the tax written down value on his main pool was £12,000. Percy is registered for VAT.

Percy makes the following acquisitions and disposals:

Acquisitions

1.5.14	Office equipment £2,400 (VAT inclusive cost)
1.8.14	Ford car for use by salesperson with CO_2 emissions of 88 g/km (see below)
1.11.14	Computer equipment £57,500 (VAT exclusive cost)

Disposals

1.8.14	Volvo car (which originally cost £10,000) used by salesperson traded in for Ford car (above). The part exchange given on the old Volvo is £4,000 and Percy pays a further £5,000 in cash (all costs VAT inclusive)
1.12.14	Machine for £2,750, original cost £2,500 (all figures are VAT exclusive)

Requirement

Using the standard format below, compute the maximum capital allowances available to Percy for the year ended 31 December 2014.

	FYA £	Main pool £	Allowances £
Period of account .... to			
TWDV b/f			
Acquisitions (FYA)			
FYA	( )		
Acquisitions (AIA)			
AIA		( )	
Disposals		( )	
		( )	
WDA	_____	( )	
TWDV c/f	_____	_____	_____
Total allowances			════════

See the **Answer** at the end of this chapter.

2.6 Special rate pool

This pool includes expenditure on:

- Long life assets

- Integral features

- Thermal insulation

- Solar panels

- Cars with CO_2 emissions in excess of 160g/km if purchased before 6 April 2013 (1 April for companies) and on or after 6 April 2009 (1 April for companies), or in excess of 130g/km if purchased on or after 6 April 2013 (1 April for companies).

The WDA on assets in the special rate pool is 8% for a 12 month period, calculated on the pool balance (after any additions and disposals) at the end of the chargeable period. [Hp140]

2.6.1 Long life assets

An item of plant and machinery is classed as a long-life asset if:

- The asset has, when new, an expected economic working life of 25 or more years; and

- The total expenditure on this kind of asset exceeds £100,000 in the 12 month accounting period (pro rata for shorter periods).

If the total expenditure is less than £100,000 in the period, the assets will be added to the main pool as usual.

The long life asset treatment does not apply to:

- Motor cars
- Plant and machinery for use in retail shops, showrooms, offices, hotels, dwelling houses
- Ships

An example of a long life asset is a crane.

Second-hand assets which were treated as long life assets when new will continue to be treated as long life assets by the new owners. However, if not treated as long life assets when new (for example because expenditure on such assets was less than £100,000), they must not be treated as such by the new owner.

2.6.2 Integral features

Items identified as integral features are:

- Electrical systems (including lighting systems)

- Cold water systems

- Space or water heating systems, powered systems of ventilation, air cooling or purification and any floor or ceiling comprised in such systems

- Lift/escalators/moving walkways

- External solar shading

Additionally, expenditure on the substantial rebuilding or replacement of integral features will be allocated to the special rate pool and will not be allowed as a revenue deduction if it represents more than 50% of the full replacement cost. In addition, where replacements are phased over time the entire cost will be treated as capital if the aggregate of expenditure on a particular asset within a 12-month period exceeds 50% of the full replacement cost. This prevents substantial rebuilding of, for example, an air conditioning system being treated as repairs.

Some integral features may be eligible for the 100% FYA on designated energy saving or water saving technologies. If an integral feature in the exam fulfils the necessary criteria it will be specifically stated.

2.6.3 Thermal insulation

Expenditure on thermal insulation of all existing buildings, other than residential property, is entitled to capital allowances.

Worked example: Special rate pool

Jason is a sole trader making up accounts to 30 November each year. The TWDVs of his plant and machinery at 1 December 2013 were:

	£
Main pool	65,300
Special rate pool	112,000

During the year ended 30 November 2014 Jason made the following acquisitions:

		£
10.4.14	Car with CO_2 emissions of 90g/km	18,000
1.3.14	Machinery	60,017
1.8.14	Thermal insulation	220,000
20.9.14	Lift installation	142,000

Jason sold a machine on 12.7.14 for £11,300.

Requirement

Calculate the maximum capital allowances that Jason can claim for the year ended 30 November 2014. Ignore VAT.

Solution

	FYA £	Main pool £	Special rate pool £	Allowances £
Period of account 1.12.13 – 30.11.14				
TWDV b/f		65,300	112,000	
Acquisitions (FYA)				
10.4.14 Low emission car	18,000			
FYA @ 100%	(18,000)			18,000
	—			
Acquisitions (AIA)				
1.8.14 Thermal insulation			220,000	
20.9.14 Lift installation			142,000	
1.3.14 Machinery		60,017		
AIA Max ((4/12 × £250,000) + (8/12 × £500,000)) = £83,333 + £333,333 = £416,667 (Note).		(54,667)	(362,000)	416,667
Disposals		(11,300)		
		59,350	112,000	
WDA @ 18%		(10,683)		10,683
WDA @ 8%		—	(8,960)	8,960
TWDV c/f		48,667	103,040	
Total allowances				454,310

Note:

The machine for £60,017 is purchased prior to 6 April 2014 but the cost is below the maximum annual AIA of £250,000 for expenditure incurred prior to this date, so the AIA is not restricted for this reason. As all the other expenditure is incurred on or after 6 April 2014, the maximum AIA of £416,667 is available against this without restriction. The AIA is claimed against expenditure in the special rate pool first (using £362,000) as this has a lower rate of WDA than expenditure in the main pool. The remainder is used against expenditure in the main pool.

2.7 WDA for small pools

If the balance on the main or special rate pool (before WDA) is less than the small pool limit at the end of the chargeable period, a WDA can be claimed up to the value of the small pool limit.

This means that the pools may be written down to nil, rather than a small balance being carried forward on which allowances have to be claimed each year.

The small pool limit is £1,000 for a 12-month period (pro rata for short and long chargeable periods).

Note: This does not apply to any of the single asset pools (short life asset, private use asset) as they have rules to write off the balance of the pool after the disposal of the asset.

3 Single asset pools

Section overview

- Some assets are not put in the main pool but have a separate pool for each asset.
- Each asset which is partly used privately by a sole trader or partner is kept in a separate pool.
- A taxpayer may elect for most assets in the main pool to be depooled except for cars or assets with private use.

3.1 Introduction

There are two types of asset which are not brought into the main pool but are given a separate pool for each asset. These are:

- Assets with some private use by the sole trader or partner
- Short life assets

We will deal with both of these in turn.

3.2 Assets with private use by sole trader or partner

Each asset which is partly used privately by a sole trader or partner is kept in a separate pool. This is because only the business element of the capital allowance can be claimed.

However, the AIA, the FYA or WDA is still calculated in full and deducted from the single asset pool.

Worked example: Cars and private use

Zoe is a sole trader making up accounts to 31 December each year.

Zoe purchased a car with CO_2 emissions of 124g/km for use in her business for £6,781 in January 2014. This car is used by an employee and has 25% private use.

Zoe purchased a second car, which has CO_2 emissions of 154g/km, for £18,890 on 1 December 2014. She uses the car 40% of the time for private purposes.

At 1 January 2014, the tax written down value of her main pool was £65,000.

Requirement

Compute the maximum capital allowances that Zoe can claim for the year ended 31 December 2014. Ignore VAT.

Solution

	Main Pool £	Car (private use) > 130g/km CO_2 £	Allowances £
Period of account 1.1.14 to 31.12.14			
TWDVs b/f	65,000		
Acquisition – cars	6,781	18,890	
WDA @ 18%	(12,921)		12,921
WDA @ 8%		(1,511) × 60%	907
TWDVs c/f	58,860	17,379	
Total allowances			13,828

Note that private use by the employee does not have any effect for capital allowances. It is only private use by a sole trader or partner which restricts allowances. Therefore the first car is added to the main pool (CO_2 emissions equal or less than 130g/km) and does not have a separate pool.

3.3 Short life assets

The taxpayer may elect for most assets in the main pool to be depooled except for cars or assets with private use. Instead of entering the main pool, the short life asset will be held in its own pool.

Normally an election is only made if the asset is expected to have a short working life although there is no requirement to show from the outset that the asset will actually have a 'short life'.

If the short-life asset has **not been disposed of by the end of:**

- **Four years** if purchased prior to 6 April 2011 (1 April for companies)
- **Eight years** if purchased from 6 April 2011 (1 April for companies)

after the end of the basis period (or chargeable period for companies) in which the expenditure was incurred, then at the beginning of the next period its **TWDV will be transferred from its separate pool to the main pool** where it will then be written down as normal.

A depooling election for a sole trader or partnership must be made by the first anniversary of 31 January following the end of the tax year in which the period of account of expenditure ends. For companies a depooling election must be made by the end of two years following the end of the accounting period of expenditure. [Hp150]

We will see an example of how the depooling election is beneficial once we have reviewed balancing adjustments.

4 Pre-trading expenditure

Section overview

- Capital expenditure incurred before a business starts is eligible for capital allowances.
- The capital expenditure is treated as incurred on the first day of trading.

4.1 Pre-trading expenditure

Capital expenditure incurred before a business starts is eligible for capital allowances.

In general, the capital expenditure is treated as incurred on the first day of trading and so included in the capital allowances computation for the first accounting period.

However, the rate of allowances available is determined by the actual date of the expenditure.

Worked example: Pre-trading expenditure and opening years

Gwen started trading on 1 May 2014 and decided to make up accounts to 31 May.

Her first period of account ran from 1 May 2014 to 31 May 2015. Her taxable trading income before capital allowances was £74,375.

Gwen bought plant and machinery as follows:

		£
1 December 2013	Machinery	7,280
1 May 2014	BMW Car (CO$_2$ emissions 171g/km)	26,700
1 September 2014	Equipment	7,188

The car is used 60% privately by Gwen.

Ignore VAT.

Requirement

Compute the taxable trading income in the opening years and the amount of any overlap profits.

Solution

Capital allowances

	Main pool £	BMW £	Allowances £
Period of account			
1.5.14 to 31.5.15			
Additions (AIA)			
1.12.13(Actual date) Machinery	7,280		
1.9.14 Equipment	7,188		
AIA	(14,468)		14,468
Additions (no AIA)			
1.5.14 Car		26,700	
WDA @ 8% × 13/12	———	(2,314) × 40%	926
TWDV c/f	–	24,386	
Allowances			15,394

Taxable trading income p/e 31 May 2015

	£
Taxable trading income before capital allowances	74,375
Less capital allowances	(15,394)
Taxable trading income	58,981

Taxable trading income for opening years

First tax year (2014/15)

Actual basis ie basis period = 1 May 2014 to 5 April 2015

11/13 × £58,981 — £49,907

Second tax year (2015/16)

Period of account longer than 12 months ending in second tax year, so use 12 months to the end of the period of account in the second tax year:

Basis period 1 June 2014 to 31 May 2015

12/13 × £58,981 — £54,444

Overlap profits

1 June 2014 to 5 April 2015
10/13 × £58,981 — £45,370

5 Disposals & cessations

Section overview

- On disposal, a balancing charge arises if too many capital allowances have been given or a balancing allowance may arise if too few capital allowances have been given.

- In the last period of account of a business, no allowances are given and all the assets are actually disposed of or deemed to have been disposed of at their market value.

5.1 Balancing adjustments

If too many capital allowances have been given on the asset, a balancing charge arises on disposal or cessation. This might happen if an asset is sold for an amount in excess of its tax written down value. The balancing charge will be taxed either by using it to reduce the capital allowances in the period of account or by adding it to the adjusted trading income computation.

If the asset is one with business and private use, only the business use element is actually chargeable.

A balancing charge can occur on the main pool, the special rate pool and on single asset pools either when the asset is sold or the business ceases.

If too few capital allowances have been given on the asset, a balancing allowance may arise on its disposal. This could happen if the asset is sold for an amount less than its tax written down value. The balancing allowance will be added to the capital allowances otherwise available for the period of account.

If the asset is one with business and private use, only the business use element is allowable as for all capital allowances.

A balancing allowance can only arise on the main pool or special rate pool if the business ceases. Balancing allowances can arise on single asset pools either when the asset is sold or the business ceases.

Where an asset is disposed of on which FYAs have been claimed, the proceeds on disposal must be deducted from the pool to which the item relates even if the balance on that pool is nil. This may create a balancing adjustment. For example, where a sole trader purchases a low emission car (a main pool asset) which is the only asset of the business the 100% FYA will mean that the balance of the main pool is £nil. If the car is disposed of, the proceeds should be deducted from the main pool and a balancing charge will be created equivalent to the sales proceeds on the car.

Worked example: Balancing adjustments

Gisala is a sole trader making up accounts to 31 August. She is not registered for VAT. The main pool at 1 September 2013 had a tax written down value of £9,500. Gisala also had a Jaguar car, purchased two years ago with 20% private use with a tax written down value of £15,000.

On 12 March 2014, Gisala sold machinery for £11,000 (original cost £12,000).

On 15 July 2014, Gisala traded in her Jaguar for an Audi with CO_2 emissions of 125g/km. The trade in value was £13,000 and she paid £7,000 in cash. The Audi also has 20% private use.

Requirements

(i) Compute the capital allowances available for Gisala for the year ended 31 August 2014.

(ii) Show the maximum capital allowances in the main pool for the year ending 31 August 2014 assuming that the machinery was sold on 12 March 2014 for only £8,700.

Solution

(i)

	Main pool £	Jaguar £	Audi £	Allowances £
Period of account 1.9.13 to 31.8.14				
TWDV b/f	9,500	15,000		
Acquisition (no AIA)				
15.7.14 Car (<130g/km CO₂)				
(£13,000 + £7,000)			20,000	
Disposals				
12.3.14	(11,000)			
	(1,500)			
Balancing Charge	1,500			(1,500)
15.7.14		(13,000)		
		2,000		
Balancing Allowance		(2,000) × 80%		1,600
WDA @ 18%			(3,600) × 80%	2,880
TWDV c/f	NIL	NIL	16,400	
Allowances				2,980

(ii)

	Main pool £	Allowances £
Period of account 1.9.13 to 31.8.14		
TWDV b/f	9,500	
Disposals		
12.3.14	(8,700)	
	800	
WDA (small pool)	(800)	800
	–	

Worked example: Short life assets

Jerry is a sole trader, making up accounts to 31 January. On 1 May 2014, he bought general plant and machinery costing £20,800. On 15 May 2014 he bought a photocopier costing £2,880.

He sold the photocopier on 30 November 2016 for £820.

Jerry is not registered for VAT. Jerry has used the full AIA on expenditure on integral features.

Requirements

Compute Jerry's capital allowances for the three years ending 31 January 2017 if:

(a) He does not make a depooling election for the photocopier; or
(b) He does make a depooling election for the photocopier.

Solution

(a) No depooling election made

	Main pool £	Allowances £
y/e 31.1.15		
Additions		
1.5.14 P&M	20,800	
15.5.14 Photocopier	2,880	
WDA @ 18%	(4,262)	4,262
TWDV c/f	19,418	
Allowances		4,262

	Main pool £	Allowances £
y/e 31.1.16		
WDA @ 18%	(3,495)	3,495
TWDV c/f	15,923	
Allowances		3,495
y/e 31.1.17		
30.11.14 Disposal	(820)	
	15,103	
WDA @ 18%	(2,719)	2,719
TWDV c/f	12,384	
Allowances		2,719

(b) Depooling election made

	Main pool £	Short life asset £	Allowances £
y/e 31.1.15			
1.5.14 P&M	20,800		
15.5.14 Photocopier		2,880	
WDA @ 18%	(3,744)	(518)	4,262
TWDVs c/f	17,056	2,362	
Allowances			4,262
y/e 31.1.16			
WDA @ 18%	(3,070)	(425)	3,495
TWDVs c/f	13,986	1,937	
Allowances			3,495
y/e 31.1.17			
30.11.16 Disposal		(820)	
		1,117	
Balancing Allowance		(1,117)	1,117
WDA @ 18%	(2,517)		2,517
TWDV c/f	11,469		
Allowances			3,634

You will see that making the depooling election has accelerated the allowances on the photocopier by giving a balancing allowance on disposal. If, however the AIA is claimed against expenditure on short life assets the depooling election would be disadvantageous as the receipt of disposal proceeds would trigger a balancing charge.

5.2 Allowances on cessation

On the cessation of trade, all the plant and machinery in the business are disposed of or deemed to have been disposed of.

Capital allowances for the final period of account are computed as follows:

- Any items acquired in the final period are added to TWDV b/f

- No WDAs or FYAs or AIAs are given for the final period of account

- The disposal value of the assets in each pool is deducted from the balance, giving rise to balancing allowances or balancing charges. Any assets taken over personally by the owner are treated as sold for market value

Worked example: Cessation of business

Ted is a sole trader, making up accounts to 31 December each year. The TWDVs of his plant and machinery at 31 December 2013 were:

	£
Main pool	24,285
Car with CO$_2$ emissions of 154g/km, purchased in 2012 (30% private use by Ted)	23,750

Ted ceased trading on 30 September 2014. He made up his final set of accounts for the nine month accounting period to 30 September 2014.

His taxable trading income before capital allowances for the period was £9,000. He had unused overlap profits of £2,000.

His purchases and sales of plant and machinery in the period to 30 September 2014 are:

		£
14 May 2014	Bought office furniture	1,850
30 September 2014	Sold all main pool items (all less than cost)	26,590
30 September 2014	Sold car	19,680

Requirement

Calculate Ted's taxable trading income for the final tax year of the business. Ignore VAT.

Solution

Capital allowances

	Main pool £	Car £	Allowances £
Period of account – 1.1.14 to 30.9.14			
TWDVs b/f	24,285	23,750	
Additions			
14.5.14 Office furniture	1,850		
	26,135		
Disposals			
30.9.14 main pool	(26,590)		
	(455)		
Balancing charge	455		(455)
30.9.14 Car		(19,680)	
		4,070	
Balancing allowance		(4,070) × 70%	2,849
Allowances			2,394

Taxable trading income p/e 30 September 2014

	£
Taxable trading income before capital allowances	9,000
Less capital allowances	(2,394)
Taxable trading income	6,606

Taxable trading income for closing year

Last tax year (2014/15)

End of previous basis period to cessation

1 January 2014 to 30 September 2014

	£	
Taxable trading income	6,606	
Less overlap relief	(2,000)	£4,606

Summary and Self-test

Summary

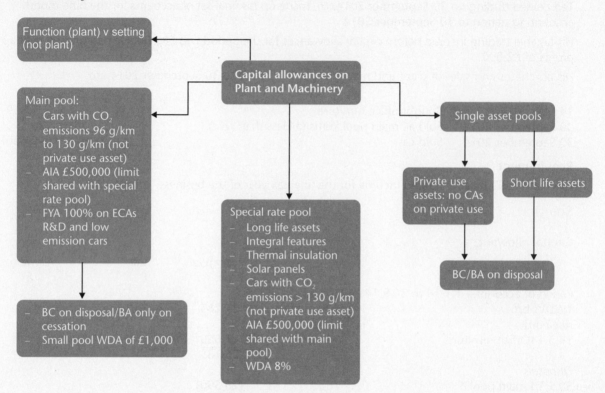

Function (plant) v setting (not plant)

Capital allowances on Plant and Machinery

Main pool:
- Cars with CO_2 emissions 96 g/km to 130 g/km (not private use asset)
- AIA £500,000 (limit shared with special rate pool)
- FYA 100% on ECAs R&D and low emission cars

- BC on disposal/BA only on cessation
- Small pool WDA of £1,000

Special rate pool
- Long life assets
- Integral features
- Thermal insulation
- Solar panels
- Cars with CO_2 emissions > 130 g/km (not private use asset)
- AIA £500,000 (limit shared with main pool)
- WDA 8%

Single asset pools

Private use assets: no CAs on private use

Short life assets

BC/BA on disposal

Self-test

Answer the following questions.

1 Happy Days, a holiday camp, incurred the following items of capital expenditure in the year ended 31 December 2014:

	£
Coach to transport guests from train station	45,000
False ceiling in restaurant to hide wiring	15,000
Moveable partitions in restaurant	5,000

How much of the expenditure qualifies as plant or machinery for capital allowances?

A £65,000
B £60,000
C £50,000
D £45,000

2 Joel is a sole trader preparing accounts to 30 June.

In the year ended 30 June 2014 his capital transactions were:

		£
4 May 2014	Bought Ford car (CO_2 emissions 127g/km)	16,580
10 May 2014	Sold Fiat car	3,525

The tax written down value of the Fiat purchased in 2010 was £4,230 on 1 July 2013.

Both cars have 10% private use by Joel.

What are the maximum capital allowances that Joel can claim for the year to 30 June 2014? Ignore VAT.

A £3,391
B £3,619
C £3,321
D £3,689

3 Assuming the AIA has been used on special rate pool assets, which **one** of the following items could be beneficially depooled as a short life asset?

A Car (no private use) to be disposed of in three years' time at less than written down value
B Plant to be sold in nine years for less than written down value
C Machinery to be scrapped (nil proceeds) in two years
D Plant to be traded in two years for 90% of its original cost

4 **Olivia**

Olivia started trading on 1 January 2015. Her first set of accounts were prepared to 30 June 2015 and to the same date each year thereafter.

She made the following purchases and sales of capital assets as follows:

Purchases

		£
1 May 2014	Machinery	10,000
30 September 2015	Car for use by employee (CO_2 emissions 125g/km)	12,200
1 October 2015	Plant	4,000
1 December 2015	Van	10,000
1 February 2017	Car for use by Olivia (CO_2 emissions 166g/km)	18,000
1 June 2017	Car for use by employee (CO_2 emissions 130g/km)	see below

Sales

		£
1 June 2017	Car bought in September 2015	see below
10 June 2017	Machinery purchased in May 2014	2,500

The car bought in September 2015 was sold in part exchange for the car purchased in June 2017. The part exchange allowance was £5,000 and Olivia also paid £3,000 in cash as the balance of the purchase price.

Private use of Olivia's car is 25%.

Taxable trading income before capital allowances is:

	£
p/e 30 June 2015	12,000
y/e 30 June 2016	26,000
y/e 30 June 2017	32,000

Requirements

(i) Compute the capital allowances for the first three periods of account, taking advantage of any beneficial elections available (ignore VAT).

(ii) Show the taxable trading income for the first four tax years of the business and compute any overlap profits. **(12 marks)**

Now go back to the Learning Objectives in the Introduction. If you are satisfied you have achieved these objectives please tick them off.

Technical reference

Legislation

References relate to Capital Allowances Act 2001 (*CAA 2001*)

Plant and machinery

Qualifying activities	ss.15 – 20
Qualifying expenditure: general	ss.21 – 38
Qualifying expenditure: first year allowances	ss.39 – 49
Pooling	ss.53 – 54
Writing down allowances	s.55
First year allowances	s.52
Long life assets	ss.90 – 102
Private use assets	ss.205 – 208
Short life assets	ss.83 – 89
Balancing adjustments	s.56
Final chargeable period	s.65
Thermal insulation of buildings	s.28
Integral features	ss.33A – 33B
Annual investment allowance	ss.38A – 38B 51A – 51N
Small pools	s.56A
Special rate expenditure and the special rate pool	ss.104A – 104E
Fixtures	s.187A

HMRC manual references

Capital allowances manual

(Found at http://www.hmrc.gov.uk/manuals/camanual/Index.htm)

PMAs: Introduction: Outline	CA20006
General: Definitions: Chargeable period, accounting period and period of account	CA11510
PMA: FYA: Expenditure on which available and rates	CA23110
PMA: Short life assets: Outline	CA23610

> This technical reference section is designed to assist you. It should help you know where to look for further information on the topics covered in this chapter.

CHAPTER

7

Answer to Interactive question

	FYA £	Main pool £	Allowances £
Period of account			
1.1.14 to 31.12.14			
TWDV b/f		12,000	
Acquisitions			
1.8.14 Low emission car	9,000		
FYA @ 100%	(9,000)		9,000
Acquisitions (AIA)			
1.5.14 Equipment (5/6 × £2,400)		2,000	
1.11.14 Computer equipment		57,500	
AIA		(59,500)	59,500
(Max (£250,000 × 3/12) + (£500,000 × 9/12) = £437,500)			
Disposals			
1.8.14 Volvo car		(4,000)	
1.12.14 Machine (restrict to cost)		(2,500)	
		5,500	
WDA @ 18%		(990)	990
TWDV c/f	–	4,510	
Total allowances			69,490

Answers to Self-test

1   C – £50,000

	£
Coach	45,000
False ceiling (setting, not active function)	n/a
Moveable partitions (active function)	5,000
Total	50,000

2   C – £3,321

	Fiat £	Ford CO$_2 \leq 130$ g/km £	Allowances £
Period of account 1.7.13 to 30.6.14			
TWDV b/f	4,230		
Acquisition (no AIA)			
4.5.14		16,580	
Disposals			
10.5.14	(3,525)		
BA	705 × 90%		635
WDA @ 18%		(2,984) × 90%	2,686
TWDV c/f		13,596	
Allowances			3,321

3   C – Machinery to be scrapped (nil proceeds) in two years

Car – cannot be depooled

Plant to be sold in nine years for less than written down value – TWDV will automatically transfer to main pool after eight years so no benefit

Plant to be traded in two years for 90% of its original cost – will create balancing charge so no benefit

4   Olivia

(i)   Capital allowances

	Main pool £	Car $CO_2 \geq 130$ g/km £	Allowances £
p/e 30 June 2015			
1.1.15 to 30.6.15			
Addition (AIA)			
1.5.14 (pre-trading)			
Machinery	10,000		
AIA	(10,000)		10,000
TWDV c/f	–		
Allowances			10,000
y/e 30 June 2016			
1.7.15 to 30.6.16			
Additions (AIA)			
1.10.15 Plant	4,000		
1.12.15 Van	10,000		
AIA	(14,000)		14,000
Addition (no AIA)			
30.9.15 Car	12,200		
	12,200		
WDA @ 18%	(2,196)		2,196
TWDV c/f	10,004		
Allowances			16,196
y/e 30 June 2017			
1.7.16 to 30.6.17			
Addition (no AIA or FYA)			
1.2.17 Car		18,000	
1.6.17 Car	8,000		
Disposals			
1.6.17 Car	(5,000)		
10.6.17 Machine	(2,500)		
	10,504		
WDA @ 18%	(1,891)		1,891
WDA @ 8%		(1,440) × 75%	1,080
TWDV c/f	8,613	16,560	
Allowances			2,971

(ii) **Taxable trading income**

	p/e 30.6.15 £	y/e 30.6.16 £	y/e 30.6.17 £
Taxable trading income before CAs	12,000	26,000	32,000
Less CAs	(10,000)	(16,196)	(2,971)
Taxable trading income	2,000	9,804	29,029

2014/15 (First tax year)

Actual basis

1 January 2015 to 5 April 2015

3/6 × £2,000 .... £1,000

2015/16 (Second tax year)

No 12-month period of account ending in 2nd tax year

First 12 months' trading

1 January 2015 to 31 December 2015

	£	
p/e 30 June 2015	2,000	
1 July 2015 to 31 December 2015		
6/12 × £9,804	4,902	£6,902

2016/17 (Third tax year)

CYB

y/e 30 June 2016 .... £9,804

2017/18 (Fourth tax year)

CYB

y/e 30 June 2017 .... £29,029

Overlap profits

	£	
1 January 2015 to 5 April 2015		
3/6 × £2,000	1,000	
1 July 2015 to 31 December 2015		
6/12 × £9,804	4,902	£5,902

CHAPTER 8

Partnerships

Learning objective

- Calculate the assessable trading profits or losses of a partnership including after a change in the profit sharing ratio or change in partners, and allocate the profits or losses to each partner including the allocation of notional profits and losses

The specific syllabus reference for this chapter is 3d.

Syllabus links

We covered the basic division of profits between partners in Chapter 7 of your Principles of Taxation study manual.

In this chapter, we review that knowledge and look at changes in partnership composition, notional profits and losses and limited liability partnerships.

Examination context

In the examination candidates may be required to:

- Allocate profits and losses between partners in an ongoing partnership, where partners are joining or leaving the partnership or where there is a change in the profit share arrangement

- Deal with the allocation of notional profits and losses

- Discuss the implication of a limited liability partnership

Better candidates have achieved excellent marks in partnership questions. Less well prepared candidates struggle with where to start partnership questions and often try to allocate profits for the tax year rather than for the accounting period.

1 Partnerships

> **Section overview**
>
> - A partnership itself is not a taxable person.
> - Each partner is liable to income tax on his share (and only his share) of the partnership taxable trading income. Similarly each partner is liable to capital gains tax on his share of any gains realised on the disposal of partnership assets.
> - The current year basis applies to continuing partnerships.
> - Opening and closing year rules apply to partners who join and leave the partnership but the continuing partners remain on the current year basis.
> - If the allocation of partnership profit results in a notional loss for one or more partners, a reallocation of profits must be made.
> - Similarly, if the allocation of partnership loss results in a notional profit for one or more partners, a reallocation of the loss must be made.

1.1 Taxation of partnerships

A partnership itself is not a taxable person. Each of the partners is liable to tax on his share of the taxable trading income of the partnership on the same basis as a sole trader.

For income tax purposes in a continuing partnership, the basis of assessment for a tax year will be the current year basis. Opening and closing year rules apply as partners join and leave the partnership.

Each partner is only liable to income tax on his share of the partnership trading income.

1.2 Allocation of partnership profits

The net profit or loss for the partnership for the period of account must be adjusted for tax purposes (in the same way as for a sole trader as we saw in Chapter 6). Partners' salaries and interest on capital are not deductible expenses and must be added back in computing profits, because they are a form of drawings.

Capital allowances for the partnership must then be computed and deducted from the adjusted trading profit. Capital allowances are available on partnership assets and are computed as for a sole trader (see Chapter 7).

The resultant taxable trading income of the partnership for the period of account is allocated between the partners according to the profit-sharing agreement for the period of account.

The agreement may specify that one or more of the partners is entitled to a 'salary' (an allocation of profits) and/or interest on capital introduced into the partnership. These amounts are allocated first and then the remaining amount of taxable trading income is allocated in accordance with the agreed profit-sharing ratios (PSR).

1.3 Change in profit sharing ratio during period of account

Where there is a change in the profit-sharing agreement during the period of account, divide the period of account into the periods of the different profit sharing agreements.

Any salaries and interest on capital as appropriate must be time-apportioned accordingly.

Worked example: Change in partnership profit allocation

Lisa, Alicia and Mary are in partnership. Partnership accounts are made up to 31 July. The partnership had taxable trading income of £90,000 for the year ended 31 July 2014.

Until 30 November 2013, the partnership had shared profits equally. From 1 December 2013 it was agreed that the partners should be paid an annual salary and the profit sharing ratios divided as follows:

	Lisa	Alicia	Mary
Salary	£24,000	£21,000	£15,000
PSR	25%	35%	40%

Requirement

Show the taxable trading income for each partner for the period of account.

Solution

	Total £	Lisa £	Alicia £	Mary £
First PSR period				
1.8.13 to 30.11.13				
PSR (1:1:1)				
£90,000 × 4/12	30,000	10,000	10,000	10,000
Second PSR period				
1.12.13 to 31.7.14				
Salaries (× 8/12)	40,000	16,000	14,000	10,000
PSR (25:35:40)	20,000	5,000	7,000	8,000
Total	90,000	31,000	31,000	28,000

1.4 Partner joining partnership

If a new partner joins a partnership, the opening year rules will apply to that partner, but the continuing partners will continue on the current year basis.

If the new partner joins the partnership part way through the partnership period of account, there will be a change in the partnership profit-sharing agreement. This change is dealt with in the same way as a change in profit-sharing agreement in a continuing partnership.

Remember that when a new partner joins a partnership part way through an accounting period, the new partner's accounting period will only commence when he joined the partnership and will therefore be a short accounting period.

It is important that you deal with the allocation of profits to each partner first, before you attempt to match those profits to tax years.

Worked example: Partner joining a partnership

Sam and Emma have been in partnership for many years making up accounts to 31 December each year. Profits have been shared equally.

On 1 June 2014, Hilary joined the partnership. From that date, profits were shared Sam 50% and Emma and Hilary 25% each.

The partnership taxable trading income for the year ended 31 December 2014 was £48,000 and for the year ended 31 December 2015 was £60,000.

Requirement

Compute the trading income taxable on Sam, Emma and Hilary for 2014/15.

Solution

First, allocate the taxable trading income between the partners:

y/e 31.12.14	Total £	Sam £	Emma £	Hilary £
First PSR period				
1.1.14 to 31.5.14 = £48,000 × 5/12				
PSR (1:1)	20,000	10,000	10,000	n/a
Second PSR period				
1.6.14 to 31.12.14 = £48,000 × 7/12				
PSR (50:25:25)	28,000	14,000	7,000	7,000
Totals	48,000	24,000	17,000	7,000

y/e 31.12.15	Total £	Sam £	Emma £	Hilary £
PSR (50:25:25)	60,000	30,000	15,000	15,000

Next, consider the basis periods for each partner for 2014/15.

Sam
CYB
y/e 31.12.14 £24,000

Emma
CYB
y/e 31.12.14 £17,000

Hilary
First tax year (2014/15)
Actual basis
Basis period 1.6.14 to 5.4.15

	£
1.6.14 to 31.12.14	7,000
1.1.15 to 5.4.15	
3/12 × £15,000	3,750
Total	10,750

1.5 Partner leaving partnership

If a partner leaves a partnership, the closing year rules will apply to that partner, but the continuing partners will continue on the current year basis.

If the partner leaves the partnership part way through the partnership period of account, there will be a change in the partnership profit-sharing agreement, dealt with in the same way as a change in profit-sharing agreement in a continuing partnership.

Again, it is important that you deal with the allocation of profits to each partner first, before you attempt to match those profits to tax years.

Interactive question 1: Partner leaving partnership [Difficulty level: Exam standard]

Richard, Charlotte and William have traded in partnership for many years. Each partner was entitled to 6% interest per annum on capital introduced into the partnership. Each partner had introduced £100,000 of capital on the commencement of the partnership. Thereafter, profits were shared in the ratio 50% to Richard, 30% to Charlotte and 20% to William. The partnership makes up accounts to 30 September each year.

On 1 May 2014, William left the partnership. Thereafter profits were shared equally between the two remaining partners and no interest was paid on capital. The partnership taxable trading income for the year to 30 September 2014 was £120,000. William had overlap profits on commencement of £5,000.

Requirement

Using the standard format below, compute the taxable trading income for each of the partners for 2014/15.

First allocate the taxable trading income between the partners:

y/e	Total £	Richard £	Charlotte £	William £
First PSR period				
.... to				
Interest				
PSR				
Second PSR period				
.... to				
PSR				
Totals				

Then match to the relevant tax years:

Richard
.... basis

£ _____

Charlotte
.... basis

£ _____

William
Last tax year
Basis period .... to ....

£

Partnership allocation
Less overlap profits
Taxable trading income

See **Answer** at the end of this chapter.

1.6 Notional profits and losses

Sometimes, if the partnership makes an overall profit, the allocation of profits results in one or more of the partners making a notional loss. In this case, the profit allocation must be adjusted.

A partner with a notional loss will have a nil amount of taxable trading income.

The total profit will then be reallocated to the remaining partners in proportion to the profit initially allocated to them.

Worked example: Notional loss

Graham, Henry and Isobel are in partnership. In the year to 31 December 2014, the partnership had taxable trading income of £44,500.

During the period, Graham was entitled to a salary of £28,000 and Henry a salary of £24,000. The remaining profits/losses are to be divided equally between the partners.

Requirement

Show the taxable trading income for each of the partners.

Solution

First, allocate the profit in accordance with the partnership sharing arrangements.

	Total £	Graham £	Henry £	Isobel £
Salaries	52,000	28,000	24,000	NIL
PSR (1:1:1)	(7,500)	(2,500)	(2,500)	(2,500)
Total	44,500	25,500	21,500	(2,500)

Isobel has a notional loss and therefore will have NIL taxable trading income.

The remaining partners will have the profit of £44,500 reallocated to them:

Graham $\dfrac{25,500}{25,500+21,500} \times £44,500$ £24,144

Henry $\dfrac{21,500}{25,500+21,500} \times £44,500$ £20,356

The taxable trading income for each of the partners is therefore:

	Total £	Graham £	Henry £	Isobel £
	44,500	24,144	20,356	NIL

A similar situation can arise where the partnership has an overall loss. In this case, the allocation of profits may result in one or more of the partners making a notional profit. The loss allocation must be adjusted.

A partner with a notional profit will have a NIL trading loss.

The total loss will then be reallocated to the remaining partners in proportion to the losses initially allocated to them.

Interactive question 2: Notional profit   [Difficulty level: Exam standard]

Jacqui, Kalid and Leslie are in partnership. In the year to 31 July 2014, the partnership had a trading loss of £(24,000).

During the period, Jacqui was entitled to a salary of £66,000. The partners share profits and losses (after Jacqui's salary) 25% to Jacqui, 25% to Kalid and 50% to Leslie.

Requirement

Using the standard format below, show the trading loss for each of the partners.

First, allocate the loss in accordance with the partnership sharing arrangements.

	Total £	Jacqui £	Kalid £	Leslie £
Salary				
PSR (............. : .... : ....)				
Total				

.... has a notional profit and therefore will have no trading loss.

The remaining partners will have the loss of £............... reallocated to them:

.... $\dfrac{.................}{.................+.................} \times £(.................)$ £( )

.... $\dfrac{.................}{.................+.................} \times £(.................)$ £( )

The trading loss for each of the partners is therefore:

	Total £	Jacqui £	Kalid £	Leslie £

See **Answer** at the end of this chapter.

1.7 Capital gains

Partnership capital transactions are treated as dealings by the individual partners rather than the partnership. Each partner is treated as owning a fractional share of each of the partnership assets.

Each partner is chargeable on his share of gains arising on disposals of partnership assets. The chargeable gain on the disposal of an asset will be allocated to the partners in accordance with the partnership profit sharing ratio.

2 Limited liability partnerships

Section overview

- The liability of partners in a limited liability partnership (LLP) is limited to their capital contributions.

- Partners in a LLP are taxed on a similar basis to unlimited liability partners.

- Certain partners (salaried members) of an LLP are treated as employees for tax purposes if the payments they receive from the LLP do not vary with the profits of the LLP.

2.1 What is a limited liability partnership?

Most partnerships are formed so that the partners each have unlimited liability for the debts of the partnership.

However, it is possible to form a limited liability partnership (LLP) under which the liability of the partners is limited to the amount of capital that they contribute to the partnership.

2.2 Income tax on limited liability partnerships

The partners of an LLP are taxed on a similar basis to those in an unlimited partnership.

Thus each of the partners is liable to tax on his share of the taxable trading income of the LLP.

2.3 Salaried members of LLP

This section is new.

Although partners (members) of an LLP are taxed like those of an unlimited partnership, from 6 April 2014, there is an exception to this in the case of 'salaried members' of an LLP. Broadly, for these purposes, 'salaried members' are partners who receive payment from the LLP in return for their services, and the payment received is fixed (or if variable, the payment does not vary with the profits of the LLP). Such partners are treated for income tax, national insurance and corporation tax purposes as if they are employees, and not partners.

In an exam question, you will be told if a partner should be treated as a salaried member. Otherwise, apply the usual tax treatment for partners, as explained in this chapter.

Summary

Partnerships:
each partner taxed on his share of
partnership taxable trading income

Continuing partnership:
CYB

Partner joins:
opening rules apply to new
partner, other partners stay
on CYB,
Partner leaves:
closing rules apply to old
partner, other partners stay
on CYB

LLP: treated in similar way
to other partnerships

Notional profit/loss:
reallocation required

CHAPTER

8

Self-test

Answer the following questions.

1 Which **two** of the following statements about partnerships are **true**?

    A   The taxable trading income of the partnership is allocated to individual partners according to the profit sharing ratio of the period of account

    B   The taxable trading income of the partnership is allocated to individual partners according to the profit sharing ratio of the tax year in which the period of account ends

    C   Each partner is liable for the income tax liability of the partnership as a whole

    D   Each partner is only responsible for the income tax liability on his share of the partnership taxable trading income

2 Arnold, Betty and Christie have been in partnership for many years. Partnership accounts have been made up to 30 April each year. Profits have been shared 20% to Arnold and Betty and 60% to Christie.

    Christie left the partnership on 30 April 2014. The taxable trading income for the partnership is as follows:

y/e 30.4.13	£70,000
y/e 30.4.14	£150,000

    Christie had overlap profits on commencement of £12,000.

    What is Christie's taxable trading income for 2014/15?

    A   £70,000
    B   £30,000
    C   £78,000
    D   £90,000

3 Simon, Ted and Angie are in partnership. They prepare accounts to 30 November each year and share profits equally.

    On 1 December 2014, Mike joins the partnership. From this date, the profit sharing agreement changes so that Mike receives a salary of £4,000 a year and the balance of the profits are shared equally.

    The taxable trading income of the partnership is

y/e 30.11.14	£15,000
y/e 30.11.15	£28,000

    What is the taxable trading income for Mike for 2014/15 and 2015/16?

A	2014/15	£4,000,	2015/16	£6,000
B	2014/15	£3,333,	2015/16	£10,000
C	2014/15	£nil,	2015/16	£10,000
D	2014/15	£3,333,	2015/16	£11,000

4 Jean, Katie and Laura are in partnership. Jean is entitled to a salary of £6,000 and Katie is entitled to a salary of £3,000. Remaining profits are shared equally.

    In the year to 31 December 2014, the partnership made a profit of £6,000.

    What is Jean's taxable trading income for the period?

    A   NIL
    B   £1,714
    C   £4,286
    D   £5,000

5 Robin, Sylvia and Taylor

Robin, Sylvia and Taylor traded in partnership for many years.

The profit sharing arrangements were:

	Robin	Sylvia	Taylor
Salaries	£7,500	£6,000	£5,000
Remaining profits	2	2	1

On 30 June 2015, Taylor left the partnership. He had no overlap profits. On 1 July 2015, Una joined the partnership.

From 1 July 2015, the profit sharing arrangements were:

	Robin	Sylvia	Una
Salaries	£9,000	£9,000	£9,000
Remaining profits	6	3	1

The partnership makes up accounts to 31 December each year and had the following taxable trading income:

	£
y/e 31 December 2014	51,000
y/e 31 December 2015	90,000
y/e 31 December 2016	120,000

Requirement

Show the taxable trading income for each of the partners for the tax years 2014/15, 2015/16 and 2016/17. **(10 marks)**

Now go back to the Learning Objectives in the Introduction. If you are satisfied you have achieved these objectives please tick them off.

Technical reference

Legislation

References relate to Income Tax (Trading and Other Income) Act 2005 (*ITTOIA 2005*)

Partnerships   ss.846 – 856

HMRC manual references

Business Income manual

(Found at http://www.hmrc.gov.uk/manuals/bimmanual/BIM82000.htm)

Partnerships: General notes   BIM82000

Partnerships: General notes: Sharing Profits/Losses   BIM82055

This technical reference section is designed to assist you. It should help you know where to look for further information on the topics covered in this chapter.

Answer to Interactive question 1

y/e 30.9.14	Total £	Richard £	Charlotte £	William £
First PSR period				
1.10.13 to 30.4.14 = £120,000 × 7/12 ie: £70,000				
Interest (7/12)	10,500	3,500	3,500	3,500
PSR (5:3:2)	59,500	29,750	17,850	11,900
Second PSR period				
1.5.14 to 30.9.14 = £50,000				
PSR (1:1)	50,000	25,000	25,000	n/a
Totals	120,000	58,250	46,350	15,400

Basis periods for 2014/15

Richard
Current year basis
y/e 30.9.14   £58,250

Charlotte
Current year basis
y/e 30.9.14   £46,350

William
Last tax year (2014/15)
End of previous basis period to cessation
Basis period 1.10.13 to 30.4.14

	£
Partnership allocation	15,400
Less overlap profits	(5,000)
Taxable trading income	10,400

Answer to Interactive question 2

First, allocate the loss in accordance with the partnership sharing arrangements.

	Total £	Jacqui £	Kalid £	Leslie £
Salary	66,000	66,000	NIL	NIL
PSR (25:25:50)	(90,000)	(22,500)	(22,500)	(45,000)
Total	(24,000)	43,500	(22,500)	(45,000)

Jacqui has a notional profit and therefore will have no trading loss.

The remaining partners will have the loss of £24,000 reallocated to them:

Kalid $\dfrac{22,500}{22,500+45,000} \times £(24,000)$ £(8,000)

Leslie $\dfrac{45,000}{22,500+45,000} \times £(24,000)$ £(16,000)

The trading loss for each of the partners is therefore:

	Total £	Jacqui £	Kalid £	Leslie £
	(24,000)	NIL	(8,000)	(16,000)

CHAPTER 8

1   A – The taxable trading income of the partnership is allocated to individual partners according to the profit sharing ratio of the period of account.

     D – Each partner is only responsible for the income tax liability on his share of the partnership taxable trading income.

2   C – £78,000

Christie

Last tax year

End of previous basis period to cessation

Basis period 1.5.13 to 30.4.14

	£
PSR (60%)	90,000
Less overlap profits	(12,000)
Taxable trading income	78,000

3   B – 2014/15 £3,333, 2015/16 £10,000

y/e 30.11.14	Total	Mike
	£	£
Salary	4,000	4,000
Balance (25% to Mike)	24,000	6,000
Totals	28,000	10,000

Mike

First tax year (2014/15)
Actual basis
Basis period 1.12.14 to 5.4.15
4/12 × £10,000   £3,333

Second tax year (2015/16)
12 month period of account ending in 2nd tax year
Basis period 1.12.14 to 30.11.15
y/e 30.11.15   £10,000

4   C – £4,286

This is a notional loss situation.

First, allocate the profit in accordance with the partnership sharing arrangements.

	Total	Jean	Katie	Laura
	£	£	£	£
Salaries	9,000	6,000	3,000	NIL
PSR (1:1:1)	(3,000)	(1,000)	(1,000)	(1,000)
Total	6,000	5,000	2,000	(1,000)

Reallocation:

Jean $\dfrac{5,000}{5,000+2,000} \times £6,000$ £4,286

5   First, allocate the profit in accordance with the partnership sharing arrangements for each period of account.

y/e 31.12.14	Robin £	Sylvia £	Taylor £	Una £	Total £
Salaries	7,500	6,000	5,000	NIL	18,500
PSR (2:2:1)	13,000	13,000	6,500	NIL	32,500
Totals	20,500	19,000	11,500	NIL	51,000
y/e 31.12.15					
1.1.15 – 30.6.15 = £45,000					
Salaries	3,750	3,000	2,500	NIL	9,250
PSR (2:2:1)	14,300	14,300	7,150	NIL	35,750
1.7.15 – 31.12.15 = £45,000					
Salaries	4,500	4,500	NIL	4,500	13,500
PSR (6:3:1)	18,900	9,450	NIL	3,150	31,500
	41,450	31,250	9,650	7,650	90,000
y/e 31.12.16					
Salaries	9,000	9,000	NIL	9,000	27,000
PSR (6:3:1)	55,800	27,900	NIL	9,300	93,000
	64,800	36,900	NIL	18,300	120,000

Now allocate to each tax year:

Robin

2014/15	y/e 31.12.14	£20,500
2015/16	y/e 31.12.15	£41,450
2016/17	y/e 31.12.16	£64,800

Sylvia

2014/15	y/e 31.12.14	£19,000
2015/16	y/e 31.12.15	£31,250
2016/17	y/e 31.12.16	£36,900

Taylor

2014/15	y/e 31.12.14	£11,500
2015/16	p/e 30.06.15 (last year)	£9,650

Una

2015/16	First tax year	
	Actual basis	
	Basis period 1.7.15 to 5.4.16	£
	1.7.15 – 31.12.15	7,650
	1.1.16 – 5.4.16 3/12 × £18,300	4,575
		12,225
2016/17	Second tax year	
	y/e 31.12.16	£18,300

CHAPTER 9

Cash basis of accounting

Introduction

Examination context

Topic List

Summary and Self-test

Technical reference

Answers to Self-test

Introduction

Tick off

Learning objective

- Calculate trading profits or losses after adjustments and allowable deductions using the cash basis of accounting

The specific syllabus reference for this chapter is 3c.

Syllabus links

We covered the basic rules of the cash basis of accounting for small businesses in Chapter 7 of your Principles of Taxation study manual.

In this chapter, we review that knowledge and look at the rules for joining and leaving the cash basis.

Examination context

In the examination candidates may be required to:

- Integrate knowledge acquired previously in the Principles of Taxation examination to compute adjusted profits computations for a trader using the cash basis

- Identify the adjustments required under the cash basis

1 Cash basis for small businesses

Section overview

- Certain small unincorporated businesses may elect to use the cash basis of accounting rather than accruals accounting for the purposes of calculating their tax adjusted trading income.

- The cash basis can be used by unincorporated businesses with receipts for the tax year that do not exceed the VAT threshold (currently £81,000).

- Taxable trading profits are calculated as total cash receipts less total allowable business expenses paid, subject to adjustments required by tax law.

- As for accruals accounting traders, the profit per the accounts must be adjusted for tax purposes. The majority of the tax adjustments are the same. The main differences relate to capital expenditure and interest payments.

- Capital payments for plant and machinery (except cars) are deductible in calculating taxable trading profits and capital allowances are not available. Capital receipts from the sale of plant and machinery (except cars) are taxable when received.

- Interest paid on a loan is a deductible expense from trading profits subject to a maximum of £500 for a 12-month period.

- The basis of assessment rules which determine in which tax year the profits of an accounting period are taxed apply in the same way as for accruals accounting traders.

- An election must be made to use the cash basis.

1.1 Introduction

Usually, businesses are required to prepare accounts using GAAP (Generally Accepted Accounting Practice) for tax purposes. This is referred to as 'accruals accounting' in this chapter.

However, certain small unincorporated businesses may elect to use the cash basis rather than accruals accounting for the purposes of calculating their tax adjusted trading income.

The cash basis is intended to simplify the tax reporting system for many small businesses who do not need to prepare accruals based accounts in order to effectively manage their business.

Under the cash basis a business is taxed on its cash receipts less cash payments of allowable expenses.

You will be told in an exam question whether a business uses the cash basis to prepare its tax-adjusted trading income. Unless told otherwise, where a question states that the business has used the cash basis to prepare its tax-adjusted trading income, you should assume that the business has also used a cash basis for its financial accounts.

1.2 Which businesses can use the cash basis?

The cash basis can only be used by unincorporated businesses (sole traders and partnerships) with receipts for the tax year that do not exceed the VAT registration threshold (currently £81,000). The limit is increased to twice the VAT registration limit (£162,000) for recipients of Universal Credit.

A trader must leave the cash basis if his receipts in the previous tax year exceeded twice the VAT registration threshold for that previous year and receipts for the current year exceed the VAT registration limit for the current year.

A trader may leave the scheme if his 'commercial circumstances' change such that the scheme is no longer appropriate for him (see below).

The above limits are proportionately reduced for accounting periods of less than 12 months.

The combined receipts of all the trader's businesses must be considered in deciding whether a trader can use the scheme.

Companies and LLPs are excluded from using the cash basis.

1.3 Capital items

Remember that under the normal accruals basis (see earlier in this Manual) capital expenditure is disallowed in computing taxable trading profits and instead capital allowances are available on plant and machinery. In addition, capital receipts are not taxable as trading receipts (unless capital allowances have been claimed in which case the proceeds are brought into the capital allowances computation) but may be subject to capital gains tax.

The main difference for cash basis traders is in relation to plant and machinery (except cars). Capital payments for plant and machinery (except cars) are deductible in calculating taxable trading profits and capital allowances are not available. Similarly, capital receipts from the sale of plant and machinery (except cars) are taxable when received.

For other assets eg land and buildings and cars, the same rules as for accruals accounting traders apply. Thus capital payments are disallowed but capital allowances can be claimed on cars.

Capital receipts and expenditure under the cash basis are dealt with in more detail below.

1.4 Calculation of taxable profits

The taxable trading profits are calculated as:

- Total cash receipts less
- Total allowable business expenses paid

subject to adjustments required by tax law.

As we saw earlier in this text for accruals accounting traders, the starting point for calculating the taxable profit is the net profit per the accounts. A number of adjustments to this net profit are then required for tax purposes.

The same approach applies when using the cash basis. Many of the tax adjustments are the same as for accruals accounting, eg expenditure not wholly and exclusively for the purposes of the business is still a disallowable expense.

There are however a number of differences. The main differences relate to the treatment of capital expenditure and interest payments, and are covered below.

1.4.1 Taxable receipts

Taxable receipts include all amounts received including cash, card receipts, cheques and payments in kind. They also include amounts received from the sale of plant and machinery which qualify for capital allowances (but not cars).

As for accruals accounting traders, the net profit per the accounts must be adjusted for:

- Receipts which have not been included in the accounts but which are   Added to net profit
taxable as trade profits eg where the trader takes goods for his own use

And

- Receipts included in the accounts which are not taxable as trade profits   Deducted from net profit
eg interest income, capital receipts

Whilst in principle the adjustments required are the same as for accruals accounting, they are adapted as follows for the cash basis:

- Where a trader takes stock out of the business for his own use without paying an arm's length price a 'just and reasonable' amount (for example the cost of the stock) should be added to the taxable profit.

    Contrast this with an accruals accounting trader where the goods are treated as sold for their market value (see earlier in this Manual).

    This principle also applies to any other 'uncommercial transactions' included in the cash accounts.

- Not all capital receipts are deducted from the net profit. Only deduct the capital receipts from the sale of cars and other assets which are not classed as plant and machinery eg land and buildings.

In addition the following adjustments, which are specific to the cash basis are required:

- Where a trader ceases to use a capital asset for the purposes of the trade, the market value of the asset at that date is treated as a taxable receipt.

- When a trader ceases to trade, the value of stock and work in progress is treated as a taxable receipt in the final period of account.

1.4.2 Allowable expense payments

Business expenses are deductible when they are paid and include capital expenditure on plant and machinery (but not cars).

The majority of the specific tax rules covered earlier in this Text concerning the deductibility of expenditure also apply to the cash basis. It should be remembered in particular that only business expenses are tax deductible so that any private element must be disallowed. The fixed rate expenses for motor vehicles and premises used for private and business purposes may be used instead.

However, some of the tax adjustments normally required in arriving at taxable trading profits are not applicable to the cash basis and there are other adjustments which are specific to the cash basis. This section deals with the differences between adjustments required for accruals accounting and the cash basis. You should refer back to earlier in this Text to remind yourself of the general rules for allowing/disallowing trading expenditure.

The main provisions which are specific to the cash basis are:

- Capital expenditure on plant and machinery: Expenditure on plant and machinery (but not cars) is an allowable expense for the cash basis (see below).

- Bad debts: Not an allowable deduction for the cash basis as income is only taxed when it is received.

- Leased cars: The 15% restriction does not apply such that amounts paid are allowable in full.

1.4.3 Capital expenditure

Payments made to acquire plant and machinery (but not cars) which would qualify for capital allowances are allowable expenses when they are made. This includes the acquisition cost of vans and motor cycles.

If an item of plant and machinery is used for both business and private purposes, only the proportion of expenditure related to business use is deductible ie add back the private use proportion to the profit per the accounts.

Where plant and machinery (except cars) is acquired under hire purchase, a deduction is allowed for each payment made under the contract.

Contrast this with an accruals accounting trader where capital allowances are available on the capital value of the asset when the contract is signed and a trading deduction is available for the finance cost over the period of the contract (see earlier in this Text). This may be more beneficial than the cash basis if the trader can claim 100% AIA on the capital value up front.

Other capital expenditure is not a deductible expense eg capital payments related to land, buildings, cars, legal fees on such acquisitions.

Capital allowance may be claimed in respect of cars in the normal way.

1.4.4 Interest paid

Interest paid on a loan is a deductible expense from trading profits (even if the loan is not wholly and exclusively for the purposes of the trade) subject to a maximum of £500 for a 12-month period.

Note that this restriction only applies to loan interest ie it does not apply to interest charges for hire purchase or leasing assets; interest charged by suppliers of goods or services; or credit card interest on allowable purchases.

Worked example: Calculation of taxable profits

Alex started to trade as a sole trader on 1 May 2014 and has elected to use the cash basis for tax purposes. The receipts figure in his accounts for the year to 30 April 2015 is analysed as follows:

	£
Cash receipts from customers	30,000
Bank transfers received from customers	36,000
Cash receipt from sale of a van	3,000
Cash receipt from sale of a car	4,500
Interest credited to business bank account	500
Total receipts	74,000

In addition, Alex took goods out of the business for his own use which had cost £400. These goods could have been sold for £530.

The expense payments figure in his accounts for the year to 30 April 2015 is analysed as follows:

	£
Cheque payments to suppliers of goods for resale	28,000
Cheque payments to other suppliers	9,000
Standing orders paid to utility companies	3,400
Cheque payment for purchase of machinery	6,300
Bank transfer for purchase of car	7,500
Payment for servicing the car	200
Payments to landlord for rental of business premises	1,950
Interest paid on bank loan to acquire machinery and car	700
Total payments	57,050

As at 30 April 2015 Alex still had a third of the goods paid for during the year, in stock.

The payments made to other suppliers include £130 paid to a restaurant where he entertained a potential supplier.

The car has CO_2 emissions of 125g/km and is used 20% of the time for private purposes and 80% for business purposes. Alex drove 12,000 miles in the car during the year.

Alex rented business premises from 1 May 2014 at a monthly rent of £150. He paid the rent for May 2015 on 21 April 2015.

Alex claims the fixed rate mileage allowance in respect of the car.

Requirement

Calculate Alex's tax adjusted profit for the year ended 30 April 2015.

Solution

Taxable receipts for year ended 30 April 2015:

	£
Total receipts per the accounts	74,000
Deduct: Receipts not taxable as trading income:	
– Receipt from sale of car	(4,500)
– Interest received	(500)
Taxable trading receipts	69,000

Allowable trading expenses for year ended 30 April 2015

	£
Total payments per the accounts	(57,050)
Add: Disallowable entertaining	130
Machinery (allowable expense)	–
Car purchase – disallowable capital addition	7,500
Car servicing – disallowed as FRMA claimed	200
Interest paid on bank loan (maximum allowed £500)	200
Deduct fixed rate mileage allowance (12,000 × 80% = 9,600 × 45p)	(4,320)
Allowable trading expenses	53,340

Note. The information concerning the year end stock and the rent prepaid to the landlord is irrelevant. Only the actual payments in the year are deductible.

Alex could have claimed capital allowances on the car, but instead claims the fixed rate mileage allowance, so cannot also claim capital allowances.

Tax adjusted profit for the year ended 30 April 2015 is:

	£
Total receipts per the accounts	69,000
Less allowable trading expenses	(53,340)
Plus removal of goods for personal use	400
	16,060

1.5 Basis of assessment

A trader using the cash basis can, like any other trader, prepare his accounts to any date in the year. The basis of assessment rules which determine in which tax year the profits of an accounting period are taxed apply in the same way for traders using the cash basis and for accruals accounting traders.

1.6 The election

An election to use the cash basis is made by ticking the 'cash basis' box in the self assessment tax return. The election applies to all the businesses run by the trader.

The election is effective for the tax year for which it is made and all subsequent tax years unless:

- The trader's receipts exceed the eligibility limit (see above), or

- There is a change of circumstances which makes it more appropriate to prepare accounts using GAAP and the trader elects to calculate profits using GAAP.

There is no definition of a 'change of circumstances' in the legislation but HMRC guidance gives examples of such changes as a business that is expanding which wishes to claim more than the maximum interest deduction.

2 Starting to use the cash basis

Section overview

- A new business can elect to use the cash basis.

- An existing business, previously using accruals accounting, can elect to use the cash basis but must make adjustments so that receipts are only taxed once and payments only deducted once.

- An adjustment will also be needed to deduct a portion of any unrelieved expenditure in a capital allowance pool which relates to plant and machinery.

2.1 New businesses

A new trader who meets the eligibility criteria, can simply elect to use the cash basis, as above, and prepare cash accounts from the date he starts to trade. He will continue to be in the scheme until he fails to meet the criteria or elects to use GAAP.

2.2 Existing businesses

An existing business which has previously prepared accounts on the accruals basis under GAAP, may elect to start using the cash basis, provided it meets the eligibility criteria.

If the fixed rate mileage allowance has previously been claimed it must continue to be used under the cash basis.

In the first year of the cash basis the following adjustments are required in order to ensure that receipts/payments are only taxed/deducted once for tax purposes.

2.2.1 Plant and machinery (except cars)

A deduction from trading profits is given for the 'relevant portion' of any balance on any capital allowance pool at the end of the previous year which relates to plant and machinery (except cars). The 'relevant portion' can be calculated on any just and reasonable basis eg by reference to the cost of the assets in the pool. Thus a tax deduction is taken for the proportion of the brought forward tax written down value on any capital allowance pool which relates to plant and machinery.

2.2.2 Adjustment income/expenditure

An adjustment must be made in the first year in which the cash basis is used to reflect the amount by which taxable profits have been under or over stated as a result of the change to the cash basis.

For example, under accruals accounting, income which has been earned but not received (represented by year end debtors) is taxed in the year it is earned. On the change to the cash basis, a deduction must be made from the cash receipts figure to reflect those receipts that relate to the previous year's debtors which have already been taxed. Conversely, an adjustment (add back to expense payments) must be made to reflect amounts owed to creditors for which a tax deduction was taken in the previous year.

A net addition to taxable profits is known as 'adjustment income' and a net deduction as 'adjustment expense'.

Worked example: Joining cash accounting

Ahmed has been running a business as a sole trader for a number of years. He prepares his accounts for the year to 31 March 2015 on the cash basis and elects to use the cash basis for tax purposes for the first time.

Ahmed's net profit (net receipt) per the accounts for the year to 31 March 2015 is £31,000. Included in this figure are the following amounts:

	£
Payment for hire of car	3,000
Purchase of bottles of whiskey for five customers	120
Purchase of furniture for office	600

The car has CO_2 emissions of 135g/km. Ahmed drove 4,000 business miles and 1,000 private miles in the car during the year.

At 1 April 2014 the tax written down value on Ahmed's capital allowances main pool was £1,400. Half of the balance relates to cars (all used for business purposes) and half to items of plant and machinery.

Ahmed's accountant has informed him that he has an adjustment expense in respect of the change to the cash basis of accounting of £2,000. This is not included in his accounts for the year.

Requirement

Calculate Ahmed's taxable trading profit for the year ending 31 March 2015 assuming he does not claim the fixed rate mileage allowance for the car hired during the year.

Solution

Taxable trading profit for the year to 31 March 2015

		£
Net profit (receipt) per accounts		31,000
Add:	Car hire: Private use (£3,000 x 1,000/5,000) (Note)	600
	Gifts of alcohol disallowed	120
	Furniture – allowable expense as plant and machinery	–
Deduct:	TWDV bfwd re plant and machinery (£1,400 × 50%)	(700)
	Adjustment expense – deducted in first year of the cash basis	(2,000)
	Capital allowances on balance of main pool (£1,400 × 50% × 18%)	(126)
Taxable trading profit		28,894

Note.   The 15% restriction for hired cars with CO_2 emissions exceeding 130g/km does not apply to the cash basis.

3   Ceasing to use the cash basis

Section overview

- If a trader leaves the cash basis, adjustments must be made for plant and machinery and in respect of income and expenditure.

- Adjustment income may be spread over the six years following the tax year of change.

When a trader leaves the cash basis the following adjustments must be made.

3.1   Plant and machinery

Any unrelieved expenditure on plant and machinery is allocated to a capital allowances pool in the next accounting period. This applies where an asset has been acquired but not fully paid for eg for a hire purchase asset where payments are still to be made under the HP agreement.

3.2   Adjustment income/expenditure

The trader must make a net adjustment income or adjustment expense calculation as above.

Any adjustment income is spread equally over six years and taxed as trading income in the six tax years following the year in which the trader leaves the cash basis, unless an election is made to accelerate the charge.

Any adjustment expense is deductible as a trading expense in the first accounting period after the trader leaves the cash basis.

4 Interaction with other taxes

Section overview

- Receipts that are taxable as trading receipts will be excluded from the charge to capital gains tax.

- A VAT registered trader must exclude the VAT from payments and receipts for tax purposes.

- A trader using the cash basis for income tax purposes must also use the VAT cash accounting scheme.

4.1 Other income tax provisions

Interest paid by an individual on a loan to invest in a partnership or to buy plant and machinery to be used by a partnership is not an allowable deduction from total income, when calculating the individual's income tax liability, where the partnership has elected to use the cash basis to prepare its accounts for tax purposes (see earlier in this Manual).

4.2 Capital gains tax

The proceeds from the sale of plant and machinery are taxable as trading receipts under the cash basis. Accordingly, they are excluded from the charge to capital gains tax.

4.3 VAT

A trader who uses the cash basis may be voluntarily registered for VAT.

Where the trader uses the cash basis for income tax purposes he must also use the VAT cash accounting scheme.

4.4 Class 4 NIC

Profits under the cash basis are used for calculating Class 4 NICs (see later in this Manual).

Summary

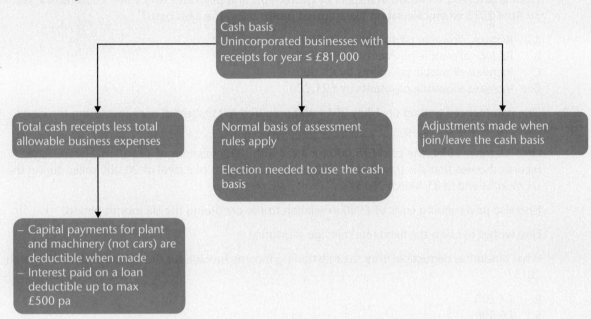

Cash basis
Unincorporated businesses with
receipts for year ≤ £81,000

Total cash receipts less total
allowable business expenses

Normal basis of assessment
rules apply

Election needed to use the cash
basis

Adjustments made when
join/leave the cash basis

– Capital payments for plant
and machinery (not cars) are
deductible when made
– Interest paid on a loan
deductible up to max
£500 pa

CHAPTER

9

Self-test

Answer the following questions.

1   A sole trader prepares accounts using the cash basis for the year to 30 April 2015. Included in the accounts is a cash payment of £12,000 in respect of the purchase of an item of machinery and a cash payment of £9,000 for the purchase of a new car.

What adjustment is needed in respect of the receipts and payments for capital items for the year to 30 April 2015 when calculating tax adjusted profits using the cash basis?

A   Reduce allowable payments by £9,000
B   Reduce allowable payments by £21,000
C   Increase allowable payments by £9,000
D   Increase allowable payments by £21,000

2   Elise commenced trading on 1 July 2014 and prepared her first set of accounts, using the cash basis, to 31 March 2015.

On 1 October 2014, she paid £18,000 for a car with CO_2 emissions of 135g/km. Her mileage records showed that she travelled 14,000 business miles out of a total of 20,000 miles during the six months ended 31 March 2015.

Elise also paid running costs of £900 in relation to the car during the six month period.

Elise wishes to claim the fixed rate mileage allowance.

What amount is deductible from taxable trading income for Elise for the period ending 31 March 2015?

A   £7,200
B   £6,300
C   £5,500
D   £6,400

3   Sally has been trading as a sole trader for a number of years. She elects to use the cash basis for tax purposes for the first time in respect of the accounts for the year to 31 March 2015.

She had the following receipts and payments in respect of capital assets in the period to 31 March 2015:

			£
1.5.14	Payment	Purchase of machinery	15,000
4.6.14	Payment	Purchase of new car (30% private use & CO_2 emissions 90g/km)	11,000
15.7.14	Receipt	Sale of used car (no private use) (CO_2 emissions 120g/km)	3,400
31.8.14	Receipt	Sale of van (CO_2 emissions 170g/km)	7,000

The car and van which were sold during the year were acquired for £18,000 and £13,500 respectively.

The balance on the capital allowances main pool as at 1 April 2014 was £5,000. It is reasonable to assume that 20% of the balance related to items of plant and machinery and 80% to cars.

Requirement

Calculate the capital allowances which may be claimed for the period ending 31 March 2015. Assume that Sally claims all available allowances.   **(5 marks)**

Now go back to the Learning Objectives in the Introduction. If you are satisfied you have achieved these objectives please tick them off.

Legislation

References relate to Income Tax (Trading and Other Income) Act 2005 (*ITTOIA 2005*)

Cash basis for small businesses	s.25A
Trade profits: cash basis	ss.31A-31F
Cash basis: capital expenditure	ss.33A

HMRC manual references

Business income manual

(Found at http://www.hmrc.gov.uk/manuals/bimmanual/index.htm)

Cash basis: eligibility	BIM70010
Cash basis: receipts: overview	BIM70015
Cash basis: receipts: capital receipts	BIM70020
Cash basis: expenses: overview	BIM70030
Cash basis: expenses: capital expenditure	BIM70035
Cash basis: expenses: interest payments and incidental costs of obtaining finance	BIM70040
Transitional adjustments: entering the cash basis: overview	BIM70060

> This technical reference section is designed to assist you. It should help you know where to look for further information on the topics covered in this chapter.

CHAPTER

9

1   A – Reduce allowable payments by £9,000

    The payment for plant and machinery is an allowable payment. The purchase of the car is not allowable and the allowable payments must be reduced by £9,000. Capital allowances can be claimed on the car.

2   C – £5,500

    Claim the fixed rate mileage allowance (FRMA) as follows:

Business miles	£
10,000 miles at 45p/mile	4,500
4,000 miles at 25p/mile	1,000
	5,500

    If Elise claims the FRMA she will receive no further deductions for the running costs of the car.

3   Capital allowances for year to 31 March 2015

	Main pool £	Private use asset (BU 70%) £	Allowances £
TWDV at 1.4.14	5,000		
Amount related to P&M expensed in first year of cash basis (£5,000 × 20%)	(1,000)		
Additions eligible for FYAs:			
4.6.14 Low emission car (BU 70%)		11,000	
100% FYA		(11,000) × 70%	7,700
15.7.14 Disposal of car	(3,400)		
	600	-	
Small pools WDA	(600)		600
TWDV c/f	-	-	
Total allowances			8,300

    Note: The machinery and van are items of plant and machinery, such that payments are deductible in full when made and receipts are taxable as trading receipts when received. Capital allowances are not available if using the cash basis in respect of plant and machinery (other than cars).

CHAPTER 10

Income tax for trusts

Introduction

Examination context

Topic List

Summary and Self-test

Technical reference

Answer to Interactive question

Answers to Self-test

Learning objective

- Calculate total taxable income and the income tax payable or repayable for trustees and beneficiaries

The specific syllabus reference for this chapter is 3n.

Syllabus links

The taxation of trusts was not covered in your Principles of Taxation Study Manual.

Examination context

In the examination candidates may be required to:

- Calculate the income tax payable by trustees or beneficiaries

- Calculate the additional tax charge due from the trustees of a discretionary trust where the tax pool is insufficient to cover the tax credit attached to distributions to beneficiaries

1 Introduction

Section overview

- A trust is a flexible alternative to gifting assets directly.

- A trust may be set up either during the settlor's lifetime or on their death.

- There are two main types of trust for income tax purposes – trusts with an interest in possession and non interest in possession (ie discretionary) trusts.

- A bare trust is treated as transparent for tax purposes – ie it is treated as a direct gift from the settlor to the beneficiary.

1.1 Terminology

Trusts help preserve family wealth while maintaining flexibility over who should benefit. The way in which a trust is taxed depends on the nature of the trust itself. In order to understand the nature of the transaction it is important to have a basic understanding of English trust law (note that Scots law is different):

Definitions

Trust: A trust is an arrangement under which a person, the settlor, transfers property to another person, the trustee, who must deal with the trust property on behalf of certain specified persons, the beneficiaries.

Interest in possession trust: A trust where one or more of the beneficiaries has the right to receive the income of the trust (an **interest in possession**), the capital passing to other beneficiaries (the remainderman) when the interest in possession comes to an end.

Discretionary trust: A trust where no beneficiary is entitled by right to any income or capital; it is left up to the discretion of the trustees which of the beneficiaries is to benefit from the trust and how they are to benefit.

Bare trust: Property in a bare trust (or 'simple' trust) is held by the trustee (or nominee) as its legal owner on behalf of the beneficiary. The beneficiary is absolutely entitled to the trust property and any income arising from it. There is no interest in possession and the trustees cannot exercise any discretion over the trust property or income.

1.2 Why use a trust

Trusts are useful vehicles for non-tax reasons such as to preserve family wealth, provide for those who are deemed to be incapable (minors and the disabled) or unsuitable (due to youth or poor business sense) to hold assets directly.

1.3 Will trusts

A trust may be set up in an individual's will. A discretionary trust allows the settlor flexibility about who may benefit from the trust and to what extent. This can be useful if there are beneficiaries of differing ages and whose financial circumstances may differ.

1.4 Lifetime trusts

Although gifts to trusts during lifetime can lead to an IHT charge (a chargeable lifetime transfer (CLT), see later in this study manual), there can be tax benefits from setting up trusts during the settlor's lifetime.

If the cumulative total of the settlor's CLTs in any seven year period does not exceed the nil rate band, there will be no lifetime tax to pay on creation of the trust. This will also impact any further charges which may be payable while the trust is in existence.

If a discretionary trust is used, the settlor can preserve maximum flexibility in the class of beneficiaries and how income and capital should be dealt with.

1.5 Bare trusts

Income arising in a bare trust is assessed on the beneficiaries of the trust. The trustees are not required to file a self-assessment return or deduct tax at source.

Such trusts are treated as transparent for tax purposes. Consequently the transfer of assets to bare trustees is treated as an outright gift to the beneficiary.

A practical application of the bare trust is when a beneficiary of a trust becomes absolutely entitled to trust property (for example, when the beneficiary of a trust for a bereaved minor becomes absolutely entitled to trust property at age 18). If the trust property is not distributed at that date a bare trust will arise in favour of the beneficiary until such time as the trust fund is handed over.

1.6 Property income

Where trust assets include a property that is rented out, you may need to calculate the property income figure to put into the trust's income tax computation.

Trustees are taxed on the full amount of the rental profits accrued in the tax year (ie from 6 April to 5 April). Property income is always taxed as non-savings income.

Profits and losses on different properties owned by the trust are automatically set off to arrive at a net amount.

If a loss is generated it will be carried forward and set against future UK property income.

Where a property is let on non-commercial terms (eg to a beneficiary at a nominal or 'peppercorn' rent), and a loss would otherwise arise in respect of that property, the deductible expenses are limited to the income from the property. Excess expenses cannot be carried forward to a later year.

2 Interest in possession trusts

Section overview

- The trustees of an interest in possession trust are taxed on the income received at the basic rate applicable to that type of income – ie non-savings, savings or dividend income.

- Trustees do not deduct trust expenses from income received although expenses relating to a specific source of income are deducted from that income – eg property income expenses such as mortgage interest.

- Interest in possession beneficiaries are treated as entitled to trust income (net of expenses) as it arises. Life tenants are taxed on all the income of the trust after the deduction of tax and expenses. The life tenant will be taxed according to the type of income received by the trust ie non-savings, interest or dividends.

- Annuitants are paid a fixed annuity each year by the trustees. The annuity is paid net of 20% tax.

2.1 Overview

In a trust, assets are legally owned by trustees, for the benefit of beneficiaries. In a trust with an interest in possession, the beneficiaries are entitled to income from the trust assets as it arises. These beneficiaries are often called life tenants, as their right to the income often lasts until their deaths.

Income is taxed in the first instance on the trustees and reported on the self-assessment trust and estate tax return, the SA900. The trustees do not have a personal allowance, nor is the trust income split into different bands of income as it is for an individual. Instead all trust income is taxed at the basic rate of tax applicable to the type of income.

Expenses relating to specific sources of income are deducted from that income, as they are for an individual. For example, letting expenses are deducted from property income. However, there is no deduction for trust management expenses.

2.2 Rates of tax

- Non savings income (such as property income) is taxed at 20%
- Savings income (such as interest) is taxed at 20%
- Dividends are taxed at 10%

Interest is usually received net of a 20% tax credit by the trust (as it is by an individual). Dividends are received with a 10% notional tax credit. As these tax credits satisfy the trustees' liability for these types of income, no further tax is due from the trustees.

Trust expenses are never deductible for the trustees of an interest in possession trust, so do not deduct them in the income tax computation. Instead they are deducted from the trust income before it is taxed on the beneficiary.

2.3 Beneficiary's tax position

The life tenant is entitled to receive the trust income once tax has been paid and expenses settled out of the net income. Expenses are treated as paid out of dividend income in priority to other income.

The beneficiary will receive a statement of income from the trust (form R185 (Trust Income)) showing the net amounts which he is entitled to receive along with the associated tax credit (ie the tax paid by the trustees). The beneficiary will then include these amounts on his own tax return.

The income paid to the beneficiary retains its nature so if it is rental income in the trustees' hands it will be taxed as non-savings income on the beneficiary, if it is interest, as savings income and so on.

Worked example: Income tax for an IIP trust

A trust receives rental income of £6,000, net bank interest of £3,200 and dividends of £1,800 in 2014/15. Trust expenses are £200. There is one life tenant.

Requirement

What are the trust's net income and the life tenant's tax position?

Solution

Trust's net income:

	Non-Savings Income £	Savings Income £	Dividend Income £
Rental income	6,000		
Interest £3,200 × 100/80		4,000	
Dividends £1,800 × 100/90			2,000
Tax @ 20%/20%/10%	1,200	800	200
Less tax credits	–	(800)	(200)
Tax due	1,200	–	–
Trust's net income (ie after tax)	4,800	3,200	1,800
Less expenses	–	–	(200)
Trust's net distributable income	4,800	3,200	1,600

The life tenant is treated as receiving income as follows:

	Net £	Tax suffered £
Non savings income	4,800	1,200
Savings income	3,200	800
Dividends	1,600	178
	9,600	

The tax suffered on the dividend income is the grossed up dividend received at 10%:

$$£1,600 \times \frac{100}{90} = £1,778 \times 10\% = £178$$

2.4 Annuitants

The trustees may have to make a fixed income payment each year, known as an annuity. This is paid to the recipient, the annuitant, net of a 20% tax credit. The trustee can deduct the gross annuity from the total trust income, from non-savings income first as a deductible payment, and must pay the 20% tax liability to HMRC.

3 Discretionary trusts

Section overview

- Trustee expenses are deductible for the purposes of computing tax for discretionary trustees. Trust expenses are deducted first from dividend income.

- Discretionary trust beneficiaries are only taxable on income paid to them or applied for their benefit.

- If there is not enough tax in a discretionary trust's tax pool to cover the 45% tax credit on payments to beneficiaries the trustees must pay the additional tax to HMRC.

3.1 Overview

In a discretionary trust trustees have complete discretion over the distribution of trust assets. They may either pay out income or accumulate it in the trust (ie not pay it out), however they choose.

3.2 Rates of tax

Trustees' expenses must be paid out of net income (ie after tax). Trustees of discretionary trusts can deduct the expenses in their income tax computation. However, as all figures in the computation are shown gross (ie before tax), the amount of income used to cover the expenses must be grossed up at 10% (if dividend income is used) or 20% (if savings income is used). Expenses are allocated against dividend income first then savings income and then non savings income.

Once expenses are deducted discretionary trusts then have a basic rate band of £1,000. The first £1,000 of taxable income is taxed at the basic rates, ie at 20% for savings and non-savings income and 10% for dividends. As for individuals, the basic rate band is applied first to non-savings income, then savings income and finally dividends. Many smaller trusts will have no further tax to pay and will not need to file a tax return.

Where a settlor has made more than one settlement the £1,000 is divided by the number of settlements made by the same settlor, with a minimum amount of £200 for each trust. In the exam, assume there is only one settlement, unless specifically stated otherwise.

Any remaining income is taxed at one of two special trust tax rates. These are equivalent to the rates that additional rate taxpaying individuals pay and are therefore 45% for non-savings and savings income; and 37.5% for dividend income. These are known as the 'trust rate' and 'trust dividend rate' respectively.

Finally the income used to pay the expenses is taxed at the basic rate, depending on the type of income used to pay them, eg 10% if paid out of dividend income.

Interactive question: Income tax for discretionary trust   [Difficulty level: Exam standard]

The Crane Trust had the following receipts and payments during the year ended 5 April 2015:

	£
Receipts	
UK rental income receivable	19,400
Dividends received (net)	1,170
Savings income	240
Payments	
Relating to rental property	2,200
Trustees' expenses	810

Requirement

Calculate the income tax payable by the trustees. No other trusts have been set up by the same settlor.

See **Answer** at the end of this chapter.

3.3 The tax pool

When the trustees make an income payment out of the trust to a beneficiary, the beneficiary is treated as receiving the payment net of a 45% tax credit. This means that the beneficiary must gross up the payment received by 100/55 to include as non-savings income in his income tax computation, and he will be able to deduct 45% of the gross amount as a tax credit. This applies even if the only income that the trustees have is dividend income taxed at 37.5% or income that has been taxed within the trust basic rate band.

This 45% tax credit comes from certain amounts of tax paid by the trustees. The most important of these are:

- Tax at the basic rates paid on trust income within the basic rate band.

- Tax at the rate applicable to trusts (45%) on trust income.

- The difference between the dividend trust and ordinary rates (ie 37.5% − 10%) = 27.5% on dividend income.

This total amount of tax that is available to cover the tax credit on distributions to the beneficiaries is known as the 'tax pool'. If the trustees have paid more tax than they need to cover the tax credits, this tax is carried forward to the next tax year.

If, however, the reverse applies, ie they have paid less tax than is required to cover the tax credits, the balance required is extra tax which must be paid over to HMRC.

Note that the 10% tax credit on dividends cannot enter the tax pool as this is not real tax paid by the trustees.

Worked example: Discretionary trust tax pool

The Crane trust (from interactive question 1) has a balance b/f on its tax pool at 6 April 2014 of £2,534.

Requirement

Show what the tax pool for 2014/15 would be assuming the trustees make a net income payment to Joseph, a beneficiary, on 1 December 2014 of either (a) £2,000; or (b) £15,000.

Solution

(a) *Payment of £2,000*

	£
Tax pool brought forward as at 6.4.14	2,534
Add tax for 2014/15 (W)	7,735
	10,269
Tax available for providing credits	
Less tax paid out as credit on payment to beneficiary (2,000 × 100/55 × 45%)	(1,636)
Carried forward at 5.4.15	8,633

(b) *Payment of £15,000*

	£
Tax pool brought forward as at 6.4.14	2,534
Add tax for 2014/15 (W)	7,735
Tax available for providing credits	10,269
Less tax paid out as credit on payment to beneficiary (15,000 × 100/55 × 45%)	(12,273)
Additional tax to pay to HMRC by trustees	(2,004)
Balance carried forward at 5.4.15	NIL

WORKING – Trust income tax liability (from solution to interactive question 1)

	£
Tax paid at 20% (basic rate band)	
£1,000 @ 20%	200
Tax paid at 45%	
£16,500 @ 45%	7,425
Tax on dividend income (excluding the 10% non-refundable tax credit)	
£400 @ (37.5 – 10%)	110
Income tax liability	7,735

3.4 Beneficiary's tax position

Beneficiaries of discretionary trusts are only taxed if they receive income payments from the trust. Any payments of income to beneficiaries are made net of tax at 45% and are non-savings income for the beneficiary.

Even if all the income of the trust is dividend income the beneficiary is still treated as receiving income net of a 45% tax credit.

The trustees will provide a statement of income (R185 (Trust Income)) to the beneficiaries showing the relevant figures. If the trustees have not paid sufficient tax to cover this tax credit, they must make an additional payment (as seen above). Beneficiaries not subject to income tax at the additional rate may obtain repayments. Additional rate taxpaying beneficiaries will have no further tax liability.

Worked example: Income tax for beneficiary of a discretionary trust

In 2014/15, Matilda received a salary of £11,000 (before deducting PAYE tax of £950). She also received a payment of £1,650 from a discretionary trust.

Requirement

What is Matilda's final tax payable or repayable for the year?

Solution

	Non savings £
Earnings	11,000
Trust income £1,650 × 100/55 (remember will be taxed as non-savings income)	3,000
Net income	14,000
Less personal allowance	(10,000)
Taxable income	4,000

Income tax	£	£
£4,000 × 20%		800
Less tax paid and suffered		
PAYE	950	
Trust income £3,000 × 45%	1,350	
		(2,300)
Repayment due		(1,500)

Summary and Self-test

Summary

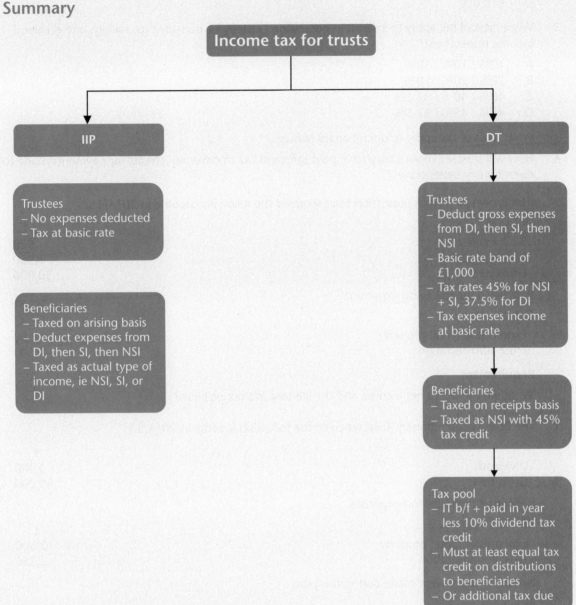

Income tax for trusts

IIP

Trustees
- No expenses deducted
- Tax at basic rate

Beneficiaries
- Taxed on arising basis
- Deduct expenses from DI, then SI, then NSI
- Taxed as actual type of income, ie NSI, SI, or DI

DT

Trustees
- Deduct gross expenses from DI, then SI, then NSI
- Basic rate band of £1,000
- Tax rates 45% for NSI + SI, 37.5% for DI
- Tax expenses income at basic rate

Beneficiaries
- Taxed on receipts basis
- Taxed as NSI with 45% tax credit

Tax pool
- IT b/f + paid in year less 10% dividend tax credit
- Must at least equal tax credit on distributions to beneficiaries
- Or additional tax due

Self-test

1 What personal allowance are trustees entitled to in 2014/15?

    A   £nil

    B   £1,000

    C   £5,000

    D   £10,000

2 What rates of tax apply to interest in possession trustees for non-savings, savings and dividend income respectively?

    A   10% / 10% / 10%

    B   20% / 20% / 10%

    C   40% / 40% / 32.5%

    D   45% / 45% / 37.5%

3 What rates of tax apply to discretionary trustees?

4 How will trustees know if they have paid sufficient tax to cover tax credits for payments made to discretionary beneficiaries?

5 The Brown interest in possession trust received the following income in 2014/15:

	£
Bank interest	920
Dividends	1,350
Gross rents	30,000

It incurred the following expenses:

	£
Expenses re rental property	4,500
Trust administration	1,500

Requirement

What are the trust's net income and the life tenant's tax position?

6 The Bristow Discretionary Trust received the following income in 2014/15:

	£
Dividends	3,000
Gross rents	30,000

It incurred the following expenses:

	£
Expenses re rental property	2,500
Trust administration	2,250

No distributions were made during the year.

Requirement

Calculate the trust's income tax liability.

7   **The Ray Trust**

In 2014/15, the Ray trust had the following income:

	£
Property income	30,800
Interest received (paid gross)	25,200
Dividends received	32,760

Payments from the trust comprised the following:

	£
Allowable property expenses	8,400
Trust admin expenses	5,040

Income distributions to beneficiaries:

	£
Charlotte	45,000

The balance brought forward on the tax pool at 6 April 2014 was £4,200.

Charlotte has no other source of income.

Requirements

(i)   Calculate the income tax payable by the trust for 2014/15.   **(10 marks)**

(ii) Calculate the amount of income tax payable/recoverable for Charlotte.   **(4 marks)**

                                                                                    (14 marks)

Now go back to the Learning Objectives in the Introduction. If you are satisfied you have achieved these objectives please tick them off.

Legislation

References are to Income Tax Act 2007 (*ITA 2007*) unless otherwise stated

Annuity paid net of basic rate tax	Income Tax (Trading & Other Income) Act 2005 s.686
Trust tax rates	s.479
Discretionary trust basic rate band	s.491
The tax pool	s.498

HMRC manual references

Trusts, settlements and estates manual

(Found at http://www.hmrc.gov.uk/manuals/tsemmanual/index.htm)

Introduction to trusts	TSEM1002
Trust income and gains	TSEM3000
Ownership and income tax	TSEM9000

> This technical reference section is designed to assist you. It should help you to know where to look for further information on the topics covered in this chapter.

Answer to Interactive question

Trust tax liability

	£	Non savings income £	Savings income £	Dividend income £
Income from UK property business	19,400			
Less letting expenses	(2,200)	17,200		
Dividends £1,170 × 100/90				1,300
Taxed interest £240 × 100/80			300	
		17,200	300	1,300
Less administration expenses (against dividends first) £810 × 100/90				(900)
Taxable income		17,200	300	400

Tax

	£
£1,000 @ 20% (non-savings income)	200
£(17,200 – 1,000 + 300) = £16,500 @ 45%	7,425
£400 @ 37.5%	150
£900 @ 10% (dividend income used to pay expenses)	90
Total tax liability	7,865
Less tax credits/paid	
£300 × 20%	(60)
£1,300 × 10%	(130)
Tax due	7,675

1   A – £nil

    Trustees are not entitled to a personal allowance.

2   B – 20% / 20% / 10%

    Trustees of an interest in possession trust are taxed at 20% for non-savings income, 20% for savings income, and 10% for dividend income. The tax liability for savings income and dividend income will therefore normally be covered by the tax credit attached to the income.

3   Trustees of a discretionary trust have a basic rate band of £1,000 (shared between all trusts created by the same settlor, subject to a minimum of £200) within which income is taxed at the basic rates. Thereafter the special trust rates apply, ie 37.5% for dividend income and 45% for all other income.

4   Trustees of a discretionary trust must maintain the 'tax pool' which comprises all the tax paid at the basic rates within the basic rate band, any tax paid at 45% and the actual tax paid on dividends, ie 37.5% minus the non-refundable 10% notional tax credit. When a payment is made to a beneficiary the tax needed to cover the tax credit on the payment must be deducted from the tax pool. If there is insufficient tax in the pool, the excess required must be paid by the trustees as part of their income tax due for the tax year.

5   Trust's net income:

	Non savings income £	Savings income £	Dividend income £
Rental income (£30,000 – £4,500)	25,500		
Interest £920 × $\frac{100}{80}$		1,150	
Dividends £1,350 × $\frac{100}{90}$			1,500
Tax @ 20%/20%/10%	5,100	230	150
Less tax credits	–	(230)	(150)
Tax due	5,100	–	–
Trust's net income (ie after tax)	20,400	920	1,350
Less expenses	–	(150)	(1,350)
Trust's net distributable income	20,400	770	NIL

The life tenant is treated as receiving income as follows:

	Net £	Tax suffered £
Non savings income	20,400	5,100
Savings income	770	193
Dividends	NIL	NIL
	21,170	

The tax suffered on the interest income is the grossed up interest received at 20%:

$$£770 \times \frac{100}{80} = £963 \times 20\% = £193$$

6　Trust's income tax liability

	Non savings income £	Dividend income £
Rental income (£30,000 – £2,500)	27,500	
Dividends (£3,000 × 100/90)		3,333
Gross income	27,500	3,333
Less expenses of trust (£2,250 × 100/90)		(2,500)
Amount chargeable at trust rates	27,500	833

	£
£1,000 @ 20%	200
£27,500 – 1,000 = £26,500 @ 45%	11,925
£833 @ 37.5%	312
£2,500 @ 10%	250
Tax liability	12,687

7　**The Ray Trust**

(a)　*Trust income tax liability*

	Non savings income £	Savings income £	Dividend income £
Property income £(30,800 – 8,400)	22,400		
Interest		25,200	
Dividends (£32,760 × $\frac{100}{90}$)			36,400
Admin expenses (£5,040 × $\frac{100}{90}$)			(5,600)
			30,800

Tax:	£
£1,000 @ 20%	200
£22,400 + £25,200 – £1,000 = £46,600 @ 45%	20,970
£30,800 @ 37.5%	11,550
Income to pay expenses £5,600 @ 10%	560
	33,280

Total liability:	£
Tax on income	33,280
Additional tax liability (charge re tax pool) (W)	2,978
Credit on dividends	(3,640)
Credit on interest (paid gross)	NIL
Income tax payable by the trustees	32,618

WORKING – Tax pool	
Pool b/f at 6.4.14	4,200
Tax paid at 20%/45% £(200 + 20,970)	21,170
Tax paid at 37.5% less credit at 10% (£30,800 × 27.5%)	8,470
	33,840
Credit on distributions to beneficiaries (£45,000 × 100/55 × 45%)	(36,818)
Additional tax to pay to HMRC by trustees	(2,978)
Tax pool c/f at 5.4.15	NIL

CHAPTER

10

(b) *Charlotte income tax computation*

	£
Trust income (£45,000 × $\frac{100}{55}$)	81,818
Personal allowance	(10,000)
	71,818
Income tax liability (taxed as non-savings income)	
£31,865 @ 20%	6,373
£39,953 @ 40%	15,981
Less credit on trust distribution	(36,818)
Refund due	(14,464)

CHAPTER 11

Chargeable gains for individuals and trustees

Introduction

Examination context

Topic List

Summary and Self-test

Technical reference

Answers to Interactive questions

Answers to Self-test

Learning objectives

- Calculate the chargeable gains and losses on assets, including pre 31 March 1982 assets

- Describe the circumstances in which the following reliefs apply and calculate the effect of full or partial relief available in a given situation:

    - Letting relief
    - Principal private residence relief (PPR)

- Calculate total taxable gains and tax payable thereon, utilising available reliefs to reduce the liability

Specific syllabus references for this chapter are 2a, 2b and 2d.

Syllabus links

In Chapter 9 of your Principles of Taxation study manual, you learnt about some of the basic principles of chargeable gains for individuals. These included chargeable and exempt persons, disposals and assets, how to compute simple gains and losses and the charge to capital gains tax. You also learnt about the treatment of chattels.

In this chapter we review those topics and look at part disposals. We also deal with some other more advanced aspects of chargeable gains and principal private residence and letting reliefs.

Examination context

In the examination candidates may be required to:

- Calculate gains as part of a personal tax question

- Consider the gains implications of transactions involving trusts

- Calculate the gain on the disposal of an individual's PPR where there are periods of deemed occupation/letting/business use

This area of the syllabus is a good discriminator between candidates.

Candidates generally like and understand PPR relief and letting relief. Good marks are achieved in this area.

1 Chargeable and exempt persons, assets and disposals

Section overview

- Chargeable persons include individuals, partners, trustees and companies.

- Chargeable disposals include sales and gifts.

- Death is not an occasion of charge for CGT and there is a tax-free uplift of the value of assets passed on death.

- Exempt assets include cars, some chattels and investments held in ISAs.

1.1 Chargeable persons

Chargeable persons include:

- Individuals

- Business partners, who are treated as owning a share of partnership assets and taxed on the disposal of that share

- Trustees

- Companies, which pay corporation tax on their chargeable gains, not CGT

Some persons are specifically exempt from capital gains. These include:

- Registered charities using gains for charitable purposes
- Friendly societies
- Local authorities
- Registered pension schemes
- Investment trusts
- Approved scientific research associations

Where a UK residential property valued at over £2m is held by a non-natural person, eg a company, it is subject to a number of tax charges including a CGT charge, rather than a corporation tax charge, on any gain arising on the disposal of the property. However, this is not examinable at TC.

1.2 Chargeable disposals

Chargeable disposals include:

- The sale of whole or part of an asset
- The gift of whole or part of an asset
- Receipts of capital sums on the surrender of rights over assets
- The loss or destruction of the whole or part of an asset
- Appropriation of assets as trading stock

If a taxpayer appropriates an asset to trading stock, there is a disposal of the asset at market value at the date it is taken into stock. The trader may elect for the disposal to be treated as one at neither a gain nor a loss. The cost of the asset for trading income is then adjusted for the gain or loss which would have occurred.

Exempt disposals include gifts to charities, art galleries, museums and similar institutions, provided that the asset is used for the purposes of the institution.

Death is not a disposal for capital gains tax purposes and there is a tax-free uplift of the value of assets passed on death.

1.3 Chargeable assets

Chargeable assets are all capital assets except those which are specifically exempted from CGT.

Chargeable assets include both tangible assets (such as land, furniture, works of art) and intangible assets (such as goodwill of a business, shares, leases).

Exempt assets include:

- Legal tender (ie cash)

- Motor cars (including vintage and classic cars)

- Wasting chattels (tangible moveable property such as furniture, moveable machinery, with a predictable life not exceeding 50 years), except assets used in a business where the owner has or could have claimed capital allowances on the assets

- Chattels which are either not wasting chattels or used in business etc, if sold for consideration which does not exceed £6,000. There is marginal relief where proceeds exceed £6,000 (see later in this chapter)

- Gilt-edged securities

- Qualifying Corporate Bonds (QCBs)

- National Savings Certificates and Premium Bonds

- Shares and investments held in an Individual Savings Account (ISA)

Definition

Qualifying corporate bond (QCB): A QCB is defined as:

- sterling denominated
- non-convertible
- loan stock representing a normal commercial loan
- the interest upon which is neither excessive nor dependent on business performance

Note that for a company, a QCB is a loan relationship receivable.

---

2 Computing net chargeable gains

Section overview

- Gains and losses are disposal proceeds less allowable costs.

- Part of the original cost of an asset is allowable on a part disposal based on the market values of the part sold and the part retained.

2.1 Overview of chargeable gain computation

	£
Disposal consideration	X
Less allowable costs	(X)
Gain before reliefs	X

2.2 Computation of gains and losses

The disposal consideration is the sale proceeds, if the asset is sold at arm's length. If the asset is not sold at arm's length (eg a gift or sale at undervalue) the disposal consideration is generally the market value of the asset. There are a few specific exceptions for 'no gain/no loss' transfers, such as between spouses (see Section 4).

Incidental costs of disposal are deducted to give the net disposal consideration. These include legal fees, estate agents' and auctioneers' fees and advertising costs.

Allowable costs are:

- Acquisition cost of the asset (purchase price if bought, market value of asset if gifted, probate value if acquired on death)

- Incidental costs of acquisition such as legal fees, surveyors' fees, stamp duty, stamp duty land tax

- Enhancement expenditure (capital costs of additions and improvements to the asset reflected in the value of the asset at the date of disposal such as extensions, planning permission and architects' fees for such extensions)

2.3 Part disposals

The definition of a chargeable disposal includes the disposal of part of a chargeable asset.

The cost for calculation of the gain or loss is:

$$\text{Cost} \times \frac{A}{A+B}$$

where A is the market value of the part disposed of and B is the market value of the part that is retained.

Any incidental costs relating wholly to the part disposal are deductible in full.

Worked example: Part disposal

Jenny bought ten hectares of land in December 2000 for £42,500. The incidental costs of purchase were £2,000.

In October 2014, she sold three hectares for £20,400 less auctioneers' fees of 5%. The market value of the remaining seven hectares was £61,200.

Requirement

Calculate the chargeable gain on sale.

Solution

	£	£
Gross proceeds	20,400	
Less auctioneers' fees (£20,400 × 5%)	(1,020)	
Net disposal consideration		19,380
Less acquisition cost		
$\frac{20,400}{20,400+61,200} \times £42,500$	10,625	
incidental costs of acquisition		
$\frac{20,400}{20,400+61,200} \times £2,000$	500	(11,125)
Gain		8,255

3 Capital gains tax payable by individuals & trustees

Section overview

- Each individual is entitled to an annual exempt amount.

- Trustees are entitled to half the annual exempt amount. If several trusts are created by the same settlor the available amount is divided equally between them subject to a minimum of 10% of the full individual's annual exempt amount.

- CGT is chargeable at 18% or 28%, depending on the individual's taxable income.

- Trustees pay CGT at a flat rate of 28%.

- CGT may be payable by instalments.

3.1 Annual exempt amount for individuals

Each individual is entitled to an annual exempt amount each year. For 2014/15 the annual exempt amount is £11,000. The annual exempt amount is deducted from chargeable gains to produce gains liable to CGT (**taxable gains**). [Hp85]

If the annual exempt amount is unused in a tax year, it is wasted and cannot be used in any other tax year.

3.2 Annual exempt amount for trustees

The annual exempt amount available to trustees is one half of that given to individuals, so it is £5,500 for 2014/15. [Hp 85] However, the full annual exempt amount is available for trustees of a bare trust or a disabled person's trust.

If several trusts are created by the same settlor, the exempt amount is divided equally between them subject to a minimum exempt amount per trust of one tenth of a full individual annual exempt amount (£1,100 for 2014/15).

3.3 Rates of capital gains tax for individuals

Individuals are taxed on their taxable gains separately from their taxable income.

Taxable gains are taxed at the rate of 18% or 28% depending on the individual's taxable income. The rate of CGT is 28% if the individual is a higher or additional rate taxpayer. If the individual is a basic rate taxpayer then CGT is payable at 18% on an amount of taxable gains up to the amount of the individual's unused basic rate band and at 28% on the excess.

When calculating the amount of unused basic rate band it must be extended for gross Gift Aid donations and gross personal pension contributions made during the tax year.

Worked example: CGT liability for individual

Olly has taxable income in 2014/15 of £28,355. He makes taxable gains of £20,000 in the year. Olly's sister Alice has taxable income of £5,000 in 2014/15. She makes taxable gains of £17,000 in the year.

Requirement

Calculate Olly's and Alice's CGT liability for 2014/15.

Solution

Olly	£
(£31,865 – £28,355) £3,510 × 18%	632
(£20,000 – £3,510) £16,490 × 28%	4,617
CGT liability	5,249

Taxable gains are already net of the annual exempt amount.

Taxable income is net of the personal allowance. Olly has £3,510 of unused basic rate band remaining and this amount of the taxable gains is taxed at 18%. The remainder of the taxable gains of £16,490 are taxed at 28%.

Alice	£
£17,000 × 18%	3,060

Alice has £26,865 unused basic rate band so her taxable gains are all taxed at 18%.

3.4 Rates of capital gains tax for trustees

The rate of tax for all trusts (except bare trusts and trusts for disabled persons) is 28%.

Worked example: CGT liability for trustees

Edith established a trust in 2005. In July 2014 the trustees realised a gain on the sale of an asset of £15,000, and a further gain of £35,000 on a disposal in January 2015.

Requirement

Calculate the capital gains tax liability of the trust.

Solution

Disposal by Trustees	£
2014/15 gains (£15,000 + £35,000)	50,000
Less annual exempt amount	(5,500)
Taxable gain	44,500
CGT @ 28%	12,460

In a bare trust, the assets are not treated as settled property and are instead treated as belonging to the beneficiary personally, so any gain (or loss) arising on the disposal of those assets is assessed on (or allowable for) the beneficiary, using the normal rules for individuals, rather than the trustees.

Interactive question 1: CGT liability [Difficulty level: Exam standard]

Madeleine had gains during 2014/15 on the following assets.

	£
Shares in XX Ltd	21,000
Shares JJ plc	19,650
Shares held in an ISA	4,170

Madeleine had taxable income in 2014/15 of £14,000 and had made a donation to charity under Gift Aid of £600 in December 2014.

Requirement

Using the standard format below, calculate Madeleine's capital gains tax liability for 2014/15.

	Gains £
Shares in XX Ltd	
Shares in JJ plc	
Shares held in ISA	
Annual exempt amount	_____
Taxable gains	_____

£.................... × ....%

Basic rate band available

(£............. (W) – £.............. – £.................)
£............. × ....%

(£........... – £.........) £.............. x ....%   _____

CGT liability   _____

	£
Basic rate band	
Gif Aid donation	_____
Extended basic rate band	_____

See **Answer** at the end of this chapter.

3.5 Payment of CGT by instalments

If the CGT arises as a result of a gift of either land, or shares in a company out of a controlling holding, or any number of shares in an unquoted company, the CGT may be paid by instalments.

The CGT is payable in ten equal yearly instalments starting on the normal due date, provided an election is made in writing to HMRC. Interest will normally be chargeable on the outstanding balance.

4 Married couples/civil partners

Section overview

- Spouses/civil partners are taxed separately.
- Disposals between spouses/civil partners are on a no gain/no loss basis.

4.1 Taxation of spouses/civil partners

In general, spouses/civil partners are taxed separately as two individual taxpayers.

Each has his own annual exempt amount. Losses cannot be shared between spouses/civil partners.

Assets owned jointly between spouses/civil partners are taxed in accordance with the underlying beneficial ownership of the asset. Where a declaration of beneficial ownership has been made for income tax purposes, this will generally also apply for capital gains tax.

4.2 Disposals between spouses/civil partners

Disposals in a tax year between spouses/civil partners who are living together in that tax year are on a no gain/no loss basis.

Married couples/civil partners are treated as living together unless they are separated under a court order or deed of separation or are, in fact, separated in circumstances which make permanent separation likely. A couple will be treated as living together in a tax year if they have satisfied this condition at any time during the tax year.

The disposal value on a no gain/no loss disposal is therefore cost.

4.3 Subsequent disposal to third party

The deemed acquisition cost of the acquiring spouse/civil partner is equal to the deemed disposal proceeds for the disposing spouse.

On a subsequent disposal to a third party the gain is simply proceeds (or market value for non arm's length disposal) less the original cost to the first spouse/civil partner.

4.4 Tax planning for spouses/civil partners

Spouses/civil partners can organise their capital disposals to ensure that as a couple they make use of both spouses'/civil partners' annual exempt amounts.

However, if an asset is transferred between spouses/civil partners, it is important that there is an outright unconditional disposal. In addition, the disposal proceeds should be retained by the spouse/civil partner making the ultimate disposal to the third party.

HMRC may otherwise contend that there was not an actual disposal between the spouses/civil partners and treat the ultimate disposal as being made by the spouse/civil partner who originally owned the asset.

5 Connected persons

Section overview

- An individual is connected with certain close relatives.
- Disposals to connected persons (other than a spouse/civil partner) are at market value.

5.1 Who are connected persons?

Definition

Connected persons: An individual is connected with his:

- Spouse/civil partner
- Relatives and their spouses/civil partners
- Spouse's/civil partner's relatives and their spouses/civil partners
- Business partners and their spouses/civil partners and relatives

In addition, a trustee of a settlement is connected with the trust settlor and anyone connected with the settlor.

A settlor and the trustees of his settlement are connected from the start of the trust, ie in respect of the initial property transferred to the trust. If the settlor dies, his relatives and spouse or civil partner and their relatives are no longer connected with the trustees.

For this purpose, relatives means brothers, sisters, ancestors and direct descendants.

Note that under the definition of connected persons, an individual is not connected with his aunt, uncle, niece, nephew or cousins.

5.2 Disposals to connected persons

A disposal by an individual to a person connected with him is always at market value at the date of the disposal.

This rule does not apply to a disposal by an individual to his own spouse/civil partner as such a disposal is on a no gain/no loss basis.

Where a settlor puts an asset into a trust or when the trustees dispose of assets out of the trust to a beneficiary, the disposal proceeds are always deemed to be the market value. The market value is also the base cost for the recipient.

6 Pre-March 1982 assets

Section overview

- To calculate a gain on the disposal of an asset acquired prior to 31 March 1982 use market value as at 31 March 1982 instead of original cost.

An individual may own assets purchased before 31 March 1982. When an individual sells such an asset the market value at 31 March 1982 is used instead of cost.

In the examination, you will be given the market value of the asset at 31 March 1982. In practice, this will be subject to negotiation with HMRC.

Worked example: Pre-31 March 1982 asset

Kevin bought a plot of land in July 1980 for £10,000. The plot was worth £12,000 on 31 March 1982.

Kevin sold the plot for £96,000 in December 2014.

Requirement

Calculate the chargeable gain on the disposal.

Solution

	£
Disposal proceeds	96,000
Less 31.3.82 MV	(12,000)
Chargeable gain	84,000

7 Chattels

Section overview

- Wasting chattels are usually exempt from CGT.

- Non-wasting chattels are usually chargeable to CGT.

- Gains on non-wasting chattels bought and sold for £6,000 or less are exempt.

- Marginal relief applies to gains on non-wasting chattels sold for more than £6,000.

- Losses are restricted on non-wasting chattels sold for less than £6,000.

- There are special rules for disposals from sets of non-wasting chattels.

7.1 Wasting chattels

A chattel is a wasting chattel if it has a predictable life at the date of disposal not exceeding 50 years. Plant and machinery is always treated as having a useful life of less than 50 years. Examples include animals, computers, clocks, watches, caravans, boats, other vehicles and mechanical objects.

Wasting chattels are usually exempt from CGT so there will be no chargeable gain or allowable loss on disposal.

However, if the asset has been used solely in a business and the owner has, or could have, claimed capital allowances on the asset, it will be treated as a non-wasting chattel.

7.2 Non-wasting chattels

A non-wasting chattel is one with a predictable life at the date of disposal of more than 50 years. Examples include antiques, jewellery and works of art. Non-wasting chattels are generally chargeable to CGT, subject to some special rules.

If the chattel is disposed of for gross disposal proceeds of £6,000 or less and a gain arises on disposal, the gain is exempt. [Hp85]

If the chattel is disposed of for gross disposal proceeds of more than £6,000, there is marginal relief for the gain. In this case, the gain cannot exceed:

$$5/3 \times \text{(gross proceeds less £6,000)}$$

If the chattel is sold for less than £6,000 and the disposal would result in a loss, the loss is restricted by assuming that the gross disposal proceeds were £6,000. This rule cannot turn a loss into a gain, only reduce the amount of the loss to nil.

If capital allowances have been claimed on the asset and a loss would arise on disposal, the allowable cost for chargeable gains purposes must be reduced by the lower of the loss and the net amount of capital allowances. For plant and machinery this means that there will be no chargeable gain nor allowable loss on the disposal. This rule also applies to assets which are not chattels.

7.3 Sets of non-wasting chattels

There is a special rule where two or more assets forming part of a set of assets which was owned by the same person are disposed of to:

- The same person; or
- Persons acting in concert; or
- Persons connected with each other.

The disposals will be treated as one disposal for the £6,000 exemption and marginal relief. The loss rules also apply in a similar way.

If the disposals are in different tax years an apportionment of the total gain will be required. This is made on the basis of disposal proceeds.

Worked example: Sets of chattels

Sue owned a set of two paintings which cost her £2,000 in July 2002.

In May 2014, she sold one of the paintings to Lloyd for £5,500. The other painting was valued at £4,500 at this time.

In December 2014, she sold the other painting to Lloyd's brother, Lewis, for £4,800.

Requirement

Show the chargeable gains on disposal.

Solution

This is a disposal from a set of chattels to persons connected with each other.

Since the total proceeds are (£5,500 + £4,800) = £10,300, marginal relief applies. However, it is still necessary to compute the actual gains on each disposal.

May 2014

	£
Disposal proceeds	5,500
Less cost (part disposal)	
$\dfrac{5,500}{5,500 + 4,500} \times £2,000$	(1,100)
Gain	4,400

December 2014

	£
Disposal proceeds	4,800
Less cost (£2,000 – £1,100)	(900)
Gain	3,900
Total gains (£4,400 + £3,900)	8,300
Gain cannot exceed 5/3 × £(10,300 – 6,000)	7,167

Apportionment:

May 2014: $\dfrac{5,500}{5,500 + 4,800} \times £7,167$ 3,827

December 2014: $\dfrac{4,800}{5,500 + 4,800} \times £7,167$ 3,340

Gains

May 2014	£3,827
December 2014	£3,340

8 Principal private residence and letting reliefs

Section overview

- No gain or loss arises on the disposal of a principal private residence (PPR).

- If an individual has more than one residence he can elect which one should be his PPR.

- Married couples/civil partners can only have one PPR between them.

- PPR relief is given for periods of actual and deemed occupation.

- The last 18 months of ownership are treated as a period of occupation.

- PPR relief is not given on a part of the property used exclusively for business purposes.

- Letting relief is available to cover a gain arising during a period when all or part of the property is let.

8.1 What is principal private residence relief?

The disposal of a principal private residence does not give rise to a chargeable gain or allowable loss.

Definition

Principal private residence (PPR): A taxpayer's only or main residence, including grounds or gardens totalling up to half a hectare or such larger area as is required for the enjoyment of the house having regard to the size and character of the house. [Hp88]

The property must usually be actually occupied as the residence of the taxpayer throughout the period of ownership to obtain full relief. Mere ownership on its own is not sufficient.

8.2 More than one residence

For the majority of taxpayers it is obvious that a property is their PPR.

An individual may only have one PPR at any one time. Spouses/civil partners may only have one PPR between them.

If an individual owns and lives in two (or more) properties, he may elect which is to be regarded as the PPR. This election must be made within two years of the acquisition of the second or further property and if jointly owned, it must be signed by all of the joint owners. [Hp102]

If spouses/civil partners each own a property before marriage/registration of the civil partnership, the election for which one of the properties is to be treated as the couple's PPR must be made within two years of the marriage/registration.

There is a special rule where an individual lives in job-related accommodation and acquires a property which he intends to occupy in the future as his PPR.

Definition

Job related accommodation: Accommodation is job related if:

(a) The accommodation is necessary for the proper performance of the employee's duties (eg caretaker); or

(b) The accommodation is provided for the better performance of the employee's duties and the employment is of a kind in which it is customary for accommodation to be provided (eg police officers); or

(c) The accommodation is provided as part of arrangements in force because of a special threat to the employee's security (eg members of the government).

In this case, it is not necessary to establish actual occupation in the property that he intends to occupy in future whilst he is occupying job-related accommodation.

8.3 Partial principal private residence relief

If a property has been occupied as a PPR for only part of the period of ownership, a chargeable gain or allowable loss may arise on disposal.

PPR relief is given for periods of actual and deemed occupation of the property in relation to the total period of ownership of the property. If the property was acquired before 31 March 1982, periods before that date are ignored.

Periods of actual occupation are based on fact and will be given in an exam question.

For most disposals on or after 6 April 2014, the last 18 months of ownership are always treated as a period of occupation if the property has at some time been the individual's PPR. This applies even if the individual has another PPR during this period. [Hp88] For disabled people, or those who are long-term resident in care homes at the date of disposal of their previous residence, the last 36 months are treated as a period of occupation.

In the exam, calculate the periods of residence and ownership to the nearest month.

Worked example: Partial PPR relief

Pam sold her house on 16 February 2015 for £130,000.

She bought the house on 16 June 2007 for £80,000 and lived in it until 16 September 2009. Pam then moved into a new house and made an election for it to be her PPR. The original house was empty until it was sold.

Requirement

Calculate the chargeable gain arising on the sale.

Solution

Gain on disposal

	£
Disposal proceeds	130,000
Less cost	(80,000)
Gain before reliefs	50,000
Less PPR relief (W)	(24,457)
Chargeable gain	25,543

WORKING

	Chargeable months	Exempt months	Total months
16.6.07 – 16.09.09 actual occupation		27	27
17.09.09 – 16.8.13 not occupied	47		47
17.8.13 – 16.2.15 last 18 months		18	18
	47	45	92

PPR relief is:

$$\frac{45}{92} \times £50,000 \qquad\qquad £24,457$$

Periods of deemed occupation are defined in statute as follows:

- Any period (or periods added together) of up to three years of absence for any reason;

- Any periods of absence during which the individual was required by his employment to live abroad;

- Any period (or periods added together) of up to four years during which the individual was required to live elsewhere due to his work (employed or self-employed) so that he could not occupy the property.

Such periods are only counted as deemed occupation if the individual does not have another PPR.

The periods of absence must usually be preceded by a period of actual occupation and followed by a period of actual occupation. However, by extra-statutory concession, an individual is not required to resume residence in the last two situations if the terms of his employment require him to work elsewhere.

In addition, by extra-statutory concession, a house is also treated as occupied as the owner's main residence for a period of up to 12 months (or longer if there is a good reason) if he was prevented from living in the house because it was being built or altered or because necessary steps were being taken to dispose of his previous residence.

The property may be let during a period of absence without affecting deemed occupation.

Interactive question 2: Deemed occupation [Difficulty level: Exam standard]

Daniel bought a house on 15 October 2003 for £60,000.

He lived in the house until 15 March 2005 when he was sent by his employer to work abroad. He returned to live in the house on 15 March 2007. The property was let in his absence.

Daniel stayed in the house until 15 September 2010 when he bought another house which he elected to be his PPR. The original house was unoccupied during this time.

Daniel sold the original house on 15 December 2014 for £240,000.

Requirement

Using the standard format below, calculate the chargeable gain on sale.

	£
Disposal proceeds	
Less cost	(_____)
Gain before reliefs	
Less PPR relief (W)	(_____)
Chargeable gain	

WORKING

	Chargeable months	Exempt months	Total months
	————	————	————
	————	————	————

PPR relief is:

.... × £........................   £————————

See **Answer** at the end of this chapter.

8.4 Business use

If part of the property is used exclusively for business purposes, the gain attributable to that part of the property will not be given PPR relief. The apportionment of the gain between the business and non-business parts is made on a just and reasonable basis.

If the business part has been used for business purposes throughout the period, the last 18-month exemption cannot apply to that part.

If, however, the business part was at some time during the ownership used for non-business purposes, then the last 18-month exemption will apply to the business part, even if it is used for business purposes during that time.

Non-exclusive business use of part of the property does not affect PPR relief.

8.5 Break-down of marriage/civil partnership

Where a marriage or civil partnership has broken down, the owner or one of the owners of the property may cease to live in it. This will result in a period of non-occupation and therefore may lead to part of the gain not qualifying for PPR relief on a subsequent disposal.

There is an extra-statutory concession which applies where the owner who has ceased to live in the property disposes of his interest in the property to the other party to the marriage/civil partnership.

In this case, he is deemed to be still in occupation provided that:

- The other party to the marriage/civil partnership continues to live in the property; and
- The owner who has left has not made an election to treat another property as his PPR.

8.6 Letting relief

If a property has been occupied as a PPR, letting relief may be available for that part of the gain which does not qualify for PPR relief.

Note that periods of absence covered by the deemed occupation rules will already be eligible for PPR relief and so letting relief is not relevant in this case.

Letting relief can apply where:

- The entire property is let out during a period of absence which would otherwise be chargeable; or
- Part of the property is let out and the owner lives in the remainder (in this case the last 18 months exemption will apply to the let part if it has at any time been used by the owner as his PPR).

Letting relief is the lowest of:

- Letting gain
- PPR relief
- £40,000 [Hp89]

Worked example: Letting relief

Lena bought a three storey house on 1 December 2006 for £120,000. She occupied the whole of the house until 1 June 2008 when she let out the top floor to a tenant. Lena sold the house for £360,000 on 1 June 2014.

Requirement

Calculate the chargeable gain on sale.

Solution

	£
Disposal proceeds	360,000
Less cost	(120,000)
Gain before reliefs	240,000
Less PPR relief (W1)	(192,000)
	48,000
Less letting relief (W2)	(40,000)
Chargeable gain	8,000

WORKINGS

(1) **PPR relief**

	Chargeable months	Exempt months	Total months
1.12.06 – 1.6.08 actual occupation		18	18
1.6.08 – 1.12.12 1/3 let, 2/3 actual occupation	18	36	54
1.12.12 – 1.6.14 last 18 months		18	18
	18	72	90

PPR relief is:

$$\frac{72}{90} \times £240,000 \qquad\qquad £192,000$$

(2) **Letting relief**

Lowest of:

Letting gain: $\dfrac{18}{90} \times £240,000$	£48,000
PPR relief	£192,000
Maximum	£40,000
Letting relief is therefore	£40,000

8.7 Principal private residence (PPR) relief for trusts

Where the trustees of any trust dispose of a property occupied by a beneficiary as the beneficiary's main residence, principal private residence (PPR) relief applies if the trustees and beneficiary make a joint claim for the relief.

The gain is wholly exempt where the beneficiary has occupied the whole of the residence throughout the trustees' period of ownership. Where occupation has been for only part of the period, the proportion of the gain exempted is:

$$\text{Total gain} \times \frac{\text{period of beneficiary's occupation}}{\text{total period of trustees' ownership}}$$

The last 18 months of ownership are usually exempt if at some time the residence has been a beneficiary's main residence.

The same periods of absence as above are deemed to be periods of occupation provided the beneficiary had no other exempt residence at that time and the period of absence was at some time both preceded by and followed by a period of actual occupation.

Letting relief may also be available, as explained above.

Summary and Self-test

Summary

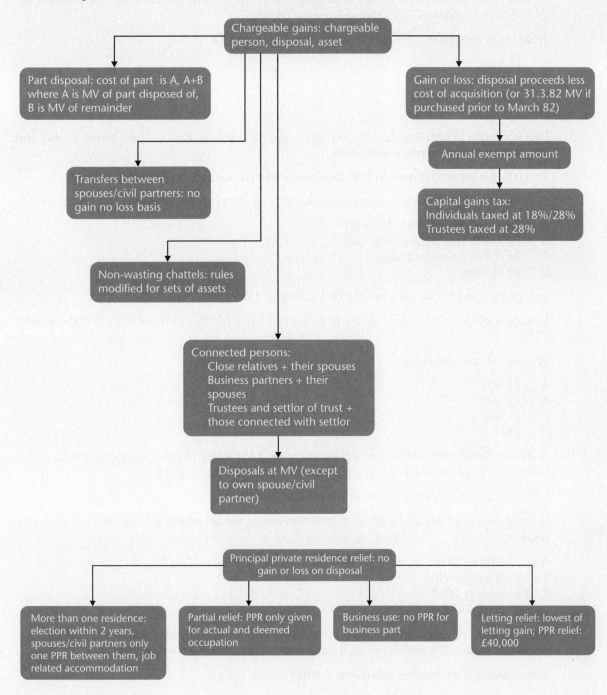

Chargeable gains: chargeable person, disposal, asset

Part disposal: cost of part is A, A+B where A is MV of part disposed of, B is MV of remainder

Transfers between spouses/civil partners: no gain no loss basis

Non-wasting chattels: rules modified for sets of assets

Connected persons:
Close relatives + their spouses
Business partners + their spouses
Trustees and settlor of trust + those connected with settlor

Disposals at MV (except to own spouse/civil partner)

Gain or loss: disposal proceeds less cost of acquisition (or 31.3.82 MV if purchased prior to March 82)

Annual exempt amount

Capital gains tax:
Individuals taxed at 18%/28%
Trustees taxed at 28%

Principal private residence relief: no gain or loss on disposal

More than one residence: election within 2 years, spouses/civil partners only one PPR between them, job related accommodation

Partial relief: PPR only given for actual and deemed occupation

Business use: no PPR for business part

Letting relief: lowest of letting gain; PPR relief: £40,000

Self-test

Answer the following questions.

1 Harold bought nine hectares of land for £60,000 in December 2005. The incidental costs of acquisition were £3,000.

He sold three hectares for £50,000 in October 2014. The remaining six hectares were valued at £75,000. The incidental costs of disposal were £6,000.

What is the chargeable gain on sale of the three hectares?

A £17,000
B £18,800
C £22,400
D £20,706

2 Paul is married to Gill. They have two children, Lucy and Emma. Paul's father, Alfred, is dead and his mother, Mary, recently married Bob.

Paul is in a business partnership with Gordon. Gordon is married to Gill's sister, Amy.

Which of the above people is Lucy connected with for the purposes of tax on chargeable gains?

A Paul, Gill, Emma, Mary and Amy
B Paul, Gill, Emma, Mary and Bob
C Paul, Gill, Emma and Mary
D All of them

3 Josh bought an antique table for £3,100 in October 1999.

In August 2014 the table was sold for gross proceeds of £7,000. Incidental costs of disposal were £500.

What is the chargeable gain?

A £3,900
B £3,400
C £1,667
D £833

4 Mark and Simon entered into a civil partnership on 2 December 2014. They jointly own a house which they have occupied as their only residence since 2 October 2014.

Mark and Simon acquire a second home on 2 March 2015.

By what date must Mark and Simon elect which one of the properties is to be their principal private residence?

A 2 October 2016
B 2 December 2016
C 31 January 2017
D 2 March 2017

5 If the principal private residence of an individual is not occupied by him due to a period of residence abroad, this period can be treated as a period of deemed occupation.

Which one of the following statements is true?

A Actual occupation is normally required before and after the absence
B The individual must be employed abroad
C The period of deemed occupation cannot exceed three years
D The period of deemed occupation cannot exceed four years

6   Alex owns a house for 60 months. One-quarter of the house is used exclusively for business purposes throughout the period of ownership.

Alex sells the house and makes a gain of £48,000.

What is the amount of PPR relief?

A   £12,000
B   £36,000
C   £39,600
D   £48,000

7   Pepe owns a house for 96 months. He occupies the house for 24 months. He then retires abroad and lets the property for the remaining 72 months of ownership. His gain on sale is £120,000.

What is the chargeable gain on sale?

A   NIL
B   £27,500
C   £67,500
D   £50,000

8   **Phoebe**

Phoebe had the following capital transactions during 2014/15:

(1)   Sold a painting for £64,000 in May 2014. She had acquired it from her husband, Edward, in August 2009 when it was worth £25,000. Edward bought it for £15,000 in April 2000.

(2)   Sold a plot of land to her brother, Robert, for its market value £50,000 in August 2014. She had acquired the land in June 2006 for £50,000.

(3)   Sold a house (which had been let out throughout her ownership) for £180,000 in February 2015. She had acquired the house in December 1980 for £36,500. The market value at 31 March 1982 was £40,000. In April 1995 an extension costing £8,000 was built.

(4)   Sold a vintage Alfa Romeo car in December 2014 for £76,500. The car had cost £17,400 in March 1994.

(5)   Sold three hectares out of a 12 hectare plot of land in December 2014. The whole plot had been bought for £18,000 in October 1997. The disposal proceeds for the three hectares were £24,000. The remaining nine hectares were valued at £48,000 in December 2014.

Phoebe had taxable income of £31,255 for 2014/15. She had paid £1,200 into her personal pension fund during 2014/15.

Requirement

Calculate Phoebe's capital gains tax payable for 2014/15.   **(8 marks)**

9   **Julius**

Julius bought a house in Kent for £39,350 on 1 April 1990.

He occupied the property as his sole residence until 1 April 1994 when he was sent by his employer to work abroad. He let the property whilst he was abroad.

On 1 January 2004, Julius returned to the UK but was immediately sent to the North of England by his employer. On 1 March 2005, he returned to Kent but lived with a friend until he could resume occupation of his house on the termination of the lease on 1 July 2005.

On 1 January 2007, Julius bought another house in Kent and made an election for it to be treated as his principal private residence. The original house was unoccupied until 1 January 2011 when it was again let until it was sold on 1 April 2015 for £410,000.

Requirement

Calculate the chargeable gain on sale.   **(8 marks)**

Now go back to the Learning Objectives in the Introduction. If you are satisfied you have achieved these objectives please tick them off.

Legislation

References relate to Taxation of Chargeable Gains Act 1992 (*TCGA 1992*)

Chargeable persons	s.2
Assets and disposals	s.21
Computation of gains and losses	ss.15 – 17
Allowable deductions	ss.37 – 39
Annual exempt amount	s.3
Rates of tax	s.4
Disposals between spouses/civil partners	s.58
Connected persons	s.286
Disposals between connected persons	s.18
Assets acquired before 31 March 1982	s.35
Chattels	s.262
Capital gains tax reform	Sch 2 FA 2008
Relief on disposal of private residences	s.222
Amount of relief	s.223
Deemed period of occupation concession	D4
Separated couples concession	D6
Business use	s.224
Letting relief	s.223(4)

HMRC manual references

Capital gains manual

(Found at http://www.hmrc.gov.uk/manuals/cgmanual/index.htm)

Persons chargeable: general	CG10700
Chargeable assets: exemptions from capital gains charge	CG12600
Computation: introduction	CG14200
Part-disposals: general	CG12730
Part-disposals: formula for apportioning expenditure	CG12731
Chattels and wasting assets: Introduction	CG76550
Private residence relief: introduction: scheme of relief	CG64200
Private residence relief: computation of relief: introduction	CG64970

Trusts, settlements and estates manual

(Found at http://www.hmrc.gov.uk/manuals/tsemmanual/index.htm)

Introduction to trusts	TSEM1002
Trust income and gains	TSEM3000

This technical reference section is designed to assist you. It should help you know where to look for further information on the topics covered in this chapter.

Answer to Interactive questions

Answer to Interactive question 1

	Gains £
Shares in XX Ltd	21,000
Shares in JJ plc	19,650
Shares held in ISA (exempt)	–
Annual exempt amount	(11,000)
Taxable gains	29,650

(£32,615 (W) – £14,000) £18,615 × 18%	3,351
(£29,650 – £18,615) £11,035 × 28%	3,090
CGT liability	6,441

WORKING

	£
Basic rate band	31,865
Gif Aid donation (£600 × 100/80)	750
Extended basic rate band	32,615

Answer to Interactive question 2

	£
Disposal proceeds	240,000
Less cost	(60,000)
Gain before reliefs	180,000
Less PPR relief (W)	(135,672)
Chargeable gain	44,328

WORKING

	Chargeable months	Exempt months	Total months
15.10.03 – 15.3.05 actual occupation		17	17
15.3.05 – 15.3.07 employed abroad		24	24
15.3.07 – 15.9.10 actual occupation		42	42
15.9.10 – 15.6.13 not occupied	33		33
15.6.13 – 15.12.14 last 18 months		18	18
	33	101	134

PPR relief is:

$\dfrac{101}{134}$ × £180,000   £135,672

The period of absence from 15 September 2010 onwards cannot be deemed occupation because he has bought another house and elected for it to be his PPR: a person may only have one PPR at any point in time. In any event, even if he did not have another PPR, as the period of absence is not followed by a period of actual occupation the deemed occupation rules would not apply. Remember though that the last 18 months are always treated as a period of deemed occupation.

1   B – £18,800

	£	£
Gross proceeds	50,000	
Less incidental costs of disposal	(6,000)	
Net disposal consideration		44,000
Less cost $\dfrac{50,000}{50,000+75,000} \times £63,000$		(25,200)
Gain		18,800

2   B – Paul, Gill, Emma, Mary and Bob

Lucy is connected with Paul and Gill (parents), Emma (sister), Mary (grandmother) and Bob (grandmother's spouse).

3   C – £1,667

	£	£
Gross proceeds	7,000	
Less costs of sale	(500)	
Net disposal proceeds		6,500
Less cost		(3,100)
Chargeable gain		3,400
Gain cannot exceed 5/3 × £(7,000 – 6,000)		1,667

4   D – 2 March 2017

Mark and Simon acquired the second home after their civil partnership. They have two years from the date of that acquisition to make the election.

5   A – Actual occupation is normally required before and after the absence

B is not true because absence abroad can be covered by the 'any reason' period of deemed occupation (for up to three years).

C and D are not true because if the individual is employed abroad, any period is treated as deemed occupation.

6   B – £36,000

75% × £48,000	£36,000

There is no PPR relief for the exclusive business part, including for the last 18 months of ownership where it has been used exclusively for business purposes throughout the period of ownership.

7 B – £27,500

	£
Gain	120,000
Less PPR relief (W1)	(52,500)
	67,500
Less letting relief (W2)	(40,000)
Gain	27,500

WORKINGS

(1) **PPR relief**

	Chargeable months	Exempt months	Total months
Actual occupation		24	24
Not occupied by owner	54		54
Last 18 months		18	18
	54	42	96

The period of absence cannot be deemed occupation as it is not followed by actual occupation

PPR relief is: $\dfrac{42}{96} \times £120,000$ £52,500

(2) **Letting relief**

Lowest of:

Letting gain: $\dfrac{54}{96} \times £120,000$	£67,500
PPR relief	£52,500
Maximum	£40,000

Letting relief is therefore £40,000

8   Phoebe

Summary:	£
Painting	49,000
House	132,000
Land	18,000
Chargeable gains	199,000
Annual exempt amount	(11,000)
Taxable gains	188,000

| |
--- | ---:
((£31,865 + (£1,200 × 100/80)) – £31,255) £2,110 × 18% | 380
(£188,000 – £2,110) £185,890 × 28% | 52,049
CGT payable | 52,429

WORKINGS

(1) *Painting*

Disposal by Phoebe

| £
--- | ---:
Disposal proceeds | 64,000
Less cost | (15,000)
Gain | 49,000

Phoebe's cost is the deemed proceeds from the previous no gain, no loss disposal between Edward and Phoebe ie Edward's original cost.

(2) *Plot of land*

| £
--- | ---:
Disposal proceeds | 50,000
Less cost | (50,000)
Gain | nil

(3) *House*

| £
--- | ---:
Disposal proceeds | 180,000
Less: 31.3.82 MV | (40,000)
enhancement | (8,000)
Gain | 132,000

(4) *Alfa Romeo*

A car is an exempt asset.

(5) *Land*

| £
--- | ---:
Net disposal proceeds | 24,000
Less cost $\dfrac{24,000}{24,000+48,000} \times £18,000$ | (6,000)
Gain | 18,000

		£
Disposal proceeds		410,000
Less cost		(39,350)
Gain before reliefs		370,650
Less PPR relief (W1)		(270,575)
		100,075
Less letting relief (W2)		(40,000)
Chargeable gain		60,075

WORKINGS

(1) **PPR relief**

	Chargeable months	Exempt months	Total Months
1.4.90 – 1.4.94 actual occupation		48	48
1.4.94 – 1.1.04 employed abroad (any period, followed by actual occupation)		117	117
1.1.04 – 1.3.05 working elsewhere (up to four years followed by actual occupation)		14	14
1.3.05 – 1.7.05 any reason (up to three years followed by actual occupation)		4	4
1.7.05 – 1.1.07 actual occupation		18	18
1.1.07 – 1.10.13 not occupied by owner and not followed by actual occupation and had elected for another house to be his PPR at that time	81		81
1.10.13 – 1.4.15 last 18 months		18	18
	81	219	300

PPR relief is:

$$\frac{219}{300} \times £370,650 \qquad\qquad £270,575$$

(2) **Letting relief**

Letting period not covered by PPR relief is 1.1.11 to 1.10.13 which is 33 months.

Lowest of:

Letting gain: $\frac{33}{300} \times £370,650$ £40,772

PPR relief   £270,575

Maximum   £40,000

Letting relief is therefore £40,000

CHAPTER 12

Shares and securities

Introduction

Examination context

Topic List

Summary and Self-test

Technical reference

Answer to Interactive question

Answers to Self-test

Learning objective

- Calculate the chargeable gains and losses on shares and securities

The specific syllabus reference for this chapter is 2a.

Syllabus links

Shares and securities is a new topic, not covered in your Principles of Taxation study manual.

However, the calculation of gains and losses will be familiar to you.

Examination context

In the examination a candidate may be required to:

- Calculate gains on a disposal of shares acquired over a period of time, including the treatment of rights issues and bonus issues

Better candidates achieve good marks on share questions, although these require a methodical approach and can be time consuming.

1 Disposals of shares and securities by individuals and trustees

Section overview

- There are matching rules to determine which shares are sold.
- The s.104 pool contains all the shares acquired prior to the date of the disposal.

1.1 Share matching rules

Where a disposal is made from a shareholding that has been acquired piecemeal over time, special rules exist to identify which shares are deemed to have been sold.

Disposals of shares are matched against acquisitions of the same class of shares in the same company in the following order: [Hp99]

- Any acquisitions made on the same day as the date of the disposal.
- Any acquisitions within the following 30 days, matching on a FIFO (first in first out) basis (ie shares acquired earlier rather than later within that 30-day period).
- Any shares in the s.104 pool which consists of all shares acquired prior to the date of disposal.

Worked example: Matching rules for individuals and trustees

James has the following transactions in the ordinary shares of A plc:

Shares acquired/(disposed of)	Date
1,000	28 April 1980
250	31 January 1985
350	28 May 1998
1,300	23 August 2001
1,500	4 September 2014
(2,600)	4 September 2014
800	17 September 2014

Requirement

Apply the matching rules to the disposal.

Solution

4 September 2014 – disposal of 2,600 shares

Same day acquisition	1,500
Acquisition in following 30 days	800
S.104 pool	300
	2,600

1.2 S.104 pool

Definition

S.104 pool: All acquisitions of shares of the same class in a company.

The s.104 pool was introduced in Finance Act 1985. It contains all acquisitions prior to the date of the current disposal. Any shares acquired prior to March 1982 will be included at 31.3.82 MV instead of cost.

Worked example: s.104 pool

Lars has acquired ordinary shares in G plc, a quoted trading company, as follows:

Date	Shares acquired	Cost £	31.3.82 MV £
16 September 1981	1,750	1,800	1,925
7 August 1990	3,500	4,025	n/a
1 October 1995	5,200	5,500	n/a

On 24 November 2014, Lars sold 7,350 shares for £29,750.

Requirement

Calculate the chargeable gain on the sale.

Solution

S.104 pool

	No. £	Cost/MV82 £
16 September 1981		
Acquisition	1,750	1,925
7 August 1990		
Acquisition	3,500	4,025
1 October 1995		
Acquisition	5,250	5,500
	10,500	11,450
24 November 2014		
Disposal	(7,350)	(8,015)
C/f	3,150	3,435

Gain

	£
Disposal proceeds	29,750
Less: cost	(8,015)
Gain	21,735

2 Bonus and rights issues

Section overview

- Bonus issue shares are acquired at nil cost.
- Bonus issue shares are allocated pro-rata to the s.104 pool.
- Rights issue shares are acquired for consideration paid to the company.
- Rights issue shares are allocated pro-rata to the s.104 pool.

2.1 Bonus issues

When a company offers a bonus issue of shares, it issues free shares to its existing shareholders in proportion to their existing shareholdings.

Bonus issues are commonly referred to as a '1 for x' bonus issue (eg '1 for 5' or '1 for 2'). This terminology means that for a '1 for 5' bonus issue, each shareholder will receive one free share for every five shares previously held.

As bonus shares are free, for taxation purposes a bonus issue is not treated as an acquisition of shares by the individual / trustee shareholder in the normal way.

The event is treated as a reorganisation of the company's share capital as follows:

- The new bonus shares are deemed to have been acquired on the same date as the original shares to which they relate.

- Bonus issues attach pro-rata to the s.104 pool. The number of shares are added into the holding at nil cost.

Worked example: Bonus issue

Maisie made the following acquisitions of ordinary shares in Q plc:

Date	Shares acquired	Cost
	£	£
3 August 1980	1,400	4,900 (31.3.82 MV £5,600)
6 May 1995	875	3,850
8 October 2001	525	2,625
10 January 2007	215	1,300

On 4 November 2006, the company made a 1 for 7 bonus issue.

In June 2014, Maisie sold her entire shareholding for £10 per share. This was her only capital disposal in 2014/15.

Requirement

Calculate the taxable gain.

Solution

S.104 holding

	No.	Cost/MV82
		£
3 August 1980		
Acquisition	1,400	5,600
6 May 1995		
Acquisition	875	3,850
8 October 2001		
Acquisition	525	2,625
	2,800	
4 November 2006		
Bonus issue 1:7	400	–
10 January 2007		
Acquisition	215	1,300
	3,415	13,375
June 2014		
Disposal	(3,415)	(13,375)
	–	–

Gain:

	£
Disposal proceeds 3,415 × £10	34,150
Less: cost	(13,375)
Chargeable gain	20,775
Annual exempt amount	(11,000)
Taxable gain	9,775

2.2 Rights issues

When a company offers a rights issue, it offers its existing shareholders the right to buy extra shares, usually at a discounted price, in proportion to their existing shareholdings. The key difference from a bonus issue is that rights shares are not issued free.

A rights issue is treated, for taxation purposes, as a reorganisation of the company's share capital as follows:

- The new rights shares are deemed to have been acquired on the same date as the original shares to which they relate.

- Rights issues attach pro rata to the s.104 pool. The number of shares are added into the holdings and the cost of the rights shares increases the cost of these holdings.

Worked example: Rights issue

Rose had the following transactions in K Ltd:

July 1980	Acquired 1,000 shares for £1,000 (31.3.82 MV £1,200)
August 1990	Acquired 1,500 shares for £2,700
June 1992	Rights 1 for 2 acquired at £2.50 per share

In November 2014, Rose sold all her shares for £4 per share.

Requirement

Calculate the chargeable gain on sale.

Solution

S.104 pool

	No.	Cost/MV82 £
July 1980		
Acquisition	1,000	1,200
August 1990		
Acquisition	1,500	2,700
	2,500	
June 1992		
Rights 1:2 @ £2.50	1,250	3,125
	3,750	7,025
November 2014		
Disposal	(3,750)	(7,025)
	–	–

Gain

	£
Disposal proceeds 3,750 × £4	15,000
Less cost	(7,025)
Gain	7,975

Interactive question: Rights issue   [Difficulty level: Exam standard]

Alan made the following acquisitions of preference shares in H plc:

Date	Shares acquired	Cost £
10 May 1979	300	975 (31.3.82 MV £1,200)
15 June 1989	1,050	4,375
12 November 2007	900	5,250

On 10 October 2010, the company made a 1 for 15 rights issue at £14 per share which Alan took up in full.

In March 2015, Alan sold his entire shareholding for £12 per share.

Requirement

Using the standard formats below, calculate the chargeable gain on sale.

S.104 holding

	No.	Cost/MV82 £

10 May 1979

Acquisition

15 June 1989

Acquisition

12 November 2007

Acquisition   _____

10 October 2010

Rights 1:15 @ £14   _____   _____

March 2015

Disposal   (_____)   (_____)

        =========   =========

Gain

                                               £

Disposal proceeds .... × £................

Less cost   (_____)

Gain   =========

Summary

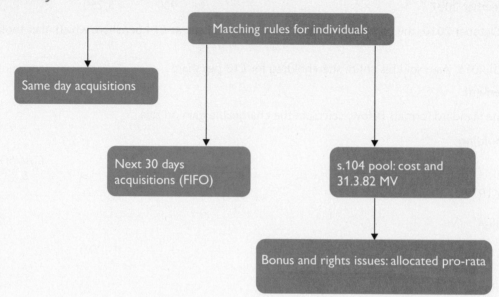

Self-test

Answer the following questions.

1 Jonathan had the following transactions in shares in S Ltd:

18 July 2014	bought	400 shares
21 July 2014	bought	400 shares
23 July 2014	bought	500 shares
23 July 2014	sold	300 shares
25 July 2014	sold	200 shares
10 August 2014	bought	200 shares

With which acquisition will the shares sold on 25 July 2014 be matched?

A   18 July 2014
B   21 July 2014
C   23 July 2014
D   10 August 2014

2 Karen bought 5,000 shares in Q plc in April 1985 for £5,500. In July 1999, Q plc made a one for five bonus issue. The Q plc shares after the bonus issue were worth £2 each.

Karen sold all her shares in December 2014 for £5 per share.

What is her chargeable gain on sale?

A   £19,500
B   £22,500
C   £24,500
D   £18,000

3 Roy bought 1,000 shares in L plc on 7 July 1999 for £1,200.

On 10 June 2003, L plc made a one for four rights issue at £1.40 per share. Roy purchased his full entitlement of rights issue shares.

On 2 January 2015, Roy sold 750 shares in L plc for £1,575.

What is the cost on disposal of the shares in L plc?

A   £950
B   £1,050
C   £900
D   £930

4 Mavis Jones acquired the following shares in Red Ltd as follows:

July 1980	1,000 shares for £3,000 (31.3.82 MV £3,750)
May 1982	2,000 shares for £8,000
April 1986	2,000 shares for £10,000
August 1999	1,000 shares for £8,000

There was a 1 for 10 rights issue in August 2006 at £10 per share. Mavis took up all her rights.

Mavis sold all her shares in November 2014 at £12 per share.

Mavis makes no other disposals in 2014/15 and has no losses brought forward. Mavis has taxable income of £19,000 in 2014/15.

Requirement

Calculate Mavis' capital gains tax payable for 2014/15.   **(5 marks)**

Now go back to the Learning Objectives in the Introduction. If you are satisfied you have achieved these objectives please tick them off.

Technical reference

> This technical reference section is designed to assist you. It should help you know where to look for further information on the topics covered in this chapter.

Answer to Interactive question

S.104 holding

	No.	Cost/MV82 £
10 May 1979 Acquisition	300	1,200
15 June 1989 Acquisition	1,050	4,375
12 November 2007 Acquisition	900	5,250
	2,250	
10 October 2010 Rights 1:15 @ £14	150	2,100
	2,400	12,925
March 2015 Disposal	(2,400)	(12,925)
c/f	–	–

Gain

	£
Disposal proceeds 2,400 × £12	28,800
Less: cost	(12,925)
Gain	15,875

1   D – 10 August 2014

Shares acquired in the next 30 days after disposal

2   C – £24,500

S.104 pool

	No.	Cost £
April 1985		
Acquisition	5,000	5,500
July 1999		
Bonus 1:5	1,000	NIL
	6,000	5,500
December 2014		
Disposal	(6,000)	(5,500)
c/f	NIL	NIL

Gain

	£
Disposal proceeds 6,000 × £5	30,000
Less cost	(5,500)
Gain	24,500

3   D – £930

	No.	Cost
L plc shares		
S.104 pool		
July 1999		
Acquisition	1,000	1,200
June 2003		
Rights issue 1 for 4 @ £1.40	250	350
	1,250	1,550
January 2015		
Disposal	(750)	(930)
c/f	500	620

4   **Mavis Jones – CGT payable 2014/15**

S.104 holding

	No.	Cost/MV82 £
July 1980 Acquisition	1,000	3,750
May 1982 Acquisition	2,000	8,000
April 1986 Acquisition	2,000	10,000
August 1999 Acquisition	1,000	8,000
	6,000	
August 2006 Rights 1:10 @ £10	600	6,000
	6,600	35,750
November 2014 Disposal	(6,600)	(35,750)
c/f	–	–

Gain

	£
Disposal proceeds 6,600 × £12	79,200
Less cost	(35,750)
Chargeable gain	43,450
Annual exempt amount	(11,000)
Taxable gain	32,450
(£31,865 – £19,000) £12,865 × 18%	2,316
(£32,450 – £12,865) £19,585 × 28%	5,484
CGT payable	7,800

CHAPTER 13

Leases

Introduction

Examination context

Topic List

Summary and Self-test

Technical reference

Answer to Interactive question

Answers to Self-test

Learning objective

- Calculate the chargeable gains and losses on leases

The specific syllabus reference for this chapter is 2a.

Syllabus links

The taxation of gains and losses arising on the disposal of leases was not covered in your Principles of Taxation study manual.

Examination context

In the examination candidates may be required to:

- Understand the terminology used regarding leases
- Calculate the gains or losses arising on the assignment or grant of a lease

This area of the syllabus is only tested in this paper and is therefore likely to be tested fairly frequently. Candidates who understand the rationale behind the treatment of each type of disposal (ie those who understand the summary diagram in section 1.3) understand how to calculate the gain for each type of disposal and are able to apply their knowledge in the exam, will do well on questions set on this area. Those who merely rote learn the technical knowledge struggle to apply that knowledge to a novel scenario in the exam.

1 Introduction

Section overview

- A lease is the right to use land and/or buildings for a specified period of time.

- A long lease is one with >50 years left to run at disposal.

- A short lease is one with ≤50 years left to run at disposal.

- The grant of a lease means the creation of a leasehold interest in land for a specified period of time. The freeholder or leaseholder retains a superior interest in the land which will revert to him at the end of the specified period.

- The assignment of a lease means the outright disposal by the leaseholder of the remaining period of the lease.

1.1 Introduction

The leasing of land and buildings has taxation implications as it will normally give rise to a chargeable gain. A lease is the right to use land and/or buildings for a specified period of time.

1.2 Terminology

The gain that arises on the disposal of a lease depends on the nature of the lease disposed of. In order to understand the nature of the transaction it is important to have a basic understanding of English property law (note that Scots law is different):

Definitions

Freehold interest: The owner of the freehold has the absolute right to occupy and use the property and to dispose of the property.

Leasehold interest: The owner of a leasehold interest has the right to occupy and use the property for a specified period of time, subject to the rights of the person retaining the freehold.

Reversionary interest: When a lease term comes to an end, the rights under the lease revert back to the holder of the superior interest, for example the freeholder. That superior interest is called 'the reversionary interest' or 'the reversion'. The holder of a reversionary interest is either a freeholder or the lessee of a head-lease.

Grant of a lease: The creation of a leasehold interest in land for a specified period of time. The freeholder or leaseholder retains a superior interest in the land which will revert to him at the end of the specified period.

Assignment of a lease: The outright disposal by the leaseholder of the remaining period of the lease:

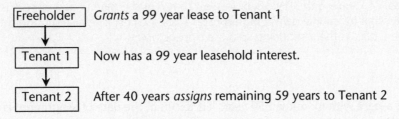

Freeholder	*Grants* a 99 year lease to Tenant 1
Tenant 1	Now has a 99 year leasehold interest.
Tenant 2	After 40 years *assigns* remaining 59 years to Tenant 2

Lease premiums: A lump sum is normally payable at acquisition of a lease in addition to any annual rent payable. This lump sum is known as the lease premium. On the grant of a short lease, some of this premium is treated as being income instead of capital.

Reverse premiums: A lump sum paid by a landlord to a prospective tenant as an inducement to enter into a lease. A reverse premium is always taxed as a revenue receipt.

Long lease: A lease is a long lease if at the time of grant or assignment it still has more than fifty years left to run. Otherwise it will be treated as a short lease.

1.3 Disposal of leases – overview

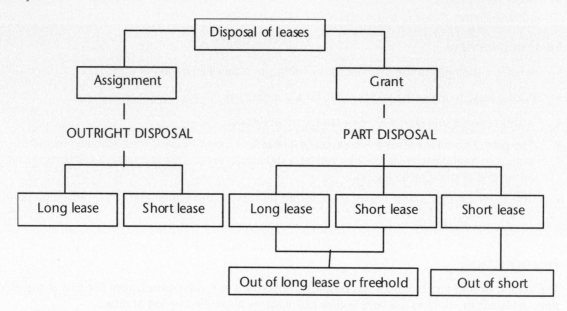

- The assignment of a lease is a complete disposal of a lease and is treated as a chargeable disposal. The whole lease premium is treated as capital proceeds in the computation of the gain.

- The grant of a long lease (> 50 years) is also a chargeable disposal and the whole lease premium is again capital proceeds.

- When a short lease is granted (≤ 50 years) the lease premium is treated as being partly capital and partly property income.

  The amount of the premium which is assessed as property income is taxable on the lessor in the year of grant. If the lessee is trading he may then claim an additional expense over the term of the lease known as 'deemed additional rent'.

- The disposal of a lease is the disposal of an interest in property so where the property qualifies for principal private residence relief (PPR), the gain on the lease will also qualify for any such exemption.

2 Assignment of leases

Section overview
- The disposal of a lease with more than 50 years left to run at the date of assignment is treated as an outright disposal for capital gains tax purposes.
- The disposal of a lease with 50 years or less left to run at the date of assignment is treated as an outright disposal for capital gains tax purposes. The base cost is adjusted using the lease percentage tables as the asset being sold is a wasting asset.

2.1 Assignment of a long lease

The disposal of a lease with more than 50 years left to run at the date of assignment is treated as an outright disposal for capital gains tax purposes.

The capital gain or allowable loss is calculated as normal.

2.2 Assignment of a short lease

The disposal of a lease with 50 years or less left to run at the date of assignment is treated as an outright disposal for capital gains tax purposes.

2.2.1 Adjusted cost on assignment of a short lease

The capital gain or allowable loss is calculated as normal but takes account of the fact that the asset being sold is a wasting asset by adjusting the original cost accordingly.

The adjusted cost is calculated using the following formula:

$$\frac{\text{\% re number of years left to run at disposal}}{\text{\% re number of years left to run at acquisition / 31 Mar 82}} \times \text{Cost/31 Mar 82 MV}$$

For companies where the asset was purchased prior to 31 March 1982 the original cost and the 31 March 1982 market value both need to be adjusted.

Remember that for individuals, assets acquired before 31 March 1982 are treated as acquired on 31 March 1982 for their value at that date.

The appropriate percentage can be found by referring to HMRC's short lease percentages table which can be found at Hp91.

Worked example: Assignment of a short lease

A 32 year lease is acquired by Mr Jones for £50,000 in March 1994. When sold in March 2016 for £30,000 it has only ten years left to run.

Requirement

Compute the chargeable gain arising.

Solution

	£
Proceeds (10 yrs)	30,000
Deemed cost £50,000 × $\left\{\dfrac{46.695\ (10\ \text{yrs})}{89.354\ (32\ \text{yrs})}\right\}$	(26,129)
Gain	3,871

Where the duration of the lease is not an exact number of years, the percentage is calculated as:

- The percentage for the whole number of years, plus
- $\frac{1}{12}$ of the difference between that and the next highest percentage for each additional month.

2.2.2 Interaction with deemed additional rent

When a short lease is granted, a proportion of the lease premium is taxed on the lessor as property income. If the lessee is a trader, the amount of the income which is treated as income for the lessor can then be deducted from trading profits over the term of the lease.

If the lessee subsequently assigns the lease, any relief given as deemed additional rent must be deducted from the original cost before it is adjusted using the wastage formula above. This prevents tax relief being given twice.

Worked example: Adjusted cost and deemed additional rent

Q Ltd was granted a 30 year lease for £20,402 in November 2007. In recent years Q Ltd has lost a major customer and has now been forced into liquidation. The liquidator sells the lease with 23 years left to run in November 2014 for £26,000. Company Q has used the lease for trading purposes throughout.

Requirement

Compute the chargeable gain arising.

Assume an RPI in November 2014 of 258.9

Solution

	£	£
Disposal proceeds		26,000
Less: Cost	20,402	
Allowable deduction from trading profits		

$\dfrac{7}{30} \times (£20,402 \times \dfrac{50-29}{50})$ (1,999)

	£	£
Subject to wastage	18,403	

Deemed wasted cost £18,403 × $\dfrac{78.055\ (23)}{87.330\ (30)}$ (16,448)

9,552

Less indexation allowance $\dfrac{258.9 - 209.7}{209.7}$ = 0.235 × £16,448 (3,865)

Chargeable gain 5,687

---

3 Grant of leases

Section overview

- The grant of a long lease from a long lease or freehold means that the lessor retains a reversionary interest in the property and it is therefore a part disposal for capital gains tax. A normal part disposal computation is required.

- The grant of a short lease from a long lease or freehold will also be a part disposal for capital gains tax. However, as only a short lease is granted, part of the lease premium is treated as being property income of the lessor. Only the capital element of the premium is treated as proceeds in the calculation of the lessor's capital gain at the date of grant.

- The grant of a short lease from a short lease will also be treated as a part disposal for capital gains purposes. As this is a disposal of a wasting asset the original cost needs to be adjusted using the lease percentage tables. In addition, as a short lease has been granted, part of the lease premium will be taxable as property income (although the whole of the premium will also be treated as sale proceeds) in the hands of the lessor.

3.1 Grant of a long lease from a freehold or long leasehold

The grant of a long lease means that the lessor retains a reversionary interest in the property and it is therefore a part disposal for capital gains tax. A normal part disposal computation is therefore required with the cost adjusted using the formula:

$$\frac{A}{A + B} \times \text{Cost/31 Mar 82 MV}$$

Where:

A = sale consideration ie the total lease premium

B = market value of the reversionary interest

There is no income element of the premium, as the lease is > 50 years long.

Worked example: Grant of a long lease

B Ltd grants a 99 year lease from a freehold for £200,000 in March 2015. The company acquired the freehold for £100,000 in March 1993. The value of the reversionary interest was £60,000.

Requirement

Compute the chargeable gain arising. Assume an indexation factor of 0.883

Solution

		£
Sale consideration = premium received		200,000
Less deemed cost $\dfrac{£200,000}{£200,000 + £60,000} \times £100,000$		(76,923)
		123,077
Less indexation to March 2015 (£76,923 × 0.883)		(67,923)
Chargeable gain		55,154

3.2 Grant of a short lease from a freehold or long leasehold

The grant of a short lease again means that the lessor has retained a reversionary interest in the property and it is therefore a part disposal for capital gains tax. Part of the premium is assessable as property income and must be excluded from the gains computation. The proceeds figure used in the gains computation is the 'capital element' of the premium (ie the total premium less the amount assessable as property income).

A normal part disposal computation is required with the cost adjusted using the formula:

$$\frac{a}{A + B} \times \text{Cost/31 Mar 82 MV}$$

Where

a = capital proceeds ie the capital element of the lease premium ie the total less the amount assessed as property income

A = the total lease premium received

B = market value of the reversionary interest

Interactive question: Leasing [Difficulty level: Exam standard]

P Ltd acquired a freehold property for £24,000 in March 1993. The property is situated in the UK and is held solely for investment purposes.

P Ltd decided to sub-let the property to an associate on 1 May 2014 for a term of eight years for a premium of £20,000 and an annual rental of £12,000. The value of the reversionary interest on 1 May 2014 was £80,000.

Requirement

Compute the property income assessment and chargeable gain resulting for P Ltd for the year to 31 December 2014. Assume an RPI for May 2014 of 256.8.

See **Answer** at the end of this chapter.

3.3 Grant of a short lease from a short lease

This transaction can be analysed as follows:

- As this is a grant of a lease, the lessor retains a reversionary interest.

- So this will be treated as a part disposal for capital gains purposes.

- It is also a disposal from a wasting asset so the original cost needs to be adjusted using the lease percentage tables. In addition as it is the grant of a short lease, some of the lease premium will be taxable as property income.

- The whole of the premium will also be treated as sale proceeds in the hands of the lessor.

The property income assessable on the sub-lease premium is calculated as:

£

$$\text{Premium} \times \frac{50-(n-1)}{50}$$ X

Less relief for premium paid on head lease:

$$\frac{\text{duration of sub-lease}}{\text{duration of head-lease}} \times \text{property income for head-lease}$$ (X)

Property income assessment for sub-lease premium   X

Where n = the duration of the lease in years

The chargeable gain on the grant of the sub-lease is:

£

Actual lease premium   X
Less deemed cost:

$$\frac{\%G-\%S}{\%A} \times \text{full premium on head-lease}$$ (X)

    X
Less indexation allowance (companies only)   (X)
Indexed gain   X
Less property income assessment for sub-lease premium   (X)
Net gain   X

Where:

%G = duration of head-lease remaining at grant of sub-lease

%S = duration of head-lease remaining at termination of sub-lease

%A = original duration of head lease at acquisition

Note that the deduction of the property income assessment cannot create or increase a loss.

Worked example: Grant of a short lease

On 1 May 2009 Z Ltd paid £80,000 for the grant of a 40 year lease of premises from which it carried on a butcher's trade. Due to an outbreak of food poisoning in the town, Z Ltd was forced to sub-let the property to J Ltd for ten years on 1 May 2014 for £12,000 plus an annual rental of £5,000.

Requirement

Compute the property income assessment for Z Ltd for the year ended 30 September 2014 and the chargeable gain resulting from the grant of the sub-lease.

Assume an RPI in May 2014 of 256.8

Solution

Property assessment

£

Income element of premium received ($£12,000 \times \frac{50-9}{50}$)   9,840

Less Proportion of income element on head lease

$$£80,000 \times \frac{50-39}{50} \times \frac{10 \text{ yrs}}{40 \text{ yrs}}$$ (4,400)

Property income assessment on premium   5,440

Rent receivable $\frac{5}{12} \times £5,000$ 2,083

Total property income assessment   7,523

Capital gains computation

	£
Consideration received	12,000
Less deemed cost £80,000 × $\dfrac{91.981\,(35\text{ yrs}) - 81.100\,(25\text{ yrs})}{95.457\,(40\text{ yrs})}$	(9,119)
Unindexed gain	2,881
Less indexation allowance $\dfrac{256.8 - 212.8}{212.8} = 0.207 \times £9,119$	(1,888)
	993
Less property income on premium (£5,440 restricted)	(993)
Chargeable gain	NIL

Summary and Self-test

Summary

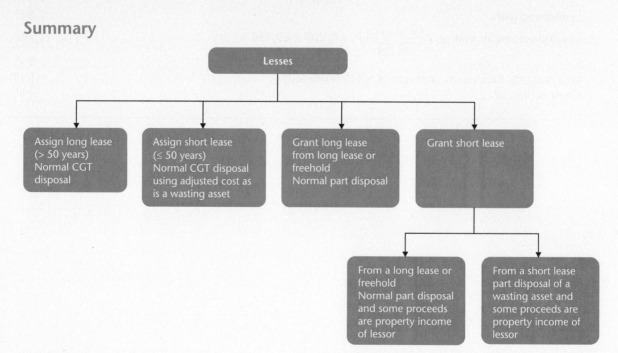

Self-test

Answer the following questions.

1 Lang Ltd acquired a 40 year lease for £30,000 on 1 January 1979 to expire on 31 December 2018. It was sold on 1 October 2014 for £43,000. The value of the lease on 31 March 1982 was £35,000.

   Requirement

   Calculate the gain arising on disposal of the lease. Assume an RPI for October 2014 of 258.7.

2 In January 1998 Mrs Corless acquired a freehold property for £41,000. In December 2014 she granted a 30 year lease at a premium of £19,500. The market value of the reversion was £52,000.

   Requirement

   Compute Mrs Corless' tax position on the grant of the lease.

3 On 1 January 1992 a 40 year lease was acquired by Sarah for £10,000. On 1 January 2015 she granted a sub-lease for 12 years for a premium of £62,000.

   Requirement

   Calculate the taxation position on the grant of the sub-lease.

Now go back to the Learning Objectives in the Introduction. If you are satisfied you have achieved these objectives please tick them off.

Technical reference

Legislation

References are to Taxation of Chargeable Gains Act 1992 (*TCGA 1992*) unless otherwise stated

Deemed additional rent	s.63 CTA 2009 & s.61 ITTOIA 2005
Disposal of lease qualifies for PPR	s.222
Leases	Schedule 8
Lease percentages tables	Para 1(6) Sch 8

HMRC manual references

Capital gains manual (Found at http://www.hmrc.gov.uk/manuals/cgmanual/Index.HTM)

Leases	CG70700

> This technical reference section is designed to assist you. It should help you to know where to look for further information on the topics covered in this chapter.

Answer to Interactive question

Property income assessment

	£
Premium (£20,000 × $\dfrac{50-7}{50}$)	17,200
Rent ($\dfrac{8}{12}$ × £12,000)	8,000
	25,200

Chargeable gain

	£
Consideration (£20,000 – £17,200)	2,800
Less deemed cost $\dfrac{£2,800}{£20,000+£80,000}$ × £24,000	(672)
	2,128
Less indexation allowance $\dfrac{256.8-139.3}{139.3}$ = 0.844 × £672	(567)
Chargeable gain	1,561

1   The allowable proportion of cost is:

% at disposal/% at acquisition × £30,000 where
        X is the percentage for 4 $^3/_{12}$ yrs
        Y is the percentage for 40 yrs
X = 21.983 + [(26.722 – 21.983) × $^3/_{12}$] = 23.168
Y = 95.457

so $\dfrac{23.168}{95.457}$ × £30,000 =   £7,281

The allowable proportion of deemed cost at 31.3.82 is:

X/Y^1 × £35,000 where
        X is the percentage for 4 $^3/_{12}$ yrs, and
        Y^1 is the percentage for 36^3/4 yrs (from 31.3.82 to 31.12.18)
        X = 23.168
        Y^1 = 92.761 + [(93.497 - 92.761) × $^9/_{12}$] = 93.313
        so $\dfrac{23.168}{93.313}$ × £35,000 =   £8,690

The gain is:

	Cost	MV 31.3.82
	£	£
Disposal value	43,000	43,000
Less allowable expenditure	(7,281)	(8,690)
Unindexed gains	35,719	34,310
Less indexation allowance		
$\dfrac{258.7-79.44}{79.44}$ (= 2.257) × £8,690	(19,613)	(19,613)
	16,106	14,697
		14,697
Lower gain chargeable		

2   As this is the grant of a short lease from a freehold or long lease, it is a part disposal for capital gains tax purpose. As it is the grant of a short lease, part of the premium is taxable as property income:

Income tax 2014/15:

Assessable to income tax £19,500 × $\dfrac{50-29}{50}$ £8,190

The balance of the premium is charged to CGT.

CGT 2014/15:

	£
Balance of premium	11,310
Less cost	
£41,000 × $\dfrac{11,310}{19,500+52,000}$	(6,485)
Capital gain	4,825

3   The grant of a short sub-lease from a short lease is a part disposal of a wasting asset. The cost therefore needs to be adjusted using the lease percentage tables. Part of the lease premium will also be treated as property income.

Property income 2014/15

	£	£
Income element of premium = £62,000 × $\dfrac{50-11}{50}$		48,360
Deduct allowance for premium paid		
$£10,000 × \dfrac{50-39}{50}$	2,200	
× $^{12}/_{40}$		(660)
Assessable to income tax		47,700

CGT computation 2014/15

	£
Premium received	62,000
Less: Allowable expenditure	
Depreciated cost (W)	(4,164)
Gain	57,836
Deduct: Property income assessment (above)	(47,700)
Gain	10,136

WORKING

	Unexpired term	Years	%
A	: on granting head lease	40	95.457
G	: on granting sublease	17	66.470
S	: on expiration of sublease	5	26.722
G – S			39.748

Depreciated cost: $\dfrac{39.748}{95.457}$ × £10,000 = £4,164

CHAPTER 14

Overseas aspects of income tax and capital gains tax

Introduction

Topic List

    1   Residence and domicile

    2   Overseas aspects of income tax

    3   Overseas aspects of capital gains tax

Summary and Self-test

Technical reference

Answers to Interactive questions

Answers to Self-test

Learning objectives

- Explain the impact of an individual's residence and domicile

- Calculate total taxable gains and tax payable thereon, utilising available reliefs to reduce the liability, including the computation of double tax relief where appropriate

- Calculate total taxable income and the income tax payable or repayable for trustees, beneficiaries, employees, company directors, partners and self-employed individuals including the computation of double tax relief where appropriate

Specific syllabus references for this chapter are 2c, 2d, 3m and 3n.

Syllabus links

The overseas aspects of income tax and capital gains tax were not covered in your Principles of Taxation study manual.

Examination context

In the examination candidates may be required to:

- Explain the implications of residence and domicile for a particular scenario

- Calculate the income tax liability for an individual with one or more sources of overseas income including income from employment or investments

- Calculate the capital gains tax liability for an individual with one or more overseas assets

Candidates must ensure that they fully understand the implications of residence and domicile for income tax and capital gains tax computations. Candidates must be able to apply the concepts to specific scenarios.

1 Residence and domicile

> **Section overview**
>
> - An individual's residence and domicile status will determine his liability to UK tax.
>
> - An individual who is UK resident is subject to tax on his worldwide income.
>
> - An individual who is non-UK resident is only subject to UK tax on UK income.
>
> - Whether an individual is UK resident is determined by a statutory residence test.
>
> - An individual is domiciled in the country of his permanent home, subject to case law decisions.

1.1 Residence

A taxpayer's residence and domicile have important consequences in establishing the treatment of his UK and overseas income. Prior to 2013/14, whether a taxpayer was resident in the UK was determined by principles derived from case law. With effect from 2013/14, a statutory residence test applies, which considers a number of different tests to assess whether an individual is UK resident. You do not need to know the details of these tests for your examination. In questions involving residence, you will be told whether a taxpayer is UK resident. However, you do need to understand the implications of residence and domicile for income tax and capital gains tax purposes.

1.2 Domicile

A person is domiciled in the country in which he has his permanent home. Domicile is distinct from nationality or residence. A person may be resident in more than one country or have dual nationality, but under UK law he can be domiciled in only one country at a time.

A person

- Acquires a domicile of origin at birth. This is normally the domicile of his father (or that of his mother if his father died before he was born or his parents were unmarried at his birth). Therefore it will not necessarily be his country of birth.

- Retains this domicile until he acquires a:

  - Different domicile of dependency (if, while he is under 16, the domicile of the person on whom he is legally dependent changes); or

  - Different domicile of choice.

A domicile of choice can only be acquired by individuals aged 16 or over.

To acquire a domicile of choice a person must sever his ties with the country of his former domicile and settle in another country with the clear intention of making it his permanent home. Long residence in another country is not in itself enough to prove that a person has acquired a domicile of choice; there must be evidence that he intends to live there permanently and even be buried there.

Individuals who are not UK domiciled may be taxed on a 'remittance' basis (see below).

For inheritance tax purposes there is an additional concept of 'deemed domicile', and in some cases it is also possible to make an election to be treated as domiciled in the UK for inheritance tax purposes (see Chapter 18).

Interactive question 1: Determining domicile [Difficulty level: Exam standard]

Juliette was born in 1977 in the USA. Juliette's parents are married to each other and are British but were working in the USA at the time. In 1987 Juliette's parents moved to Japan and adopted Japan as their permanent home, obtaining Japanese nationality and severing all ties with the UK and the USA. In 2012, Juliette moved to France. She became a French national, renouncing all other nationalities. Juliette also pre-booked her funeral and burial plot in a Parisian cemetery.

Requirement

Explain Juliette's domicile in 1977, 1987 and 2012.

See **Answer** at the end of this chapter.

2 Overseas aspects of income tax

Section overview

- Most UK resident individuals are subject to income tax on an arising or receipts basis. The income is taxed according to the type of income, ie non-savings income, savings income or dividend income.

- Where UK resident individuals are subject to income tax on a remittance basis, the income is taxable as non-savings income.

- The residence and domicile status of an employee (and, in some cases, whether he carries out his duties in the UK or outside it and the residency of his employer) determine the tax treatment of his earnings.

- Other income from overseas sources is taxed on a similar basis to UK income. It may be charged on a remittance basis for non-UK domiciled individuals.

- The remittance basis must usually be claimed and may be subject to payment of the remittance basis charge (RBC).

- Double taxation relief (DTR) is available where income is taxed in more than one country. DTR is calculated on a source by source basis as if the overseas income were taxed as the top slice of income in the UK.

- The DTR is the lower of the UK tax on the overseas income and the actual overseas tax paid.

Generally, a UK resident individual is liable to UK income tax on his worldwide income whereas a non-resident individual is liable to UK income tax only on income arising in the UK.

Most UK resident individuals are subject to income tax on their worldwide income on an arising or receipts basis. The income is taxed according to the type of income, ie non-savings income, savings income or dividend income. This is what we have seen so far in earlier chapters.

A non-UK resident's income tax liability on certain types of UK income is broadly limited to any tax deducted at source (this excludes UK trading, employment and rental income). So, where interest is received gross (eg NS&I accounts), the interest is not taxed but if the interest is received net (eg bank interest), the interest is taxable but the tax liability is limited to the basic rate tax deducted at source.

However, UK resident individuals who are non-UK domiciled may be taxed on a remittance basis, ie only when the income is remitted into the UK. This is explained further later in this chapter. In this case, such income is taxable as non-savings income.

The diagram below provides a broad summary of how an individual is taxed, based on his residence (R) and domicile (D) status. The detail for specific types of income is covered further below.

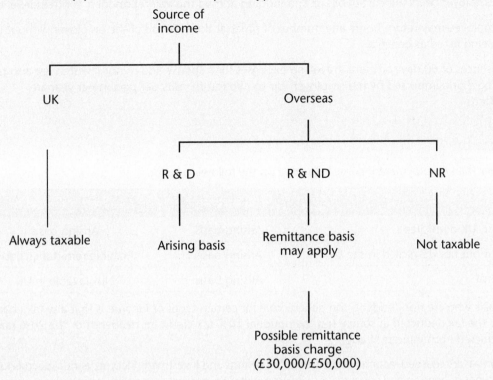

2.1 Employment income

2.1.1 Basis of assessment

Employment income is taxable on the following basis:

	Duties performed wholly or partly in the UK		Duties performed wholly outside the UK
	In the UK	Outside the UK	
UK resident and UK domiciled	Arising basis	Arising basis	Arising basis
UK resident but not UK domiciled	Arising basis	Arising basis	Possible remittance basis or Amount earned
Not UK resident	Arising basis	Not taxable	Not taxable

A non-UK domiciled person who is resident in the UK may be taxed on 'overseas earnings' on a remittance basis provided the employer is also non-UK resident. If the employer is UK resident then the earnings will be taxed on a receipts basis.

The remittance basis is explained further in section 2.3.

2.1.2 Income tax and national insurance contributions (NICs)

An employer must deduct tax (under the PAYE system) if any employees are in receipt of UK taxable earnings even if the duties are performed wholly outside the UK.

In general, an individual is subject to the social security legislation in the country in which he works. However, if working abroad temporarily for a UK employer in the European Union, UK NICs are applicable for at least the first 12 months.

2.1.3 Relief for expenses when employed abroad

- If the employer bears the cost of board and lodging abroad this will represent a tax-free benefit.

- The employee may return home any number of times at the expense of the employer without the costs being taxed as benefits.

- For absences of 60 days or more, travelling expenses for a spouse and minor children are also tax free if paid or reimbursed by the employer. Up to two return visits per person per year are permitted.

2.2 Other income

Income other than employment income is taxable on the following basis:

	UK income	Overseas income
UK resident, UK domiciled	Arising basis	Arising basis
UK resident but not domiciled in the UK	Arising basis	Possible remittance basis
Non-resident	Arising basis	Not taxable in UK

For individuals who are non-resident, the general rule for certain types of income is that any tax charge is limited to the tax deducted at source (eg the notional 10% tax credit for dividends or the 20% tax actually deducted from interest, if any).

This is known as 'disregarded income' and includes UK savings and investment income, annual payments and certain types of pension and social security income, but does not include trading, employment or rental income. However, where an individual is treated as non-resident for only part of a tax year, this treatment does not apply.

Where income tax is limited in this way personal allowances are not available and thus any UK income which has not been disregarded may incur a higher tax liability.

2.2.1 Profits of an overseas trade

- Profits of an overseas trade are computed as for UK trades.

- Profits of an overseas property business are also calculated in the same way as for a UK property business.

- An overseas property which is outside the European Economic Area cannot qualify as a furnished holiday let.

2.2.2 Foreign dividends

- Foreign dividends are taxed in the UK in the same way as UK dividends, ie at 10% in the basic rate band, at 32.5% in the higher rate band and at 37.5% in the additional rate band.

- From 6 April 2009, **all** foreign dividends have a 10% tax credit as long as the company pays the foreign equivalent of corporation tax. For the purposes of your exam you should assume that the paying company does pay the equivalent of corporation tax and therefore you should always gross up the foreign dividend received.

2.3 The remittance basis

Individuals who are resident in the UK but not domiciled in the UK may be able to use the remittance basis for their foreign income, so it is only taxed when it is brought into the UK.

The remittance basis applies automatically in the following two cases:

- Individuals who are not UK domiciled with unremitted foreign income and gains of less than £2,000; or

- The individual

    - Is not UK domiciled; and

    - Has no UK income or gains or only has taxed UK investment income of £100 or less; and

    - Does not remit any foreign income or gains; and

    - Either has been UK resident in not more than 6 out of the previous 9 tax years, or is under 18 years old for the whole tax year.

Where the remittance basis applies automatically the individual personal allowances and the capital gains tax annual exempt amount still apply and there is no liability to pay the remittance basis charge (see below).

Other individuals must **claim** the remittance basis and become a remittance basis user (RBU) and

- Lose their entitlement to UK personal allowances and the capital gains tax annual exempt amount, and

- May have to pay a remittance basis charge (RBC) of £30,000 per annum, or £50,000 per annum if they have been UK resident for 12 out of the previous 14 years.

Foreign investment income (ie interest and dividends) will be taxed as non-savings income where the remittance basis applies. However, it still needs to be included in the income tax computation gross.

2.3.1 Claiming the remittance basis

- Individuals wishing to claim the remittance basis must make a claim on a Self Assessment form.

- Individuals aged under 18 or those who have not been UK resident for at least seven out of the last nine tax years do not need to pay the RBC.

- The RBC is in addition to any tax due on remitted income and gains.

- If individuals do not claim the remittance basis, they will be taxed on an arising basis with full entitlement to UK personal allowance and annual exempt amount.

- The decision whether to make a claim should be considered year by year.

Worked example: Claiming the remittance basis

Jem has been resident in the UK for tax purposes since 2005 but is not UK domiciled.

In 2014/15, he has the following income:

UK trading income	£40,000
Non-UK trading income	£155,000

He remits £52,000 of his non-UK trading income into the UK.

Requirement

Calculate Jem's income tax liability for 2014/15 assuming he:

- Does not claim the remittance basis in 2014/15; and
- Does claim the remittance basis in 2014/15.

Solution

Remittance basis

If Jem uses the remittance basis he will need to make a claim for it to apply and will therefore be liable to pay the remittance basis charge and lose his entitlement to both the personal allowance and the annual exempt amount. Jem will be taxed on his UK income and his world-wide income which he remits to the UK.

	£
UK trading income	40,000
Non-UK trading income remitted to the UK	52,000
Taxable income (no personal allowance as claimed to be remittance basis user)	92,000

His income tax liability will therefore be:

£31,865 × 20%	6,373
£60,135 × 40%	24,054
Remittance basis charge (present for at least 7 but fewer than 12 years)	30,000
Income tax payable	60,427

Arising basis

If Jem does not make a claim for the remittance basis to apply, he will instead be taxed on his world-wide income on an arising basis.

	£
UK trading income	40,000
Non-UK trading income	155,000
Taxable income (no personal allowance as income exceeds £120,000)	195,000

His income tax liability will therefore be:

£31,865 × 20%	6,373
£118,135 × 40%	47,254
£45,000 × 45%	20,250
Income tax payable	73,877

2.4 Personal allowances

Personal allowances, eg personal allowance, married couple's age allowance and blind person's allowance, may be claimed by all UK residents subject to the remittance basis rules described above. Personal allowances may only be claimed by non-UK residents if they are:

- Citizens of the EEA
- Resident in the Isle of Man or Channel Islands
- Current or former Crown servants and their widows or widowers
- Resident in certain territories with which the UK has a double tax agreement
- Former residents who have left the UK for health reasons

2.5 Double taxation relief

Where overseas income is taxable both in the UK and overseas, double taxation relief (DTR) will be available. Where a double tax treaty exists relief may be given via the exemption method ie the income will be exempt in one of the countries. Where no double tax treaty exists unilateral relief will apply instead.

2.5.1 Unilateral/credit relief

The overseas income is treated as follows:

- Overseas income is included in the UK income tax computation gross of overseas taxes suffered.
- DTR, on a source by source basis, is given as the lower of the

    - Overseas tax suffered
    - UK tax on the overseas income

The steps for calculating the UK tax on overseas income are as follows:

Step 1
- Calculate the UK income tax liability (before DTR) including all sources of income.

Step 2
- Exclude the overseas source of income suffering the highest rate of overseas tax.
- Treat this source of overseas income as the top slice of income.

Step 3
- Re-calculate the UK income tax liability (obeying all normal rules regarding savings/non-savings income). The difference is the UK income tax on this overseas source of income.

Step 4
- Exclude the next source of overseas income (if applicable).

Step 5
- Repeat Step 3, now excluding both sources. The difference is the UK income tax on this second source of income.

Worked example: Income tax and DTR

Sue works partly in the UK and partly abroad. She is resident and domiciled in the UK. Her income for 2014/15 is as follows:

Employment income – UK duties	£32,550
Employment income – overseas duties (gross)	£15,000
Savings income – UK interest received	£2,450

Sue paid overseas tax of £5,500.

Requirement

Calculate Sue's total UK tax payable for 2014/15.

Solution

	Non-savings Income £	Savings Income £	Total £
Income			
Employment income – UK	32,550		32,550
Employment income – overseas	15,000		15,000
Interest x 100/80		3,063	3,063
Total income	47,550	3,063	50,613
Personal allowance	(10,000)		(10,000)
Taxable income	37,550	3,063	40,613

	£
Tax	
£31,865 @ 20%	6,373
£8,748 @ 40%	3,499
	9,872
Less DTR (W1)	(4,749)
Income tax liability	5,123
Less tax deducted at source (£3,063 × 20%)	(613)
Income tax payable	4,510

WORKING 1 – DTR

Excluding overseas income, UK income tax would be:

Taxable income	22,550	3,063	25,613
			£
Tax			
£25,613 @ 20%			5,123
Income tax liability			5,123

Thus UK income tax on the overseas income is £9,872 – £5,123 = £4,749

DTR is the lower of the actual overseas tax of £5,500 and the UK tax on the overseas income ie the DTR is £4,749.

Interactive question 2: Multiple sources of overseas income

[Difficulty level: Exam standard]

Danielle has UK employment income of £32,400 for 2014/15. In addition she has two sources of overseas income in 2014/15:

Overseas debenture interest (including overseas tax of £1,120)	£6,400
Overseas rental income (including overseas tax of £4,000)	£8,200

Danielle is single and is resident and domiciled in the UK.

Requirement

Calculate Danielle's income tax liability for 2014/15.

See **Answer** at the end of this chapter.

3 Overseas aspects of capital gains tax

Section overview

- CGT applies primarily to individuals resident in the UK.

- If an individual is resident in the UK but not UK domiciled, overseas gains may be taxable on the remittance basis, ie to the extent that the gains are remitted to the UK (see Section 2). Individuals claiming the remittance basis cannot claim the annual exempt amount (£11,000 for 2014/15).

- An individual who is not UK resident has no liability to UK CGT even for assets situated in the UK.

3.1 Basis of assessment

A liability to capital gains tax depends on an individual's residence status:

	UK gains & losses	Overseas gains & losses
UK resident and domiciled in the UK (Note)	Arising basis	Arising basis
UK resident but not UK domiciled in the UK	Arising basis	Possible remittance basis*, limited relief for overseas losses
Not UK resident	Not taxable in UK	Not taxable in UK

*See remittance basis in Section 2.

3.2 Overseas assets

Where an asset is bought and/or sold in an overseas currency, it must be translated into sterling using the rate applicable at the time of purchase or sale. The gain or loss is always calculated based on sterling figures.

Double taxation relief (DTR) is available to offset any double taxation suffered on assets disposed of abroad.

Remember that the AEA and the 18% tax rate can be used in the most effective way possible to maximise the amount of DTR available. In other words the AEA and the 18% basic rate band should always be set against UK gains in priority to foreign gains, thereby ensuring that the UK tax on the foreign gain is maximised. For example, compare the taxation of UK and foreign gains of £16,000 each, when the basic rate band remaining is £5,000:

UK CGT liability – treat foreign gains as top slice	*UK Gains* £	*Foreign Gains* £
Gains	16,000	16,000
Less AEA (treat as set against UK gains only)	(11,000)	–
Taxable gains	5,000	16,000
Basic rate band remaining is £5,000		
£5,000 @ 18%	900	–
£0 + £16,000 @ 28% (treat as if foreign gains are top slice)	–	4,480
Total CGT due	900	4,480
Less double tax relief		
Lower of:		
UK tax on overseas gains £4,480		
Overseas tax paid is £3,100	–	(3,100)
	900	1,380

Total CGT liability = £900 + £1,380 = £2,280

UK CGT liability – treat UK gains as top slice	*UK Gains* £	*Foreign Gains* £
Gains	16,000	16,000
Less AEA (treat as set against overseas gains only)	–	(11,000)
Taxable gains	16,000	5,000
Basic rate band remaining is £5,000		
£5,000 @ 18%	–	900
£16,000 @ 28% (treat as if UK gains are top slice)	4,480	–
Total CGT due	4,480	900
Less double tax relief		
Lower of:		
UK tax on overseas gains £900		
Overseas tax paid is £3,100	–	(900)
	4,480	Nil

Total CGT liability = £4,480 + £0 = £4,480

Interactive question 3: CGT & DTR   [Difficulty level: Intermediate]

Will Gates is resident and domiciled in the UK. During 2014/15 he earns £50,000. He has a villa in Spain which he sells in October 2014 for £80,000, incurring Spanish taxes of £8,000. The full amount of Spanish tax suffered is eligible for relief against UK capital gains tax as double taxation relief. This is his only gain of 2014/15. He had bought the villa in June 1996 for £25,000, and uses it only for holidays.

Requirement

Calculate Will's capital gains tax liability for 2014/15.

See **Answer** at the end of this chapter.

Summary

Domicile
- Origin, dependency or choice
- Difficult to change

Income Tax

Status	Employment Income	Other Income
UKR + UKD	world-wide income taxed on receipts basis	world-wide income taxed on arising basis
UKR + non-UKD	receipts basis except possibly for foreign earnings	UK income taxed on receipt basis, remittance basis may apply to overseas income
Non-UKR	UK income taxed on receipts basis otherwise exempt	UK income taxed on receipts basis otherwise exempt

- DTR available for income taxed in UK and overseas
  - Source by source basis
  - Computed as if overseas income is top-slice of income

- Remittance basis needs to be claimed if unremitted foreign income / gains > £2,000
- Otherwise tax on arising basis
- RBC of £30,000 payable if resident for 7 out of previous 9 years, £50,000 if resident for 12 out of 14 years
- Entitled to UK personal allowances lost

CGT

Basis
- UKR + UKD
  = world-wide gains taxed
- UKR + non-UKD
  = UK gains taxed as arise, remittance basis may apply to overseas gains
- Non-UKR
  = world-wide gains exempt

Self-test

Answer the following questions.

1   Jennifer Spears is a new personal tax client of your firm. You have been asked to calculate her UK income tax liability for 2014/15. During your interview with Jennifer in May 2014 you obtain the following information:

- Jennifer has always been resident and domiciled in the UK.

- Her P60 for 2014/15 shows taxable pay of £44,000, with PAYE deducted of £8,900.

- In 2012/13, when on holiday in Spain, she decided to buy a holiday apartment. She spends four weeks a year there on holiday and for the rest of the time the apartment is let through a Spanish agency. In 2014/15 the agent paid £4,200 into Jennifer's Spanish bank account, which was net of Spanish tax of £800. Jennifer always leaves the money in her Spanish bank account to spend when on holiday.

- Jennifer is single and has no children. She is aged 36.

Requirements

(a)   Calculate Jennifer's income tax liability for 2014/15.

(b)   Explain how your answer would differ if Jennifer were domiciled in Spain (but resident in the UK for the last fifteen years).

(Ignore the provisions of the UK-Spain double tax treaty.)

2   Julian is domiciled in Ecuador but moved to the UK on 1 March 2010 and immediately became UK resident. Julian has been a client of our firm for a few years. He has decided to purchase a property in the UK and has sold the following assets in 2014/15 in order to realise the requisite capital to fund the property purchase (all amounts are translated into a sterling equivalent where appropriate):

- 42,000 shares in Shipton plc to his friend Jemimah for £62,000. Shipton plc is an investment company quoted on the London stock exchange with 280,000 issued shares. When he sold the shares they were quoted at 305-310p with marked bargains of 303p, 307p and 309p, and Julian had paid £56,450 for them in March 2012.

- A lease on a UK house for £60,000 with ten years left to run at the time of sale. Julian bought the lease for £72,000 exactly five years before he sold it. Julian lived in the house until its sale.

- Jewellery which cost £4,750 was sold at auction for £9,100 less auctioneer's fees of £364.

- The remaining six hectares of some land in Ecuador for £54,000. Julian originally bought 11 hectares of land in May 1999 for £68,000, but sold the other five hectares for £42,000 in July 2012. At that time the remaining six hectares were valued at £30,000. Julian has paid £7,500 of tax in Ecuador in respect of the latest disposal.

All proceeds have been remitted to the UK except for the cash from the sale of the land, which is currently held in Julian's bank account in Ecuador.

Julian has net income for 2014/15 of £31,305. The UK has no Double Tax Treaty with Ecuador. Julian is not automatically entitled to the remittance basis and must make a claim for it to apply.

Requirement

Calculate the capital gains tax payable by Julian for 2014/15, showing the amount of any available reliefs, assuming he:

- Does not claim the remittance basis in 2014/15; and
- Does claim the remittance basis in 2014/15.

3   Niamh is 37 years old and has been resident in the UK since she was 19. Niamh was born in Australia and intends to return there in the future. She pays £10,000 into her personal pension each year.

In 2014/15 she received a salary of £29,588 (PAYE deducted of £4,297). She drives a diesel company car with a list price of £22,000 and a CO_2 emission rate of 165g/km. Her employer provides fuel for both private and business use.

Niamh received interest of £250 from her National Savings & Investments Direct Saver account and £800 from her UK bank deposit account. She also received a dividend of £4,000 from her holding of 50,000 £1 ordinary shares in Red plc, a UK quoted company and a dividend of £1,800 from Black Inc, a company quoted overseas. Withholding tax of 19% had been deducted at source. She only sent £450 of this net dividend to the UK.

Niamh owns two properties that she rents out. One is situated in Overseaslandia and she receives £1,000 rent (after expenses) per month. Withholding tax of 38% is deducted at source from the payments she receives. She sent the full net amount to her UK bank account during 2014/15. The other property is in the UK and she receives £1,500 rent per month (net of expenses). She pays £250 per month interest on a loan she took out to purchase the UK property.

Requirements

(i)   Explain the basis on which Niamh will be charged to income tax given her residence and non-UK domicile status.   **(5 marks)**

(ii)   Calculate the amount of income tax due for 2014/15 assuming Niamh is taxed on the remittance basis automatically.   **(20 marks)**

                                                                                        (25 marks)

Now go back to the Learning Objectives in the Introduction. If you are satisfied you have achieved these objectives please tick them off.

Legislation

Overseas aspects of Income Tax

References are to Income Tax Act 2007 (*ITA 2007*)

Remittance basis	ss.809A-809Z10
Disregarded income	s.811
Residence etc	ss.829-832

Overseas aspects of Capital Gains Tax

References are to Taxation of Chargeable Gains Act 1992 (*TCGA 1992*)

Residence etc	ss.9-14A

HMRC manual references

Employment Income Manual (Found at http://www.hmrc.gov.uk/manuals/eimanual/index.htm)

Remittance basis (Found at http://www.hmrc.gov.uk/international/remittance.htm)

Capital gains manual (Found at http://www.hmrc.gov.uk/manuals/cgmanual/index.htm)

Effects of residence and domicile	CG10900+

> This technical reference section is designed to assist you. It should help you to know where to look for further information on the topics covered in this chapter.

Answer to Interactive question 1

As Juliette's parents were married and her father was British she had a British domicile of origin. Her place of birth is irrelevant.

In 1987 Juliette was only 10 years old and therefore her domicile would change if her father's domicile changed. It appears that Juliette's father adopted Japan as his domicile of choice and therefore it also became Juliette's domicile of dependence.

In 2012 Juliette was aged over 16 and appears to have chosen France as her new domicile by renouncing all ties with her previous country of domicile. Her intention to be buried in France indicates her intention to remain permanently.

Answer to Interactive question 2

	Non-savings income £	Savings income £	Total £
Income			
UK Employment income	32,400		32,400
Overseas property business	8,200		8,200
Overseas debenture interest		6,400	6,400
Total income	40,600	6,400	47,000
Personal allowance	(10,000)		(10,000)
Taxable income	30,600	6,400	37,000

Tax	£
£31,865 @ 20%	6,373
£5,135 @ 40%	2,054
£37,000	8,427
Less DTR (W1)	(3,787)
Income tax liability	4,640

WORKING 1 – DTR

Excluding overseas income on a source by source basis exclude the income taxed at the highest rate overseas first. This will maximise the rate at which it is taxed in the UK and hence also maximise the DTR. Excluding the rental income first, UK income tax would be:

Taxable income	£22,400	£6,400	£28,800

Tax		£
£28,800 @ 20%		5,760
Income tax liability		5,760

Thus UK income tax on the overseas rental income is £8,427 – £5,760 = £2,667

DTR is the lower of the actual overseas tax of £4,000 and the UK tax on the overseas income ie the DTR is £2,667.

Then exclude the debenture interest:

Taxable income	£22,400		£22,400

Tax		£
£22,400 @ 20%		4,480
Income tax liability		4,480

Thus UK income tax on the overseas income is £5,760 – £4,480 = £1,280

DTR is the lower of the actual overseas tax of £1,120 and the UK tax on the overseas income ie the DTR is £1,120.

Total DTR is thus £2,667 + £1,120 = £3,787

Answer to Interactive question 3

Will Gates

Calculation of gain on villa

	£
Proceeds	80,000
Cost	(25,000)
Capital gain	55,000
Less Annual exempt amount	(11,000)
Taxable amount	44,000
Capital gains tax @ 28%	12,320
Less DTR	(8,000)
UK tax payable	4,320

1 **Jennifer Spears**

(a) **Income tax computation – 2014/15**

			£
Employment income			44,000
Overseas Property Income (gross)			5,000
Net income			49,000
Less personal allowance			(10,000)
Taxable income (all non-savings)			39,000

			£
Analysed			
UK			34,000
Overseas (top slice)			5,000
			39,000

Income tax	£		£
Basic rate band	31,865	@ 20%	6,373
Higher rate band	7,135	@ 40%	2,854
	39,000		
			9,227

Less double tax relief – Lower of		
(1) Overseas tax suffered (£800)		(800)
(2) UK tax at UK rate on overseas income		
[£5,000 × 40%] = £2,000		
UK income tax liability		8,427

(b) **Difference if Jennifer domiciled in Spain**

If Jennifer were domiciled in Spain, she would not qualify for the remittance basis automatically, however she could make a claim to have her overseas rents taxed on the remittance basis.

As she has been resident in the UK for at least 12 out of the last 14 years, she would also need to pay the RBC of £50,000 and would lose her personal allowance. This is clearly not worthwhile in her situation.

2 **Julian**

	£
Chargeable gains	
Shares in Shipton plc	
Proceeds (OMV) (W1)	128,520
Less cost	(56,450)
Chargeable gain	72,070

	£
Lease	
Proceeds	60,000
Less cost $\dfrac{\%10\text{years}}{\%15\text{years}} = \dfrac{46.695}{61.617} \times £72,000$	(54,564)
	5,436
Less PPR – occupation	(5,436)
Chargeable gain	NIL

	£
Jewellery	
Proceeds	9,100
Less costs of disposal	(364)
	8,736
Less cost	(4,750)
Chargeable gain	3,986

Gain cannot exceed 5/3 rule:
$(£9,100 - £6,000) \times 5/3 = £5,167$

Chargeable gain | £3,986

Ecuadorian land

	£
Proceeds	54,000
Less cost $\dfrac{30,000}{30,000+42,000} \times £68,000$	(28,333)
Chargeable gain	25,667

UK CGT liability

	RB claim £	No RB claim £
Total UK gains = £72,070 + £0 + £3,986	76,056	76,056
Ecuadorian gain	–	25,667
	76,056	101,723
Less AEA (treat as set against UK gains only)	–	(11,000)
Taxable gains	76,056	90,723
Basic rate band remaining (W2) is:		
£560 / £10,560 @ 18%	101	1,901
£75,496/ £80,163 @ 28% (treat as if foreign gains are top slice)	21,139	22,446
Total CGT due	21,240	24,347
Less double tax relief		
Lower of:		
UK tax on overseas gains £0/£25,667 × 28% = £7,187	–	(7,187)
Overseas tax £7,500		
	21,240	17,160

WORKINGS

(1) Shipton plc Lower of

$\frac{1}{4}$ up $= 305 + \frac{1}{4} \times (310\text{-}305) = 306.25$

Mid bargain $\dfrac{303+309}{2} = 306$

$42,000 \times £3.06 = £128,520$

(2) Basic rate band remaining	RB claim £	No RB claim £
Net income	31,305	31,305
Less personal allowance	NIL	(10,000)
Taxable income	31,305	21,305
Basic rate band remaining = £31,865 less taxable income	560	10,560

3 **Niamh**

As Niamh is not UK domiciled it is possible that she can use the remittance basis for her overseas income, ie her overseas income will only be taxed when she brings it into the UK.

An election for this basis is required once an individual has been UK resident for at least seven out of the last nine tax years and has more than £2,000 of unremitted overseas income and gains. Although Niamh satisfies the residency condition her unremitted overseas income and gains is less than £2,000 ($[£1,350 \times {}^{100}/_{81} \times {}^{100}/_{90}] = £1,852$) so she can use the remittance basis without needing to make the election.

Additional benefits of not needing to make the election are:

(a) She will not need to pay the £50,000 (as she has been UK resident for 12 of the last 14 years) tax charge (that represents tax on any unremitted overseas income) that is required when a remittance basis election is made.

(b) She will not lose her personal allowance.

Niamh - Income tax computation 2014/15

	Non savings income £	Savings income £	Dividend Income £
Salary	29,588		
Benefits (W1)	12,673		
NS&I Direct Saver		250	
Bank interest (£800 × $^{100}/_{80}$)		1,000	
UK dividends (£4,000 × $^{100}/_{90}$)			4,444
Foreign dividends remitted (£450 × $^{100}/_{81}$) = £556 × $^{100}/_{90}$ (Note)	617		
Foreign rents remitted £1,613 × 12 (gross amount)	19,356		
UK rents £(1,500 – 250) × 12	15,000		
Net income	77,234	1,250	4,444
Less personal allowance	(10,000)		
	67,234	1,250	4,444

Income tax	£
£31,865 × 20%	6,373
£12,500 × 20% (W2)	2,500
£(22,869 + 1,250) × 40%	9,648
£4,444 × 32.5%	1,444
	19,965
Less DTR	
On rent (W3)	(7,355)
On dividends (W4)	(106)
	12,504
Less tax deducted:	
UK dividends	(444)
Foreign dividends £617 × 10%	(62)
PAYE	(4,297)
Bank interest	(200)
Income tax due	7,501

Note: Foreign dividends taxed on the remittance basis are taxed as non savings income. They are still treated as if received net of a non-repayable 10% UK tax credit.

WORKINGS

(1) *Benefits*

	£
Car benefit (165 – 95)/5 = 14 + 12 = 26 + 3 (diesel) = 29%	
Benefit £22,000 × 29%	6,380
Fuel benefit £21,700 × 29%	6,293
Total benefit	12,673

(2) *Extension of the basic rate band*

Contributions: £10,000 ×100/80 = £12,500 gross

3 *DTR on rent*

Lower of

(i) UK tax:

	67,234	1,250	4,444
Taxable income with foreign income	67,234	1,250	4,444
Less: overseas rental income	(19,356)		
Without overseas rental income	47,878		

Income tax	£
£31,865 × 20%	6,373
£12,500 × 20% (W2)	2,500
£3,513 × 40%	1,405
£1,250 × 40%	500
£4,444 × 32.5%	1,444
Tax without overseas rental income	12,222
Tax with overseas rental income (above)	(19,965)
Tax relating to overseas rental income	7,743

(ii) Overseas tax: £19,356 @ 38% = £7,355

ie £7,355

4 *DTR on foreign dividend*

Lower of

(i) UK tax:

	47,878	1,250	4,444
Taxable income with foreign dividend	47,878	1,250	4,444
Less foreign dividend	(617)		
Without overseas foreign dividend	47,261		

Income tax	£
£31,865 × 20%	6,373
£12,500 × 20% (W2)	2,500
£2,896 × 40%	1,158
£1,250 × 40%	500
£4,444 × 32.5%	1,444
Tax without overseas rental income or foreign dividend	11,975
Tax without overseas rental income (above)	(12,222)
Tax relating to overseas dividend income	247

(ii) Overseas tax: £556 @ 19% = £106

ie £106

CHAPTER

14

CHAPTER 15

National insurance and further administrative matters

Learning objectives

- Identify the different classes of national insurance contributions ☐

- Calculate the national insurance due on employment income and the assessable trading profits of the self-employed ☐

- Explain and apply annual maxima rules for the payment of national insurance contributions ☐

- Calculate the total national insurance contributions payable by employees, employers and self-employed individuals ☐

Specific syllabus references for this chapter are 4a, 4b, 4c and 4d.

Syllabus links

You have already covered the basic principles of National Insurance Contributions (NICs) in Chapter 8 of your Principles of Taxation study manual.

In this chapter, we extend your knowledge to class 1B contributions payable by employers, NICs on company directors and the principles of annual maximum contributions.

We also cover an additional self assessment topic – reduction of payments on account.

Examination context

In the examination candidates may be required to:

- Calculate class 1 NICs where the employee is either contracted out of S2P or is a director

- Use knowledge of classes 1, 2 and 4 NICs to compute NIC liabilities

- Calculate class 1A and 1B NICs

- Calculate the maximum NICs payable for an individual where he either has more than one job or both employment and self employment

- Understand the implications of making a claim to reduce the payments on account of an individual

1 Administration of National Insurance Contributions (NICs)

Section overview

- Class 1 contributions are paid by employee and employers.

- Class 1A and class 1B contributions are paid by employers.

- Class 2 and class 4 contributions are paid by self-employed individuals.

- NICs are administered by the National Insurance Contributions Office (NICO).

1.1 Classes of NIC

There are five classes of national insurance contributions relevant to this exam:

Class 1	Paid by employees and their employers on earnings (mostly cash earnings)
Class 1A	Paid by employers on most taxable benefits provided to employees
Class 1B	Paid by employers on the grossed-up value of earnings in a PAYE settlement agreement
Class 2	Paid by self-employed individuals
Class 4	Paid by self-employed individuals

1.2 Payment of NICs

National insurance contributions are administered by the National Insurance Contributions Office (NICO), part of HMRC:

- Class 1 contributions are collected under the PAYE system on a monthly basis.

- Class 1A contributions are paid in one amount by 19 July (22 July if by electronic payment) following the end of the tax year. [Hp159]

- Class 1B contributions are paid in one amount by 19 October (22 October if by electronic payment) following the end of the tax year.

- Class 2 contributions are paid direct to NICO either by a monthly direct debit (four months in arrears) or twice yearly on 31 January in the tax year and 31 July following the tax year (in line with the self-assessment interim payment dates).

- Class 4 contributions are collected under self-assessment.

2 Class 1 contributions

Section overview

- Class 1 contributions are based on the employee's earnings period – weekly, monthly or annually.

- No contributions are due on earnings below the earnings threshold.

- Employees make contributions at a lower rate for earnings above the upper earnings limit.

- There are lower contributions payable if an individual is a member of a salary related occupational pension scheme and contracted out of the State Second Pension (S2P).

- An employment allowance reduces employer's secondary Class 1 contributions by £2,000 per annum.

- Directors have an annual earnings period.

C H A P T E R

15

2.1 Basis of charge to class 1 contributions

The amount of class 1 NICs payable depends on the age of the employee, the level of the employee's earnings in the **earnings period** and whether he is **contracted out** of the State Second Pension (S2P) via an occupational pension scheme.

All employees aged between 16 and state retirement age (currently 65 for men, approximately 62 for women, depending on date of birth, rising to 65 by 2018) are liable to pay class 1 primary NICs. Payments start on the employee's 16th birthday and cease when he or she reaches state retirement age. Employers must pay class 1 secondary NICs for all employees aged over 16. There is no upper age limit. [Hp151]

From December 2018 the state retirement age for both men and women will start to increase to reach 66 in October 2020, with further increases likely.

Definition

Earnings: An employee's gross pay before any allowable deductions (eg pension contributions, payroll giving, allowable expenses). Gross pay means cash payments, payment of marketable assets which are readily convertible into cash (eg gold, wine) and vouchers exchangeable for cash, goods or services.

Regardless of actual business miles per year, for NIC purposes the statutory mileage rate is the higher rate ie 45ppm. Earnings will include payments in excess of the 45ppm statutory mileage rate.

Definition

Earnings period: The period to which earnings paid to an employee are deemed to relate.

Where earnings are paid at regular intervals, the earnings period will be defined by the payment interval eg weekly or monthly. An earnings period cannot be less than seven days long. Directors have an annual earnings period which we will discuss later in this chapter.

Part of class 1 NICs are used to fund the S2P. If the employee has contracted out of the S2P by being a member of his employer's occupational pension scheme, the class 1 NICs are payable at a reduced rate.

Contracting out is only available for salary-related schemes. Therefore individuals cannot contract out of S2P if they are members of a personal pension scheme.

2.2 Primary class 1 contributions

The primary class 1 NICs for 2014/15 for employees are as follows: [Hp152]

Employee's earnings	Non-contracted out primary contributions payable	Contracted out primary contributions payable
Below lower earnings limit (LEL) (£111 per week, £481 per month, £5,772 per year)	NIL	NIL
Between LEL and primary earnings threshold (PT) (£153 per week, £663 per month or £7,956 per year)	0%	Rebate – Earnings between LEL and PT × 1.4%
Between PT and upper accrual point (UAP) (£770 per week, £3,337 monthly, £40,040 per year)	Earnings less PT × 12%	Earnings less PT × 10.6%
Between UAP and upper earnings limit (UEL) (£805 per week, £3,489 monthly, £41,865 per year)	Earnings less PT × 12%	UAP less PT × 10.6% + Earnings less UAP × 12%
In excess of UEL	UEL less PT × 12% + Earnings less UEL × 2%	UAP less PT × 10.6% + UEL less UAP × 12% + Earnings less UEL × 2%

The LEL is relevant to social security benefits. An employee qualifies for certain benefits which are based on NICs previously paid. An employee is treated as having made such contributions if his earnings fall between the LEL and PT. You will also see that there is a rebate for those who are contracted out of S2P.

Worked example: Primary contracted out contributions

Laura is employed by H Ltd and is paid £3,760 monthly. She is contracted out of S2P through her employer's salary related occupational pension scheme.

Requirement

Compute the monthly class 1 primary contributions payable by Laura.

Solution

	£
(£663 – £481) = £182 × 1.4% rebate	(3)
(£3,337 – £663) = £2,674 × 10.6%	283
(£3,489 – £3,337) = £152 × 12%	18
(£3,760 – £3,489) = £271 × 2%	5
Total	£303

In the examination, you might be asked to work out the annual NICs payable by an employee, in which case you should use the annual limits.

2.3 Secondary class 1 contributions

The secondary class 1 NICs for 2014/15 payable by employers are as follows: [Hp152]

Employee's earnings	Non-contracted out secondary contributions payable	Contracted out secondary contributions payable
Below LEL (£111 per week, £481 per month, £5,772 per year)	NIL	NIL
Between LEL and ST (£153 per week, £663 per month or £7,956 per year)	0%	Rebate – earnings between LEL and ST × 3.4%
Between ST and UAP (£770 per week, £3,337 monthly, £40,040 per year)	Earnings less ST × 13.8%	Earnings less ST × 10.4%
In excess of UAP	Earnings less ST × 13.8%	UAP less ST × 10.4% plus Earnings less UAP × 13.8%

Interactive question 1: Secondary contracted out contributions

[Difficulty level: Exam standard]

Laura is employed by H Ltd and paid £3,760 monthly. She is contracted out of S2P through her employer's salary related occupational pension scheme.

Requirement

Using the standard format below, compute the monthly class 1 secondary contributions payable by H Ltd.

£

(£.................... – £....................) = £.................... × ....% rebate   (   )

(£.................... – £....................) = £.................... × ....%

(£.................... – £....................) = £.................... × ....%   _____

Total   £ _____

See **Answer** at the end of this chapter.

Again, if you are required to compute the annual secondary NICs payable by an employer, you should use the annual limits.

2.4 Employment allowance

This section is new.

From 6 April 2014, the total secondary Class 1 NICs of most employers is reduced by £2,000 per year. This is an allowance per employer, not per employee. Therefore, if the employer's total secondary Class 1 NIC liability is less than £2,000 for 2014/15, the employer pays no secondary Class 1 NIC for the year. The allowance is taken off the first available PAYE payments of NIC in the year. For example, if the employer's secondary Class 1 NICs are £1,250 each month, in April £1,250 of the allowance is used, and the remaining £750 is used to reduce the NIC payment for May.

2.5 Directors

Where an individual is a director of a company at the start of a tax year, his earnings period is the tax year, regardless of whether he is paid at regular intervals.

Worked example: NICs for directors

Robin is a director of S Ltd. In 2014/15 he is paid £37,000, payable in 12 monthly instalments. He also received a bonus of £8,000 in December 2014. Robin is not contracted out of S2P.

Requirement

Compute the primary and secondary contributions payable.

Solution

Total earnings (£37,000 + £8,000)	£45,000

Primary contributions

	£
(£41,865 – £7,956) = £33,909 × 12%	4,069
(£45,000 – £41,865) = £3,135 × 2%	63
Total	4,132

Secondary contributions

(£45,000 – £7,956) = £37,044 × 13.8%	£5,112

The annual earnings period applies to the whole tax year, even if the individual ceases to be a director during the year.

3 Class 1A and class 1B contributions

Section overview

- Class 1A contributions are payable by employers on taxable benefits provided to employees.
- Class 1B contributions are payable by employers on the grossed-up value of earnings in a PAYE settlement agreement.

3.1 Class 1A contributions

Employers are also liable to pay class 1A contributions on taxable benefits provided to employees at the rate of 13.8%. [Hp159]

The value of the taxable benefits for NICs is generally the same as the taxable value for income tax. However, any benefits taxed as earnings under class 1 are not also subject to a class 1A charge.

3.2 Class 1B contributions

Employers are liable to pay class 1B contributions on the grossed-up value of earnings in a PAYE settlement agreement at the rate of 13.8%. [Hp159]

A PAYE settlement agreement is one between an employer and HMRC where the employer pays income tax on small employee benefits and expense payments as one amount. This means that it is not necessary to keep separate records of such amounts or enter them on forms P11D or P9D.

Worked example: Class 1B contributions

Beryl, a higher rate taxpayer, is employed by Z plc. During 2014/15, she receives an expense allowance of £120.

The expense allowance is subject to a PAYE settlement agreement.

Requirement

Calculate the class 1B contributions payable by Z plc.

Solution

Class 1B contributions = Grossed up earnings × 13.8% (£200 × 13.8%)   £28

$$\text{Grossed up earnings} = \frac{100}{60} \times £120 = £200$$

4 Class 2 and class 4 contributions

Section overview

- Class 2 contributions are paid by the self-employed at a fixed weekly rate unless the net accounting profit is less than the small earnings exception.
- Class 4 contributions are based on taxable trading income.

4.1 Class 2 contributions

A self-employed individual aged between 16 and state retirement age is required to pay flat weekly rate class 2 contributions (£2.75 per week for 2014/15). Payments start on the individual's 16th birthday and cease when the individual reaches state retirement age. [Hp159]

No contributions are payable if the individual's earnings are below the small earnings exception (£5,885 for 2014/15).

Earnings for class 2 purposes means the financial accounts net profit (not the taxable trading income) earned over the tax year.

4.2 Class 4 contributions

In addition to the flat rate class 2 liability, self-employed individuals may be liable to pay class 4 NICs based on their taxable trading income as liable to income tax. An individual is liable to pay class 4 contributions if aged 16 or over at the start of the tax year. He ceases to be liable if he has reached his retirement age at the start of the tax year. In a partnership, each partner is responsible for paying his own class 2 and class 4 contributions based on his own share of partnership profits.

Class 4 NICs for 2014/15 are: [Hp161]

Earnings	Class 4 contributions payable
Not above lower profits limit (£7,956)	Nil
Between lower profits limit (£7,956) and upper profits limit (£41,865)	Earnings less lower profits limit × 9%
In excess of upper profits limit (£41,865)	Upper limit less lower profits limit × 9% plus Earnings less upper profits limit × 2%

Interactive question 2: NIC for self employed individuals   [Difficulty level: Exam standard]

Barry is a sole trader. He makes up accounts to 5 April each year.

In the year ended 5 April 2015, Barry had taxable trading income of £44,000.

Requirement

Using the standard format below, calculate the total national insurance contributions payable by Barry for 2014/15.

              £

Class 2 contributions
.... × £.....................

Class 4 contributions
y/e 5.4.15

              £

(£..................... – £.....................) = £..................... × ....%
(£..................... – £.....................) = £..................... × ....%
Total NICs for 2014/15

See **Answer** at the end of this chapter.

5 Maximum annual contributions

Section overview

- There is a maximum annual limit on the amount of class 1 and class 2 NICs payable by an individual.
- There is also a maximum annual limit on the amount of class 4 contributions.

5.1 Introduction

The method of computing NICs could lead to excessive contributions being payable.

For example, an employed earner may have more than one employment during the tax year (at the same time or successively) or may be both employed and self employed.

5.2 Class 1 and class 2 maximum annual contributions

There is an annual maximum limit for an individual's liability to primary class 1 contributions and class 2 contributions or to class 1 primary contributions from more than one employment.

In the case where an individual has two employments, and the earnings from one exceed the upper earnings limit (2014/15: £41,865 pa), HMRC may agree to defer payment of NICs on the other employment. Contributions on earnings from this employment will only be payable at 2%.

Worked example: Class 1 NIC maximum

James had two employments. He has a salary of £49,000 from his work for J plc, and a salary of £6,000 from his work for K Ltd.

Requirement

Assuming HMRC has agreed to a deferment, what are the class 1 contributions payable by James on his K Ltd salary?

Solution

James has a salary exceeding the upper earnings limit from J plc.

Therefore class 1 on K Ltd salary is

2% × £6,000 = £120

In the case where an individual is both employed and self employed, and earnings from the employment exceed the upper earnings limit, payment of class 2 contributions may be deferred.

5.3 Class 4 maximum annual contributions

An individual who is both employed and self-employed may be liable to class 1, class 2 and class 4 contributions.

There is an annual maximum amount of class 4 contributions in this case.

Details of the computation of this annual maximum amount are not in your syllabus.

If the individual's earnings from employment exceed the upper earnings limit, payment of the class 4 contributions may be deferred so that they are only payable at 2%.

6 Self-assessment payments on account

Section overview

- An individual may be required to make payments on account of income tax and class 4 NICs based on his previous year's tax liability.

- A claim may be made to reduce payments on account.

- Fraudulent or negligent claims may result in a penalty being imposed.

- Interest will be payable on any excess reduction in a payment on account.

6.1 Payments on account

A taxpayer may be required to make two payments on account (POAs) of his liability to income tax and Class 4 NICs. The first POA is due by 31 January in the tax year. The second payment on account is due by 31 July following the end of the tax year. [Hp12]

Interest is payable on late paid POAs. There is no penalty for late paid POAs.

The amount of each POA is generally half of the income tax and class 4 NICs paid under self-assessment for the previous year.

Payments on account are not required where the amount of the tax paid under self-assessment in the previous tax year was less than: [Hp12]

- £1,000; or
- 20% of the total income tax and class 4 liability.

6.2 Reduction in POAs

A taxpayer may wish to reduce his POAs, for example if there was an unusually large liability in the previous tax year which is not likely to be repeated in the current tax year or there is a change in his personal circumstances (eg retirement).

He may make a claim to reduce his POAs stating that he believes his liability will be:

- A stated amount which is less than the liability for the previous year; or
- Nil.

He must state the grounds for his belief in the claim.

6.3 Penalties for incorrect reduction

If the taxpayer's actual liability is higher than his estimate when making the claim to reduce his POAs, a penalty may be imposed if the claim was made fraudulently or negligently.

The maximum amount of the penalty is the difference between the amount that would have been paid but for the incorrect statement and the amount of the payments on account actually made.

6.4 Interest on reduced payments on account

Interest will be payable if the taxpayer's actual liability is higher than his estimate when making the claim to reduce his POAs.

The general rule is that interest is payable on each POA on the lower of:

- The reduced POA plus 50% of the balancing payment; and
- The amount which would have been payable had no claim for reduction been made,

less the POA actually paid.

Interest runs from the original due date to the day before payment of the balance of the POA is made.

Worked example: Reduction in POAs

Aileen had an income tax/class 4 liability of £12,000 for 2013/14.

She made a claim to reduce her POAs for 2014/15 to £4,500 each. She paid the first POA on 25 January 2015 and the second POA on 20 August 2015.

Aileen's actual liability to income tax/class 4 for 2014/15 was £10,000. Aileen made a balancing payment of £1,000 on 28 January 2016.

Requirement

Calculate the interest payable on the POAs. Assume an interest rate of 3% pa and work to the nearest day and pound.

Solution

Aileen was originally due to pay £6,000 (£12,000 × 50%) as her POA. She reduced this to £4,500.

Interest will be charged on the lower of:

- Reduced POA (£4,500) plus 50% of balancing payment (£500) = £5,000
- Original POA (£12,000/2) = £6,000

ie £5,000 less the POA actually paid (£4,500) = £500.

First POA
Due 31 January 2015, paid on time
Interest on excessive reduction in POA
1 February 2015 to 27 January 2016

	£
Interest on £500 × 3% × $\dfrac{361}{365}$	15

Second POA
Due 31 July 2015, paid on 20 August 2015
Interest on late paid POA
1 August 2015 to 19 August 2015

Interest on £4,500 × 3% × $\dfrac{19}{365}$	7

Interest on excessive reduction in POA
1 August 2015 to 27 January 2016

Interest on £500 × 3% × $\dfrac{180}{365}$	7
Total interest payable	29

Summary and Self-test

Summary

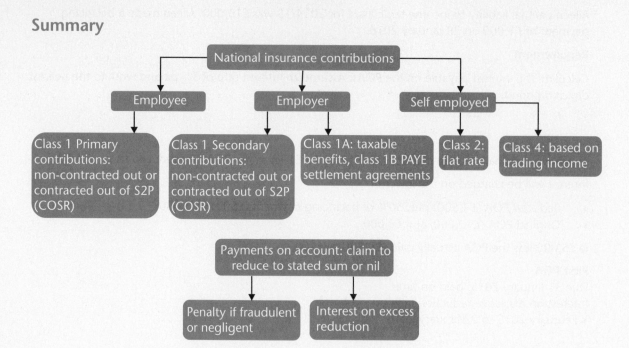

National insurance contributions

Employee

Employer

Self employed

Class 1 Primary contributions: non-contracted out or contracted out of S2P (COSR)

Class 1 Secondary contributions: non-contracted out or contracted out of S2P (COSR)

Class 1A: taxable benefits, class 1B PAYE settlement agreements

Class 2: flat rate

Class 4: based on trading income

Payments on account: claim to reduce to stated sum or nil

Penalty if fraudulent or negligent

Interest on excess reduction

Self-test

Answer the following questions.

1 Julie works part time for D Ltd earning £15,000 per year. In 2014/15, she benefits for the first time from childcare vouchers provided by D Ltd of £55 per week for 50 weeks in the tax year. Julie has a company car on which there is a taxable benefit of £4,500 per year.

Julie is also self-employed and has taxable trading income of £8,000 for 2014/15.

What National Insurance contributions are Julie and D Ltd (in respect of Julie) required to make?

	Julie	D Ltd
A	Class 1 on £17,750, class 4 on £8,000	Class 1 on £17,750, class 1A on £4,500
B	Class 1 on £15,000, class 4 on £8,000	Class 1 on £15,000, class 1A on £7,250
C	Class 1 on £17,750, class 2, class 4 on £8,000	Class 1 on £17,750, class 1A on £4,500
D	Class 1 on £15,000, class 2, class 4 on £8,000	Class 1 on £15,000, class 1A on £4,500

2 Alan is a director of Y plc.

Alan receives a salary of £34,000 in 2014/15, paid monthly. He also receives a bonus of £12,000 in March 2015.

Alan is contracted out of S2P through the company's salary related occupational pension scheme.

What are the primary class 1 contributions payable by Alan for 2014/15?

A £4,152
B £3,734
C £3,703
D £3,672

3 In 2014/15 Richard had taxable trading income of £10,500 and employment income of £6,000.

During 2014/15 he paid a personal pension contribution of £1,200.

What is his trading income for class 4 NICs?

A £10,500
B £9,300
C £15,000
D £16,500

4 Dwayne has two employments during 2014/15. In employment 1, he earns £8,000 and in employment 2 he earns £47,000.

What are Dwayne's class 1 contributions for employment 1?

A NIL
B £160
C £5
D £960

5 Serena's POAs for 2014/15 based on her previous year's liability were £1,500.

She made a claim to reduce her payments on account to £250. Both POAs were paid on time.

Serena's actual liability for 2014/15 was £4,000.

On what POA amount will interest be payable?

A NIL
B £1,250
C £1,750
D £2,000

6   **Keith**

Keith is self-employed. He makes up his accounts to 5 April each year.

The following information relates to 2014/15:

(1)   Keith's taxable trading income for the year to 5 April 2015 was £15,040. This is after taking account of any employer's national insurance contributions.

(2)   Keith has two weekly paid employees, John and Louise. They receive wages of £8,840 and £12,480 gross per year. He also paid John a bonus of £700 during the week commencing 18 December 2014.

John has occasional use of a pool car from Keith. Louise receives medical insurance cover for her family which costs Keith £1,040 pa. Keith also provides small benefits for both John and Louise valued at £200 per year, which are covered by a PAYE settlement agreement.

Requirement

Calculate all the national insurance contributions which Keith should account to HMRC for 2014/15 and state how they will be paid.   **(10 marks)**

Now go back to the Learning Objectives in the Introduction. If you are satisfied you have achieved these objectives please tick them off.

Technical reference

Legislation

National insurance contributions

References relate to Social Security Contributions and Benefits Act 1992 (*SSCBA 1992*)

Class 1 contributions	ss.5 – 9
Class 1A contributions	s.10
Class 1B contributions	s.10A
Class 2 contributions	s.11
Class 4 contributions	ss.15 – 16

Self-assessment payments on account

References relate to Taxes Management Act 1970 (*TMA 1970*)

Claim to reduce payments on account	s.59A
Interest	s.86

HMRC manual references

National insurance manual

(Found at http://www.hmrc.gov.uk/manuals/nimmanual/index.htm)

Class 1 Structural Overview: General	NIM01001
Class 2 Liability: Liability for class 2 NICs	NIM20004
Class 4 NICs Liability: General	NIM24001

Income Tax Self Assessment: The Legal Framework

(Found at http://www.hmrc.gov.uk/manuals/salfmanual/Index.htm)

Payment of Tax: Payments on Account	SALF303

> This technical reference section is designed to assist you. It should help you know where to look for further information on the topics covered in this chapter.

CHAPTER

15

Answer to Interactive question 1

	£
(£663 – £481) = £182 × 3.4% rebate	(6)
(£3,337 – £663) = £2,674 × 10.4%	278
(£3,760 – £3,337) = £423 × 13.8%	58
Total	330

Answer to Interactive question 2

Class 2 contributions

	£
52 × £2.75	143

Class 4 contributions

y/e 5.4.15

	£	£
(£41,865 – £7,956) = £33,909 × 9%	3,052	
(£44,000 – £41,865) = £2,135 × 2%	43	3,095
Total NICs for 2014/15		3,238

1 D – Julie class 1 on £15,000, class 2, class 4 on £8,000, D Ltd class 1 on £15,000, class 1A on £4,500

Julie and D Ltd pay class 1 contributions on Julie's earnings. Childcare vouchers up to £55 per week are exempt as her earnings and taxable benefit are at the basic rate level.

Class 1A contributions are payable by D Ltd on the taxable benefit of the car.

2 D – £3,672

Total earnings (£34,000 + £12,000)   £46,000

Primary contributions

	£
(£7,956 – £5,772) = £2,184 × 1.4% rebate	(31)
(£40,040 – £7,956) = £32,084 × 10.6%	3,401
(£41,865 – £40,040) = £1,825 × 12%	219
(£46,000 – £41,865) = £4,135 × 2%	83
Total	£3,672

3 A – £10,500

Taxable trading income for class 4 = £10,500

Personal pension contributions are not deductible for class 4 NICs.

4 B – £160

£8,000 × 2% = £160

As employment 2 earnings of £47,000 exceed the upper earnings limit of £41,865 Dwayne will pay 2% NIC on his earning from employment 1.

5 B – £1,250

Interest will be charged on the lower of:

- Reduced POA (£250) plus 50% of balancing payment (£1,750) = £2,000
- Original POA (£1,500)

ie £1,500 less the POA actually paid (£250) = £1,250

6 Keith – National insurance contributions accountable 2014/15

Class 1 primary NICs

Deducted by Keith from employee's gross pay.

		£
John	(£170 – £153) × 12% × 51 weeks	104
	(£805 – £153) × 12% × 1 week	78
	(£870 – £805) × 2% × 1 week	1
Total for John		183
Louise	(£240 – £153) × 12% × 52 weeks	543
Total class 1 primary NICs		726

Paid via PAYE monthly

Class 1 secondary NICs

Payable by Keith as employer

		£
John	(£170 – £153) × 13.8% × 51 weeks	120
	(£870 – £153) × 13.8% × 1 week	99
Louise	(£240 – £153) × 13.8% × 52 weeks	624
Total class 1 secondary NICs		843

This would be paid via PAYE monthly but because this is less than £2,000 (the employment allowance), no Class 1 secondary NIC is due in 2014/15.

Class 1A NICs

Payable by Keith as employer

£1,040 × 13.8%   £144

Pool car is exempt benefit.

Payable in one sum by 19 July 2015 (22 July 2015 if paid electronically).

Class 1B NICs

Payable by Keith as employer

Both employees are basic rate taxpayers so grossed up benefits subject to PAYE settlement agreement are:

$$\frac{100}{80} \times £200 = £250$$

£250 × 13.8% × 2   £69

Payable in one sum by 19 October 2015 (22 October 2015 if paid electronically).

Class 2 NICs

Payable by Keith as self-employed person

£2.75 × 52   £143

Payable direct to NICO either by a monthly direct debit (four months in arrears) or twice yearly on 31 January in the tax year and 31 July following the tax year (in line with the self-assessment interim payment dates)

Class 4 NICs

Payable by Keith as self-employed person

Taxable trading income for class 4

(£15,040 – £7,956) × 9%   £638

Paid with income tax under self-assessment.

CHAPTER 16

Inheritance tax – basic principles

Introduction

Examination context

Topic List

Introduction

Learning objectives

- Explain the principles of inheritance tax and identify the different classes of taxpayer liable to pay inheritance tax ☐

- Explain when the lifetime transfer of an asset gives rise to an inheritance tax liability, calculate the inheritance tax payable on chargeable lifetime transfers in straightforward scenarios ☐

- Calculate the death tax due on lifetime transfers ☐

- Describe the circumstances in which taper relief applies and calculate the amount of relief available in a given situation ☐

Specific syllabus references for this chapter are 2e, 2g, 2h and 2j.

Syllabus links

Inheritance tax was not covered in your Principles of Taxation study manual.

Examination context

In the examination candidates may be required to:

- Compute the value of a transfer after deducting available exemptions

- Calculate tax payable on lifetime gifts both when made, and on the death of the donor, taking account of taper relief

Candidates sometimes have difficulty in applying the nil rate band to transfers. However easy marks are usually available for deducting the relevant exemptions.

1 Scope of Inheritance Tax (IHT)

Section overview

- IHT is chargeable on a transfer of value of chargeable property made by a chargeable person.

- A transfer of value is a disposition which results in a diminution of the transferor's estate (eg a gift).

- The creation of a trust may be a transfer of value.

- Certain dispositions are specifically excluded from being transfers of value (eg for maintenance of family).

- Chargeable property is all property with the exception of excluded property.

- All individuals are liable to IHT but non-UK domiciled individuals are only chargeable on assets situated in the UK.

1.1 Transfers of value

A charge to IHT arises if a **transfer of value** of **chargeable property** is made by a **chargeable person** (the **transferor**). This charge may arise during the lifetime of the transferor or on his death, for example when property passes under the terms of his will.

A transfer of value is a **disposition** (eg a gift) of assets by a transferor which results in a fall in the value of the transferor's estate.

The fall in value of the transferor's estate is known as the **diminution in value** and it is the starting point in calculating the value of a gift for inheritance tax purposes.

In general, the diminution in the value of an estate as a result of a gift is equivalent to the open market value of the asset transferred at the time of the transfer. However this is not always the case. We will look at the situation where the diminution in value is something other than the value of the asset transferred later in this study manual.

A charge to IHT often arises when an individual (a **settlor**) creates a **settlement** (also known as a **trust**) by giving assets to **trustees** who hold the assets under the terms of the settlement for the benefit of the **beneficiaries** of the settlement.

1.1.1 Discretionary trusts

For IHT purposes, since no beneficiary of a discretionary trust has a right to any of the property in the trust, the trust property does not form part of the estate of an individual beneficiary. Therefore, special IHT rules apply to discretionary trust property. You do not need to know these special rules in your examination. However, you will be expected to deal with the IHT consequences of the creation of a discretionary trust both during the lifetime of the settlor or on his death.

1.1.2 Interest in possession trusts

Where an interest in possession trust was created before 22 March 2006, the beneficiary with the interest in possession is treated as if he owned the trust property outright and it is therefore part of his estate for IHT purposes.

This rule still applies to interest in possession trusts created on the death of the settlor, and a limited number of qualifying interest in possession trusts created in the settlor's lifetime from 22 March 2006.

This rule no longer applies to non-qualifying interest in possession trusts created in the settlor's lifetime from 22 March 2006. In this case, the trust property will be subject to the same rules as for discretionary trusts.

You will be expected to deal with the IHT consequences of the creation of an interest in possession trust during the lifetime of the settlor or on his death. You will also be expected to deal with the IHT implications of the death of the life tenant. The IHT chargeable on the interest in possession trust itself is outside the scope of your syllabus.

1.1.3 Bare trusts

Such trusts are treated as transparent for tax purposes. Consequently the transfer of assets to bare trustees is treated as an outright gift to the beneficiary and will be a PET by the settlor.

As the beneficiary of a bare trust is absolutely entitled to the trust property, that property will be included in the value of the beneficiary's free estate on death, not his settled property (see later in this study manual). Lifetime transfers of trust property by the trustee will be treated as transfers by the beneficiary.

In the examination, you will be told which type of trust the settlor has created and, in the case of an interest in possession trust created after 22 March 2006, whether it is a qualifying trust. You will not be expected to know the definitions of the different types of trust.

1.2 Dispositions which are not transfers of value

Inheritance tax covers dispositions of property, or interests in property. However, some dispositions are not treated as transfers of value for inheritance tax purposes.

The most important dispositions outside of the scope of IHT are:

- Dispositions without gratuitous intent (eg genuine commercial transactions which result in a loss and consequent reduction in the value of the transferor's estate);

- Dispositions made for the maintenance of the transferor's family, including spouses/civil partners, children, dependant relatives;

- Gratuitous dispositions which constitute allowable expenditure for the purposes of income tax and corporation tax (eg payments made by an employer into a pension fund for the benefit of employees).

1.3 Chargeable property

All property is chargeable property for IHT purposes unless it is defined as **excluded property**.

The main example of excluded property which is examinable is foreign assets of a non-UK domiciled individual, that is, property situated outside the UK which is owned by a person who, in general terms, does not have his permanent home in the UK.

1.4 Chargeable persons

All individuals are chargeable persons for IHT, but the extent of their liability depends on their domicile status.

An individual who is domiciled in the UK is liable to IHT in relation to all of his worldwide property.

An individual who is not domiciled in the UK is liable to IHT only in relation to property situated in the UK. His non-UK property is excluded property.

Trustees are also chargeable persons for IHT, but you will not be expected to deal with charges to IHT on trustees in your examination.

2 Exempt transfers

Section overview

- An exempt transfer has no effect for IHT.

- A transfer to a spouse/civil partner is exempt (lifetime and death).

- A transfer to a charity is exempt (lifetime and death).

- A transfer to a qualifying political party is exempt (lifetime and death).

- Lifetime transfers up to £3,000 per tax year are exempt (annual exemption).

- Lifetime transfers on the occasion of a marriage/civil partnership are exempt up to certain amounts.

- Lifetime transfers up to £250 per transferee per tax year are exempt.

- Lifetime transfers made as part of normal expenditure out of income are exempt.

2.1 Introduction

There are a number of transfers of value which are specifically defined as exempt transfers.

An exempt transfer has no effect for IHT so no IHT can be payable on it and it does not form part of the cumulation of transfers (see later in this chapter).

An exempt transfer can be a transfer of value which is wholly exempt or it can be part of a larger transfer of value.

Some exemptions only apply when the transfer is made by the transferor in his lifetime.

Some exemptions apply where the transfer is made during the lifetime of the transferor or where the transfer is made on his death.

2.2 Transfer to spouse/civil partner

A transfer of value is an exempt transfer if the transferee is the transferor's spouse/civil partner.

The transfer may be:

- A lifetime transfer or a transfer on death to the spouse/civil partner;

- A lifetime transfer to an interest in possession trust for the spouse/civil partner (provided it was before 22 March 2006 or was to a qualifying interest in possession trust); or

- A transfer on death to an interest in possession trust for the spouse/civil partner.

2.3 Gifts to charities

A transfer of value is an exempt transfer if the transferee is a charity. This applies to a lifetime transfer or a transfer made on death.

The property transferred must be used by the charity for charitable purposes following the transfer.

2.4 Gifts to political parties

A transfer of value is an exempt transfer if the transferee is a qualifying political party. This applies to a lifetime transfer or a transfer made on death.

Definition

Qualifying political party: A political party which, at the last general election before the transfer of value was made, had:

- Two Members of Parliament elected to the House of Commons; or
- One Member of Parliament elected to the House of Commons and not less than 150,000 votes were given to candidates who were members of that party.

2.5 Annual exemption

Lifetime transfers of value made by a transferor in any one tax year are exempt to the extent that they do not exceed £3,000 (the **annual exemption**). [Hp104]

If one or more transfers of value exceed £3,000 in any one tax year, £3,000 of the total amount of the transfers is exempt. If there is more than one transfer of value in the tax year, the annual exemption is used against transfers in chronological order even if a transfer is a PET, which is initially exempt.

If the transferor does not use all of his annual exemption in a tax year, the unused excess can be carried forward to be used in the next tax year, but not any further. However, the current year's annual exemption is used first.

Worked example: Annual exemption

Daniel made the following cash gifts to his children:

1 July 2012	£1,300 to son	15 May 2013	£800 to son
22 October 2012	£3,700 to daughter	26 June 2014	£7,500 to son

Requirement

Show the amount of each of the transfers after deduction of the annual exemption.

Solution

1 July 2012

	£
Cash	1,300
Less CY annual exemption 2012/13 (part)	(1,300)
Transfer	NIL

22 October 2012

	£
Cash	3,700
Less: CY annual exemption 2012/13 (balance)	(1,700)
PY annual exemption 2011/12 b/f	(2,000)
Transfer	NIL

15 May 2013

	£
Cash	800
Less CY annual exemption 2013/14 (part)	(800)
Transfer	NIL

26 June 2014

	£
Cash	7,500
Less: CY annual exemption 2014/15	(3,000)
PY annual exemption 2013/14 (balance) b/f	(2,200)
Transfer	2,300

ICAEW

2.6 Marriage/civil partnership exemption

Lifetime transfers of value made by a transferor are exempt if the transfer is made to one of the parties to a marriage/civil partnership in consideration of that marriage/civil partnership taking place.

The transfer is exempt to the extent that it does not exceed: [Hp105]

- £5,000 where the transferor is a parent of one of the parties to the marriage/civil partnership

- £2,500 where the transferor is a remoter ancestor (eg grandparent) of one of the parties to the marriage/civil partnership or where the transferor is one of the parties to the marriage/civil partnership

- £1,000 in any other case

If the transfer of value exceeds the relevant amount, the part of the transfer up to the relevant amount is exempt.

Where the marriage/civil partnership exemption and the annual exemption are both available in relation to the same transfer, use the marriage/civil partnership exemption in priority to the annual exemption.

2.7 Small gifts exemption

Lifetime transfers of value made by a transferor in any one tax year are exempt if they do not exceed £250 to any one transferee. [Hp104]

Note that, unlike the annual exemption and the marriage exemption, it is not possible to use the small gifts exemption to exempt part of a larger gift.

Interactive question 1: Exemptions   [Difficulty level: Intermediate]

Paula made the following gifts:

10 April 2013	£2,000 to grandson
16 August 2013	£12,000 to the Save the Children Fund (a registered charity)
22 November 2013	£3,800 to daughter
8 April 2014	£5,500 to niece on her marriage
12 June 2014	£225 to friend

Requirement

Using the standard format below, calculate the value of each of the transfers after deduction of all exemptions.

10 April 2013

	£
Cash	
Less exemption	(_____)
Transfer	

16 August 2013

	£
Cash	
Less exemption	(_____)
Transfer	

22 November 2013

	£
Cash	
Less: exemption	(_____)
Exemption	(_____)
Transfer	

8 April 2014

	£
Cash	
Less: exemption	( )
exemption	( )
Transfer	

12 June 2014

	£
Cash	
Less exemption	( )
Transfer	

See **Answer** at the end of this chapter.

2.8 Normal expenditure out of income exemption

A lifetime transfer of value is exempt if, or to the extent that:

- It is made as part of the normal expenditure out of income of the transferor; and

- It is made (taking one year with another) out of the transferor's income; and

- After taking account of all transfers which are part of his normal expenditure out of income, he is left with sufficient income to maintain his usual standard of living.

The amount of the exemption is not limited to a specific amount, but, of course, it will be limited in relation to the transferor's income.

In order to qualify as normal expenditure out of income, it must be shown that the transfer is part of a regular pattern of giving or, at least, that the transferor intended it to be part of such a regular pattern.

3 Lifetime transfers

Section overview

- A lifetime transfer of value can be a chargeable lifetime transfer (CLT) or a potentially exempt transfer (PET).

- The creation of any trust (other than a bare trust or qualifying IIP) is now a CLT.

- Lifetime tax is chargeable on a CLT and additional tax may be payable if the transferor dies within seven years of making the CLT.

- The additional tax on death is chargeable at a reduced rate if the transferor survives between three and seven years (taper relief).

- A transfer of value to another individual (other than spouse/civil partner) or a bare trust is a PET.

- The creation of an interest in possession trust for another individual (other than spouse/civil partner) or an accumulation and maintenance trust before 22 March 2006 is a PET.

- The creation of a **qualifying** interest in possession trust for another individual (other than spouse/civil partner) after 22 March 2006 is still a PET.

- A PET is treated as an exempt transfer during the lifetime of the transferor and is an exempt transfer if he survives seven years.

- If the transferor does not survive seven years from making a PET, it is a chargeable transfer and IHT may be payable on it, subject to taper relief.

- Where a lifetime transfer falls in value between the date of the gift and the transferor's death, fall in value relief is given.

3.1 Types of lifetime transfer

There are two types of lifetime transfer:

- Chargeable lifetime transfer (CLT)
- Potentially exempt transfer (PET)

A CLT is immediately chargeable to IHT when it is made. In addition, further tax may be payable on a CLT if the transferor dies within seven years of making the transfer.

A PET is treated as an exempt transfer during the lifetime of the transferor. If the transferor survives seven years from making the transfer, the PET is an exempt transfer and has no IHT consequences. However, if the transferor dies within seven years of making the PET, it is a chargeable transfer and IHT may be payable.

3.2 Chargeable lifetime transfers – calculation of lifetime tax

We will first consider the calculation of lifetime tax on a chargeable lifetime transfer.

A chargeable lifetime transfer is made on the creation of a relevant property trust:

- A discretionary trust
- A non-qualifying interest in possession trust on or after 22 March 2006

Lifetime IHT on a CLT made in 2014/15 is chargeable at the following rates of tax: [Hp103]

Chargeable transfer of value	Rate of tax
£0 – £325,000	0%
£325,001 onwards	20%

The band on which the 0% rate of tax is chargeable is called the **nil rate band**. This band is not exempt from tax, but is chargeable at 0%. You will see why this is important when we look at the situation where the transferor makes more than one chargeable transfer.

The nil rate band is £325,000 for 2014/15.

First, let us consider the situation where there is only one chargeable transfer.

Worked example: Chargeable lifetime transfer

On 1 July 2014, Seth created a discretionary trust and gave £342,000 in cash to the trustees. This was the first transfer of value that Seth had made. The trustees agreed to pay any IHT due on the transfer.

Requirement

Compute the IHT payable on the transfer.

Solution

As this is the first transfer of value made by Seth, he can set his annual exemption for 2014/15 against the cash gift and also his 2013/14 annual exemption:

	£
Cash	342,000
Less: annual exemption 2014/15	(3,000)
annual exemption 2013/14 b/f	(3,000)
Gross transfer of value	336,000
Less nil rate band 2014/15	(325,000)
Excess over nil band	11,000
IHT on £11,000 @ 20%	2,200

Note the calculation of the **gross transfer of value**. This will be important later.

IHT is a cumulative tax. This means that you need to look back seven years from the date of a chargeable transfer to see whether some or all of the nil rate band has been used up by gross chargeable transfers in that **seven year cumulation period**.

Worked example: Previous chargeable lifetime transfers

On 1 July 2014, Delia created a discretionary trust and gave £65,000 in cash to the trustees. This was the first transfer of value that Delia had made.

On 10 December 2014, Delia gave the trustees a further £400,000 in cash.

The trustees agreed to pay any IHT due on the transfers.

Requirement

Compute the IHT payable on the transfers.

Solution

1 July 2014

	£
Cash	65,000
Less: annual exemption 2014/15	(3,000)
annual exemption 2013/14 b/f	(3,000)
Gross transfer of value	59,000
Less nil rate band 2014/15	(325,000)
Excess over nil band	NIL

There is no IHT payable on this transfer.

10 December 2014

	£	£
Cash (no annual exemptions due so also gross transfer of value)		400,000
Nil rate band 2014/15	325,000	
Less gross transfer of value in 7 years before CLT (after 10 December 2007)	(59,000)	
Nil rate band available		(266,000)
Excess over nil band		134,000
IHT on £134,000 @ 20%		26,800

You may have noticed that, in the two examples we have looked at so far, the trustees paid the IHT due. However the trustees only pay the lifetime tax if they specifically agree to do so for each transfer. The transferor is otherwise liable for the lifetime tax.

If the transferor pays the IHT, this is a further diminution in his estate. He has made a **net chargeable transfer of value** of the amount of the transfer to the trustees, but we must compute tax on the gross chargeable transfer of value.

You have already met the idea of grossing up interest and dividends in the income tax computation, but the process is a little more complicated for IHT because of the nil rate band.

Where the transferor makes a net chargeable transfer of value, the amount of the transfer in excess of the available nil rate band will grossed up by:

$$\frac{100}{(100-20)}$$

The grossed up amount is then taxed at 20%.

We can simplify this calculation by saying that the tax on the amount of the transfer in excess of the available nil rate band is:

$$\frac{100}{(100-20)} \times \frac{20}{100} = \frac{20}{80}$$

The gross transfer of value is the net transfer of value plus the IHT paid by the transferor.

In the examination assume that the transferor pays the lifetime tax on each transfer, unless the question specifically states otherwise.

Worked example: Net transfer of value

On 12 August 2014, Wilma created a non-qualifying IIP trust and gave £378,000 in cash to the trustees. This was the first transfer of value that Wilma had made.

Requirement

Compute the IHT payable on the transfer and the amount of the gross chargeable transfer carried forward in the cumulation.

Solution

	£
Cash	378,000
Less: annual exemption 2014/15	(3,000)
annual exemption 2013/14 b/f	(3,000)
Net transfer of value	372,000
Less nil rate band 2014/15	(325,000)
Excess over nil band	47,000
IHT on £47,000 @ 20/80 (Wilma pays the tax)	11,750
Net transfer of value	372,000
Add IHT paid by transferor	11,750
Gross chargeable transfer of value	383,750

Note: You can check whether you have grossed up correctly by working out the IHT on the gross chargeable transfer of value:

	£
Gross transfer of value	383,750
Less nil rate band 2014/15	(325,000)
Excess over nil band	58,750
IHT on £58,750 @ 20%	11,750

The nil rate band can change every tax year. You may have to deal with transfers from previous years. The most important thing to remember is that once a transfer has a value as a gross chargeable transfer of value, this amount does not change, even if the nil rate band changes.

Worked example: Changes in nil rate band

On 13 December 2008, Robin created a discretionary trust and gave £324,000 in cash to the trustees. This was the first transfer of value that Robin had made. The nil rate band for 2008/09 was £312,000.

On 15 June 2014, Robin gave the trustees £300,000 in cash. The trustees agreed to pay any IHT due on this transfer.

Requirement

Compute the IHT payable on the transfers.

Solution

13 December 2008

	£
Cash	324,000
Less: annual exemption 2008/09	(3,000)
annual exemption 2007/08 b/f	(3,000)
Net transfer of value	318,000
Less nil rate band 2008/09	(312,000)
Excess over nil band	6,000
IHT on £6,000 @ 20/80 (Robin pays the tax)	1,500
Net chargeable transfer of value	318,000
Add IHT paid by transferor	1,500
Gross chargeable transfer of value	319,500

15 June 2014

	£	£
Cash		300,000
Less: annual exemption 2014/15		(3,000)
annual exemption 2013/14 b/f		(3,000)
Gross transfer of value		294,000
Nil rate band 2014/15	325,000	
Less gross transfer of value in 7 years before CLT (ie since 15.6.07)	(319,500)	
Nil rate band available		(5,500)
Excess over nil band		288,500
IHT on £288,500 @ 20%		57,700

3.3 Chargeable lifetime transfers – calculation of additional tax on death

If the transferor of a chargeable lifetime transfer dies within seven years of making the transfer, additional IHT may be payable on the transfer. The IHT is calculated using the nil rate band at the date of death (**not** the date of the CLT). However, you still need to look back seven years from the date of the CLT (**not** seven years from the date of death) to see whether any of the nil rate band has been used up.

Additional IHT on a CLT where the transferor dies in 2014/15 is chargeable at the following rates of tax: [Hp103]

Chargeable transfer of value £	Rate of tax
0 – 325,000	0%
325,001 onwards	40%

The above rates assume that the transfer has not claimed any unused nil rate band on the death of a spouse/civil partner. The consequences of such a claim are covered in the next chapter.

The primary liability for additional tax on a CLT as the result of the transferor's death falls on the transferee. This means there is no grossing up calculation required.

Remember that this is a charge to **additional** tax: if the death tax is equal to or less than the lifetime tax paid, there is no additional tax due. However, there is no repayment of lifetime tax in this situation.

Worked example: Additional IHT on death

On 1 November 2012, Mary created a non-qualifying trust in which her son had an interest in possession and gave £553,000 in cash to the trustees. This was the first transfer of value that Mary had made.

Mary died on 10 March 2015.

Requirement

Compute the additional IHT payable on the transfer as a result of Mary's death.

Solution

First, you need to work out the lifetime tax paid by Mary in 2012/13.

	£
Cash	553,000
Less: annual exemption 2012/13	(3,000)
annual exemption 2011/12 b/f	(3,000)
Net transfer of value	547,000
Less nil rate band at date of gift ie 2012/13 (less any gross transfers since 1.11.05)	(325,000)
Excess over nil band	222,000
IHT on £222,000 @ 20/80	55,500
Net chargeable transfer of value	547,000
Add IHT paid by transferor	55,500
Gross chargeable transfer of value	602,500

Now use the gross chargeable transfer of value to work out the additional tax payable by the trustees on Mary's death in 2014/15:

	£
Gross transfer of value	602,500
Less nil rate band at time of death ie 2014/15 (less any gross transfers since 1.11.05)	(325,000)
Excess over nil band	277,500
IHT on £277,500 @ 40%	111,000
Less lifetime tax paid	(55,500)
Additional tax payable by trustees	55,500

If the transferor survives more than three years after the CLT, but less than seven years, the additional tax on death is charged at the following percentages of the full amount: [Hp110]

Period between CLT and death	% chargeable
More than 3 years but not 4 years	80%
More than 4 years but not 5 years	60%
More than 5 years but not 6 years	40%
More than 6 years but not 7 years	20%

This reduction in tax is called **taper relief.**

Interactive question 2: Taper relief
[Difficulty level: Intermediate]

On 15 July 2005, Eric made a gross chargeable transfer of value of £62,000.

On 21 November 2011, Eric created a discretionary trust and gave the trustees £424,000 in cash. The trustees agreed to pay any lifetime IHT due on the transfer.

Eric died on 9 March 2015.

Requirement

Using the standard format below, compute any additional IHT payable by the trustees on Eric's death.

Once again, you need to look at the lifetime position first:

21 November 2011

	£	£
Cash		
Less: annual exemption 20 ...../.....		( )
annual exemption 20 ...../..... b/f		( )
Gross chargeable transfer of value		
Nil rate band 20 ...../.....		
Less gross transfer of value in 7 years before CLT (after ....)	( )	
Nil rate band available		( )
Excess over nil band		
IHT on £........................ @ ....%		

Then think about the position on Eric's death:

9 March 2015

	£	£
Gross transfer of value		
Less: nil rate band 20 ...../.....		
gross transfer of value in 7 years before CLT (after ....)	( )	( )
Excess over nil band		
IHT on £........................ @ ....%		
Transferor survived .... years but not .... years		
Chargeable ....% × £........................		
Less: lifetime tax paid		( )
Additional tax payable by trustees		

See **Answer** at the end of this chapter.

3.4 Potentially exempt transfers

3.4.1 Transfers treated as PETs

A PET is made on a transfer by the transferor to:

- An individual (other than his spouse/civil partner)

- A trust in which an individual (other than the settlor or his spouse/civil partner) has an interest in possession where the trust was made before 22 March 2006

- A trust in which an individual (other than the settlor or his spouse/civil partner) has an interest in possession where the trust was made after 22 March 2006 and is treated as a **qualifying** trust (unusual)

- A bare trust

- A special type of discretionary trust for children called an accumulation and maintenance (A&M) trust created before 22 March 2006

3.4.2 Allocation of exemptions

There is no lifetime charge to IHT on a PET. Remember that the annual exemption and marriage exemption (if applicable) are deducted from the gift to find the amount of the PET which may become chargeable in the future.

Remember that if there is more than one transfer of value in the tax year, the annual exemption is used against transfers in chronological order even if a transfer is a PET, which is initially exempt. So if a PET is made before a CLT in the same tax year, the annual exemption will be allocated to the PET first and any unused balance can then be allocated to the CLT. If the donor survives seven years from making the PET the exemption allocated to the PET will have been wasted as the PET will be completely exempt.

3.4.3 Treatment in lifetime

Whilst the transferor is alive, it is assumed that a PET is an exempt transfer. Therefore, during the lifetime of the transferor, no IHT is chargeable on the PET and it should not be included in the cumulation when working out lifetime tax on CLTs.

3.4.4 Treatment on death

If the transferor dies more than seven years after making a PET, the PET is an exempt transfer. This is particularly important to note when looking back at transfers in the seven year cumulation period. Only if a PET becomes chargeable will it use up the nil rate band for calculating the death tax on later gifts or the death estate. So if a PET never becomes chargeable it is not taken into account when calculating the remaining nil rate band.

If the transferor dies within seven years of making the PET, the PET is a chargeable transfer. IHT is calculated on the PET in a similar way to the additional tax on a CLT. The only difference is that there will be no lifetime tax to deduct. Again, it will be the transferee who has primary liability to pay the IHT due and so there is no grossing up calculation required.

Remember to use the nil rate band at the date of death, but look back seven years from the date the PET was made to see if there are any chargeable transfers to cumulate.

Worked example: PETs

Graham made the following gifts during his life:

11 July 2007	Cash of £105,000 to son on his son's marriage
12 September 2008	Land valued at £265,000 to daughter
23 December 2010	Cash of £75,000 to son

Graham died on 22 October 2014.

Requirement

Compute the IHT payable as a result of Graham's death.

Solution

11 July 2007

	£
Cash gift to son	105,000
Less: marriage exemption	(5,000)
annual exemption 2007/08	(3,000)
annual exemption 2006/07 b/f	(3,000)
Potentially exempt transfer	94,000

Transferor survived more than seven years from making this PET and therefore it is an exempt transfer.

12 September 2008

	£
Land given to daughter	265,000
Less annual exemption 2008/09	(3,000)
Potentially exempt transfer	262,000
Less nil rate band at death 2014/15	(325,000)
Excess over nil band	NIL

There is no IHT payable on this transfer.

23 December 2010

	£	£
Cash gift to son		75,000
Less: annual exemption 2010/11		(3,000)
annual exemption 2009/10 b/f		(3,000)
Potentially exempt transfer		69,000
Nil rate band at death 2014/15	325,000	
Less gross transfer of value in 7 years before PET (after 23 December 2003)	(262,000)	
Nil rate band available		(63,000)
Excess over nil band		6,000
IHT on £6,000 @ 40%		2,400
Transferor survived three years but not four years		
Chargeable 80% × £2,400		1,920

3.5 Fall in value relief

Where property is transferred within seven years before the transferor's death and either:

- The open market value on the transferor's death is less than it was at the time of the transfer, if the transferee still owns the property; or

- The property has been sold (bona fide to unconnected person) by the transferee before the transferor's death and the sale proceeds were less than the value at the time of the original transfer;

then the transferee may claim that the IHT payable by him on the transferor's death shall be computed by reference to the lower value.

For CLTs no alteration is made to the value of the original computation and the claim cannot result in a repayment of tax.

For both PETs and CLTs, the claim does not alter the value of the transfer in the cumulative total used for calculating the nil band for subsequent transfers or the death estate.

The relief does not apply to plant and machinery nor to chattels with a useful life of 50 years or less.

Worked example: Fall in value relief

Sumira made the following gifts during her life:

1 January 2004	Gross chargeable transfer of £329,000
10 December 2010	House worth £131,000 to a discretionary trust.

Sumira died on 1 December 2014. At her death the house was worth £126,000. Sumira's death estate was valued at £190,000.

Requirement

Compute the IHT payable on the gift on 10 December 2010 and as a result of Sumira's death.

Solution

10 December 2010 – Lifetime tax

	£
Gift to trustees	131,000
Less: annual exemption 2010/11	(3,000)
annual exemption 2009/10 b/f	(3,000)
	125,000
Tax @ 20/80	31,250

Gross value of transfer is £125,000 + £31,250 = £156,250

Note the 2010/11 nil band of £325,000 is already used by the chargeable transfer on 1 January 2004.

10 December 2010 – Additional IHT payable on death

	£
Gross transfer	156,250
Less fall in value (131,000 – 126,000)	(5,000)
	151,250
Less nil rate band as at death remaining (£325,000 – £329,000)	(NIL)
Excess over nil band	151,250
Tax @ 40%	60,500
Transferor survived 3 years but not 4 years	
Chargeable 80% × £60,500	48,400
Less lifetime tax paid	(31,250)
Additional IHT payable by trustees	17,150

1 December 2014 – IHT on death estate

	£
Value of the estate on death	190,000
Less: nil band remaining after gross chargeable transfers since 1.12.07	
£325,000 – £156,250 (before fall in value relief)	(168,750)
Excess over nil band	21,250
Tax @ 40%	8,500

Summary

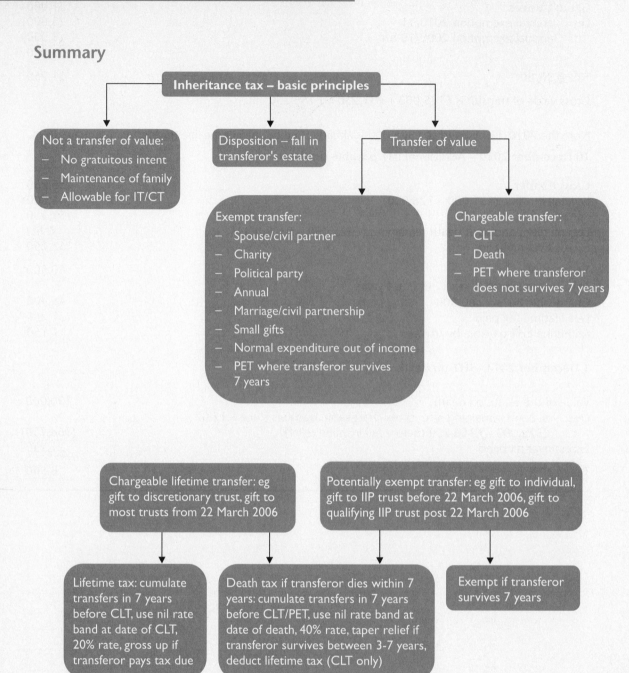

Inheritance tax – basic principles

Not a transfer of value:
- No gratuitous intent
- Maintenance of family
- Allowable for IT/CT

Disposition – fall in transferor's estate

Transfer of value

Exempt transfer:
- Spouse/civil partner
- Charity
- Political party
- Annual
- Marriage/civil partnership
- Small gifts
- Normal expenditure out of income
- PET where transferor survives 7 years

Chargeable transfer:
- CLT
- Death
- PET where transferor does not survives 7 years

Chargeable lifetime transfer: eg gift to discretionary trust, gift to most trusts from 22 March 2006

Potentially exempt transfer: eg gift to individual, gift to IIP trust before 22 March 2006, gift to qualifying IIP trust post 22 March 2006

Lifetime tax: cumulate transfers in 7 years before CLT, use nil rate band at date of CLT, 20% rate, gross up if transferor pays tax due

Death tax if transferor dies within 7 years: cumulate transfers in 7 years before CLT/PET, use nil rate band at date of death, 40% rate, taper relief if transferor survives between 3-7 years, deduct lifetime tax (CLT only)

Exempt if transferor survives 7 years

Self-test

Answer the following questions.

1   Prior to June 2014, Mark had made no dispositions.

In June 2014, he gave £10,000 to Oxfam, a registered charity. He paid his son's school fees of £3,000 in September 2014. He gave £9,000 to his sister on the occasion of the formation of her civil partnership in January 2015.

Mark died in March 2015.

What amount (if any) is chargeable to IHT in respect of these events on his death?

A   £2,000
B   £3,000
C   £5,000
D   £15,000

2   Ron had made no gifts until January 2014.

On 15 January 2014, he gave cash of £1,600 to his daughter. On 18 August 2014, he gave cash of £200 to his grandson. On 22 December 2014 he gave cash of £10,000 to his son.

On 10 January 2015, Ron died.

What amount (if any) is chargeable to IHT in respect of these events on his death?

A   £4,000
B   £5,600
C   £5,800
D   £7,000

3   Teresa had made no gifts until July 2014.

On 10 July 2014, she gave £380,000 to the trustees of a non-qualifying trust in which her son had an interest in possession.

The trustees agreed to pay the IHT due.

How much IHT is payable on the transfer in Teresa's lifetime?

A   NIL
B   £9,800
C   £11,000
D   £12,250

4   On 1 June 2010, William made a gross chargeable transfer of £332,250 (his only lifetime transfer) when he made a gift to a discretionary trust. Lifetime IHT of £1,450 was paid.

On 15 August 2015, William died.

What is the IHT payable or repayable, if any, as a result of William's death?

A   £290 repayable
B   £1,450 payable
C   NIL
D   £1,160 payable

5 Keira made the following transfers of value in her lifetime:

10 August 2004   Gross chargeable lifetime transfer of £71,000
17 September 2006 Potentially exempt transfer of £27,000
20 July 2011   Potentially exempt transfer of £319,000

Keira died on 15 November 2014.

What is the IHT payable as a result of Keira's death? Ignore the annual exemption.

    A   £20,800
    B   £29,440
    C   £26,000
    D   £36,800

6 **Jonathon**

Jonathon made the following cash gifts in his lifetime:

Date	Amount	Transferee
21 May 2003	£268,000	Trustees of discretionary trust, trustees paid IHT due
18 November 2007	£59,600	Trustees of discretionary trust, Jonathon paid IHT due
21 August 2009	£18,750	Daughter on her marriage
15 July 2012	£300,000	Son on his 21st birthday
12 April 2013	£25,000	Oxfam, a registered charity

Jonathon died on 10 October 2014.

Requirements

(a) Compute the inheritance tax payable during Jonathon's lifetime on his lifetime gifts.

(4 marks)

(b) Compute the inheritance tax payable as a result of Jonathon's death on his lifetime gifts.

(6 marks)

Now go back to the Learning Objectives in the Introduction. If you are satisfied you have achieved these objectives please tick them off.

Legislation

All references are to Inheritance Tax Act 1984 (*IHTA 1984*)

Charge to IHT	s.1
Chargeable transfers and exempt transfers	s.2
Dispositions as transfers of value	s.3

Dispositions which are not transfers of value:

• No gratuitous intent	s.10
• Maintenance of family	s.11
• Allowable for income tax or corporation tax	s.12
Excluded property	s.6

Exempt transfers:

• Spouse/civil partner	s.18
• Charity	s.23
• Political party	s.24
• Annual	s.19
• Marriage	s.22
• Small gifts	s.20
• Normal expenditure out of income	s.21
Potentially exempt transfers	s.3A
Rates of IHT and taper relief	s.7

HMRC manual references

Inheritance Tax Manual (Found at http://www.hmrc.gov.uk/manuals/ihtmanual/index.htm)

How Inheritance Tax is charged	IHTM04000
Structure of the charge: what is property?	IHTM04030

This technical reference section is designed to assist you. It should help you know where to look for further information on the topics covered in this chapter.

Answer to Interactive question 1

10 April 2013

	£
Cash	2,000
Less annual exemption 2013/14 (part)	(2,000)
Transfer	NIL

16 August 2013

	£
Cash	12,000
Less charity exemption	(12,000)
Transfer	NIL

22 November 2013

	£
Cash	3,800
Less: annual exemption 2013/14 (balance)	(1,000)
annual exemption 2012/13 b/f	(2,800)
Transfer	NIL

8 April 2014

	£
Cash	5,500
Less: marriage exemption	(1,000)
annual exemption 2014/15	(3,000)
Transfer	1,500

12 June 2014

	£
Cash	225
Less small gifts exemption	(225)
Transfer	NIL

Answer to Interactive question 2

Once again, you need to look at the lifetime position first:

21 November 2011

	£	£
Cash		424,000
Less: annual exemption 2011/12		(3,000)
annual exemption 2010/11 b/f		(3,000)
Gross chargeable transfer of value		418,000
Nil rate band 2011/12	325,000	
Less gross transfer of value in 7 years before CLT (after 21 November 2004)	(62,000)	
Nil rate band		(263,000)
Excess over nil band		155,000
IHT on £155,000 @ 20%		31,000

Then think about the position on Eric's death:

9 March 2015

	£	£
Gross transfer of value		418,000
Less: nil rate band 2014/15	325,000	
gross transfer of value in 7 years before CLT (after 21 November 2004)	(62,000)	(263,000)
Excess over nil band		155,000
IHT on £155,000 @ 40%		62,000
Transferor survived three years but not four years		
Chargeable 80% × £62,000		49,600
Less lifetime tax paid		(31,000)
Additional tax payable by trustees		18,600

Answers to Self-test

1   A – £2,000

June 2014 – Exempt transfer to charity

September 2014 – Disposition not a transfer of value – for maintenance of family

January 2015

	£
Cash	9,000
Less: marriage exemption	(1,000)
annual exemption 2014/15	(3,000)
annual exemption 2013/14 b/f	(3,000)
PET chargeable as dies within seven years	2,000

2   B – £5,600

15 January 2014

	£
Cash	1,600
Less annual exemption 2013/14 (part)	(1,600)
Transfer	NIL

18 August 2014

	£
Cash	200
Less small gifts exemption	(200)
Transfer	NIL

22 December 2014

	£
Cash	10,000
Less: annual exemption 2014/15	(3,000)
annual exemption 2013/14 (balance) b/f	(1,400)
PET chargeable as dies within seven years	5,600

3   B – £9,800

A gift to a non-qualifying interest in possession trust for the transferor's son from 22 March 2006 is a CLT.

	£
Cash	380,000
Less: annual exemption 2014/15	(3,000)
annual exemption 2013/14 b/f	(3,000)
Gross transfer of value	374,000
Less nil rate band at gift 2014/15	(325,000)
Excess over nil band	49,000
IHT on £49,000 @ 20%	9,800

4   C – NIL

	£
Gross transfer of value	332,250
Less nil rate band at death – 2014/15	(325,000)
Excess over nil band	7,250
IHT on £7,250 @ 40%	2,900
Transferor survived 5 years but not 6 years	
Chargeable 40% × £2,900	1,160
Less lifetime tax paid	(1,450)
Additional tax payable by trustees	NIL

5   A – £20,800

10 August 2004

CLT – no additional IHT payable as transferor survived seven years. However, this transfer still remains in the cumulation.

17 September 2006

PET – now exempt as transferor survived seven years. Does not enter into the cumulation.

20 July 2011

	£	£
PET now chargeable		319,000
Nil rate band at death – 2014/15	325,000	
Less gross transfer of value in 7 years before PET (after 20 July 2004)	(71,000)	
Nil rate band available		(254,000)
Excess over nil band		65,000
IHT on £65,000 @ 40%		26,000

Transferor survived three years but not four years
Chargeable 80% × £26,000   20,800

6   **Jonathon**

   (a)   **Lifetime tax**

   21 May 2003

	£
Cash	268,000
Less: annual exemption 2003/04	(3,000)
annual exemption 2002/03 b/f	(3,000)
Gross transfer of value	262,000
Less nil rate band at gift – 2003/04	(255,000)
Excess over nil band	7,000
IHT on £7,000 @ 20%	1,400

   18 November 2007

	£	£
Cash		59,600
Less: annual exemption 2007/08		(3,000)
annual exemption 2006/07 b/f		(3,000)
Net transfer of value		53,600
Nil rate band at gift – 2007/08	300,000	
Less gross transfer of value in 7 years before CLT (after 18.11.00)	(262,000)	
Nil rate band available		(38,000)
Excess over nil band		15,600
IHT on £15,600 @ 20/80		3,900
Net chargeable transfer of value		53,600
Add IHT paid by transferor		3,900
Gross chargeable transfer of value		57,500

   21 August 2009

	£
Cash	18,750
Less: marriage exemption	(5,000)
annual exemption 2009/10	(3,000)
annual exemption 2008/09 b/f	(3,000)
PET	7,750

No lifetime IHT on a PET.

15 July 2012

	£
Cash	300,000
Less: annual exemption 2012/13	(3,000)
annual exemption 2011/12 b/f	(3,000)
PET	294,000

No lifetime IHT on a PET.

12 April 2013

	£
Cash	25,000
Less charity exemption	(25,000)
Transfer	NIL

(b) **Death tax**

21 May 2003

Transferor survived more than seven years – no additional IHT payable

18 November 2007

	£	£
Gross transfer of value		57,500
Nil rate band at death – 2014/15	325,000	
Less gross transfer of value in 7 years before CLT (after 18.11.00)	(262,000)	
Nil rate band available		(63,000)
Excess over nil band		NIL
IHT		NIL

21 August 2009

	£	£
PET now chargeable transfer		7,750
Nil rate band at death – 2014/15	325,000	
Less gross transfers of value in 7 years before PET (after 21.8.02)		
(£262,000 + £57,500)	(319,500)	
Nil rate band available		(5,500)
Excess over nil band		2,250
IHT on £2,250 @ 40%		900

Transferor survived five years but not six years

Chargeable 40% × £900		360

15 July 2012

	£	£
PET now chargeable transfer		294,000
Nil rate band at death – 2014/15	325,000	
Less gross transfers of value in 7 years before PET (after 15.7.05)		
(£57,500 + £7,750)	(65,250)	
Nil rate band available		(259,750)
Excess over nil band		34,250

Transferor did not survive three years so no taper relief

IHT on £34,250 @ 40%		13,700

12 April 2013

Transfer already exempt

CHAPTER 17

Inheritance tax – death estate and valuation

Introduction

Examination context

Topic List

Summary and Self-test

Technical reference

Answers to Interactive questions

Answers to Self-test

Introduction

Learning objectives

- Calculate the value of an individual's estate at death and the inheritance tax due

- Describe the circumstances in which quick succession relief applies and calculate the amount of relief available in a given situation

Specific syllabus references for this chapter are 2i and 2j.

Syllabus links

Inheritance tax was not covered in your Principles of Taxation study manual.

Examination context

In the examination candidates may be required to:

- Calculate inheritance tax payable on a death estate after taking account of reliefs and exemptions

- Calculate the value of transfers of assets with special valuation rules

- Calculate the inheritance tax payable on a death estate which includes settled property and quick succession relief

Candidates can usually make a good attempt at the calculation of inheritance tax on death. However weaker candidates often have difficulty correctly applying quick succession relief where there is settled property in the death estate.

1 IHT on the death estate

> **Section overview**
>
> - IHT is chargeable on the death estate when an individual dies.
>
> - The value of the death estate is calculated as total assets less allowable debts and funeral expenses.
>
> - Allowable debts are those incurred for full consideration and those imposed by law eg tax.
>
> - Quick succession relief applies where there are two charges to IHT within five years.

1.1 What to include in the death estate

When an individual dies, he is treated as making a transfer of value of the amount of his **death estate.**

The **death estate** consists of all the assets to which the deceased was beneficially entitled at his death less debts and funeral expenses (see later in this section). It includes anything acquired by reason of his death, such as the proceeds (rather than the surrender value) of a life assurance policy. The estate at death may include:

- Settled property which is the subject of a qualifying interest in possession in which the deceased was a life tenant

- Free estate – ie everything else less any debts and funeral expenses

The life tenant of settled property which is the subject of a qualifying interest in possession is treated for the purposes of inheritance tax as though he owned the trust capital. You will always be told whether the trust is a qualifying interest in possession trust.

It is important to keep the two classes of property separate in the death estate computation as responsibility for paying the death tax due depends on the type of property:

- Tax on settled property is payable by the trustees.
- Tax on the free estate is payable by the personal representatives.

1.2 Charge to IHT on the death estate

The death estate is chargeable to IHT, subject to the exemptions available on death where assets pass to:

- Spouse/civil partner (outright or to a trust in which the spouse/civil partner has an interest in possession)

- Charity

- Qualifying political party

Where assets pass on death to anyone else (eg children, grandchildren, any type of trust for anybody other than the spouse/civil partner), a charge to IHT arises on those assets.

The chargeable transfers made by the deceased in the seven years before his death are cumulated to calculate the nil rate band remaining for use when calculating the tax on the death estate. Remember that this will include potentially exempt transfers within the seven years before death.

Worked example: Death estate

Ryan died on 12 July 2014. His death estate was as follows:

	£
Trust assets of a qualifying interest in possession trust	235,000
House	500,000
Cash	163,000
Quoted investments	120,000
Personal chattels	50,000
Gross assets	1,068,000
Less allowable debts and funeral expenses	(40,000)
Net assets	1,028,000

Ryan had made a gross chargeable transfer of value of £41,000 in July 2008. He also made a potentially exempt transfer of £67,000 in October 2012 (after deduction of annual exemptions).

Ryan left his estate as follows:

- £10,000 to RSPCA (a registered charity)
- House and personal chattels to his wife

The trust assets pass to Ryan's brother (the remainderman) on Ryan's death. The rest of his estate passes to his son.

Requirement

Compute the IHT payable on Ryan's death estate and state who is liable to pay the IHT due and how much each person is required to pay.

Solution

Ryan death estate – 12 July 2014

	£	£
Free estate		833,000
Less allowable debts and funeral expenses		(40,000)
		793,000
Less: Spouse exemption:		
House	500,000	
Chattels	50,000	(550,000)
Charity exemption		(10,000)
Chargeable free estate		233,000
Settled property		235,000
		468,000
Nil rate band 2014/15	325,000	
Less gross transfer of value in 7 years before death (after 12.7.07)		
(£41,000 + £67,000)	(108,000)	
Nil rate band		(217,000)
Excess over nil band		251,000
IHT on £251,000 @ 40%		100,400

The trustees of the interest in possession trust are responsible for paying the IHT due on the trust assets. The personal representatives are responsible for paying the IHT due on the free estate.

The deceased's debts and funeral expenses are set-off against the free estate. The exemptions do not relate to the settled property. Tax payable by the trustees is therefore:

£235,000/£468,000 × £100,400 = £50,415

Tax payable by the personal representatives is:

£233,000/£468,000 × £100,400 = £49,985

1.3 Debts and expenses

The following debts and expenses can be deducted from the free estate in the computation of the death estate:

- Debts incurred for full consideration eg credit card bills for goods bought prior to death, rent due accrued to date of death, but not gaming debts as such debts are not incurred for consideration

- Taxes imposed by law eg income tax, capital gains tax

- Reasonable funeral expenses, including the cost of a tombstone

- Unpaid debts only if they remain unpaid for a commercial reason and not as part of an arrangement to obtain a tax advantage

Where a debt is charged on specific property, eg a mortgage on a house, the debt is deductible primarily from the property on which it is charged.

No deduction is allowed for loans obtained to acquire or enhance excluded property. Excluded property (see later in this Text) is that which is situated outside the UK and the individual entitled to it is domiciled outside the UK.

1.4 Quick succession relief

If the deceased had acquired property in the five years before his death on which there was a charge to IHT (either a lifetime transfer on which IHT was paid or a death transfer), quick succession relief (QSR) may reduce the IHT payable on the death estate.

It is not necessary for the property originally given to still be part of the death estate: it is sufficient that there are two IHT charges within five years. If the deceased inherited a painting three years ago and sold it prior to his death, QSR will still be available on the value of the painting when calculating the death tax due on the deceased's estate.

QSR is calculated as: [Hp107]

$$\text{Tax paid on first transfer} \times \frac{\text{net transfer}}{\text{gross transfer}} \times \text{relevant \%}$$

The net transfer is the amount actually received by the transferee after IHT. The gross transfer is the amount chargeable to IHT.

The relevant % relates to the period of time between the first transfer and the date of death:

	Relief %
One year or less	100
One year but less than two years	80
Two years but less than three years	60
Three years but less than four years	40
Four years but less than five years	20

Worked example: Quick succession relief

Petra died on 14 August 2010. Her chargeable death estate was £335,000 and she left the whole of her estate to her son, Michael. Petra had made no lifetime transfers.

Michael died on 15 February 2015. His chargeable death estate was £602,000 and he left the whole of his estate to his daughter, Lianne. Michael had made no lifetime transfers.

Requirement

Compute the IHT payable on Michael's death.

Solution

Michael – Death estate 15 February 2015

	£
Chargeable estate	602,000
Less nil rate band 2014/15	(325,000)
Excess over nil band	277,000
IHT on £277,000 @ 40%	110,800
Less QSR (W)	(790)
IHT payable	110,010

WORKING

IHT on Petra's death:

	£
Chargeable estate	335,000
Less nil rate band 2010/11	(325,000)
Excess over nil band	10,000
IHT on £10,000 @ 40%	4,000
Net transfer is (£335,000 – £4,000)	331,000

Period between death of Petra and Michael is more than four years but less than five years. QSR is therefore:

$$£4,000 \times \frac{£331,000}{£335,000} \times 20\% \qquad\qquad 790$$

QSR is deducted from the IHT calculated on the whole estate ie before apportioning between the free estate (payable by personal representatives) and settled property (payable by the trustees). The QSR therefore does not attach to the particular asset gifted.

2 Transfer of nil rate band

Section overview

- Unused nil rate band from the death of a spouse/civil partner can be transferred to the surviving spouse/civil partner when he/she subsequently dies.

- The nil rate band on the death of the survivor is increased by the proportion that corresponds to the proportion of the nil rate band unused by the first spouse/civil partner to die.

- There is a maximum 100% increase in the nil rate band of the survivor if there is more than one previous spouse/civil partner.

- A claim must be made by the personal representatives on the death of the surviving spouse/civil partner.

2.1 What is the transfer of the nil rate band?

This rule allows a claim to be made for the part of the nil rate band which is unused on the death of the first spouse/civil partner to be transferred to the surviving spouse/civil partner when he/she dies.

This increases the nil rate band available on the death of the second spouse/civil partner, and hence covers additional tax due on CLTs and PETs made within seven years of death as well as the death estate.

2.2 Calculation of the unused nil rate band to transfer

The nil rate band available to the survivor will be increased according to the proportion of the nil rate band that was unused at the death of the first spouse.

The proportion of unused nil rate band is computed by reference to the nil rate band in force at the date of the first death. That unused proportion is applied to the nil rate band in force at the date of the survivor's death in order to calculate the value of the nil rate band he/she has available on his/her death.

Worked example: Transfer of unused nil rate band (100%)

Aliyah's husband Samuel died in July 2008.

Samuel had made no lifetime transfers. His chargeable death estate was £330,000 and he left all of his estate to Aliyah.

Aliyah died on 10 February 2015.

Requirement

Calculate the amount of nil rate band that is available on Aliyah's death.

Solution

Samuel died having made no lifetime transfers and leaving all of his estate to his spouse, which is an exempt transfer. Samuel did not use any of his nil rate band of £312,000.

On the death of Aliyah her nil rate band can be increased by the proportion of the nil rate band that was unused at Samuel's death ie 100%.

Aliyah will have a nil rate band of (£325,000 + (100% × £325,000)) £650,000 on her death.

The value of the exempt death estate on the first death does not matter. In the above example, if Samuel had left an estate valued at £200,000 (below the value of the nil rate band at the date of his death of £312,000), he would still have 100% of the nil rate band unused. Aliyah would therefore still have a nil rate band of £650,000 at her death.

Worked example: Transfer of unused nil rate band (less than 100%)

Joseph's wife Mollie died in January 2007. Mollie had a chargeable estate at death of £114,000 which she left to her daughter. Mollie had made no lifetime transfers.

Joseph died on 21 October 2014. He had a chargeable estate of £580,000.

Joseph had made no lifetime transfers.

Requirement

Compute the IHT payable on Joseph's death.

Solution

Mollie used £114,000 of the £285,000 nil rate band available at her death. This left an unused proportion of:

$$\frac{£285,000 - £114,000}{£285,000} = 60\%$$

The nil rate band on the death of Joseph can be increased by 60%. Remember that you should always assume that such beneficial claims are made unless told otherwise.

Joseph – death estate 21 October 2014

	£
Chargeable estate	580,000
Less nil rate band 2014/15 plus transfer from spouse ((100% + 60%) × £325,000)	(520,000)
Excess over nil rate band	60,000
IHT on £60,000 @ 40%	24,000

2.3 What if the surviving spouse/civil partner has made lifetime transfers?

If the surviving spouse/civil partner has made PETs or CLTs within seven years of death, the transferred nil rate band is available to set against these when calculating the tax due on the surviving spouse's/civil partner's death.

Worked example: Lifetime transfers

Mervyn's wife Emily died in May 2007 leaving her whole estate to Mervyn. She had made no lifetime gifts.

In June 2008 Mervyn made a CLT of £400,000 to a discretionary trust, the trustees paid the IHT due of £17,600. Mervyn died on 19 January 2015. He had a chargeable estate of £350,000.

Requirement

Compute the IHT payable as a result of Mervyn's death.

Solution

Emily used none of the £300,000 nil rate band available at her death. The nil rate band on Mervyn's death can be increased by 100%. Remember that you should assume the claim to do this is made.

Mervyn

CLT June 2008

	£
CLT	400,000
Less nil rate band at death – 2014/15 plus transfer from spouse (2 × £325,000)	(650,000)
Excess over nil rate band	NIL

No IHT is payable, but none of the lifetime tax paid of £17,600 is repayable.

Death estate 19 January 2015

	£	£
Chargeable estate		350,000
Nil rate band 2014/15 plus transfer from spouse (2 × £325,000)	650,000	
Less gross transfers in 7 years before death	(400,000)	
		(250,000)
Excess over nil rate band		100,000
IHT on £100,000 @ 40%		40,000

2.4 What if the first spouse/civil partner had made lifetime transfers?

When determining how much of the nil rate band remains unused on the death of the first spouse/civil partner, both the value of chargeable lifetime transfers made by the first spouse/civil partner in the seven years prior to his/her death and the value of the chargeable death estate of the first spouse/civil partner must be deducted.

2.5 What if there is more than one deceased spouse/civil partner?

Nil rate bands can be transferred from more than one deceased spouse or civil partner.

However there is a limit of one additional nil rate band being available on the death of the survivor.

Suppose Mr A dies leaving 70% of his nil rate band unused. Mrs A then remarries Mr B. Mr B dies leaving 60% of his nil rate band unused. When Mrs A dies in January 2014 the increase in her nil rate band as a result of the transfers from Mr A and Mr B is limited so that her nil rate band is only increased by 100%, to £650,000.

2.6 Claiming the transfer of the unused nil rate band

When the surviving spouse/civil partner dies, the personal representatives need to make a claim to transfer the unused nil rate band.

The claim must be made by the later of:

- Two years from the end of the month of death of the survivor, or
- Three months from the date the personal representatives first act for the survivor.

HMRC can accept a late claim.

3 Reduced rate for estates leaving 10% or more to charity

Section overview

- IHT will be charged at 36% on the value of the chargeable death estate if 10% or more of the estate has been left to charity.

- The reduced rate is automatic. An election may be made for the reduced rate not to apply.

IHT is automatically charged at 36% (rather than at 40%) where an individual dies and leaves at least 10% of his 'net chargeable estate' to charity. [Hp103]

The 'net chargeable estate' is the value of the estate after deducting all available reliefs, exemptions and remaining nil rate band (as increased by any amount transferable from a spouse or civil partner), but without deducting the charitable legacy itself.

If the individual's free estate includes certain jointly owned property and/or he also has any settled property, the 10% test applies to each component separately, with the nil rate band split proportionately between them. If the 10% test for an individual component is passed, IHT is charged on that particular component at 36%.

If one component satisfies the 10% test the PRs can make an election to merge either or both of the other components.

Worked example: Estates containing settled property

Trevor died on 24 July 2014 having made no lifetime gifts and leaving a total estate of £500,000, made up of his free estate of £400,000 and an interest in settled property valued at £100,000.

Requirement

Explain, with supporting calculations, how much of the estate would need to be gifted to charity in order for the estate to qualify for the 36% rate of IHT.

Solution

The free estate element for determining whether the 36% rate applies is, after apportioning the nil rate band between the two elements, £140,000 [£400,000 – (£325,000 × 4/5)] and the settled property element is £35,000 [£100,000 – (£325,000 × 1/5)].

To qualify for the reduced IHT rate on each element, £14,000 of the free estate and £3,500 of the settled property would need to pass to charity.

Alternatively, if £17,500 of one of the elements is left to charity (10% × (£500,000 – £325,000)), Trevor's PRs could make an election to treat the two elements as one, so the 10% test would be satisfied for the whole estate and the reduced rate of IHT would apply to all of it.

The personal representatives can elect for the reduced rate not to apply if, for example, the benefit obtained from applying the reduced rate is likely to be minimal and they do not wish to incur additional costs of valuing items left to charity.

The above applies to both charitable legacies made by will and also by a deed of variation.

Worked example: Reduced rates for estates leaving 10% or more to charity

Irene died on 10 August 2014. Her death estate was as follows:

	£
House	500,000
Cash	234,000
Personal chattels	50,000
Allowable debts and funeral expenses	30,000

Irene had made a gross chargeable transfer of value of £80,000 in August 2010.

Irene left her £60,000 of her estate to Oxfam (a registered charity). The rest of her estate was left to her son.

Requirement

Compute the IHT payable on Irene's death estate.

Solution

Irene death estate – 10 August 2014

	£	£
House		500,000
Cash		234,000
Chattels		50,000
		784,000
Less debts and funeral expenses		(30,000)
		754,000
Less charity exemption		(60,000)
Chargeable estate		694,000
Nil rate band 2014/15	325,000	
Less gross transfer of value in 7 years before death (after 10.8.07)	(80,000)	
Nil rate band		(245,000)
Excess over nil band		449,000
Baseline:		
Chargeable estate before charitable exemption		754,000
Less available nil rate band		(245,000)
Baseline		509,000
Charitable exemption % (£60,000/£509,000)		11.8%
IHT on £449,000 @ 36%		161,640

4 Valuation

Section overview

- The value of a transfer of value is the diminution in value of the transferor's estate, usually the value of the asset transferred.

- Assets transferred are usually valued at open market value.

- For lifetime transfers where part of an asset is given away, the position before and after the transfer must be considered.

- Quoted shares are valued at the lower of ¼ up and average marked bargain.

- Unit trust units are valued at bid price.

- Proceeds of a life assurance policy owned by a person on his own life are part of his death estate.

- There is a discount for valuing land held jointly (except related property).

- Related property is taken into account when valuing certain assets eg unquoted shares, land held jointly.

4.1 Principles of valuation for IHT

As explained earlier in this study manual, the amount of a transfer of value is the diminution in value of the transferor's estate.

Usually, this calculation involves valuing the asset transferred in accordance with valuation rules which we will cover in this section. In general, the value of any asset for the purposes of IHT is the price which the asset might reasonably be expected to fetch if it were sold on the open market at the time of the transfer.

4.2 Lifetime transfers – diminution in value

In the case of lifetime transfers there is a further aspect which needs to be considered if the transferor gives away part of an asset. In this case, it is necessary to look at the situation before the transfer of value and after the transfer of value. This is particularly relevant where the transfer is part of a shareholding of unquoted shares.

The valuation of unquoted shares mainly depends on the voting power that the shares confer on the shareholder.

For example, if a shareholder has 75% or more of the shares of the company, he has a great deal of power over the conduct of the company's business and so his shares will be valued in relation to the net assets of the company.

A shareholder in an unquoted company who holds less than 25% of the shares in the company will have virtually no power over the conduct of the company's business and so his shares will be valued in relation to the income that he can expect to receive from the shares.

Values of unquoted shares are negotiated with the Shares and Assets Valuation office of HMRC.

Worked example: Diminution of value

Simon owns 80% of the shares in T Ltd. He gives a 20% shareholding to his son, Edward, on 10 February 2015. The values agreed with HMRC are:

	£
80% holding	400,000
60% holding	260,000
20% holding	40,000

Requirement

Show the transfer of value made by Simon.

Solution

	£
Before: 80% holding	400,000
After: 60% holding	(260,000)
Transfer of value	140,000

Note that for CGT purposes, in calculating the gain on the gift, the market value of the shares transferred is £40,000 ie the value of the actual holding transferred – the diminution in value rule only applies for IHT.

Related property must also be taken into account (see later in this section).

4.3 Quoted shares

Shares which are listed on the Stock Exchange are valued at the lower of:

- The quarter up rule; and
- The average of the highest and lowest marked bargains on the day of the transfer.

The quarter up rule is:

Lower quoted price + ¼ (higher quoted price less lower quoted price)

These rules also apply when valuing quoted shares for CGT purposes.

Interactive question 1: Quoted share valuation   [Difficulty level: Intermediate]

Penny gifts all of her portfolio of shares to her son which consists of:

Company	No. of shares	Quoted at	Marked bargains
J plc	8,750	330p – 346p	332p, 336p, 343p
K plc	1,700	102p – 108p	100p, 104p, 106p

Requirement

Using the standard format below, compute the value of the shares transferred for IHT.

J plc shares

Lower of:

¼ up

.... + 1/4 (....................... – ....)   _____

Average bargain

(....................... + ...)/.........................   _____

ie .... shares @ ....   £ _____

K plc shares

Lower of:

¼ up

.... + 1/4 (....................... – ....)   _____

Average bargain

(....................... + ...)/.........................   _____

ie .... shares @ ....   £ _____

See **Answer** at the end of this chapter.

4.4 Unit trusts

Units in an authorised unit trust are shown at two prices:

- Bid price (the amount at which the units will be bought by the unit trust manager)
- Offer price (the amount at which the units will be sold by the unit trust manager)

For IHT purposes, the units are valued at the bid price (the lower of the two prices).

4.5 Life assurance policies

An individual may own a life assurance policy on his own life or on the life of someone else (eg spouse/civil partner).

If the individual dies owning a life assurance policy on his own life not written in trust, the proceeds (rather than the market value) of the policy are included in his estate for IHT purposes.

It is common for such a policy to be written in trust so that the proceeds do not form part of the individual's estate but are held on the terms of the trust for specified beneficiaries. Thus no IHT will then be paid on the proceeds.

If the individual dies owning a life assurance policy on the life of someone else, the market value (rather than the potential proceeds) of the policy is included in his estate for IHT purposes.

4.6 Assets held jointly

Where an asset is owned by more than one individual and one of the joint owners makes a transfer of value in relation to the joint asset, that individual's interest must be valued.

Sometimes, the joint owners will have set out their interests in the asset (eg A owns 40% and B owns 60%) or the interests may be ascertained from the circumstances of the acquisition of the asset.

Particularly where land is held jointly, it may not be possible for the individual's interest to be disposed of freely.

A discount of between 5% and 15% will be allowed from the full value of the interest. However, this does not apply where related property is held (see further in next section).

4.7 Related property

Rules apply to prevent taxpayers avoiding IHT by fragmenting ownership of assets to reduce the value of their estates for IHT. These are called the **related property rules**. The related property rules are usually used for valuing land held jointly and for unquoted shares.

Definition

Related property: property related to the property comprised in the transferor's estate which is:

- Comprised in the estate of his spouse/civil partner; or
- Held (or has been held within the previous five years) by;
    - A charity; or
    - A political party,

    as the result of a transfer made by the transferor or his spouse/civil partner.

Where there is related property, two valuations need to be compared:

- The value of the transferor's interest as if there were no related property; and
- The proportion held by the transferor of the value of the whole of the transferor's interest plus related property.

The higher value applies.

For most property other than shares (eg land or a set of jewellery), the proportion is calculated by using the formula based on unrelated values:

$$\frac{\text{Value of property transferred at unrelated value}}{\text{Value of property transferred plus value of related property}} \times \text{value of total related property owned}$$

Worked example: Related property – land

Trevor and Olive, a married couple, own a piece of land in the proportions 40%:60%. Trevor dies, leaving his share of the land to his son.

The relevant values are:

40% interest	£15,000
60% interest	£42,000
Value of whole interest owned by Trevor & Olive	£80,000

Requirement

Show the value of Trevor's interest for IHT.

Solution

Valuation ignoring related property

40% interest	£15,000

Valuation with related property

When valuing Trevor's share, the interest of Olive must also be taken into account. Between them Trevor and Olive own the whole of the land.

Trevor's interest is therefore valued at:

$$\frac{15,000}{15,000 + 42,000} \times £80,000 \qquad £21,053$$

Therefore the related property value of £21,053 applies (this will usually be the case).

For shares, the proportion is calculated by the number of shares, not the value of the shareholdings.

Worked example: Related property – shares

J Ltd, an investment company, has an issued capital of 10,000 £1 ordinary shares.

Norman owned 6,000 shares. His wife, Lynn, owned 1,000 shares. Lynn died and left her shares to her daughter.

The following values have been agreed:

1,000 shares	£20,000
7,000 shares	£210,000

Requirement

Show the value of Lynn's shares for IHT.

Solution

Valuation ignoring related property

1,000 shares	£20,000

Valuation with related property

$$\frac{1,000}{1,000 + 6,000} \times £210,000 \qquad £30,000$$

Therefore the related property value of £30,000 applies.

To calculate the diminution in value of a lifetime transfer, the related property rules have to be applied to value the estate both before and after the gift.

Interactive question 2: Diminution in value with related property
[Difficulty level: Exam standard]

H Ltd, an unquoted investment company, has an issued share capital of 20,000 £1 ordinary shares owned as follows:

	No. of shares
Philip	7,000
Sarah (Philip's wife)	3,200
Joanne (Philip's daughter)	5,000
Unconnected persons	4,800
	20,000

The value of shareholdings in H Ltd are as follows:

	Price per share
0% – 25%	£10
26% – 50%	£15
51% – 75%	£25
76% – 100%	£35

Philip gives 1,000 shares to his grand-daughter.

Requirement

Using the standard format below, compute the diminution in value as a result of the transfer.

Shareholdings

	Before transfer	After transfer
Philip		
Related property	————	————
	————	————
Total %	..........%	..........%

Valuation ignoring related property

£

Before:
.... shares × £.......................... (..........................% interest)

After:
.... shares × £.......................... (..........................% interest)   (_____)

Diminution in value

Valuation with related property

£

Before:
(...................... × £......................) × .... / ....

After:
(...................... × £......................) × .... / ....   (_____)

Diminution in value

Therefore the .... valuation of £_____ applies.

See **Answer** at the end of this chapter.

For examination purposes, unless you are specifically asked to show the two computations, you may use the related property valuation only.

Summary

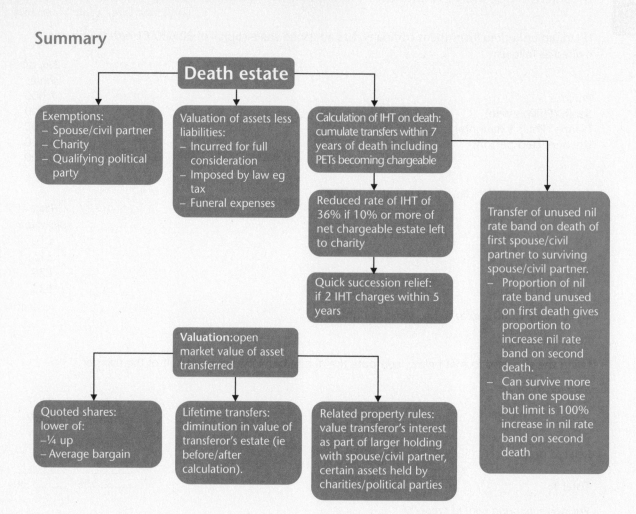

Death estate

Exemptions:
- Spouse/civil partner
- Charity
- Qualifying political party

Valuation of assets less liabilities:
- Incurred for full consideration
- Imposed by law eg tax
- Funeral expenses

Calculation of IHT on death: cumulate transfers within 7 years of death including PETs becoming chargeable

Reduced rate of IHT of 36% if 10% or more of net chargeable estate left to charity

Quick succession relief: if 2 IHT charges within 5 years

Transfer of unused nil rate band on death of first spouse/civil partner to surviving spouse/civil partner.
- Proportion of nil rate band unused on first death gives proportion to increase nil rate band on second death.
- Can survive more than one spouse but limit is 100% increase in nil rate band on second death

Valuation: open market value of asset transferred

Quoted shares: lower of:
- ¼ up
- Average bargain

Lifetime transfers: diminution in value of transferor's estate (ie before/after calculation).

Related property rules: value transferor's interest as part of larger holding with spouse/civil partner, certain assets held by charities/political parties

ICAEW

Self-test

Answer the following questions.

1   Susan died on 12 March 2015. Her chargeable death estate was £390,000 and she left the whole of her estate to her son, Mark. Susan had made no lifetime transfers.

Susan had been the sole beneficiary of her aunt's estate. Her aunt died on 27 August 2013. Her chargeable estate amounted to £250,000 and IHT of £20,000 was charged on her death.

What is the IHT chargeable on Susan's estate?

A   £11,280
B   £14,720
C   £14,960
D   £26,000

2   Y Ltd is an unquoted investment company with a share capital of 10,000 shares. John owns 5,500 shares, his wife Lucinda owns 2,500 and their son Lewis owns the remaining 2,000 shares.

John gives 2,500 shares to Lewis. At that date, the shares in the company were valued as follows:

% shareholding	Value per share
100	£25
80	£20
75	£20
55	£15
30	£12
25	£12

What is the transfer of value?

A   £30,000
B   £46,500
C   £65,000
D   £77,500

3   Paul owns 40 acres of Bluebell Meadow. His civil partner, Peter, owns the other 60 acres of Bluebell Meadow. The respective values of the plots of land are:

Paul's land	£30,000
Peter's land	£50,000

The total value of 100 acres of Bluebell Meadow as a whole is £120,000.

What is the value of Paul's land for IHT estate purposes?

A   £30,000
B   £32,000
C   £45,000
D   £48,000

4   Kevin dies in October 2013 leaving a death estate valued at £240,000. He leaves all of his estate to his wife Rebecca.

Rebecca dies in July 2014. Her chargeable estate is valued at £830,000, all of which is left to her daughter. Neither Rebecca nor Kevin had made any lifetime transfers.

How much IHT is payable on Rebecca's death estate?

A   £69,600
B   £72,000
C   £199,600
D   £202,000

5   Neil died on 28 March 2015, leaving a wife, Elizabeth, and two adult children, Annie and George, surviving him.

Neil had made the following transfers in his lifetime:

8 April 2010	Gift of 16,000 quoted shares to his nephew. On this day the shares were quoted at 550p – 602p each. There were no marked bargains.
10 July 2012	Gift of quoted shares to a discretionary trust for the benefit of his nephews. The shares were valued at £336,250. The trustees paid the IHT due.
19 October 2012	Gave cash of £20,000 to Annie on the occasion of her marriage.
28 November 2012	Gave George 5,000 ordinary shares in S Ltd, an unquoted investment company. The company share capital immediately before the transfer was held as follows:

	No. of shares
Neil	8,000
Elizabeth	4,000
Neil's brother, Ralph	3,000
Neil's sister, Amy	3,000
Neil's father, Ronald	2,000
	20,000

Each shareholder had held his or her shares for many years. HMRC has agreed the following values for the shares:

Holding	Value per share £
75% or more	100
More than 50% but less than 75%	80
Exactly 50%	70
More than 25% but less than 50%	60
Exactly 25%	40
Less than 25%	30

Neil's death estate comprised the following assets:

	£
Personal chattels	15,750
House	430,000
Quoted shares	26,000
Cash	5,823
Life assurance policy on his own life	75,000
Painting (see below)	10,000
Shares in S Ltd	see below

The painting had been inherited by Neil from his uncle who died on 9 July 2012. The painting was then worth £8,000 and tax of £1,200 had been paid out of the residue of the uncle's estate.

In respect of the shares in S Ltd, HMRC agreed that the values in November 2012 still applied at Neil's death.

Debts due at death amounted to £8,880 and the funeral expenses were £507.

Under his will, Neil left his house, personal chattels and quoted shares to Elizabeth, the remaining shares in S Ltd to George and the residue of his estate to Annie.

Neil was the life tenant of a qualifying interest in possession trust set up by his father many years ago. The capital of the trust passed to Neil's brother on Neil's death. At the date of Neil's death the trust capital consisted of £15,000.

Requirement

Compute the inheritance tax payable as a result of Neil's death. State who is liable to pay the death tax due on the death estate and how much each person is liable to pay. **(25 marks)**

Now go back to the Learning Objectives in the Introduction. If you are satisfied you have achieved these objectives please tick them off.

Legislation

All references are to Inheritance Tax Act 1984 (*IHTA 1984*)

Death estate

Meaning of estate	s.5
Changes on death	s.171
Liabilities	s.162
Funeral expenses	s.172
Quick succession relief	s.141

Valuation

Market value	s.160
Life policies	s.167
Related property	s.161

Transfer of unused nil rate band

ss.8A, 8B

HMRC manual references

Inheritance Tax Manual (Found at http://www.hmrc.gov.uk/manuals/ihtmanual/index.htm)

Structure of the charge: what is the value transferred?	IHTM04028
Exemptions: contents	IHTM11000

This technical reference section is designed to assist you. It should help you to know where to look for further information on the topics covered in this chapter.

CHAPTER

17

Answer to Interactive question 1

J plc shares

Lower of:

¼ up

330p + 1/4 (346p – 330p)   334p

Average bargain

(343 + 332)/2   337.5p

ie 8,750 shares @ 334p   £29,225

K plc shares

Lower of:

¼ up

102p + 1/4 (108p – 102p)   103.5p

Average bargain

(100 + 106)/2   103p

ie 1,700 shares @ 103p   £1,751

Answer to Interactive question 2

Shareholdings

	Before transfer	After Transfer
Philip	7,000	6,000
Related property	3,200	3,200
	10,200	9,200
Total %	51%	46%

Valuation ignoring related property

                                                                          £

Before:

7,000 shares × £15 (35% interest)   105,000

After:

6,000 shares × £15 (30% interest)   (90,000)

Diminution in value   15,000

Valuation with related property

                                                                          £

Before:

$(10,200 \times £25) \times \dfrac{7,000}{7,000 + 3,200}$ 175,000

After:

$(9,200 \times £15) \times \dfrac{6,000}{6,000 + 3,200}$ (90,000)

Diminution in value   85,000

Therefore the related property valuation of £85,000 applies.

It is acceptable to use the following simplification computation where you are given a value per share:

                                                                          £

Before:

£25 × 7,000   175,000

After:

£15 × 6,000   (90,000)

Diminution in value   85,000

1   A – £11,280

   Susan – Death estate 12 March 2015

	£
Chargeable estate	390,000
Less nil rate band 2014/15	(325,000)
Excess over nil band	65,000
IHT on £65,000 @ 40%	26,000
Less QSR (W)	(14,720)
IHT payable	11,280

   WORKING

   Susan survived her aunt by one year but not two years.

   $£20,000 \times \dfrac{£230,000}{£250,000} \times 80\%$ 14,720

2   C – £65,000

	£
Before: (5,500 shares × £20) (80% holding with Lucinda)	110,000
After: (3,000 shares × £15) (55% holding with Lucinda)	(45,000)
	65,000

3   C – £45,000

   The related property rules apply, so Paul's plot is valued at:

   $\dfrac{30,000}{30,000 + 50,000} \times £120,000$ £45,000

   This value applies since the value of Paul's share in isolation is lower (£30,000). Note that the physical number of acres owned by Paul and Peter is not relevant.

4   B – £72,000

	£
Chargeable estate	830,000
Less: nil rate band 2014/15	
increased by 100% due to transfer of Kevin's unused nil rate band	(650,000)
	180,000
IHT on £180,000 @ 40%	72,000

5   **Neil – IHT payable as a result of death**

   Death tax on lifetime transfers

   8 April 2010

   Potentially exempt transfer within seven years of death

	£
Quoted shares	
16,000 shares @ [550p + 1/4 (602p – 550p)]	90,080
Less: annual exemption 2010/11	(3,000)
annual exemption 2009/10 b/f	(3,000)
Potentially exempt transfer now chargeable	84,080
Nil rate band at death – 2014/15	(325,000)
Excess over nil band	NIL

   There is no IHT payable on this transfer as a result of Neil's death.

10 July 2012

Chargeable lifetime transfer

	£	£
Quoted shares		336,250
Less: annual exemption 2012/13		(3,000)
annual exemption 2011/12 b/f		(3,000)
Gross chargeable transfer		330,250
Nil rate band at death – 2014/15	325,000	
Less gross transfers of value in 7 years before CLT (after 10 July 2005)	(84,080)	
Nil rate band available		(240,920)
Excess over nil band		89,330
IHT on £89,330 @ 40%		35,732
No taper relief as within 3 years of death		
Less lifetime IHT paid (W)		(1,050)
Death IHT due		34,682

WORKING

	£
Gross chargeable transfer	330,250
Nil rate band at gift – 2012/13	(325,000)
Excess over nil band	5,250
IHT on £5,250 @ 20%	1,050

19 October 2012

Potentially exempt transfer within seven years of death

	£	£
Cash		20,000
Less marriage exemption		(5,000)
Potentially exempt transfer now chargeable		15,000
Nil rate band at death – 2014/15	325,000	
Less gross transfers of value in 7 years before PET		
(after 19 October 2005) (£84,080 + 330,250)	(414,330)	
Nil rate band available		(NIL)
Excess over nil band		15,000
IHT on £15,000 @ 40%		£6,000

No taper relief as within three years of death

28 November 2012

Potentially exempt transfer within seven years of death

	£	£
Shares in S Ltd		
Before: part of 60% holding with related property		
8,000 @ £80		640,000
After: part of 35% holding with related property		
3,000 @ £60		(180,000)
		460,000
Nil rate band at death – 2014/15	325,000	
Less gross transfers of value in 7 years before PET		
(after 28 November 2005) (£84,080 + 330,250 + 15,000)	(429,330)	
Nil rate band available		(NIL)
Excess over nil band		460,000
IHT on £460,000 @ 40%		£184,000

No taper relief as within three years of death

Death estate

28 March 2015

	£	£
Chattels		15,750
House		430,000
Quoted shares		26,000
Cash		5,823
Life assurance		75,000
Painting		10,000
Shares in S Ltd = 3,000 @ £60		180,000
Gross free estate		742,573
Less: debts	8,880	
funeral expenses	507	(9,387)
Net free estate		733,186
Less: spouse exemption		
chattels	15,750	
house	430,000	
quoted shares	26,000	(471,750)
Chargeable free estate		261,436
Settled property		15,000
Total chargeable estate		276,436
Nil rate band 2014/15	325,000	
Less gross transfers of value in 7 years before death (after 28.03.08)		
(£84,080 + 330,250 + 15,000 + 460,000)	(889,330)	
Nil rate band available		(NIL)
Excess over nil band		276,346
IHT on £276,346 @ 40%		110,574
Less QSR (W)		(626)
IHT payable		£109,948

WORKING

QSR

$$\frac{£8,000}{£8,000 + £1,200} \times £1,200 \times 60\% \ (2 - 3 \text{ yrs}) = £626$$

The tax payable by the executors is $\dfrac{£261,436}{£276,436} \times £109,948 = \underline{£103,982}$

The tax payable by the trustees is $\dfrac{£15,000}{£276,436} \times £109,948 = \underline{£5,966}$

CHAPTER 18

Inheritance tax – other aspects

Introduction

Examination context

Topic List

    1   Overseas aspects of IHT

    2   Administration of IHT

    3   Interaction of IHT and CGT

Summary and Self-test

Technical reference

Answer to Interactive question

Answers to Self-test

Introduction

Learning objectives

Tick off

- Explain the impact of an individual's domicile and deemed domicile on their inheritance tax liability ☐

- Calculate the inheritance tax payable on chargeable lifetime transfers in straightforward scenarios and state the due date for payment ☐

- Calculate the death tax due on lifetime transfers and state the due date for payment ☐

- Calculate the value of an individual's estate at death and the inheritance tax due and state the due date for payment ☐

- Calculate the interest and penalties due in respect of late payment of inheritance tax ☐

Specific syllabus references for this chapter are 2f, 2g, 2h, 2i and 2k.

Syllabus links

Inheritance tax was not covered in your Principles of Taxation study manual.

Examination context

In the examination candidates may be required to:

- Explain the implications of domicile and deemed domicile to a particular scenario

- Calculate the inheritance tax due on a lifetime transfer or death estate where assets are held overseas

- Explain the administration required for inheritance tax purposes

- Explain who is liable to pay the inheritance tax due in a given scenario and state the due date for payment

- Calculate the interest and penalties due for a particular scenario

Candidates must ensure that they fully understand the implications of domicile and deemed domicile for inheritance tax computations. Candidates must be able to apply the concepts to specific scenarios. Inheritance tax administration questions should be relatively straight forward providing you have practised questions and make prodigious use of the information available in your open book.

1 Overseas aspects of IHT

Section overview

- UK domiciled or deemed UK domiciled individuals are liable to IHT on assets situated anywhere in the world.

- Non domiciled individuals are liable to IHT on UK assets only (not including the Channel Islands or Isle of Man).

- Assets are generally situated where they are physically held, registered shares are situated where the company is registered, bank accounts are located where the branch is, debts are located where the debtor resides and life insurance proceeds are located where the proceeds are payable.

- Transfers made by a UK domiciled person to a non-UK domiciled spouse/civil partner are only exempt up to £325,000 (the level of the prevailing nil rate band). This is a cumulative lifetime limit.

- Non UK domiciled individuals who are married or in a civil partnership with a UK domiciled person can elect to be treated as UK domiciled for IHT purposes.

1.1 Basis of assessment

An individual's liability to inheritance tax is determined by his domicile status:

	UK assets	Overseas assets
UK domiciled or deemed UK domiciled	Assessable	Assessable
Non-UK domiciled	Assessable	Exempt

Therefore overseas assets of a non-UK domiciled individual are excluded property for inheritance tax.

Definition

Deemed UK domicile: An individual will be deemed to have UK domicile for IHT purposes:

- If the individual has been resident in the UK for 17 out of the last 20 tax years (including the tax year of the chargeable transfer or death); or

- For 36 months after ceasing to be UK domiciled under general law.

Transfers between spouses/civil partners are exempt.

Where a transfer is made by a UK domiciled person to a non-UK domiciled spouse/civil partner, only transfers up to the value of the nil rate band are exempt. This applies for transfers from 6 April 2013 and thus the current limit is £325,000. For transfers before 6 April 2013 this limit was £55,000. This is a cumulative lifetime total.

Alternatively, the non-UK domiciled transferee spouse/civil partner of a UK domiciled spouse/civil partner, may make an election to be treated as UK domiciled for IHT purposes (only, ie not for income tax or capital gains tax) so that the whole of any transfer is exempt without limit. However, the non-UK domiciled spouse's assets are then fully within the charge to UK IHT, even where they would ordinarily have been exempt. An election to be treated as UK domiciled cannot be revoked, but ceases to be effective if the individual is non-UK resident for four consecutive tax years.

Transfers where both spouses/civil partners are non-UK domiciled are totally exempt.

Where assets included in the death estate are situated abroad, additional expenses incurred of up to 5% of the value of the asset may be deducted from the value of the overseas property.

1.2 Double taxation relief

Where assets are subject to double taxation, relief is available against the UK inheritance tax liability.

DTR applies to transfers (during lifetime and on death) of assets situated overseas which may suffer tax overseas as well as IHT in the UK. Relief may be given under a treaty, but if not then the following rules apply.

DTR is given as a tax credit against the IHT payable on the overseas asset. The amount available as a tax credit is the lower of the foreign tax liability and the IHT (at the average rate) on the asset.

Worked example: Double taxation relief

Joseph died on 1 January 2015 leaving a chargeable estate of £306,000. Included in this total is a foreign asset valued at £96,000 in respect of which foreign taxes of £18,000 were paid.

Requirement

Calculate the IHT payable on the estate assuming that Joseph made a gross chargeable lifetime transfer of £182,000 one year before his death.

Solution

	£
Death estate	306,000
Less: nil rate band £(325,000 – 182,000)	(143,000)
Chargeable estate	163,000
IHT @ 40%	65,200

(Average rate: £65,200/£306,000 = 21.307%)

Less DTR: lower of:
- (a)   £18,000
- (b)   £96,000 × 21.307% = £20,455

	£
Less DTR	(18,000)
IHT payable on the estate	47,200

1.3 Location of assets

If an individual is not domiciled in the UK the location of assets becomes very important. The location of some common assets is as follows:

Type of asset	Location
Land and buildings	Where physically situated
Debt	Where the debtor resides
Life policies	Where the proceeds are payable
Registered shares and securities	Where they are registered
Bearer securities	Where the certificate of title is located at the time of transfer
Bank accounts	At the branch where the account is kept
Interest in a partnership	Where the partnership business is carried on
Goodwill	Where the business to which it is attached is carried on
Tangible property	At its physical location

2 Administration of IHT

Section overview

- IHT is administered by HMRC Inheritance Tax.
- An account must usually be delivered by the end of 12 months following an IHT event occurring.
- HMRC can make a notice of determination of the IHT liability against which the taxpayer can appeal.
- IHT is usually payable at the end of six months following an IHT event.
- An election can be made to pay IHT by ten annual instalments in certain cases.
- Penalties apply on late delivery of an account and on failure to submit an account.

2.1 Accounts, determinations and appeals

IHT is administered by HMRC Inheritance Tax.

When an IHT event occurs, an account must be delivered to HMRC specifying details of the property chargeable and its value.

The account must be delivered as follows: [Hp112]

Event	Person responsible	Latest date
CLT – lifetime IHT	Transferor	12 months after end of month in which gift made
PET	Transferee	12 months after end of month in which death occurred
Death estate	Personal representatives (PRs) eg executors appointed in will, administrators if no will	12 months after end of month in which death occurred or, if later, three months following the date they become PRs

In practice, accounts are usually delivered before the latest date.

In the case of CLTs and PETs, the IHT due will be payable well before the date for submission of the account so usually the account will be submitted when the IHT is paid. Usually, the PRs will include details of CLTs and PETs in the death account. In this case, it is not necessary for the transferee of a PET to make a separate account. There is no separate account required for a CLT on the death of the transferor.

In the case of the death estate, the account must be submitted and the IHT paid before the grant of probate or letters of administration can be issued and so this is usually done as soon as possible after the death.

There are some excepted transfers and excepted estates, on which no IHT is payable and certain other conditions are satisfied, where no IHT account needs to be submitted.

When an account is submitted, HMRC issues a **notice of determination** showing the value of the transfer for IHT purposes and the amount of IHT payable. A notice of determination may also be made where an officer of HMRC believes there to be an IHT liability. Such a determination is made on the basis of the officer's judgement.

An **appeal against a notice of determination** must be made in writing within thirty days of the service of the notice. The First-tier Tribunal will hear the appeal. There is a right of appeal, with permission from the First-tier Tax Chamber, to the Finance and Tax Chamber in the Upper Tribunal. Questions of land valuation are heard by the Lands Tribunal.

2.2 Payment of IHT and interest

2.2.1 Standard payment dates

Payment of IHT due is as follows: [Hp114]

Event	Person primarily liable	Due date
CLT – lifetime IHT	Transferor	Later of:
		6 months after end of month in which CLT made; and
		30 April in tax year following the tax year of CLT
CLT – death IHT	Transferee	6 months after end of month in which death occurred
PET	Transferee	6 months after end of month in which death occurred
Death estate	Personal representatives	On delivery of IHT account

Usually, the whole of the IHT due on a transfer is payable in full on the due date. For lifetime transfers, interest will run from the due date on unpaid IHT. For the death estate, interest will run from the end of six months following the date of death. Interest runs until the day before payment of IHT.

Interactive question: Accounts and payment of IHT   [Difficulty level: Intermediate]

Selina made a transfer of value to a discretionary trust on 10 July 2009. The IHT payable on the transfer was £10,000 which was payable by her. She also made a transfer of value to her daughter, Barbara, on 15 September 2010.

Selina died on 2 January 2015. She left her entire death estate to her son.

Additional IHT of £8,000 was payable on the transfer to the discretionary trust. IHT on the transfer to her daughter was £5,000. The IHT on the death estate was £60,000.

Requirements

Using the standard format below:

(1)   State who should make an IHT account for each of the transfers and by what date the account should be submitted.

(2)   State when the amounts of IHT payable are due and from what date interest will run in each case.

(1)   **Accounts**

   Transfer to discretionary trust – 10 July 2009

   .... transfer

   Account due:

   Submitted by:

   Transfer to daughter – 15 September 2010

   .... transfer

   Account due:

   Submitted by:

   Death estate – 2 January 2015

   Account due:

   Submitted by:

(2) **Payment of IHT**

Transfer to discretionary trust – 10 July 2009

Lifetime IHT due:

Payable by:

Interest runs from:

Additional death IHT due:

Payable by:

Interest runs from:

Transfer to daughter – 15 September 2010

IHT due:

Payable by:

Interest runs from:

Death estate – 2 January 2015

IHT due:

Payable by:

Interest runs from:

See **Answer** at the end of this chapter.

2.2.2 Payment by instalments

In some circumstances the taxpayer can make a written election to HMRC to pay the IHT due in ten equal annual instalments. Payment by instalments can be made for:

- Lifetime IHT on a CLT where the transferee pays the IHT;

- Additional IHT on death on a CLT, and IHT on death on a PET (but only if the transferee still owns the transferred property at the transferor's death or, in the case of a PET, his own death if earlier);

- IHT on the death estate.

For lifetime transfers, the due date for the first instalment is the due date if the IHT were to be paid in one amount. In relation to the death estate, the first instalment is due at the end of the six months following the date of death. The other instalments follow at annual intervals.

The election for instalments may be made on the following property [Hp109]:

- Land and buildings;
- Most unquoted shares and securities;
- A business or interest in a business.

If the instalment property is sold, the IHT on it immediately becomes payable in full.

Instalments may be interest-free or interest-bearing. For the purposes of this exam only interest-bearing instalments are examinable.

2.2.3 Interest-bearing instalments

Interest-bearing instalments carry interest on the outstanding IHT balance from the date the first instalment is due to the date each instalment is due. The interest is added to that instalment.

In addition, if an instalment is paid late it will bear interest from the due date for that instalment until the day before the IHT is paid.

Interest-bearing instalments are available on:

- Unquoted shares and securities which are either not a controlling holding or are in certain companies such as investment companies and property trading companies

- Businesses and interests in businesses (including partnerships) which are investment businesses or businesses in property trading

- Land

Worked example: Instalment option

Stephen died on 16 November 2014 leaving a death estate as follows:

	£
House	750,000
Land	350,000
Cash and quoted investments	275,000
	1,375,000

Stephen had made no lifetime transfers of value. He left his entire estate to his son.

Requirements

(1) Compute the IHT due on Stephen's death and state when the IHT is due, assuming no election is made.

(2) Advise whether an election may be made to pay the IHT by instalments and briefly describe how the instalments would be paid.

Solution

(1) **Death estate – 16 November 2014**

	£
House	750,000
Land	350,000
Cash and quoted investments	275,000
Chargeable estate	1,375,000
Less nil band available 2014/15	(325,000)
Excess over nil band	1,050,000
IHT on £1,050,000 @ 40%	420,000

Due on submission of the IHT account by the executors.

(2) **Instalment option**

House

IHT payable on house is:

$$\frac{750,000}{1,375,000} \times £420,000 = \qquad £229,091$$

This can be paid in ten equal annual instalments of £22,909 starting on 31 May 2015. The unpaid balance will be subject to interest which will be added to each instalment.

Land

IHT payable on land is:

$$\frac{350,000}{1,375,000} \times £420,000 = \qquad £106,909$$

This can be paid in ten equal annual instalments of £10,691 starting on 31 May 2015. The unpaid balance will be subject to interest which will be added to each instalment.

Where IHT is overpaid, interest supplement is payable by HMRC from the date the payment was made to the date that the repayment order is issued.

2.3 Penalties

If an IHT account is submitted late to HMRC, penalties apply as follows:

- Immediate £100 fixed penalty, regardless of whether the tax has been paid (note that the £100 still applies even if the tax due is £0)

- Daily fixed penalties of up to £10 per day if the return is more than three months late (for a maximum of 90 days)

- Where the delay is greater than 6 months but less than 12 months a tax geared penalty of 5% of the tax due

- Where the delay is greater than 12 months the following tax geared penalties apply:

  - 100% of tax due where withholding of information is deliberate and concealed
  - 70% of tax due where withholding of information is deliberate but not concealed
  - 5% of tax due in other cases

The tax geared penalties are all subject to a minimum of £300 and can be reduced for disclosure, with higher reductions if the disclosure is unprompted.

The minimum and maximum penalties are as follows:

Behaviour	Maximum penalty	Minimum penalty with unprompted disclosure	Minimum penalty with prompted disclosure
Deliberate and concealed	100%	30%	50%
Deliberate but not concealed	70%	20%	35%

Note that these are the new penalty regime rules. They are being implemented over a number of years, however only the new late filing penalties explained here are examinable in 2015.

A standardised penalty regime also applies for late payment of IHT. An initial penalty of 5% of the tax unpaid runs from the filing date for the particular IHT account. Further 5% penalties are charged where the tax is still unpaid 6 and 12 months after the filing date.

3 Interaction of IHT and CGT

Section overview

- Gifts on death are subject to inheritance tax but are exempt from capital gains tax.
- A lifetime gift can be subject to both inheritance tax and capital gains tax.

3.1 Gifts on death

On death inheritance tax may be payable on the death estate and on lifetime gifts made within the previous seven years.

Capital gains tax is not payable on the death estate. Donees receive assets at their probate value (market value at death), and so receive a free capital gains tax uplift in value.

3.2 Lifetime gifts

When someone makes a gift during lifetime, we have seen that there are IHT consequences. The gift will either be a chargeable lifetime transfer (CLT) if made to a relevant property trust, a potentially exempt transfer (PET) if made to another individual (or a bare or disabled person's trust) or completely exempt (eg gifts to a spouse or civil partner or gifts to charity).

At the time of the gift there may also be capital gains tax (CGT) consequences if the asset is chargeable to CGT.

Once the assets are in the trust there may be CGT implications if the trustees sell the assets.

3.3 Potentially exempt transfers

Potentially exempt transfers (gifts to individuals or bare trusts) have no immediate inheritance tax charge.

The capital gains tax position depends on the asset gifted. The asset may be

- Exempt, for example cash, or
- Chargeable to capital gains tax.

If the asset is chargeable to capital gains tax, the gain is calculated using market value for the sale proceeds.

If the disposal is to a spouse or civil partner then it will be exempt from both inheritance tax and capital gains tax.

3.4 Chargeable lifetime transfers

A chargeable lifetime transfer may be subject to an immediate inheritance tax charge and an immediate capital gains tax charge.

To alleviate this problem, the gain arising on the transfer may be deferred using a special form of gift relief (details of this relief are outside the scope of this syllabus).

Summary

```
                                    ┌─────────────┐
                                    │     IHT     │
                                    └─────────────┘
        ┌───────────────────────────────┼───────────────────────────────┐

┌──────────────────────────┐  ┌──────────────────────────┐  ┌──────────────────────────┐
│ Basis                    │  │ –  Only first £325k of   │  │ Deemed domicile          │
│ –  Domiciled or deemed   │  │    transfer to non-dom   │  │ –  Resident 17 out of    │
│    domile                │  │    spouse/civil partner  │  │    previous 20 years; or │
│    = world-wide assets   │  │    is exempt             │  │ –  36 months since       │
│ –  Non-UK domiciled      │  │ –  Non UK dom            │  │    ceased to be UK       │
│    = UK assets only      │  │    spouse/civil partner  │  │    domiciled             │
│                          │  │    can elect to be       │  │                          │
│                          │  │    treated as UK dom     │  │                          │
│                          │  │    for IHT               │  │                          │
└──────────────────────────┘  └──────────────────────────┘  └──────────────────────────┘
```

```
                              ┌──────────────────────┐
                              │    Administration    │
                              └──────────────────────┘
        ┌─────────────────────────────┼─────────────────────────────┐

┌──────────────────────────┐  ┌──────────────────────────┐  ┌──────────────────────────────────┐
│ Accounts: submit by end  │  │ Payment: usually by end  │  │ Interest: on late-paid and       │
│ of 12 months from event  │  │ of 6 months from event   │  │ over-paid tax                    │
└──────────────────────────┘  └──────────────────────────┘  │ Penalties: eg on late submission │
                                          │                  │ of account                       │
                             ┌────────────┴────────────┐     └──────────────────────────────────┘
            ┌──────────────────────────┐  ┌──────────────────────────┐
            │ Payment by non-interest: │  │ Payment by interest-     │
            │ bearing instalments      │  │ bearing instalments      │
            └──────────────────────────┘  └──────────────────────────┘
```

```
                    ┌────────────────────────────────┐
                    │    Interaction of IHT and CGT  │
                    └────────────────────────────────┘
        ┌───────────────────────┼───────────────────────┐

┌──────────────────────┐  ┌──────────────────────┐  ┌──────────────────────┐
│ Death estate:        │  │ PETs:                │  │ CLTs:                │
│ no CGT payable       │  │ no immediate IHT     │  │ immediate IHT        │
│                      │  │ possible CGT         │  │ immediate CGT        │
└──────────────────────┘  └──────────────────────┘  └──────────────────────┘
```

Self-test

Answer the following questions.

1   Mustafa (domiciled in Switzerland) was resident in the UK for 15 years immediately prior to his death in April 2015. At the time of his death he owned the following assets:

	£
House in Spain	455,550
Leasehold flat in UK	345,000
Bank balances held at:	
London Branch of Swiss Bank	22,000
London Branch of UK Bank	33,450
Spanish Branch of UK Bank	22,700
Shares in House plc, incorporated in UK, wholly trading in USA	98,341
Chattels in storage in Switzerland	442,189

The personal representatives arranged management of the house in Spain pending its transfer to a beneficiary. Additional costs of £4,000 were incurred as a result.

Requirement

Calculate the value of Mustafa's death estate.

2   Donald died on 6 June 2014 leaving a chargeable estate of £380,000.

By what date must his personal representatives submit an account to HMRC?

A   31 December 2014
B   6 April 2015
C   6 June 2015
D   30 June 2015

3   John gave his son £200,000 on 30 June 2011 and died on 19 August 2014.

When is the IHT on the gift due for payment?

A   30 April 2012
B   19 February 2015
C   28 February 2015
D   30 April 2015

4   Irene died in August 2014. Her death estate consisted of:

	£
House	500,000
Shares in M Ltd, unquoted investment company	100,000
Cash and quoted investments	200,000
	800,000

For which property can an election for payment by instalments be made?

A   House, cash and quoted investments
B   House, shares in M Ltd
C   Shares in M Ltd only
D   All of the estate

5 Mrs Dante and Mr Dante

You are a tax accountant with Keats, Kipling and Partners. You have been allocated Mr Edward Dante's file to prepare assorted tax computations for a meeting between Edward Dante and your senior manager this afternoon. Your first task is to review the inheritance tax issues arising from the death of Mrs Dante, his wife, in May 2014.

In August 2000, Mrs Dante gave her son, Victor, a house worth £150,000. On 10 April 2008 Mrs Dante gave Victor £228,000 in cash. In June 2008 Mrs Dante gave her other son, Hugo, half of her shares in Inferno Ltd, an unquoted investment company. Mrs Dante had owned 10% of Inferno Ltd's shares for many years and a further 15% were owned by Edward Dante at the date of the gift. Both Edward and Hugo still owned these shares in May 2014. The Inferno Ltd shares were valued as follows:

Holding %	June 2008 £	May 2014 £
5%	250,000	375,000
10%	525,000	787,500
15%	885,000	1,327,500
20%	1,175,000	1,762,500
25%	1,475,000	2,212,500

Mrs Dante was a regular donor to major political parties and had given away £100,000 each year since January 2009. The only other gift made by Mrs Dante during her lifetime was in February 2012 when she gave £400,000 in cash to a discretionary trust. The trustees agreed to pay any inheritance tax due.

At the date of her death, in addition to the Inferno Ltd shares, Mrs Dante owned the following assets:

- A 50% share in the marital home. The property was worth £4.6 million in May 2014 and was mortgaged to Horse Bank plc for £1.25 million. Mrs Dante also held a £1.25 million life insurance policy, taken out under a declaration of trust, with Horse Bank plc as beneficiary

- Remaining shares in Inferno Ltd

- Jewellery worth £1,467,000 and an art collection worth £2,456,000

- Cash deposits of £1,500,110 with Horse Bank plc

Mrs Dante's funeral cost £42,456. She died leaving unpaid store and credit card bills of £62,145 and an income tax bill of £16,320. Mrs Dante left her entire estate to her children, Victor and Hugo.

Requirements

(i) Calculate the inheritance tax due as a result of Mrs Dante's death. **(17 marks)**

(ii) State the due date for payment of the inheritance tax and who is liable to make the payment.

(3 marks)

(20 marks)

Now go back to the Learning Objectives in the Introduction. If you are satisfied you have achieved these objectives please tick them off.

Technical reference

Legislation

References are to Inheritance Tax Act 1984 (*IHTA 1984*)

Overseas aspects of IHT

Transfers between spouses or civil partners	s.18
Double taxation relief	ss.158-9
Persons treated as domiciled in UK	s.267

Administration

Submission of accounts	s.216
Notice of determination	s.221
Appeals	s.222
Payment of IHT	s.226
Interest	s.233
Instalment option	ss.227 – 228
Interest on instalments	s.234
Interest on overpaid tax	s.235
Penalties relating to accounts	s.245
Penalty for failure to notify variation	s.245A

HMRC manual references

Inheritance Tax Manual (Found at http://www.hmrc.gov.uk/manuals/ihtmanual/index.htm)

Domicile	IHTM13000
Domicile: Introduction	IHTM13001

> This technical reference section is designed to assist you. It should help you to know where to look for further information on the topics covered in this chapter.

Answer to Interactive question 1

(1) **Accounts**

Transfer to discretionary trust – 10 July 2009

Chargeable lifetime transfer

Account due:	31 July 2010
Submitted by:	Selina

Transfer to daughter – 15 September 2010

Potentially exempt transfer

Account due:	31 January 2016
Submitted by:	Barbara

(Unless full details given by executors in their account)

Death estate – 2 January 2015

Account due:	31 January 2016
Submitted by:	Selina's executors

(2) **Payment of IHT**

Transfer to discretionary trust – 10 July 2009

Lifetime IHT due:	30 April 2010
Payable by:	Selina
Interest runs from:	30 April 2010
Additional death IHT due:	31 July 2015
Payable by:	Trustees of discretionary trust
Interest runs from:	31 July 2015

Transfer to daughter – 15 September 2010

IHT due:	31 July 2015
Payable by:	Barbara
Interest runs from:	31 July 2015

Death estate – 2 January 2015

IHT due:	On submission of account
Payable by:	Selina's executors
Interest runs from:	31 July 2015

CHAPTER

18

1 As Mustafa is domiciled in Switzerland his estate is only liable to UK IHT on UK situated assets unless he has deemed UK domicile. As Mustafa was only UK resident for 15 of the last 20 years, this is insufficient for deemed UK domicile to apply.

	£
House in Spain	0
Leasehold flat in UK	345,000
Bank balances held at:	
London Branch of Swiss Bank	22,000
London Branch of UK Bank	33,450
Spanish Branch of UK Bank	0
Shares in House plc, incorporated in UK, wholly trading in USA	98,341
Chattels in storage in Switzerland	0
Total	498,791

No relief is available for expenses incurred disposing of or managing overseas assets as they are not chargeable assets for a non-UK domiciled individual.

2 D – 30 June 2015

The PRs must submit an account within 12 months after the end of the month of death.

3 C – 28 February 2015

IHT on a PET is payable six months following the end of the month in which date of death of the transferor falls.

4 B – House, shares in M Ltd

Instalment option is always available on land. It is also usually available on unquoted shares.

5 **Mrs Dante and Mr Dante**

(i) **Inheritance tax as a result of Mrs Dante's death**

Death tax on lifetime transfers

August 2000

Potentially exempt transfer more than 7 years before death, exempt transfer so no IHT payable as a result of Mrs Dante's death

10 April 2008

Potentially exempt transfer

	£
Cash	228,000
Less: annual exemption 2008/09	(3,000)
annual exemption 2007/08 b/f	(3,000)
Potentially exempt transfer now chargeable	222,000
Nil rate band at death – 2014/15	(325,000)
Excess over nil band	NIL

There is no IHT payable on this transfer as a result of Mrs Dante's death.

June 2008

Potentially exempt transfer

	£	£
Transfer of value (W) = chargeable value as AEs already used		296,250
Nil rate band at death – 2014/15	325,000	
Less gross transfers of value in 7 years pre CLT (after June 2001)	(222,000)	
Nil rate band available		(103,000)
Excess over nil band		193,250
IHT on £193,250 @ 40%		77,300
Transferor survived five years but not six years		
Chargeable 40% × £77,300		30,920
Less no lifetime IHT paid as a PET		NIL
Death IHT due		30,920

WORKING

	£
Before transfer: owns $\dfrac{10\%}{10\%+15\%} \times £1,475,000$	590,000
After transfer: owns $\dfrac{5\%}{5\%+15\%} \times £1,175,000$	(293,750)
Loss to transferor's estate	296,250

Political donations

Donations to qualifying political parties are exempt transfers

February 2012

Chargeable lifetime transfer

	£	£
Cash		400,000
Less: annual exemption 2011/12		(3,000)
annual exemption 2010/11 b/f		(3,000)
Gross chargeable transfer		394,000
Nil rate band at death – 2014/15	325,000	
Less gross transfers of value in 7 years before CLT		
(after February 2005) (£222,000 + 296,250)	(518,250)	
Nil rate band available		(NIL)
Excess over nil band		394,000
IHT on £394,000 @ 40%		157,600
No taper relief as within 3 years of death		
Less lifetime IHT paid (W)		(13,800)
Death IHT due		143,800

WORKING

	£	£
Gross chargeable transfer		394,000
Nil rate band at gift – 2011/12	325,000	
Less gross transfers of value in 7 years pre CLT (after Feb 2005)		
NB ignore PETS made as were not chargeable in lifetime	(NIL)	
Nil rate band available		(325,000)
Excess over nil band		69,000
IHT on £69,000 @ 20%		13,800

Death estate – May 2014

	£	£
House × 50%		2,300,000
(Ignore mortgage as insurance will be paid direct to mortgagor)		
Jewellery, art and cash		5,423,110
Shares in Inferno Ltd		
$\dfrac{5\%}{5\%+15\%} \times £1,762,500$		440,625
Gross chargeable estate		8,163,735
Less: liabilities		
funeral	42,456	
bills	62,145	
income tax	16,320	(120,921)
Net chargeable estate		8,042,814
Nil rate band 2014/15	325,000	
Less gross transfers of value in 7 years before CLT		
(after May 2007) (£222,000 + 296,250 + £394,000)	(912,250)	
Nil rate band available		(NIL)
Excess over nil band		8,042,814
IHT on £8,042,814 @ 40%		3,217,126

(ii)

Event	Person primarily liable	Due date
CLT – death IHT	Transferee	6 months after end of month in which death occurred ie 30 November 2015
PET	Transferee	6 months after end of month in which death occurred ie 30 November 2015
Death estate	Personal representatives	On delivery of IHT account but interest will run from 30 November 2015

CHAPTER 19

Corporation tax

Introduction

Examination context

Topic List

Summary and Self-test

Technical reference

Answers to Interactive questions

Answers to Self-test

Introduction

Learning objectives

- Explain the relevance of the distinction between revenue and capital for both receipts and expenses and apply the distinction in a given scenario

- Recognise the effect on trading profits of the treatment of provisions and capitalised revenue expenditure

- Calculate trading profits or losses after adjustments and allowable deductions (including capital allowances on plant and machinery)

- Recognise the effect of the following issues on corporation tax payable:

    - Having a period of account less than or more than 12 months in length; and

    - Having one or more associated companies

- Calculate the taxable total profits and the tax payable or repayable for companies

- Identify the key features of the self-assessment system for companies, determine due dates for returns, payments and payments on account, and calculate the interest and penalties due for late submission of returns, incorrect returns and late or incorrect payments of tax

Specific syllabus references for this chapter are 5a, 5b, 5c, 5d, 5e and 5f.

Syllabus links

In Chapter 10 of your Principles of Taxation study manual, you learnt about the charge to corporation tax, how to compute simple taxable total profits and the computation of corporation tax. In Chapter 13 of your Principles of Taxation study manual, you learnt about the basics of corporation tax administration.

In this chapter, we build on this knowledge by covering computation of taxable total profits for long periods of account. We then look at more complex situations for computation of corporation tax such as dealing with associated companies and where an accounting period falls within more than one financial year. Finally, we consider the administrative implications of a company having a long period of account and payment of corporation tax instalments for a short accounting period.

Examination context

In the examination a candidate may be required to:

- Compute the taxable total profits of a company

- Calculate the corporation tax payable for a single company or one of a number of associated companies

- Explain when returns should be filed or payments should be made

Candidates generally perform well on corporation tax calculations, provided they have practised using a pro forma computation.

It is essential that candidates have a thorough understanding of corporation tax computations.

1 Charge to corporation tax

Section overview

- Corporation tax is payable by a UK resident company on its worldwide taxable total profits.
- Corporation tax is chargeable for accounting periods.
- An accounting period cannot exceed 12 months.

1.1 Chargeability to corporation tax

Corporation tax is paid by a company on its taxable total profits.

A UK resident company is liable to corporation tax on its worldwide profits.

A company is resident in the UK if either:

- It is incorporated in the UK; or
- It is incorporated outside the UK, but its central control and management are exercised in the UK.

The second test is a matter of fact. Usually it is the directors of the company who have control and management of the company and if they exercise those functions in the UK, the company will be resident in the UK.

Non-UK resident companies are only liable to UK corporation tax on the taxable total profits of any permanent establishments operating in the UK.

1.2 Accounting periods

Companies are charged to corporation tax in respect of accounting periods. A company's period of account will usually also be its accounting period.

An accounting period starts:

- When the company begins to trade or acquires a source of chargeable income; or
- When the previous accounting period ends and the company is still within the charge to corporation tax.

An accounting period ends on the earliest of:

- The end of 12 months from the start of the accounting period; or
- The date the company begins or ceases to trade; or
- The date the company ceases to be resident in the UK; or
- The date the period of account ends.

If the company has a period of account exceeding 12 months, there will be two accounting periods. The first accounting period of a long period of account will be the first 12 months of the long period of account and the second accounting period will be the remainder of the period of account. We deal with how to calculate taxable total profits for each accounting period later in this chapter.

2 Taxable total profits

Section overview

- Taxable total profits consists of income received (trading income, property income, non-trading loan relationships and miscellaneous income) and chargeable gains less qualifying donations.

- Income, gains and qualifying donations in a long period of account are allocated to accounting periods in accordance with special rules.

2.1 Computing taxable total profits

Overview of corporation tax computation

	£
Trading income	X
Property income	X
Non-trading loan relationships (investment interest)	X
Miscellaneous income	
Income not otherwise charged	X
Chargeable gains	X
Qualifying donations	(X)
Taxable total profits	X

Here is a summary of the main points:

Profit/expenditure	Treatment
Trading income	Profit for period of account adjusted for tax purposes.
	No private use adjustments, no appropriation of profit (eg an owner director's salary).
	Includes interest paid/received for trading loan relationships.
	The changes to capital allowances (the AIA) that apply to individuals from 6 April 2014, similarly apply to companies from 1 April 2014 (see Chapter 7).
Property income – profits of a UK property business	Accruals basis for income and expenses.
	Received gross.
	Includes lease premiums on grant of short leases.
	Interest on loans to buy or improve let property dealt with under non-trading loan relationships not property income.
Non-trading loan relationships	Interest paid/received from non-trading loan relationships (more details later in this study manual).
	Received gross.
Miscellaneous income	Received gross.
Chargeable gains	Generally computed as for individuals, but companies receive indexation allowance to date of disposal, and no annual exempt amount (see later in this study manual).
Qualifying donations	Qualifying charitable donation.
	Amount paid is gross amount deducted.
Exempt dividends received	Not included in taxable total profits.

Worked example: Computation of taxable total profits

B Ltd makes up its accounts to 31 March each year. For the year ended 31 March 2015, it had the following results:

	£
Trading profits before interest and capital allowances	1,000,000
Capital allowances	19,900 →
Building society interest received	295,000
Chargeable gain on sale of office block	350,000
Interest received on loan stock in C Ltd	61,400
Qualifying charitable donation paid to Oxfam	9,240
Interest paid on loan stock to D Ltd	100,000 →
Dividend received from E plc, exempt from UK taxation	8,000
Dividend paid	40,000

Note: The building society interest (BSI) and loan stock interest received are the cash amounts received. The following are the accrued amounts:

	BSI	Loan stock interest
	£	£
Accrued income b/f	20,000	1,000
Accrued income c/f	25,000	3,600

The loan stock interest paid to D Ltd represents both the cash amount paid and the accrued amount. It relates to loan stock issued to raise finance for trading purposes.

Requirement

Calculate B Ltd's taxable total profits.

Solution

	£
Trading income (W1)	880,100
Non-trading loan relationships (W2)	364,000
Chargeable gain	350,000
	1,594,100
Less Qualifying donation	(9,240)
Taxable total profits	1,584,860

WORKINGS

(1)   Trading profits

	£
Trading profits before interest and capital allowances	1,000,000
Less: trading loan relationship debit	(100,000)
capital allowances	(19,900)
Trading profits	880,100

(2)   Non-trading loan relationships (non-trading interest)

	£	£
BSI accrued income b/f	(20,000)	
Add: cash received	295,000	
closing accrual	25,000	300,000
Loan stock income b/f	(1,000)	
Add: cash received	61,400	
closing accrual	3,600	64,000
		364,000

In the next two chapters we will deal with some further aspects of the calculation of taxable total profits such as chargeable gains, research and development, intangible fixed assets, more about property income, loan relationships, and royalty payments and receipts.

2.2 Long periods of account

If a period of account exceeds 12 months, the period is split into two accounting periods, each giving rise to a separate corporation tax liability.

The first accounting period of a long period of account will be the first 12 months of the long period of account and the second accounting period will be the remainder of the period of account.

Special rules are required to allocate income and expenditure between the accounting periods:

Profit/expenditure	Allocation
Trading income before capital allowances	Time apportioned
Capital allowances	Computed separately for each accounting period
Property income	Time apportioned
Non-trading loan relationships	Accruals basis
Income not otherwise charged	Time apportioned
Chargeable gains	Date of disposal
Qualifying donations	Date of payment

Capital allowances for companies are computed for accounting periods, not periods of account. This means that capital allowances for companies can never be computed for a period longer than 12 months. Thus if a company has a long period of account, two capital allowances computations will be required: one for the first accounting period of 12 months, and one for the second accounting period for the remainder of the period of account.

Interactive question 1: Long period of account   [Difficulty level: Intermediate]

K plc makes up accounts for a 15 month period to 31 March 2015.

K plc had trading income before capital allowances of £180,000. It received bank interest of £3,000 on 31 December 2014 which was the amount accrued for that year. It received bank interest of £4,500 on 31 December 2015 which was the amount accrued for that year.

K plc disposed of shares in an investment company on 1 April 2014 realising a gain of £9,000.

The company made a qualifying charitable donation of £2,000 on 1 March 2015.

Maximum capital allowances were claimed by K plc. The tax-written down value of the main pool at 1 January 2014 was £32,000. An item of plant and machinery was sold on 10 January 2015 for £4,000 (less than original cost).

Requirement

Using the standard format below, compute the taxable total profits for the accounting periods.

	1.1.14 – 31.12.14 £	1.1.15 – 31.3.15 £
Trading income (............... : ....)		
Less capital allowances (W)	( )	( )
Trading income		
Non-trading loan relationships:		
Chargeable gains	————	————
Less qualifying donation	( )	( )
Taxable total profits	════	════

WORKING

	Main pool £	Allowances £

Accounting period
1.1.14 – 31.12.14

Accounting period
1.1.15 – 31.3.15

See **Answer** at the end of this chapter.

3 Computation of corporation tax

Section overview

- The rate of corporation tax depends on the augmented profits of a company and the financial year (FY) in which the accounting period falls.

- There are two rates of corporation tax: main rate and small profits rate.

- Marginal relief may apply where augmented profits fall between the upper and lower limits.

- Upper and lower limits must be scaled down in a short accounting period.

- Upper and lower limits are apportioned between a company and its associated companies.

- Where an accounting period falls in more than one FY and the rates/limits in those FYs are different, taxable total profits, augmented profits and the limits are time apportioned for each FY.

3.1 Rates of corporation tax

The rate of corporation tax depends on the augmented profits of the company and the financial year in which the accounting period falls.

Definition

Augmented profits: Taxable total profits plus franked investment income (FII), where FII is exempt dividends and tax credits received from UK and overseas companies, other than those received from companies which are 51% subsidiaries of the receiving company or from a company which is a 51% subsidiary of a company of which the receiving company is a 51% subsidiary.

Dividends received by a company are usually exempt. For the purposes of the exam, assume that all UK dividends received by a company are exempt dividends. You will be told whether foreign dividends received are taxable in the UK.

There are two rates of corporation tax: [Hp119]

	FY 2014	FY 2013
The main rate (where augmented profits exceed £1,500,000)	21%	23%
The small profits rate (where augmented profits are £300,000 or less)	20%	20%

Marginal relief applies where augmented profits are over £300,000 (lower limit) but do not exceed £1,500,000 (upper limit). Corporation tax is computed at the main rate on taxable total profits and then the following deduction is made:

$(U – A) \times N/A \times$ standard fraction

where   U = upper limit
         A = augmented profits
         N = taxable total profits
         Standard fraction = 1/400 (FY 2013 3/400)

Where there is no FII the rate of corporation tax in the margin between the lower and upper limits is 21.25% (FY 2013 23.75%).

3.2 Short accounting periods

The limits for augmented profits relate to a 12 month accounting period. If the accounting period is less than 12 months, the limits must be scaled down. [Hp119]

Worked example: Short accounting period

A Ltd has the following taxable total profits for the eight months to 31 March 2015:

	£
Trading income	340,000
Property income	10,000
	350,000
Less qualifying donation	(80,000)
Taxable total profits	270,000

On 1 December 2014, A Ltd received a dividend of £9,000 from an unconnected UK company.

Requirement

Compute the corporation tax liability of A Ltd.

Solution

	£
Taxable total profits	270,000
Add FII £9,000 × 100/90	10,000
Augmented profits	280,000

Limits for marginal relief for eight month period:

Upper limit (£1,500,000 × 8/12) = £1,000,000
Lower limit (£300,000 × 8/12) = £200,000

Marginal relief applies

	£
£270,000 × 21%	56,700
Less (£1,000,000 – £280,000) × $\frac{270,000}{280,000}$ × $\frac{1}{400}$	(1,736)
Corporation tax liability	54,964

3.3 Associated companies

The upper and lower limits apply to a company and its associates. [Hp119]

A company is associated with another company if:

- One company is under the control of the other; or
- Both are under common control of a third party (individual, partnership or another company).

Control means over 50% of the issued share capital or voting power; or distributable profits; or assets if the company should cease to exist.

Sub-subsidiaries, ie where one company controls another, which in turn controls another, are also included as associated companies.

Worked example: Associated companies

M Ltd has three subsidiaries: N Ltd (owns 80% of shares), O Ltd (owns 51% of shares) and P Ltd (owns 30% of shares).

For the year to 31 March 2015, M Ltd had taxable total profits of £400,000. It received a dividend of £27,000 from N Ltd and a dividend of £22,500 from P Ltd.

Requirement

Compute the corporation tax liability of M Ltd.

Solution

	£
Taxable total profits	400,000
Add FII £22,500 × 100/90	25,000
Augmented profits	425,000

The dividend from N Ltd is ignored because it is a 51% or more subsidiary of M Ltd.

M Ltd has two associated companies: N Ltd and O Ltd as it owns more than 50% of the shares of each company. P Ltd is not an associated company as M Ltd only owns 30% of the shares of this company.

Limits for marginal relief for M Ltd with its two associated companies (three associated companies in total) are:

Upper limit (£1,500,000/3) = £500,000

Lower limit (£300,000/3) = £100,000

Marginal relief applies

	£
£400,000 × 21%	84,000
Less (£500,000 – £425,000) × $\dfrac{400,000}{425,000}$ × $\dfrac{1}{400}$	(176)
Corporation tax liability	83,824

Associated companies include non-UK companies. Dormant companies (companies not carrying on a trade or business) are ignored.

Companies which are associated for part of the accounting period are deemed to have been associated for the whole of the accounting period.

Interactive question 2: Associated companies   [Difficulty level: Intermediate]

G Ltd is resident in the UK. It owns the following shareholdings during the 12 month accounting period ending 31 March 2015:

H Ltd (UK) 70%
I Ltd (non-UK) 55%
J Ltd (UK) 80%
K Ltd (UK) 60%

J Ltd does not at present carry on any trade or business. The shareholding in K Ltd was sold on 1 January 2015.

G Ltd has taxable total profits of £300,000 for the 12 month accounting period ending 31 March 2015. It did not receive any dividends during the period.

Requirement

Using the standard format below, compute the corporation tax liability of G Ltd.

Associated companies

	Yes – why?	No – why?
H Ltd		
I Ltd		
J Ltd		
K Ltd		

Limits for marginal relief for G Ltd with.. associated companies are:

Upper limit (£1,500,000/...........) = £.......................................

Lower limit (£300,000/...........) = £.......................................

Marginal relief applies

£

£.......................... × 21%

Less (£.......................... – £..........................) × ....   (   )
Corporation tax liability

See **Answer** at the end of this chapter.

3.4 Accounting period in more than one financial year

An accounting period may fall within more than one financial year. For example, a 12-month chargeable accounting period ending 31 December 2014 has three months to 31 March 2014, falling within FY 2013 and nine months to 31 December 2014, falling within FY 2014.

If the rates and limits for corporation tax are the same in both financial years, tax can be computed for the accounting period as if it fell within one financial year. If the rates and/or limits for corporation tax are different in the financial years, taxable total profits and augmented profits are time apportioned between the financial years. The limits for marginal rate relief will also need to be scaled down appropriately.

In FY 2013 the main rate of corporation tax was 23% and the marginal relief fraction was 3/400. The small profits rate of corporation tax was the same as FY2014 at 20%.

Worked example: Financial year straddle

K Ltd makes up its accounts to 31 December each year. In the year to 31 December 2014, the company has taxable total profits of £1,450,000 and receives franked investment income of £100,000.

Requirement

What is the corporation tax liability of K Ltd?

Solution

		y/e 31.12.14 £
Taxable total profits		1,450,000
FII		100,000
Augmented profits		1,550,000

	FY2013 3/12 £	FY2014 9/12 £
Taxable total profits	362,500	1,087,500
FII	25,000	75,000
Augmented profits	387,500	1,162,500
Corporation tax limits:		
Upper limit £1,500,000 × 3/12 / × 9/12	375,000	1,125,000
Lower limit £300,000 × 3/12 / × 9/12	75,000	225,000
FY2013: taxable total profits × 23% = £362,500 × 23%	83,375	
FY2014: taxable total profits × 21% = £1,087,500 × 21%		228,375
Total corporation tax liability		311,750

Note. Once it is determined that K Ltd pays tax at the main rate the corporation tax liability could be calculated as follows.

	£
FY2013: 3/12 × £1,450,000 × 23%	83,375
FY2014: 9/12 × £1,450,000 × 21%	228,375
Total corporation tax liability	311,750

Worked example: Financial year straddle with marginal relief

G Ltd makes up its accounts to 30 September each year. In the year to 30 September 2014, the company has taxable total profits of £650,000 and receives franked investment income of £50,000.

Requirement

What is the corporation tax liability of G Ltd?

Solution

		y/e 30.09.14 £
Taxable total profits		650,000
FII		50,000
Augmented profits		700,000

	FY2013 6/12 £	Marginal relief applies FY2014 6/12 £
Taxable total profits	325,000	325,000
FII	25,000	25,000
Augmented profits	350,000	350,000
Corporation tax limits:		
Upper limit £1,500,000 × 6/12	750,000	750,000
Lower limit £300,000 × 6/12	150,000	150,000

	£	£
FY2013: taxable total profits × 23% = £325,000 × 23%	74,750	
FY2014: taxable total profits × 21% = £325,000 × 21%		68,250
Less marginal relief		

FY2013: $(£750,000 - £350,000) \times \dfrac{325,000}{350,000} \times \dfrac{3}{400}$ (2,786)

FY2014: $(£750,000 - £350,000) \times \dfrac{325,000}{350,000} \times \dfrac{1}{400}$ (929)

	71,964	67,321
Total corporation tax liability		£139,285

4 Administration of corporation tax

Section overview

- The corporation tax return must usually be submitted 12 months after the end of the period of account.

- There are special rules for long periods of account.

- Large companies are required to pay corporation tax by instalments.

- Interest is payable on underpaid or overpaid instalments.

4.1 Submission of corporation tax return

The corporation tax return (CT600 Version 2) must be submitted to HMRC on or before the filing date. This is the **latest** of the following: [Hp126]

- If the period of account is 12 months long or less, 12 months after the **end** of the period of account (which will also be the accounting period);

- If the period of account is more than 12 months long but does not exceed 18 months, 12 months after the **end** of the period of account;

- If the period of account is more than 18 months long, 30 months from the **start** of the period of account; and

- Three months from the date on which a notice requiring the return to be made is issued.

Thus, in a long period of account of 18 months or less there will be two accounting periods and a corporation tax return will be required for each accounting period. However, the date of submission of both returns relates to the end of the long period of account and not to the end of each accounting period, ie they will both be due at the same time.

Penalties for late submission of the corporation tax return are as follows:

- Immediate £100 fixed penalty, regardless of whether the tax has been paid (note that the £100 still applies even if the tax due is £0)

- Daily fixed penalties of up to £10 per day if the return is more than three months late (for a maximum of 90 days)

- Where the delay is greater than 6 months but less than 12 months a tax geared penalty of 5% of the tax due

- Where the delay is greater than 12 months the following tax geared penalties apply:

  - 100% of tax due where withholding of information is deliberate and concealed
  - 70% of tax due where withholding of information is deliberate but not concealed
  - 5% of tax due in other cases

The tax geared penalties are all subject to a minimum of £300 and can be reduced for disclosure, with higher reductions if the disclosure is unprompted.

The minimum and maximum penalties are as follows:

Behaviour	Maximum penalty	Minimum penalty with unprompted disclosure	Minimum penalty with prompted disclosure
Deliberate and concealed	100%	30%	50%
Deliberate but not concealed	70%	20%	35%

Interactive question 3: Submission of CT returns and penalties

[Difficulty level: Intermediate]

First, show the accounting period(s) for each period of account. Then state the maximum penalties for the following events, briefly stating the reason for your answer. Assume that tax is paid at the same time as the submission of the return.

Question	Answer
Tax return for eight month period of account ended 31 August 2014, notice issued 30 September 2014, submitted 31 October 2016, tax due £10,000	
Tax return for 12 month period of account ended 30 June 2014, notice issued 1 September 2014, submitted 31 March 2016, tax due £30,000	

See **Answer** at the end of this chapter.

4.2 Payment of tax by instalments

A large company is required to pay corporation tax in instalments. A large company is one which pays corporation tax at the main rate. [Hp127]

However, a company is not treated as large if:

- It has a tax liability of less than £10,000; or

- It was not a large company in the preceding 12 months and it has augmented profits of not more than £10 million in the current accounting period.

If the company has companies associated with it, the £10 million limit is divided between the company and its associated companies. For this purpose, associated companies are only taken into account if they are associated at the **end** of the previous accounting period (or the start of the current accounting period if there is no previous accounting period).

Worked example: Instalments and associated companies

The following information relates to J Ltd:

	Taxable total profits £	Augmented profits £
y/e 31.12.14	500,000	600,000
y/e 31.12.15	3,600,000	4,000,000

J Ltd has two associated companies, K Ltd and L Ltd. It acquired its shares in K Ltd on 1 March 2014 and those in L Ltd on 1 July 2015.

Requirement

Explain whether J Ltd will be required to pay corporation tax by instalments for the year ended 31 December 2015.

Solution

J Ltd will not have to pay corporation tax by instalments for the year ended 31 December 2015 because:

- It was not a large company in the previous year ie y/e 31 December 2014. The upper limit for that year was £1,500,000/2 = £750,000 (note that K Ltd is treated as associated for the whole of this accounting period for the purpose of ascertaining the upper limit); and

- It has augmented profits of less than £10,000,000/2 = £5,000,000 in the current year ie y/e 31 December 2015. K Ltd is an associated company as it satisfied that definition at the end of the previous accounting period, but L Ltd does not.

The first instalment is the lower of:

- $3 \times CT/n$ where CT is the corporation tax for the accounting period and n is the number of months in the accounting period; and

- The corporation tax for the accounting period.

Where the whole of the corporation tax is not paid by the first instalment, subsequent instalments are calculated in the same way until the amount paid equals the corporation tax due.

In practice, the company will estimate its corporation tax liability for the accounting period and will make revised estimates of how much each instalment should be as the accounting period progresses.

If the company has a 12-month accounting period, this calculation gives four equal instalments.

The first instalment is due by the 14th day of the 7th month following the start of the accounting period.

Subsequent instalments are due at three-month intervals, with the final instalment due by the fourteenth day of the fourth month following the end of the accounting period.

For a 12-month accounting period, this means that instalments are due by the 14th day of the 7th, 10th, 13th and 16th months from the start of the accounting period.

Interest runs from the due date on underpaid (or overpaid) instalments to the day before payment or repayment. Interest is calculated after the corporation tax return is submitted.

Worked example: Instalments for short period of account

(a) Y Ltd makes up accounts for an eight month period of account to 30 June 2014. The company initially estimated that its corporation tax liability would be £600,000.

Requirement

Show the amount of the instalments due assuming that the actual corporation tax liability equals the estimated liability and state the due date of each instalment.

(b) Y Ltd revised its estimate of its corporation tax liability in July 2014 to £660,000. It adjusted its second instalment accordingly and paid the extra amount of the first instalment on the due date for the second instalment.

The actual corporation tax due is £672,000. The final instalment is paid on the due date.

Requirement

Show the amount of the second and final instalments and calculate the interest payable by the company. Assume interest on underpaid instalments is 3%.

Solution

(a) *First instalment*
$3 \times £600,000/8$ £225,000
Due 14 May 2014

Second instalment
$3 \times £600,000/8$ £225,000
Due 14 August 2014

Final instalment
Balance (£600,000 – £225,000 – £225,000)   £150,000
Due 14 October 2014

(b) *Second instalment*
$3 \times £660,000/8$ £247,500

Final instalment
Balance (£672,000 – £247,500 [adjusted first instalment] – £247,500)   £177,000

Based on the eventual corporation tax due, the first two instalments should have been:

$3 \times £672,000/8$ £252,000

Interest due is:
£

First instalment
14 May 2014 – 13 August 2014

$(£252,000 – £225,000) = £27,000 \times \dfrac{92}{365} \times 3\%$ 204

14 August 2014 – 13 October 2014

$(£252,000 – £247,500) = £4,500 \times \dfrac{61}{365} \times 3\%$ 23

Second instalment
14 August 2014 – 13 October 2014

$(£252,000 – £247,500) = £4,500 \times \dfrac{61}{365} \times 3\%$ 23

Total interest payable   250

4.3 Business payment support service

The Business Payment Support Service (BPSS) was launched by HMRC to help businesses that, because of the economic conditions, are having difficulty in making payments of tax. In these circumstances BPSS will seek to agree to spread the tax payments over a period to meet the needs of the business.

Where a company is making a trading loss in the current tax year, BPSS will take into account the anticipated loss in rescheduling tax payments.

Note that the BPSS also applies for payments of income tax, national insurance contributions, amounts collected via PAYE, and VAT.

Summary

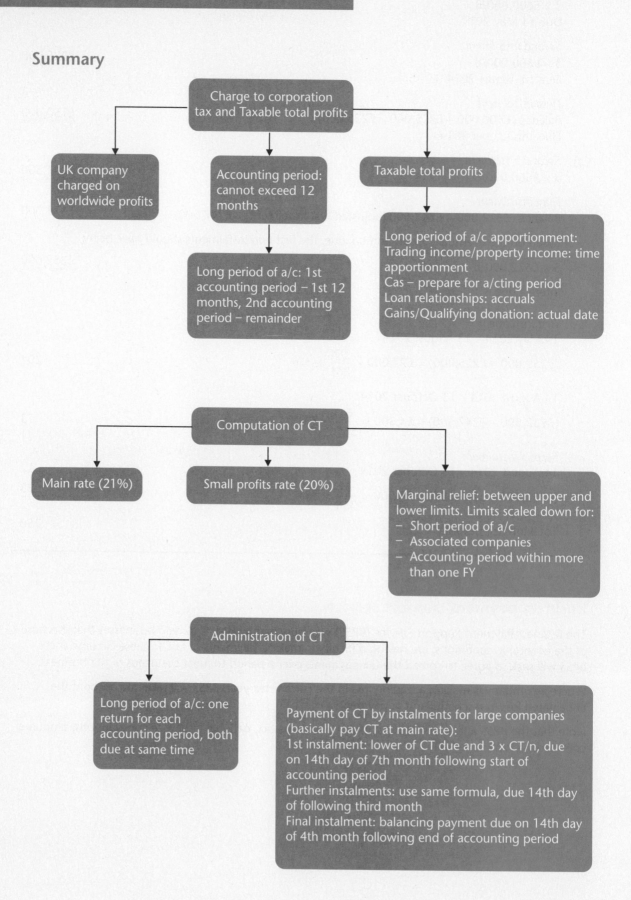

Charge to corporation tax and Taxable total profits

UK company charged on worldwide profits

Accounting period: cannot exceed 12 months

Long period of a/c: 1st accounting period – 1st 12 months, 2nd accounting period – remainder

Taxable total profits

Long period of a/c apportionment:
Trading income/property income: time apportionment
Cas – prepare for a/cting period
Loan relationships: accruals
Gains/Qualifying donation: actual date

Computation of CT

Main rate (21%)

Small profits rate (20%)

Marginal relief: between upper and lower limits. Limits scaled down for:
– Short period of a/c
– Associated companies
– Accounting period within more than one FY

Administration of CT

Long period of a/c: one return for each accounting period, both due at same time

Payment of CT by instalments for large companies (basically pay CT at main rate):
1st instalment: lower of CT due and 3 x CT/n, due on 14th day of 7th month following start of accounting period
Further instalments: use same formula, due 14th day of following third month
Final instalment: balancing payment due on 14th day of 4th month following end of accounting period

Self-test

Answer the following questions.

1 E Ltd started trading on 1 November 2013 and made up its first set of accounts to 31 December 2014. It had the following results:

	£
Trading income	2,800,000
Non-trading loan relationships (accrued evenly throughout period)	70,000
Chargeable gain (June 2014)	140,000

What is the corporation tax payable in respect of the second accounting period for this period of account?

A £546,000
B £567,667
C £90,300
D £86,100

2 Z Ltd has the following results for its nine-month period of account ended 31 December 2014:

	£
Trading income	62,000
Non-trading loan relationships	23,000
Qualifying charitable donation paid	2,000
Dividend received from wholly owned UK subsidiary	28,000

What is Z Ltd's corporation tax liability?

A £22,822
B £16,600
C £22,200
D £17,430

3 T Ltd has three associated companies. For the year ended 31 March 2015, it had taxable total profits of £70,000. It also received a dividend from an unconnected UK company of £8,000.

What is T Ltd's corporation tax liability?

A £14,700
B £13,937
C £14,043
D £14,000

4 Jam Ltd has no associated companies and taxable total profits of £1,470,000 for the year ended 31 December 2014. During the accounting period Jam Ltd received exempt dividends from UK companies of £36,000.

What is Jam Ltd's corporation tax liability for the year ended 31 December 2014?

A £316,050
B £308,700
C £324,650
D £338,100

5 S Ltd made up accounts for the 18-month period to 30 September 2014.

What is the due date for the submission of the corporation tax return for the first accounting period for this period of account?

A 30 September 2014
B 31 March 2015
C 30 September 2015
D 31 March 2016

6   G Ltd has been paying corporation tax at the main rate for many years. It has a five-month accounting period to 30 November 2014 and the corporation tax due is £2,000,000.

What is the amount of the final instalment and when is it due?

A   £1,200,000 due on 14 October 2014
B   £1,200,000 due on 14 January 2015
C   £800,000 due on 14 January 2015
D   £800,000 due on 14 March 2015

7   **W Ltd**

W Ltd prepared accounts for the year to 31 March 2015 as follows:

	£	£
Gross trading profit		710,775
Rental income received (Note 1)		1,750
Bank interest receivable (Note 2)		20,800
Debenture interest receivable (Note 3)		9,900
Profit on sale of investment property (Note 4)		37,200
Dividend from UK company, U plc		6,600
		787,025
Less:		
Allowable distribution costs	160,500	
Allowable administration expenses	166,900	
Directors' salaries and benefits	82,500	
Depreciation	79,700	
Debenture interest payable (Note 5)	81,000	
Interest on bank overdraft	39,300	
Qualifying charitable donation to RSPCA	1,600	(611,500)
Net profit for year		175,525

Notes

1   Rental income relates to a property let on 1 January 2015 at a rent of £1,750 per month payable quarterly in arrears on 31 January, 30 April, 31 July and 31 October.

2   Bank interest actually received during the year amounted to £18,000.

3   The company acquired £371,250 of 8% debenture stock for non-trade purposes on 1 December 2014. Interest is receivable half yearly on 30 April and 31 October. Therefore W Ltd did not actually receive any interest during the year.

4   The disposal of the investment property gave rise to a chargeable gain of £8,450.

5   W Ltd issued £900,000 of 9% debentures to finance its trade on 1 April 2014. The interest is payable annually on 1 January.

6   Capital allowances for the year ended 31 March 2015 are £54,050.

W Ltd has one wholly owned subsidiary, Z Ltd, which also carries on a trade.

W Ltd submitted its corporation tax return (notice issued on 1 May 2015) on 13 November 2016 and paid the corporation tax due on that date.

Requirements

(a)   Compute the taxable total profits.   **(8 marks)**

(b)   Compute the corporation tax liability.   **(2 marks)**

(c)   Compute the maximum penalty payable by W Ltd for late submission of its corporation tax return to 31 March 2015.   **(2 marks)**

                                                                                                                                    (12 marks)

Now go back to the Learning Objectives in the Introduction. If you are satisfied you have achieved these objectives please tick them off.

Technical reference

References are to Corporation Tax Act 2009 (*CTA 2009*) unless otherwise stated

Charge to corporation tax	s.2
Accounting periods	s.9
Computation of income	s.35
Marginal relief	CTA 2010 s.19
Penalty for failure to make return	Sch 55 paras 2 – 5 FA 2009
Payment by instalments	SI 1998/3175

HMRC manual reference

Company Taxation manual

(Found at http://www.hmrc.gov.uk/manuals/ctmanual/index.htm)

This technical reference section is designed to assist you. It should help you to know where to look for further information on the topics covered in this chapter.

Answers to Interactive questions

Answer to Interactive question 1

	1.1.14 – 31.12.14 £	1.1.15 – 31.3.15 £
Trading profits (12:3)	144,000	36,000
Less capital allowances (W)	(5,760)	(1,001)
Trading income	138,240	34,999
Non-trading loan relationships:		
y/e 31.12.14	3,000	
p/e 31.3.15 3/12 × £4,500		1,125
Chargeable gains 1.4.14	9,000	
	150,240	36,124
Less qualifying donation 1.3.15		(2,000)
Taxable total profits	150,240	34,124

WORKING

	Main pool £	Allowances £
Accounting period 1.1.14– 31.12.14		
TWDV b/f	32,000	
WDA @ 18%	(5,760)	5,760
TWDV c/f	26,240	
Accounting period 1.1.15 – 31.3.15		
Disposal 10.1.15	(4,000)	
	22,240	
WDA @ 18% × 3/12	(1,001)	1,001
TWDV c/f	21,239	

Answer to Interactive question 2

Associated companies

	Yes – why?	No – why?
H Ltd	✓	
I Ltd	✓ (residence of company is not relevant)	
J Ltd		✕ (dormant company ignored)
K Ltd	✓ (sold after nine months but deemed associated for whole of accounting period)	

Limits for marginal relief for G Ltd with three associated companies are:

Upper limit (£1,500,000/4) = £375,000
Lower limit (£300,000/4) = £75,000

Marginal relief applies

	£
£300,000 × 21%	63,000
Less (£375,000 – £300,000) × $\frac{1}{400}$	(188)
Corporation tax liability	62,812

Answer to Interactive question 3

Question	Answer
Tax return for eight month period of account ended 31 August 2014, notice issued 30 September 2014, submitted 31 October 2016, tax due £10,000	Accounting period 1 January 2014 to 31 August 2014. Maximum penalty is £2,000 – return due 31 August 2015, more than 12 months late so £100 + (90 × £10) + (5% × £10,000) + (5% × £10,000). This could be increased if the failure to file the return after 12 months from the due date is deemed to be deliberate and concealed or deliberate but not concealed.
Tax return for 12 month period of account ended 30 June 2014, notice issued 1 September 2014, submitted 31 March 2016, tax due £30,000	Accounting period 1 July 2013 to 30 June 2014. Maximum penalty is £2,500 – return due 30 June 2015, between 6 months late and 12 months late so £100 + (90 × £10) + (5% × £30,000)

1   D – £86,100

	1.11.13 – 31.10.14 £	1.11.14– 31.12.14 £
Trading income	2,400,000	400,000
Non-trading loan relationships	60,000	10,000
Capital gain (June 2014)	140,000	
Taxable total profits	2,600,000	410,000

For second accounting period upper limit is £1,500,000 × 2/12 = £250,000

Main rate applies

£410,000 × 21%	£86,100

2   B – £16,600

	£
Trading income	62,000
Non-trading loan relationships	23,000
	85,000
Less qualifying donation	(2,000)
Taxable total profits	83,000

Dividend from 51% or more subsidiary is ignored so augmented profits = Taxable total profits.

Limits for marginal relief for Z Ltd with one associated company for nine month accounting period are:

Upper limit (£1,500,000/2) × 9/12 = £562,500
Lower limit (£300,000/2) × 9/12 = £112,500

Small profits rate applies

£83,000 × 20%	£16,600

3   C – £14,043

	£
Taxable total profits	70,000
Add: FII £8,000 × 100/90	8,889
Augmented profits	78,889

Limits for marginal relief for T Ltd with three associated companies are:

Upper limit (£1,500,000/4) = £375,000
Lower limit (£300,000/4) = £75,000

Marginal relief applies

	£
£70,000 × 21%	14,700

Less (£375,000 – £78,889) × $\dfrac{70,000}{78,889}$ × $\dfrac{1}{400}$

	(657)
Corporation tax liability	14,043

4 A – £316,050

	Y/e 31 December 2014 £
Taxable total profits	1,470,000
FII (£36,000 × 100/90)	40,000
Augmented profits	1,510,000

Main rate applies

FY13 3/12 × £1,470,000 × 23%	84,525
FY14 9/12 × £1,470,000 × 21%	231,525
Corporation tax payable	316,050

5 C – 30 September 2015

Where the period of account is more than 12 months long, but does not exceed 18 months, the returns for both accounting periods in the period of account are due 12 months after the end of the period of account.

6 D – £800,000 due on 14 March 2015

The first instalment was:

3 × £2,000,000/5 £1,200,000

The final instalment was therefore:

(£2,000,000 – £1,200,000) £800,000

This is due by the fourteenth day of the fourth month following the end of the accounting period.

7 W Ltd

(a) **Taxable total profits y/e 31 March 2015**

	£
Trading income (W1)	126,525
Non-trading loan relationships (W2)	30,700
Property income (W3)	5,250
Chargeable gain	8,450

Less: Qualifying do[...]
Taxable total profits

WORKINGS

(1) Trading income

Net profit per [...]
Less: non-trad[...]
rental in[...]
bank int[...]
debentu[...]
profit on[...]
dividend[...]

Add: deprecia[...]
qualifyin[...]

Trading profit[...]
Less capital all[...]
Trading incom[...]

Debenture inte[...]
relationship.

(2) Non-trading loan relationships

Accruals basis

	£
Bank interest	20,800
Debenture interest	9,900
Non-trading loan relationships	30,700

(3) Property income

Accruals basis

1 January 2015 to 31 March 2015

3 × £1,750	£5,250

(b) **Corporation tax liability**

	£
Taxable total profits (part (a))	169,325
Add FII £6,600 × 100/90	7,333
Augmented profits	176,658

Limits for marginal relief for W Ltd with one associated company are:

Upper limit (£1,500,000/2) = £750,000
Lower limit (£300,000/2) = £150,000

Marginal relief applies

	£
£169,325 × 21%	35,558
Less (£750,000 – £176,658) × $\dfrac{169,325}{176,658}$ × $\dfrac{1}{400}$	(1,374)
Corporation tax liability	34,184

(c) Maximum penalty for late submission of return y/e 31 March 2015

Return for y/e 31 March 2015 should have been submitted by 31 March 2016. Actually submitted on 13 November 2016, so more than six months late but less than 12 months late.

Maximum penalty is therefore:

	£
Initial fixed penalty	100
Between three and six months late – daily fixed penalty	900
Over six months late (5% × £34,184)	1,709
	2,709

CHAPTER 20

Chargeable gains for companies

Introduction

Examination context

Topic List

    1 Computing chargeable gains for companies

    2 Pre-March 1982 assets

    3 Disposals of shares and securities by companies

    4 Bonus and rights issues

    5 Substantial shareholding exemption

Summary and Self-test

Technical reference

Answers to Interactive questions

Answers to Self-test

Learning objective

- Calculate the taxable total profit for companies

Specific syllabus reference for this chapter is 5e.

Syllabus links

In Chapter 10 of your Principles of Taxation study manual you learnt the basic computation of chargeable gains for companies. In this chapter, we cover more detailed aspects such as shares owned by companies.

Examination context

In the examination a candidate may be required to:

- Compute gains on disposals of assets by a company, including the disposal of shares and recognise when the substantial shareholding exemption applies

Candidates can achieve good marks on the calculation of gains, but often spend too much time on this area. Repeated practice is required in order to speed up.

1 Computing chargeable gains for companies

Section overview

- Companies calculate chargeable gains which are charged to corporation tax.
- Gains and losses are disposal proceeds less available costs.
- Indexation allowance is available for companies.

1.1 Introduction

Companies are liable to corporation tax on their chargeable gains arising in an accounting period. As we saw earlier in this study manual chargeable gains are included in the computation of taxable total profits and the gains are therefore charged to corporation tax at the same rate as the rest of the company's profits.

Companies, unlike individuals, are not generally liable to capital gains tax. There is an exception. Where a UK residential property valued at over £2m is held by a non-natural person, eg a company, it is subject to a number of new tax charges including a CGT charge, rather than a corporation tax charge, on any gain arising on the disposal of the property. However, this is not examinable at TC.

Companies' chargeable gains and allowable losses are however computed in accordance with the capital gains tax provisions. These provisions, as they relate specifically to companies, are set out below. The rules for the computation of gains on a disposal of a lease were covered earlier in this study manual.

1.2 Overview of chargeable gain computation for companies

	£
Disposal consideration	X
Less: allowable costs	(X)
indexation allowance	(X)
Chargeable gain	X

1.3 Indexation allowance

Companies are allowed an indexation allowance which is deducted in arriving at the chargeable gain.

Each item of acquisition cost is indexed from the date when the expenditure was incurred. Costs incurred in the same month can be added together.

The indexation factor is: $\dfrac{RD - RI}{RI}$

where RD is the Retail Prices Index (RPI) for the month of disposal and RI is the RPI for the month in which the expenditure was incurred. If RD is less than RI (ie the RPI falls) then the indexation factor is nil. [Hp177]

The indexation factor is rounded to three decimal places and applied to the item of allowable cost as appropriate to produce the indexation allowance for that item.

Indexation allowance cannot create or increase a loss.

1.4 Net chargeable gains

A capital loss is first set off against other gains for the accounting period in which the loss arose. Any remaining loss is carried forward to be set against the first available gains.

A capital loss incurred by a trading company cannot be set against income.

A company's net chargeable gains for its accounting period are the sum of its gains and losses for that period less any capital losses brought forward from earlier accounting periods. The total net figure is included in the company's Taxable Total Profits computation for that accounting period.

2 Pre-March 1982 assets

Section overview

- Rebasing was introduced to compute gains and losses based on 31 March 1982 market value instead of original cost.

- Usually two computations must be made: cost and 31 March 1982 market value.

- An election can be made to use only 31 March 1982 market value in all relevant computations.

2.1 Introduction

Major changes were made to the computation of chargeable gains during the 1980s.

Indexation allowance was introduced to give relief for gains created by inflation from March 1982. This allowed a company to compute indexation allowance on the higher of the original cost of the asset and the 31 March 1982 market value of the asset.

Subsequently, legislation was introduced with the intention that only gains or losses arising from March 1982 should be chargeable or allowable, by using the value of the asset at 31 March 1982 as the cost of the asset instead of the original cost. This was called **rebasing**.

However, it was realised that this treatment could result in a larger gain or smaller loss than a computation based on the original cost. Therefore, the legislation provides for two computations to be made, one based on original cost and one on 31 March 1982 market value.

It is possible for the company to elect to use only 31 March 1982 values for all their assets, as we will see later in this section.

In the examination, you will be given the market value of the asset at 31 March 1982. In practice, this will be subject to negotiation with HMRC.

2.2 Computations for assets held at 31 March 1982

If an asset was held at 31 March 1982, two computations need to be prepared. One is based on original cost plus any enhancement expenditure up to March 1982, and the other is based on 31 March 1982 market value.

In both cases, indexation allowance will be calculated on the higher of original cost plus enhancement and 31 March 1982 market value.

Indexation allowances will always run from March 1982 (RPI 79.44).

If the computations produce two gains, take the smaller gain.

If the computations produce two losses, take the smaller loss.

If one computation produces a gain and one computation produces a loss, there is neither a gain nor a loss.

Worked example: Pre-31 March 1982 asset

Table Ltd bought a plot of land in July 1980 for £10,000.

The plot was worth £12,000 on 31 March 1982.

Table Ltd sold the plot for £96,000 in December 2014. (Assumed RPI 260.2)

Requirement

Calculate the chargeable gain.

Solution

	Cost	31 March 1982 MV
	£	£
Disposal proceeds	96,000	96,000
Less cost/31.3.82 MV	(10,000)	(12,000)
Unindexed gain	86,000	84,000
Less indexation allowance		
$\dfrac{260.2-79.44}{79.44} = 2.275 \times £12,000$	(27,300)	(27,300)
Chargeable gain	58,700	56,700
Two gains, take smaller gain		
Chargeable gain		56,700

2.3 Election to use 31 March 1982 market value

A company can make an election to use 31 March 1982 market value only. In this case, only the computation based on 31 March 1982 market value is made. Indexation allowance is also always based on 31 March 1982 market value.

Key points are:

- The election is irrevocable

- The election applies to all assets held by that company at 31 March 1982 (with minor exceptions)

- The election must be made within two years of the end of the accounting period in which the first disposal of an asset held at 31 March 1982 is made (or such later date as HMRC may allow)

3 Disposals of shares and securities by companies

Section overview

- On a disposal of shares by a company, there are rules to match share acquisitions which are different from those for individuals.

- Shares are matched first with same day acquisitions, then with acquisitions in the previous nine days, then with the s.104 pool and finally with the 1982 pool.

3.1 Share matching rules for companies

The share matching rules for companies are different from those for individuals. [Hp100]

Disposals of shares owned by a company are matched against acquisitions of the same class of shares in the same company in the following order:

- Any acquisitions made on the **same day** as the date of the disposal

- Any acquisitions within the **previous nine days**, matching on a FIFO (first-in, first-out) basis (ie shares acquired earlier rather than later within that nine day period)

- Any shares in the **s.104 pool** which consists of shares acquired on or after 1 April 1982

- Any shares in the **1982 pool** which consists of shares acquired between 6 April 1965 and 31 March 1982 inclusive

- Any shares acquired before 6 April 1965 (details not in your syllabus)

No indexation allowance is available on shares matched under the previous nine days rule, even where the acquisition and disposal fall in different months.

Worked example: Disposal of shares by company

A plc acquired the following shares in B Ltd, an investment company:

Date	No.	Cost £
12 December 1980	10,000	5,000 (31 March 1982 MV £6,000)
10 August 1986	6,000	7,200
15 December 2000	5,000	15,000
28 May 2014	4,000	20,000

A plc sold 21,000 of the shares in B Ltd on 2 June 2014 for £109,200.

Requirement

Apply the matching rules to the disposal

Solution

2 June 2014 – disposal of 21,000 shares

Acquisitions within the previous nine days – 28 May 2014		4,000
Shares in the s.104 pool		
10 August 1986	6,000	
15 December 2000	5,000	11,000
Shares in the 1982 pool		
12 December 1980 (part)		6,000
		21,000

3.2 S.104 pool

Definition

S.104 pool: All acquisitions of shares of the same class in a company since 1 April 1982.

The s.104 pool was introduced in Finance Act 1985. However, it includes acquisitions between 1 April 1982 and 1 April 1985. Such acquisitions are indexed from acquisition to April 1985 to create the basis of the s.104 pool.

Worked example: Creation of s.104 pool

M Ltd had the following acquisitions of shares in P Ltd:

Date	Shares acquired	Cost £	RPI
11 December 1983	1,000	2,000	86.89
15 July 1984	2,000	6,000	89.10

Requirement

Show the s.104 pool at 1 April 1985 (RPI 94.78).

Solution

	No.	Cost £	Indexed cost £
11 December 1983			
Acquisition	1,000	2,000	2,000
IA to April 1985			
$\dfrac{94.78-86.89}{86.89} = 0.091 \times £2,000$			182
15 July 1984			
Acquisition	2,000	6,000	6,000
IA to April 1985			
$\dfrac{94.78-89.10}{89.10} = 0.064 \times £6,000$			384
Pool at 5 April 1985	3,000	8,000	8,566

From 1 April 1985, the pool will be adjusted for each **operative event**. An operative event occurs whenever shares are acquired or disposed of. The indexed rise in the indexed cost pool in this case only is **not** rounded to three decimal places.

Worked example: s.104 pool

D Ltd has acquired ordinary shares in G plc, a quoted trading company, as follows:

Date	Shares acquired	Cost £	RPI
16 September 1988	1,750	1,925	108.4
7 August 1990	3,500	4,025	128.1
1 October 1995	5,250	5,500	149.8

On 24 November 2014, D Ltd sold 7,350 shares for £29,750.

Requirement

Calculate the chargeable gain on sale. RPI November 2014 = 258.9 (assumed)

Solution

S.104 pool

	No.	Cost £	Indexed cost £
16 September 1988			
Acquisition	1,750	1,925	1,925
7 August 1990			
Indexed rise			
$\dfrac{128.1-108.4}{108.4} \times £1,925$			350
Acquisition	3,500	4,025	4,025
			6,300
1 October 1995			
Indexed rise			
$\dfrac{149.8-128.1}{128.1} \times £6,300$			1,067
Acquisition	5,250	5,500	5,500
			12,867

24 November 2014
Indexed rise

$$\frac{258.9 - 149.8}{149.8} \times £12,867$$

	10,500	11,450	9,371 22,238
Disposal	(7,350)	(8,015)	(15,567)
c/f	3,150	3,435	6,671

Gain

	£
Disposal proceeds	29,750
Less cost	(8,015)
Unindexed gain	21,735
Less indexation (£15,567– £8,015)	(7,552)
Chargeable gain	14,183

Interactive question 1: Share disposals [Difficulty level: Exam standard]

J Ltd bought the following ordinary shares in K Ltd, an unquoted trading company:

Date	Shares acquired	Cost £	RPI
14 July 1992	4,650	24,760	138.8
11 August 1997	3,500	39,375	158.5

There were 20,000 ordinary shares in issue in K Ltd.

In December 2014, J Ltd sold 4,375 shares for £61,500.

Requirement

Using the standard format below, calculate the chargeable gain on sale. RPI December 2014 = 260.2 (assumed).

S.104 pool

	No.	Cost £	Indexed cost £
July 1992			
August 1997			
Indexed rise			
$$\frac{\ldots - \ldots}{\ldots} \times £\ldots$$			
Acquisition			_____
December 2014			
Indexed rise			
$$\frac{\ldots - \ldots}{\ldots} \times £\ldots$$			
Disposal	(_____)	(_____)	(_____)
c/f			

Gain

	£
Disposal proceeds	
Less cost	(_____)
Unindexed gain	
Less indexation (£.......... – £..........)	(_____)
Chargeable gain	

See **Answer** at the end of this chapter.

3.3 1982 pool

Definition

1982 pool: All acquisitions of shares of the same class in a company between 6 April 1965 and 1 April 1982.

The pool consists of two elements: cost and the value of the shares at 31 March 1982.

On a disposal of shares from the 1982 pool, two computations are made. One computation is based on cost and one computation is based on 31 March 1982 market value.

Indexation allowance will always run from March 1982 (RPI 79.44).

If the computations produce two gains, take the smaller gain.

If the computations produce two losses, take the smaller loss.

If one computation produces a gain and one computation produces a loss, there is neither a gain nor a loss.

Worked example: 1982 pool

G Ltd bought the following ordinary shares in J plc:

Date	Shares acquired	Cost £
29 July 1976	9,000	13,500
7 November 1981	7,000	14,000

The market value of each share at 31 March 1982 was £1.60.

On 16 October 2014, G Ltd sold 12,000 shares for £73,000.

Requirement

Calculate the indexed gain on sale. RPI October 2014= 258.7 (assumed).

Solution

1982 pool

	No.	Cost £	31.3.82 MV £
29 July 1976	9,000	13,500	
7 November 1981	7,000	14,000	
	16,000	27,500	25,600
16 October 2014	(12,000)	(20,625)	(19,200)
c/f	4,000	6,875	6,400

Gains

	Cost £	31 March 1982 MV £
Disposal proceeds	73,000	73,000
Less cost/31.3.82 MV	(20,625)	(19,200)
Unindexed gain	52,375	53,800
Less indexation allowance		

$$\frac{258.7 - 79.44}{79.44} = 2.257 \times £20,625$$

	(46,551)	(46,551)
Indexed gain	5,824	7,249

Two gains, take smaller gain

Chargeable gain	£5,824

4 Bonus and rights issues

Section overview

- Bonus issue shares are acquired at nil cost.
- Bonus issue shares are allocated pro-rata to the 1982 pool and the s.104 pool.
- Rights issue shares are acquired for consideration paid to the company.
- Rights issue shares are allocated pro-rata to the 1982 pool and the s.104 pool.
- Indexation allowance on rights issue shares applies from the date of their acquisition or March 1982 if later.

4.1 Bonus issues

When a company offers a bonus issue of shares, it issues free shares to its existing shareholders in proportion to their existing shareholdings.

Bonus issues are commonly referred to as a '1 for x' bonus issue (eg '1 for 5' or '1 for 2'). This terminology means that for a '1 for 5' bonus issue, each shareholder will receive one free share for every five shares previously held.

As bonus shares are free, for taxation purposes a bonus issue is not treated as an acquisition of shares by the individual shareholder in the normal way.

The event is treated as a reorganisation of the company's share capital as follows:

- The new bonus shares are deemed to have been acquired on the same date as the original shares to which they relate
- Bonus issues attach pro-rata to the 1982 pool and the s.104 pool. The number of shares are added into the holdings at nil cost
- When added into the s.104 pool, the pool is not indexed up prior to recording the bonus issue as a bonus issue is not an operative event. It represents merely a reorganisation of share capital and not a new issue of shares

Worked example: Bonus issue

M Ltd made the following acquisitions of ordinary shares in Q plc:

Date	Shares acquired	Cost £
3 August 1980	1,400	4,900 (31.3.82 MV £5,600)
6 May 1995	875	3,850

On 4 November 2006, Q plc made a 1 for 7 bonus issue.

In June 2014, M Ltd sold the entire shareholding of 2,600 shares for £12 per share.

RPIs March 1982 79.44, May 1995 149.6, June 2014 256.4 (assumed).

Requirement

Calculate the chargeable gains on sale.

Solution

S.104 pool

	No.	Cost £	Indexed Cost £
6 May 1995 Acquisition	875	3,850	3,850
4 November 2006 Bonus 1:7	125	NIL	NIL
			3,850

June 2014
Indexed rise

$$\frac{256.4 - 149.6}{149.6} \times £3,850$$

	No.	Cost £	Indexed Cost £
			2,749
	1,000	3,850	6,599
Disposal	(1,000)	(3,850)	(6,599)
c/f	NIL	NIL	NIL

Gain

	£
Disposal proceeds 1,000 × £12	12,000
Less cost	(3,850)
Unindexed gain	8,150
Less indexation (£6,599 – £3,850)	(2,749)
Chargeable gain	5,401

1982 pool

	No.	Cost £	31.3.82MV £
3 August 1980	1,400	4,900	5,600
4 November 2006 Bonus 1:7	200	NIL	NIL
	1,600	4,900	5,600
June 2014	(1,600)	(4,900)	(5,600)
c/f	NIL	NIL	NIL

Gains

	Cost £	31 March 1982 MV £
Disposal proceeds 1,600 × £12	19,200	19,200
Less cost/31.3.82 MV	(4,900)	(5,600)
Unindexed gain	14,300	13,600
Less indexation allowance		

$$\frac{256.4 - 79.44}{79.44} = 2.228 \times £5,600$$

	Cost £	31 March 1982 MV £
	(12,477)	(12,477)
Indexed gain	1,823	1,123

Two gains, take smaller gain

Chargeable gain	£1,123

CHAPTER 20

4.2 Rights issues

When a company offers a rights issue, it offers its existing shareholders the right to buy extra shares, usually at a discounted price, in proportion to their existing shareholdings. The key difference from a bonus issue is that rights shares are not issued free.

A rights issue is treated, for taxation purposes, as a reorganisation of the company's share capital as follows:

- The new rights shares are deemed to have been acquired on the same date as the original shares to which they relate.

- Rights issues attach pro-rata to the 1982 pool and the s.104 pool. The number of shares is added into the holdings and the cost of the rights shares increases the cost of these holdings.

- The acquisition of rights issue shares in the s.104 pool is an operative event so an indexed rise in the pool is calculated.

- Indexation allowance on rights issue shares in the 1982 pool applies from the date of the rights issue.

Worked example: Rights issue

R Ltd had the following transactions in K Ltd:

July 1980	Acquired 1,000 shares for £1,000 (31.3.82 MV £1,200)
August 1990	Acquired 1,500 shares for £2,700
June 1992	Rights 1 for 2 acquired at £2.50 per share

In November 2014, R Ltd sold all the shares for £5 per share.

RPIs March 1982 79.44, August 1990 128.1, June 1992 139.3, November 2014 258.9 (assumed).

Requirement

Calculate the chargeable gains on sale.

Solution

S.104 pool

	No.	Cost £	Indexed cost £
August 1990			
Acquisition	1,500	2,700	2,700
June 1992			
Indexed rise			
$\frac{139.3-128.1}{128.1} \times £2,700$			236
Rights 1:2 @ £2.50	750	1,875	1,875
			4,811
November 2014			
Indexed rise			
$\frac{258.9-139.3}{139.3} \times £4,811$			4,131
	2,250	4,575	8,942
Disposal	(2,250)	(4,575)	(8,942)
c/f	NIL	NIL	NIL

Gain

	£
Disposal proceeds 2,250 × £5	11,250
Less cost	(4,575)
Unindexed gain	6,675
Less indexation (£8,942 – £4,575)	(4,367)
Chargeable gain	2,308

1982 pool

	No.	Cost £	31.3.82 MV £	Rights £
July 1980	1,000	1,000	1,200	
June 1992 Rights 1 for 2 @ £2.50	500			1,250
	1,500	1,000	1,200	1,250
November 2014	(1,500)	(1,000)	(1,200)	(1,250)
c/f	NIL	NIL	NIL	NIL

Gains

	Cost £	31 March 1982 MV £
Disposal proceeds 1,500 × £5	7,500	7,500
Less: cost/31.3.82 MV	(1,000)	(1,200)
rights	(1,250)	(1,250)
Unindexed gain	5,250	5,050
Less: indexation allowance on original shares		
$\dfrac{258.9-79.44}{79.44} = 2.259 \times £1,200$	(2,711)	(2,711)
indexation allowance on rights shares		
$\dfrac{258.9-139.3}{139.3} = 0.859 \times £1,250$	(1,074)	(1,074)
Gains	1,465	1,265

Two gains, take smaller gain

Chargeable gain $\underline{\underline{£1,265}}$

Interactive question 2: Rights issue [Difficulty level: Exam standard]

A Ltd made the following acquisitions of preference shares in H plc:

Date	Shares acquired	Cost £
10 May 1979	300	975 (31.3.82 MV £1,200)
15 June 1989	1,050	4,375

On 10 October 2007, the company made a 1 for 15 rights issue at £14 per share which A Ltd took up in full.

In March 2015, A Ltd sold the entire shareholding of 1,440 shares for £15 per share.

RPIs March 1982 79.44, June 1989 115.4, October 2007 208.9, March 2015 262.3 (assumed).

Requirement

Using the standard formats below, calculate the chargeable gains on sale.

S.104 pool

	No.	Cost £	Indexed cost £
15 June 1989			
Acquisition			
10 October 2007			
Indexed rise			
$\dfrac{\ldots\ldots - \ldots\ldots}{\ldots\ldots} \times £\ldots\ldots$			
Rights 1:15 @ £14			

March 2015

Indexed rise

$\dfrac{\ldots\ldots\ldots - \ldots\ldots\ldots}{\ldots\ldots\ldots\ldots} \times$ £...........................

    ———   ———   ———

Disposal   (   )   (   )   (   )

c/f

Gain

                                          £

Disposal proceeds .... × £.............................

Less cost   (   )

Unindexed gain

Less indexation (£........................... – £...........................) (   )

Chargeable gain

1982 pool

	No.	Cost £	31.3.82 MV £
10 May 1979			
10 October 2007 Rights 1:15 @ £14	———	———	———
March 2015 c/f	( )	( )	( )

Gains

		Cost £	31 March 1982 MV £
Disposal proceeds .... × £.........................			
Less cost/31.3.82MV		( )	( )
Unindexed gain			
Less indexation allowance on original shares			

$\dfrac{\ldots\ldots\ldots - \ldots\ldots\ldots}{\ldots\ldots\ldots\ldots} = \ldots\ldots\ldots\ldots\ldots\ldots \times$ £.........................   (   ) (   )

Indexation allowance on rights shares

$\dfrac{\ldots\ldots\ldots - \ldots\ldots\ldots}{\ldots\ldots\ldots\ldots} = \ldots\ldots\ldots\ldots\ldots\ldots \times$ £.........................   (   ) (   )

Gains

Two gains, take lower gain

Chargeable gain

5 Substantial shareholding exemption

Section overview

- The substantial shareholding exemption applies to certain disposals of shares in a trading company by a trading company.

5.1 Substantial shareholding exemption

If a trading company, or member of a trading group, disposes of shares in another trading company (or holding company of a trading group) out of a **substantial shareholding**:

- Any capital gain arising is exempt from corporation tax
- Any capital loss is not allowable

Definition

Substantial shareholding: One where the investing company owns at least 10% of the ordinary share capital and is beneficially entitled to at least 10% of the:

- Distributable profits; and
- Assets on a winding up;

and these conditions have been satisfied for a continuous period of 12 months during the 2 years preceding the disposal.

The investing company must have been a trading company (or member of a trading group) throughout the period:

- Beginning with the start of the latest 12 month period in which the substantial shareholding conditions were satisfied
- Ending with the time of the disposal

The exemption applies to the disposal of the whole or part of the substantial shareholding.

Worked example: Substantial shareholding

M Ltd and T Ltd are trading companies.

M Ltd acquired 6% of the ordinary shares in T Ltd on 1 August 2012 and a further 7% of the ordinary shares in T Ltd on 10 September 2012.

M Ltd sold 4% of the ordinary shares on 15 May 2014, 5% of the ordinary shares on 13 December 2014 and the remaining 4% of ordinary shares on 18 June 2015.

Requirement

Explain whether the substantial shareholding exemption applies to each of the disposals.

Solution

Shareholding history

	%
1 August 2012	6
10 September 2012	7
	13
15 May 2014	(4)
	9
13 December 2014	(5)
	4
18 June 2015	(4)
	NIL

15 May 2014

In the two year period starting on 15 May 2012, the 10% test is satisfied by M Ltd from 10 September 2012 to 14 May 2014 which is more than 12 months.

The substantial shareholding exemption therefore applies to this disposal.

13 December 2014

In the two year period starting on 13 December 2012, the 10% test is satisfied by M Ltd from 13 December 2012 to 14 May 2014 which is more than 12 months.

The substantial shareholding exemption therefore applies to this disposal.

18 June 2015

In the two years period starting on 18 June 2013, the 10% test is satisfied by M Ltd from 18 June 2013 to 14 May 2014 which is less than 12 months.

The substantial shareholding exemption therefore does not apply to this disposal.

Summary

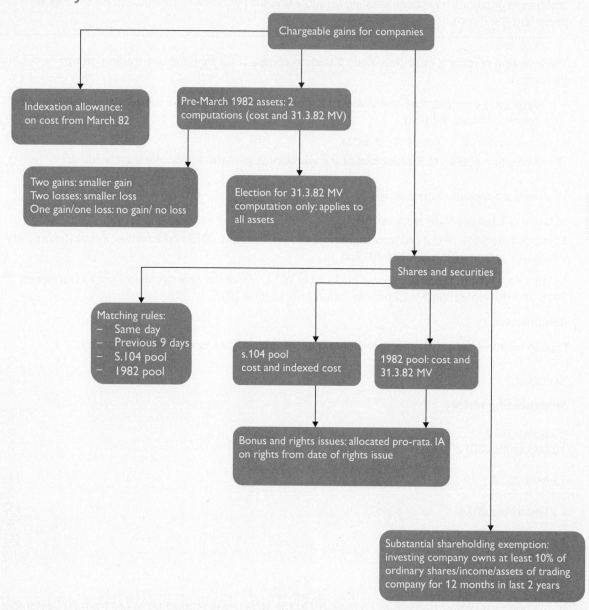

Chargeable gains for companies

Indexation allowance: on cost from March 82

Pre-March 1982 assets: 2 computations (cost and 31.3.82 MV)

Two gains: smaller gain
Two losses: smaller loss
One gain/one loss: no gain/ no loss

Election for 31.3.82 MV computation only: applies to all assets

Shares and securities

Matching rules:
– Same day
– Previous 9 days
– S.104 pool
– 1982 pool

s.104 pool
cost and indexed cost

1982 pool: cost and 31.3.82 MV

Bonus and rights issues: allocated pro-rata. IA on rights from date of rights issue

Substantial shareholding exemption: investing company owns at least 10% of ordinary shares/income/assets of trading company for 12 months in last 2 years

ICAEW

Self-test

Answer the following questions.

1   Which **two** of the following statements are **true?**

    A   The s.104 pool starts at 6 April 1985

    B   The 1982 pool is an unindexed pool

    C   Rights issue shares have indexation allowance from the date of the acquisition of the original shares to which they relate

    D   A bonus issue of shares is not an operative event in the s.104 pool

2   K Ltd bought 5,000 shares in Q plc in April 1985 (RPI 94.78) for £5,500. In July 1999, Q plc made a one for five bonus issue. The Q plc shares after the bonus issue were worth £2 each.

    K Ltd sold all its shares in December 2014 for £5 per share. RPI December 2014 260.2 (assumed).

    What is the chargeable gain on sale?

    A   £14,902
    B   £9,401
    C   £14,901
    D   £24,500

3   Z Ltd has the following transactions in shares in R plc:

July 1985 (RPI 95.23)	Acquired 10,000 shares for £11,500
May 1986 (RPI 97.85)	Rights 1 for 10 at £1.30 per share
October 2014 (RPI 258.7, assumed)	Sold all shares

    What is the indexation allowance on this disposal?

    A   £21,877
    B   £21,561
    C   £21,895
    D   £19,741

4   I Ltd disposes of an asset in December 2014. I Ltd had acquired the asset in August 1980.

    The computation on cost resulted in a loss of £(10,000).

    The computation on 31 March 1982 market value resulted in a loss of £(12,000).

    No election has been made to use 31 March 1982 market value.

    What is the allowable loss?

    A   NIL
    B   £(10,000)
    C   £(11,000)
    D   £(12,000)

5   N Ltd and J Ltd are both trading companies. N Ltd has owned 18% of the shares in J Ltd since 2001. On 1 March 2014 N Ltd sold a 10% stake in J Ltd.

    By what date must N Ltd sell the remaining 8% shareholding in J Ltd in order that the gain on disposal would be exempt?

    A   1 March 2013
    B   1 March 2014
    C   1 March 2015
    D   1 March 2016

6   Epsilon Ltd, a manufacturer of cuddly toys, prepares accounts to 31 December each year.

Epsilon Ltd has the following results for the year ended 31 December 2014:

	£
Trading income	653,000
Debenture interest receivable	12,000

Epsilon Ltd sold a factory on 10 October 2014 for £520,000. It had cost £138,000 to construct in February 1981. It had a market value at 31.3.82 of £157,000.

Epsilon Ltd also disposed of its holdings of shares in Teds Ltd, a trading company, in November 2014. It had purchased 1,500 shares (a 5% holding) in June 2011 for £23,000, and a further 2,400 shares (an 8% holding) in April 2012 for £31,000.

Requirement

Calculate the corporation tax payable by Epsilon Ltd for the year ended 31 December 2014. RPIs October 2014 258.7, November 2014 258.9 (assumed).

Now go back to the Learning Objectives in the Introduction. If you are satisfied you have achieved these objectives please tick them off.

Legislation

All references are to Taxation of Chargeable Gains Act 1992 (*TCGA 1992*).

Indexation allowance	ss.53 – 54
Assets acquired before 31 March 1982	s.35
Share matching rules:	
Same day	s.105
Previous nine days	s.107
S.104 pool	s.104
1982 pool	s.109
Bonus and rights issues	s.126
Consideration for rights issue	s.127
Indexation allowance on rights issue shares	s.131
Substantial shareholding exemption	Sch. 7AC
Exemption	para 1
Substantial shareholding definition	para 8

HMRC manual references

Capital gains manual

(Found at http://www.hmrc.gov.uk/manuals/CGmanual/index.HTM)

Share identification rules: introduction	CG50500
Introduction and computation; rebasing to 31 March 1982	CG16700

> This technical reference section is designed to assist you. It should help you know where to look for further information on the topics covered in this chapter.

Answer to Interactive question 1

S.104 pool

	No.	Cost £	Indexed cost £
July 1992			
Acquisition	4,650	24,760	24,760
August 1997			
Indexed rise			
$\dfrac{158.5-138.8}{138.8} \times £24,760$			3,514
Acquisition	3,500	39,375	39,375
			67,649
December 2014			
Indexed rise			
$\dfrac{260.2-158.5}{158.5} \times £67,649$			43,406
	8,150	64,135	111,055
Disposal	(4,375)	(34,428)	(59,615)
c/f	3,775	29,707	51,440

Gain

	£
Disposal proceeds	61,500
Less cost	(34,428)
Unindexed gain	27,072
Less indexation (£59,615 – £34,428)	(25,187)
Chargeable gain	1,885

Answer to Interactive question 2

S.104 pool

	No.	Cost £	Indexed cost £
15 June 1989			
Acquisition	1,050	4,375	4,375
10 October 2007			
Indexed rise			
$\dfrac{208.9-115.4}{115.4} \times £4,375$			3,545
Rights 1:15 @ £14	70	980	980
			8,900
March 2015			
Indexed rise			
$\dfrac{262.3-208.9}{208.9} \times 8,900$			2,275
	1,120	5,355	11,175
Disposal	(1,120)	(5,355)	(11,175)
c/f	NIL	NIL	NIL

Gain

	£
Disposal proceeds 1,120 × £15	16,800
Less cost	(5,355)
Unindexed gain	11,445
Less indexation (£11,175 – £5,355)	(5,820)
Chargeable gain	5,625

1982 pool

	No.	Cost	31 March 1982 MV
		£	£
10 May 1979	300	975	1,200
10 October 2007 Rights 1:15 @ £14	20	280	280
	320	1,255	1,480
March 2015	(320)	(1,255)	(1,480)
c/f	NIL	NIL	NIL

Gains

	Cost	31 March 1982 MV
	£	£
Disposal proceeds 320 × £15	4,800	4,800
Less cost / 31.3.82 MV	(1,255)	(1,480)
	3,545	3,320

Less: indexation allowance on original shares

$$\frac{262.3 - 79.44}{79.44} = 2.302 \times £1,200$$

	Cost	31 March 1982 MV
	(2,762)	(2,762)

indexation allowance on rights shares

$$\frac{262.3 - 208.9}{208.9} = 0.256 \times £280$$

	Cost	31 March 1982 MV
	(72)	(72)
Gain	711	486

Two gains, take lower gain

Chargeable gain	£486

1 B – The 1982 pool is an unindexed pool.

   D – A bonus issue of shares is not an operative event in the s.104 pool.

   A is incorrect. The s.104 pool starts at 6 April 1982.

   C is incorrect. Rights issue shares have indexation allowance from the date of the rights issue.

2 C – £14,901

S.104 pool

	No.	Cost £	Indexed cost £
April 1985 Acquisition	5,000	5,500	5,500
July 1999 Bonus 1:5	1,000	NIL	NIL
			5,500
December 2014 Indexed rise $\frac{260.2 - 94.78}{94.78} \times £5,500$			9,599
	6,000	5,500	15,099
Disposal	(6,000)	(5,500)	(15,099)
c/f	NIL	NIL	NIL

Gain

	£
Disposal proceeds 6,000 × £5	30,000
Less cost	(5,500)
Unindexed gain	24,500
Less indexation (£15,099 – £5,500)	(9,599)
Chargeable gain	14,901

3 A – £21,877

S.104 pool

	No.	Cost £	Indexed cost £
July 1985 Acquisition	10,000	11,500	11,500
May 1986 Indexed rise $\frac{97.85 - 95.23}{95.23} \times £11,500$			316
Rights 1:10 @ £1.30	1,000	1,300	1,300
			13,116
October 2014 Indexed rise $\frac{258.7 - 97.85}{97.85} \times £13,116$			21,561
	11,000	12,800	34,677
Disposal	(11,000)	(12,800)	(34,677)
c/f	NIL	NIL	NIL
Indexation allowance (£34,677 – £12,800)			£21,877

ICAEW

4   B – (£10,000)

Two losses – take smaller loss

If I Ltd is within the time limit for making an election to use 31.3.82 MV, it should consider doing so because this would allow it to use the larger loss of £(12,000).

5   C – 1 March 2015

The substantial shareholding exemption will continue to apply until 1 March 2015 (a 10% holding is required in 12 months of the 24 months prior to sale).

6   **Corporation tax computation**

Epsilon Ltd

Year ended 31 December 2014

	£
Trade profits	653,000
Loan relationships	12,000
Chargeable gain (W1), (W2)	8,651
Taxable total profits	673,651
Corporation tax	
FY13/FY14	
FY2013: 3/12 × 673,651 × 23%	38,735
FY2014: 9/12 × 673,651 × 21%	106,100
Less marginal relief	
FY2013: (1,500,000 – 673,651) × 3/400 × 3/12	(1,549)
FY2014: (1,500,000 – 673,651) × 1/400 × 9/12	(1,549)
Corporation tax liability	141,737

WORKINGS

(1)   Disposal of factory

	Cost	31 March 1982 MV
	£	£
Disposal proceeds	520,000	520,000
Less cost/ 31.3.82 mv	(138,000)	(157,000)
Unindexed gain	382,000	363,000
Less indexation allowance		
$\dfrac{258.7 - 79.44}{79.44} = 2.257 \times £157,000$	(354,349)	(354,349)
Indexed gains	27,651	8,651
Two gains, take smaller gain		
Chargeable gain		£8,651

(2)   Substantial shareholding exemption

Epsilon Ltd owned 13% of the shares in Teds Ltd from April 2012 until November 2014. The disposal of shares in Teds Ltd is exempt under the substantial shareholding exemption.

CHAPTER 21

Additional aspects of corporation tax

Introduction

Examination context

Topic List

Introduction

Learning objectives

Tick off

- Recognise the effect on trading profits of the treatment of intangible assets

- Calculate trading profits or losses after adjustments and allowable deductions

- Calculate the taxable total profits and the tax payable or repayable for companies including the computation of double tax relief where appropriate

Specific syllabus references for this chapter are 5b, 5c and 5e.

Syllabus links

In Chapter 10 of your Principles of Taxation study manual you learnt the basic computation of loan relationships. In this chapter, we cover some more detailed aspects such as incidental costs of loan finance.

Pension spreading, intangible fixed assets, research and development expenditure, details of property income for companies and double taxation relief were not covered in your Principles of Taxation study manual.

Examination context

In the examination a candidate may be required to:

- Calculate the correct adjustment to profit required to spread an employer's pension contributions in accordance with the legislation

- Identify the correct treatment for loan relationships

- Identify the correct treatment of intangible assets owned by a company

- Calculate the relief given to different sized companies for research and development expenditure

- Identify the differences in taxation of property income for companies compared to individuals

- Calculate the corporation tax liability for a UK based company with one or more sources of overseas income

At least one of the areas covered by this chapter is likely to be included in the exam. Candidates often fail to gain good marks, on areas such as loan relationships and intangible assets, due to not recognising the issues within the questions.

1 Pension contributions

Section overview

- An employer will obtain tax relief for pension contributions made when calculating trading profits for the period of account in which they are made, not accrued.

- There is no limit on the amount of tax deductible contributions an employer can make.

- Spreading provisions apply for large contributions.

1.1 Tax relief

All contributions made by an employer are made gross. The employer will usually obtain tax relief for the contribution by deducting it as an expense in calculating trading profits for the period of account in which the payment is made, not accrued.

However, HMRC may seek to disallow a contribution which it considers is not a revenue expense or is not made wholly and exclusively for the purposes of the trade. Circumstances which might lead to HMRC questioning the contributions include:

(a) Where a contribution is made on behalf of a controlling director (or close associate) at a disproportionately high level, or

(b) Where contributions are made in connection with the sale or cessation of a trade.

1.2 Pension spreading

Second, although there is no limit on the amount an employer may contribute, there are 'spreading provisions' for large contributions, so that part of the contribution is treated as paid in a later period of account. Spreading provisions do not apply where no contribution was paid in the previous year, eg the pension scheme has only just been set up.

These provisions apply where:

- The amount of the pension contribution in the current period exceeds 210% of that paid in the previous period, and

- The amount exceeding 110% of that paid in the previous period is at least £500,000. This amount is known as 'the excess'.

Then the maximum relief for the current period is 110% of the previous period's contribution plus a proportion of the excess:

Amount of excess contributions	Fractions and chargeable periods
Less than £500,000	No spreading required
£500,000 or more but less than £1m	½ treated as paid in current period, ½ treated as paid in the next chargeable period
£1m or more but less than £2m	⅓ treated as paid in the current period, ⅓ treated as paid in each of the next two chargeable periods
£2m or more	¼ treated as paid in the current period, ¼ treated as paid in each of the next three chargeable periods.

Worked example: Pension spreading

Aspic Ltd makes up accounts to 31 December each year. In the year ended 31 December 2015, it made a contribution of £3,000,000 to the pension scheme of one of its directors. In the year ended 31 December 2014, the corresponding pension contribution was £600,000.

Requirement

Show how the pension contribution for year ended 31 December 2015 will be given tax relief for Aspic Ltd.

Solution

Step 1   Does the contribution for year ended 31 December 2015 exceed 210% of the contributions for year ended 31 December 2014?

£600,000 × 210% = £1,260,000

The contribution of £3,000,000 exceeds this, so this test is met.

Step 2   What is the excess contribution for the rules?

The excess contribution is £3,000,000 – (600,000 × 110%) = £2,340,000

As the excess is greater than £500,000 this second part of the test is met and the spreading provisions will apply.

Step 3   Identify how the spreading provisions apply.

Current year (year ended 31 December 2015)

	£
Amount not subject to spreading provisions £(3,000,000 – 2,340,000)	660,000
Amount subject to spreading provisions 1/4 × £2,340,000	585,000
Total amount for tax relief	1,245,000

Next three years (years ended 31 December 2016, 31 December 2017 and 31 December 2018)

1/4 × £2,340,000 =   585,000

Remember that the amount which is not treated as an excess contribution will be given tax relief in the period of account in which it is paid.

In order for tax advantages to apply to a pension scheme, the scheme must be registered with HMRC.

Note that pension spreading rules also apply to unincorporated businesses.

2 Loan relationships

Section overview

- Loan relationships arise where a company borrows or lends money.

- Debits on a trading loan relationship are an allowable trading expense.

- Debits and credits on non-trading loan relationships are combined: a net credit is taxable as a profit on loan relationships, a net debit can be relieved (not in your syllabus).

- Incidental costs of loan relationships are debits.

- The loan relationship rules apply to all profits and losses (income or capital).

2.1 Trading and non-trading loan relationships

A company has a **loan relationship** if it loans money as a creditor or is loaned money as a debtor. It does not include trade debts.

All profits and losses on loans (whether the company is a lender or borrower) are treated as income. Interest payments are taxed or relieved on an accruals basis.

If the company has been lent money for trade purposes there is a **trading loan relationship**.

Examples of a trading loan relationship include a bank overdraft, debentures and loan stock which the company issues, and loans to buy plant and machinery. Interest payable on a trading loan relationship is an allowable trading expense to set against trading income. A company will not usually have receipts from a trading loan relationship unless its trade is that of money lending.

If the company has been lent money or lends money for a non-trade purpose, there is a **non-trading loan relationship**.

Examples of a non-trading loan relationship include a loan to purchase or improve a let property, a loan to acquire shares in another company and where interest is paid on overdue corporation tax. Interest paid on such relationships is a non-trading loan relationship debit.

Examples of receipts from non-trading loan relationships include interest on bank and building society accounts, gilt-edged securities, holding of debentures and loan stock, and where there is a repayment of overpaid corporation tax. Income from these sources is a non-trading loan relationship credit.

The non-trading loan relationship credits and debits are combined. If there is a net credit, this amount is taxable.

If there is a net debit, there will be no amount taxable as a non-trading loan relationship. Relief for the net debit is outside the scope of this syllabus.

2.2 Incidental costs of loan finance

The incidental costs of loan finance are debits under the loan relationship rules.

Examples include the costs of:

- Bringing a loan relationship into existence (even if not subsequently brought into existence)

- Entering into or giving effect to any related transaction (disposal or acquisition of rights or liabilities under a loan relationship)

- Making payments under a loan relationship or related transaction

- Taking steps to ensure the receipt of payments under the loan relationship or related transaction

2.3 Capital profits and losses on disposal

The loan relationship rules mean that all profits or losses arising from loan relationships must be treated as credits or debits, whether they are of an income or capital nature.

Therefore, a capital profit arising on a disposal of a debenture, loan stock or gilt-edged security is taxable as a loan relationship. Similarly, a capital loss arising on such a disposal is allowable as a loan relationship debit.

Note that the profit or loss is simply calculated as disposal proceeds less cost.

Interactive question 1: Taxable total profits and loan relationships
[Difficulty level: Intermediate]

G Ltd is a manufacturing company, making up accounts to 31 March each year.

The following information relates to the year to 31 March 2015:

- The company had tax adjusted trading income (before taking into account the items below) of £800,000.

- On 1 April 2014, the company sold debenture stock for £16,000 in W Ltd which it had acquired for £14,500 on 1 April 2011 as an investment.

- On 1 July 2014, the company issued £100,000 of 6% loan stock for the purpose of raising finance for its trade. The costs of issuing the loan stock amounted to £4,000.

- On 31 January 2015, it paid £600 interest on overdue tax to HMRC for the period from 1 January 2015 to 30 January 2015.

- On 31 March 2015, it received bank interest accrued for the year ending on that date of £3,750.

Requirement

Using the standard format below, compute the taxable total profits.

	£
Trading income (W1)	
Non-trading loan relationships (W2)	_____
Taxable total profits	======

WORKINGS

(1) **Trading income**

	£	£
Tax adjusted trading income		
Less trading loan relationship debits		
	_____	(_____)
Trading income		======

(2) **Non-trading loan relationship**

	£
Non-trading loan relationship credits:	
	_____
Less non-trading loan relationship debit:	(_____)
Net credit taxable as non-trading loan relationship	======

See **Answer** at the end of this chapter.

3 Intangible fixed assets

Section overview

- Special rules apply to intangible fixed assets such as patents and goodwill.

- Debits include payment of royalties and losses on sale of intangible fixed assets and are allowable as trading expenses.

- Credits include receipt of royalties and profits on sale of intangible fixed assets and are taxable as trading receipts.

- Normally, these rules mean that no adjustment is necessary to the accounting profit or loss in respect of such items.

3.1 What are intangible fixed assets?

Special rules apply to companies in relation to intangible fixed assets acquired or created on or after 1 April 2002.

Definition

Intangible fixed assets: Intangible assets acquired or created for use on a continuing basis in the course of a company's activities including:

- Intellectual property such as patents and copyrights
- Goodwill
- Agricultural quotas such as a milk quota

In your examination, all intangible fixed assets will be treated as being held for the purposes of the trade.

3.2 Treatment of intangible fixed assets

The rules in this section cover all profits and losses in relation to intangible fixed assets, whether income or capital in nature. Therefore the rules cover the payment and receipt of patent and copyright royalties, and profits and losses on the purchase and sale of patents, copyrights and goodwill.

A debit relating to an intangible fixed asset will arise, for example:

- When expenditure is written off as it is incurred eg payment of a patent royalty, loss on sale of intangible fixed asset

- On amortisation of capitalised cost

A debit is allowable as a trading expense.

A credit relating to an intangible fixed asset will arise, for example:

- When receipts are recognised as they accrue eg receipt of a patent royalty, profit on sale of intangible fixed asset

- When an asset is revalued in the accounts

A credit is taxable as a trading receipt.

If a company's accounts have been prepared in accordance with normal accounting practice, there will be no need to make any adjustment to the accounting profit or loss in respect of these items.

Read the examination question carefully to see what information you are given.

You may be given a figure for the tax adjusted trading profit **before** dealing with items such as interest from loan relationships and royalties (see Interactive question 1 above). In this type of question, you would need to deduct a patent royalty payable as this is an allowable trading expense.

Alternatively, you may be given a set of accounts (see Interactive question 2 below) which already includes profits and income receivable from intangible fixed assets and deducts items allowed for accounting purposes. In this type of question, you would not need to make any adjustment, for example, to a copyright royalty paid since it is an allowable trading expense as well being allowable as for accounting purposes.

Interactive question 2: Taxable total profits and intangible fixed assets

[Difficulty level: Intermediate]

J Ltd is a trading company. It has prepared accounts for the year to 31 March 2015 as follows:

	£	£
Gross trading profit		531,400
Profit on sale of investment land (indexed gain £15,100)		23,000
Profit on sale of patent		5,000
Patent royalties receivable		9,300
Bank interest receivable		400
		569,100
Less:		
Allowable manufacturing costs	150,400	
Allowable administrative costs	62,800	
Director's salaries and benefits	72,500	
Depreciation	43,700	
Patent royalties payable (accrued amount)	12,300	
Amortisation of goodwill	1,400	
		(343,100)
Net profit for the year		226,000

Requirement

Using the standard format below, compute the taxable total profits.

	£
Trading income (W)	
Loan relationships: bank interest	
Chargeable gain	_____
Taxable total profits	========

WORKING

Trading income

	£	£
Net profit per accounts		
Less non trading income		
	_____	(_____)
Add disallowable expenditure		
		_____
Trading income		========

See **Answer** at the end of this chapter.

4 Research and development expenditure

Section overview

- Qualifying R&D involves developing or improving the science or technology of a company's products, processes and services.

- Qualifying R&D is an allowable deduction against trading income.

- Where a company incurs qualifying R&D expenditure in an accounting period, it may deduct an additional amount representing 125% (small and medium companies) or 30% (large companies) of the actual expenditure.

4.1 What is research and development (R&D) expenditure?

R&D for tax purposes is defined with reference to guidelines produced by the government.

Examples of projects which would qualify as R&D are ones intended to:

- Extend overall knowledge or capability in a field of science or technology; or

- Create a process, material, device, product or service which incorporates or represents an increase in overall knowledge or capability in a field of science or technology; or

- Make an appreciable improvement to an existing process, material, device, product or service through scientific or technological changes; or

- Use science or technology to duplicate the effect of an existing process, material, device, product or service in a new or appreciably improved way.

The project must also seek to achieve an advance in overall knowledge or capability in a field of science or technology, not just the company's own state of knowledge or capability. It can include the production of a prototype, and trial production where it is needed to resolve technological uncertainty.

Routine or cosmetic improvements are not qualifying R&D.

Qualifying R&D expenditure includes revenue expenditure on:

- Staff directly (or indirectly if can be treated as R&D expenditure under UK GAAP) engaged on R&D

- External staff provider who (directly or indirectly through a staff controller) provides staff to be directly engaged on R&D

- Consumable or transformable materials

- Computer software

- Power, water and fuel

- Expenditure of the same nature subcontracted by a SME

Where staff are indirectly engaged in R&D, the expenditure only qualifies if it is specifically identifiable as a particular part of the activity of an R&D project eg training, maintenance, secretarial or payroll directly required for the R&D project. In order to qualify it must also be capable of being accounted for as R&D expenditure under UK GAAP or IAS.

For externally provided workers and subcontracted expenditure, only some of the expenditure may be allowable as qualifying R&D expenditure. If the workers are supplied by an unconnected company then only 65% of the payments made in respect of them will be qualifying expenditure. Where the provider is a connected company then the qualifying expenditure will be that paid up to a maximum of the provider's relevant expenditure in providing the staff. The company can elect for any company to be treated as a connected company.

In addition, capital expenditure on R&D (excluding the cost of land, if any) is also wholly allowable as a trading deduction ie 100% allowances are available in the year of purchase. If the capital assets are subsequently sold, the proceeds are taxed as a trading receipt.

In the case of computer related expenditure, computer software is included in the qualifying expenditure eligible for the additional deduction from trading profits. Computer hardware is eligible for a 100% initial capital allowance as capital expenditure relating to R&D.

4.2 Additional deduction against trading income for R&D expenditure

Where a company incurs qualifying R&D expenditure, it may deduct the income expenditure as an allowable trading expense under the usual rules. R&D capital expenditure is eligible for a 100% first year allowance as explained above.

Where a company incurs qualifying R&D expenditure in an accounting period, it may take an additional trading deduction.

The amount of the additional deduction depends on whether the company is small/medium-sized or is a large company.

Definition

Small or medium sized enterprise (SME) for R&D: A company which has:

- Fewer than 500 employees; and
- Either:
    - An annual turnover not exceeding 100 million Euros; or
    - An annual balance sheet total not exceeding 86 million Euros.

A company which is not within this definition is a large company. In the examination, you will be told whether a company is a SME or a large company.

A SME may make an additional 125% deduction against trading income. [Hp121]

R&D relief on expenditure on an R&D project for a SME is capped at 7.5 million euros. SMEs may be able to claim reliefs under the large company scheme for expenditure exceeding the cap. The additional deduction is only available where the SME's last accounts were prepared on a going concern basis, and the company is not in liquidation or administration.

A large company may take an additional 30% deduction against trading income.

In general, a large company can only claim for R&D expenditure if it carries out the R&D itself. If a SME undertakes work as a subcontractor on behalf of a large company (ie the work is subcontracted to the SME), it can claim an additional 30% deduction instead of the usual 125%.

Worked example: R&D expenditure

Y Ltd is a small company. In the year to 31 March 2015, it has the following results:

	£
Trading income (before taking into account R&D expenditure)	265,000
Qualifying R&D expenditure (no capital expenditure)	108,000
Bank interest receivable	2,000
Chargeable gain	28,000

Requirement

Compute the taxable total profits of Y Ltd for the year ended 31 March 2015.

Solution

	£
Trading income before R&D expenditure	265,000
Less 225% R&D deduction	(243,000)
Trading income	22,000
Non-trading loan relationships	2,000
Chargeable gain	28,000
Taxable total profits	52,000

5 Property income

Section overview

- Property income is generally taxable on a company in the same way as property income for an individual.

- There are slightly different rules relating to losses, expenses and qualifying holiday accommodation.

5.1 Property income

In general, the rules for property income for companies are the same as for property income for individuals which were explained in Chapter 3. There are a few differences which are dealt with in the rest of this section.

Note in particular the rules on the grant of short leases.

5.2 Losses

A property loss is first set off against total profits for the accounting period in which the loss arose.

Any remaining loss is carried forward to the next accounting period as if it were a property loss of that accounting period (ie can be offset against total profits of that accounting period, not just against property income) and so on, until the loss is completely relieved.

5.3 Interest paid to buy or improve property

Interest paid to buy or improve property is dealt with under the loan relationships rules. Therefore, such interest is not an allowable expense against property income.

5.4 Landlord's energy saving allowance

Landlords can have an allowable expense of up to £1,500 per dwelling for loft/cavity floor insulation, draught proofing and hot water system insulation.

6 Double taxation relief

Section overview

- A UK resident company is liable to UK corporation tax on its world-wide profits.

- Where a UK resident company operates both in the UK and overseas, it may suffer both UK corporation tax and overseas tax on its overseas profits.

- Double taxation relief (DTR) exists to give relief either via treaty relief or unilateral relief where no such treaty exists.

- Any overseas income received should be grossed up and included in the corporation tax computation of the UK company.

- Dividends received from overseas companies are usually exempt from tax. They may form part of franked investment income (FII). The dividend received is grossed up by 100/90 for the purposes of FII. Any overseas taxes suffered in respect of the dividend are ignored.

- Each overseas source of income is considered separately when calculating the amount of DTR available.

- Consideration should be given to the allocation qualifying charitable donations to UK income in priority to overseas income in order to maximise DTR available.

- Unrelieved foreign tax on most foreign sources of income is lost.

A UK resident company which also operates overseas will be liable to UK corporation tax on its world-wide profits.

A UK company may receive other income from overseas, for example rental income from an overseas property, which will be taxable in the UK. Many countries also deduct tax on income remitted overseas (withholding tax).

It is likely that the foreign income will be subject to both foreign and UK corporation tax. There are three principal ways in which double taxation relief can be given:

- Under the terms of a double tax treaty (treaty relief); or
- Unilateral double tax relief where no double tax treaty exists (unilateral relief); or
- Expense relief.

For the purposes of your exam you should always use unilateral relief in exam questions.

6.1 Treaty relief

The UK has a network of double taxation treaties with a number of other countries. Most such treaties allow the UK company a credit for tax suffered on income and gains derived from the other country. The basic principles of treaty relief are as follows:

- Treaties always take precedence over UK tax law

- If double tax relief is given under a double tax treaty, then unilateral relief via the UK tax provisions cannot be given, unless claimed in preference

- Most double tax treaties follow the standard OECD model

6.2 Unilateral relief

Where no double tax treaty provision applies, unilateral relief allows double taxation relief (DTR) as a credit against the UK corporation tax liability on the foreign income.

6.3 Expense relief

Where a company has overseas income but its UK tax liability is nil or very small, the UK company can choose to treat the overseas tax as an expense and include the overseas income in the corporation tax computation net of the overseas tax.

6.4 Classification of overseas income

The following overseas income is examinable:

- Non-trading loan relationships – income from overseas securities eg interest from debentures in an overseas company

- Property income eg foreign rental income

- Foreign dividend income

6.5 Foreign dividend income

All dividends received, whether received from UK companies or overseas companies, are treated in the same way. All dividends received are exempt from corporation tax if they fall within a prescribed list of exemptions.

The list of exemptions available for dividends is wide ranging and in almost all cases therefore foreign dividends received will be exempt dividends. From 1 July 2009 the repatriation of profits of overseas subsidiaries is therefore unlikely to be subject to UK corporation tax. The DTR position in cases where the exemptions do not apply is considered briefly below.

Exempt foreign dividends received from non-associated companies are included in franked investment income (FII) and are therefore taken into account when determining the rate of tax charged. The amount included in FII is the amount of the dividend received grossed up by 100/90. Any overseas tax suffered in respect of the dividend is ignored.

You will be told in the exam whether foreign dividends received are taxable in the UK.

6.6 Taxing overseas income

Overseas income is received by UK resident companies net of foreign tax, but the gross amount of this income is assessable to UK corporation tax. Overseas income must therefore be grossed up for any overseas tax suffered for inclusion in the UK corporation tax computation.

Foreign taxes are classified as either withholding tax (WHT) or underlying tax (UT).

- WHT is a direct tax on income and is always potentially recoverable on any source of income. It relates to tax withheld on remittances of income to the UK.

- UT is the overseas tax suffered on an overseas company's profits out of which foreign dividends are paid. It is now largely irrelevant for UK tax purposes as almost all foreign dividends are now exempt from UK corporation tax, and it is not included when calculating FII.

Worked example: Unilateral relief, single source of income

The board of R plc, a large company, has decided to expand into Europe. As a first step R plc bought 20% of the ordinary share capital of Axis SpA early in 2014.

R plc prepares its accounts to 31 March each year and in the year ended 31 March 2015 made a trading profit of £1,400,000.

In addition on 1 January 2015 R plc received from Axis SpA a dividend of £90,440 after 12% withholding tax. The dividend is exempt for corporation tax in the UK.

R plc also owns an overseas investment property from which it received rental income, after 5% withholding tax, of £47,500 during the year ended 31 March 2015.

No double tax treaty exists between the UK and Axis SpA's country of residence.

Requirement

Compute the augmented profits and state the corporation tax rate payable by R plc for the year ended 31 March 2015.

Solution

R plc – Year ended 31 March 2015

	£
Trading income	1,400,000
Property income (£47,500 × 100/95)	50,000
Taxable total profits	1,450,000
Add FII: Exempt dividend received × 100/90	
£90,440 × 100/90	100,489
Augmented profits	1,550,489

The company therefore pays the main rate of tax (21%) for the year to 31 March 2015.

6.7 Calculating DTR

In computing the DTR available to a company, each source of income must be considered separately. The DTR is the lower of:

- The UK tax on the overseas income ie gross overseas income x company's average UK corporation tax rate; and

- The overseas tax suffered in respect of each separate source.

Each source of income is considered separately when calculating the amount of double taxation relief available.

6.8 Interaction of qualifying donations & DTR

Where a company has deductions from total profits, such as qualifying charitable donations, it can choose to offset them in such a manner as to maximise its DTR. This is achieved by offsetting the deductions against UK income first followed by foreign income which has suffered the lowest marginal rate of overseas tax.

Worked example: Unilateral relief, multiple sources of income

SAM Ltd has received rental income from two properties situated in Utopia and Ruritania.

SAM Ltd has the following results for the year ended 31 March 2015:

	£
Trading income	200,000
Property income (gross Utopian rental income)	100,000
Property income (gross Ruritanian rental income)	100,000
Qualifying charitable donations	210,000
Foreign tax has been suffered as follows	
Property income (Utopian rental income)	10,000
Property income (Ruritanian rental income)	40,000

Requirement

Calculate SAM Ltd's corporation tax liability for the year ended 31 March 2015.

Solution

Corporation tax computation – year ended 31 March 2015

	£
Trading income	200,000
Property income Utopia	100,000
Property income Ruritania	100,000
	400,000
Qualifying charitable donations	(210,000)
Taxable total profits	190,000
Corporation tax @ 20%	38,000
DTR (Working)	(30,000)
Corporation tax liability	8,000

WORKING

	Trading income	Property Income Utopia	Property income Ruritania	Total
	£	£	£	£
Profits	200,000	100,000	100,000	400,000
Qualifying charitable donations	(200,000)	(10,000)	–	(210,000)
Taxable total profits	–	90,000	100,000	190,000
Corporation tax @ 20%	–	18,000	20,000	38,000
Double tax relief				
Lower of – £18,000				
– £10,000	–	(10,000)	–	(10,000)
Lower of – £20,000	–	–	(20,000)	(20,000)
– £40,000				
Corporation tax payable	–	8,000	–	8,000

The unrelieved overseas tax of £20,000 (£40,000 – £20,000) from the Ruritanian rental income is lost.

Note: If the surplus donations of £10,000 had been offset against the Ruritanian source of property income, the double tax relief would be reduced to £18,000 on that source.

6.9 DTR on taxable foreign dividends

As noted above, the majority of foreign dividends received by a UK company are exempt from corporation tax. However, if a UK company receives a non-exempt dividend, it may still be able to claim DTR to offset its corporation tax liability on the dividend.

DTR is available in respect of:

* Withholding taxes, and

- Where the UK company controls at least 10% of the voting rights in the foreign company, the underlying corporate tax paid by the company on the profits from which the dividend is paid.

The amount of the dividend is grossed up for both withholding tax and underlying tax to determine the amount of taxable income. The DTR calculation is then the same as for other sources of income.

6.9.1 Underlying tax

The amount of underlying tax which is taken into account is calculated as:

(Gross dividend received/Profit available for distribution per the accounts) × Tax paid

Where a dividend resolution specifies the period for which a dividend is paid, the calculation is done with reference to the tax paid and accounts for that period. Where it does not, you should look to the accounts and profits of the last period for which the paying company draws up accounts ending before the dividend was paid.

The amount of DTR which is attributable to a dividend is capped at the UK tax attributable to the dividend, under the 'mixer cap' provisions. In practice, this is only relevant where a dividend is paid through a chain of companies before reaching the UK. If a dividend is received directly in the UK, the limitation of the DTR to the lower of the foreign tax or the UK tax on the same income will achieve the same result.

Worked example: Underlying tax

Ball Ltd (a member of a large global group) has a 25% shareholding in Foot SA, which is a company resident in Fantopia. Dividends received from Foot SA are not exempt from corporation tax.

In the year ended 31 March 2015, Ball Ltd's only income was a dividend of £12,750 from Foot SA. This was after deduction of Fantopian withholding tax of 15%. The dividend was paid out of Foot SA's profits for the year ended 31 December 2014. Its accounts for that period showed distributable profits of £106,500, and its tax return shows a tax payment of £8,300.

Requirement

Calculate Ball Ltd's corporation tax liability for the year ended 31 March 2015.

You should assume that it is liable to corporation tax at the main rate.

Solution

Corporation tax computation – year ended 31 March 2015

	£
Net dividend	12,750
Add WHT (15/85 × £12,750)	2,250
Gross dividend	15,000
Underlying Tax: (£15,000/ £106,500) × £8,300	1,169
Taxable total profits	16,169
Corporation tax @ 21%	3,395
DTR lower of : UK tax of £3,395, and	
overseas tax of (£2,250 + £1,169) = £3,419	(3,395)
Corporation tax liability	-

6.10 Unrelieved foreign tax

Where the overseas tax exceeds the amount of UK tax on the foreign income, unrelieved foreign tax (UFT) is created. UFT on foreign sources of rental income, dividend income and income from foreign non-trading loan relationships is simply lost.

Summary and Self-test

Summary

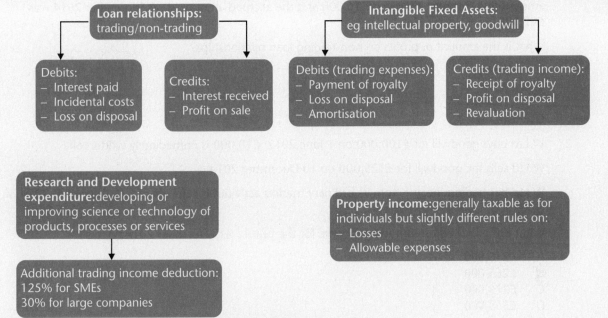

Loan relationships:
trading/non-trading

Debits:
– Interest paid
– Incidental costs
– Loss on disposal

Credits:
– Interest received
– Profit on sale

Intangible Fixed Assets:
eg intellectual property, goodwill

Debits (trading expenses):
– Payment of royalty
– Loss on disposal
– Amortisation

Credits (trading income):
– Receipt of royalty
– Profit on disposal
– Revaluation

Research and Development expenditure: developing or improving science or technology of products, processes or services

Additional trading income deduction:
125% for SMEs
30% for large companies

Property income: generally taxable as for individuals but slightly different rules on:
– Losses
– Allowable expenses

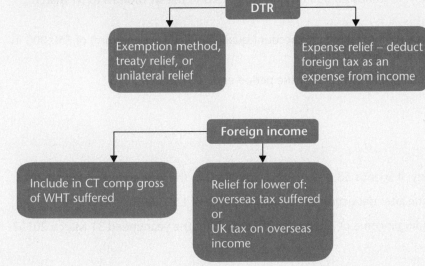

DTR

Exemption method, treaty relief, or unilateral relief

Expense relief – deduct foreign tax as an expense from income

Foreign income

Include in CT comp gross of WHT suffered

Relief for lower of:
overseas tax suffered
or
UK tax on overseas income

Self-test

Answer the following questions.

1   D Ltd made up accounts for the year to 30 September 2014.

It made an interest payment of £12,000 on 30 September 2014 on a loan to acquire shares in another company. This amount was also the amount accrued for the year. The costs of making the payment were £100.

D Ltd received £20,000 of bank interest on 31 March 2014 for the year to that date. The accrued amount at 1 October 2013 was £16,000 and the accrued amount at 30 September 2014 was £22,000.

What is the amount of profits on non-trading loan relationships?

A   £7,900
B   £9,900
C   £13,900
D   £14,000

2   W Ltd buys goodwill for £100,000 on 1 June 2012. £10,000 is immediately written off.

W Ltd sells the goodwill for £125,000 on 10 December 2014.

W Ltd has trading income from its ordinary trading activities for the year to 31 December 2014 of £240,000.

What is the final adjusted trading income for the year to 31 December 2014?

A   £240,000
B   £265,000
C   £275,000
D   £365,000

3   H Ltd is a small company. It spends £8,000 on qualifying R&D in the six months to 31 March 2015.

H Ltd has trading income (before taking into account qualifying R&D expenditure) of £50,000 in the period. It has no other income or gains.

What are the taxable total profits of H Ltd for the period ended 31 March 2015?

A   NIL
B   £32,000
C   £40,000
D   £42,000

4   Z Ltd is a large company. It spends £8,000 on qualifying R&D in the year ended 31 March 2015.

Z Ltd has trading income after deduction of the R&D expense of £503,000.

What is the taxable trading income of Z Ltd after R&D relief, for the year ended 31 March 2015?

A   £511,000
B   £503,000
C   £500,600
D   £492,600

5 Leopard Ltd

Leopard Ltd is a UK resident company that manufactures and sells specialist security equipment. Leopard Ltd prepares accounts to 31 January and the results for the year ended 31 January 2015 are as follows:

	Notes	£
Adjusted trading profit before interest, royalties and capital allowances		733,943
Interest receivable		4,000
Patent royalties payable	(1)	22,500
Dividends received from UK companies (all shareholdings < 5%)		2,650
Profit on the sale of shares in Grant Ltd	(2)	16,898
Profit on the sale of old office premises, No. 5b Bay Mews	(3)	233,794
Interest payable	(4)	3,789
Qualifying charitable donation paid to Red Cross		2,500

Notes

(1) The patent royalties relate to an infra red security alarm that Leopard Ltd manufactures for the commercial market. The royalties are paid to a company. This amount includes an accrual of £7,500 to 31 January 2015.

(2) Grant Ltd is a company which provides security personnel for high profile public events. Leopard Ltd purchased 11,000 shares in Grant Ltd in October 2003 for £424,800. The shares represented a 12.5% stake in the company. The shares were sold in January 2015 for £441,698.

(3) Leopard Ltd purchased No. 5b Bay Mews in June 1999 for £314,890, plus stamp duty land tax and legal fees totalling £8,740. The property was sold in September 2014 at auction for £568,880 and had always been used by Leopard Ltd for the purposes of its trade. Leopard Ltd incurred fees of £15,875 in connection with the sale.

(4) The interest comprises the following:

	£
Hire purchase interest on agreement to purchase a forklift truck The agreement was entered into on 12 December 2014 The cash price of the forklift truck was £11,184	466
Debenture interest payable on finance raised to fund the purchase of the factory	1,248
Bank overdraft interest	883
Interest on a loan taken out to purchase 5b Bay Mews	1,192
	3,789

The tax written down values brought forward at 1 February 2014 were as follows:

Main pool	£384,885
Short life asset	£11,250

In addition to the forklift truck, the following acquisitions and disposals were made by Leopard Ltd during the year.

Acquisitions

		£
1 April 2014	Car for Leopard Ltd's marketing director which was used 80% for private purposes; CO_2 emissions 125g/km	23,900
26 July 2014	Computer equipment	4,719
30 July 2014	Machinery	19,865

Disposals

		£
15 July 2014	Van (purchased for £5,588)	1,400
3 January 2015	Car, CO_2 emissions 128g/km (purchased for £10,700)	8,800

Leopard Ltd has no associated companies.

Requirement

Calculate the corporation tax payable by Leopard Ltd for the year ended 31 January 2015, assuming all beneficial claims and elections are made. Show your treatment of all sources of income received by the company. **(18 marks)**

Retail prices index:

June 1999	165.6
October 2003	182.6
September 2014	258.7 (assumed)
January 2015	259.4 (assumed)

6 Holmes Ltd is a large UK resident company with the following results for the year ended 31 March 2015.

	£
Trading income	300,500
Foreign rental income (inclusive of overseas tax of £50,000)	150,000
Dividends received from foreign companies in different tax territories (no double tax treaty applies to any of the territories)	
Reichenbach Ltd (inclusive of £10,000 WHT) – taxable in the UK	250,000
Lestrade Ltd (after £13,500 WHT) – exempt in the UK	76,500
Qualifying charitable donations paid	50,500

Note:

Holmes Ltd owns the following holdings in the ordinary share capital of the following foreign companies:

	%
Reichenbach Ltd	100
Lestrade Ltd	5

Requirement

Calculate the UK corporation tax payable by Holmes Ltd, explaining the relief for foreign tax suffered. **(10 marks)**

Now go back to the Learning Objectives in the Introduction. If you are satisfied you have achieved these objectives please tick them off.

Technical reference

Legislation

All references are to Corporation Tax Act 2009 (*CTA 2009*)

Loan relationships

Taxation of loan relationships	s.295
Meaning of loan relationship	s.302
Bringing amounts into account	s.296
Incidental costs	s.307(4)

Intangible Fixed Assets

Definition of Intangible Fixed Assets		s.712 – s.713
Debits:	Expenditure written off as incurred	s.728
	Amortisation	s.729
Credits:	Receipts recognised as they accrue	s.721 – s.722
	Revaluation	s.723

R&D expenditure

Entitlement	s.1044, s.1050
Qualifying R&D	s.1051 – s.1053
Subcontracted expenditure	s.1127 – s.1132

Property income

Furnished Holiday Accommodation	s.265

Double taxation relief

All references are to Taxation (International and Other Provisions) Act 2010 *(TIOPA 2010)*

Treaty relief	ss.2 & 18
Unilateral relief	ss.8 & 18
Limit on credit against corporation tax	s.42
Allocation of deductions	s.52

HMRC manual references

Company Taxation manual

(Found at http://www.hmrc.gov.uk/manuals/ctmanual/index.htm)

> This technical reference section is designed to assist you. It should help you to know where to look for further information on the topics covered in this chapter.

Answer to Interactive question 1

	£
Trading income (W1)	791,500
Loan relationships (W2)	4,650
Taxable total profits	796,150

WORKINGS

(1) **Trading income**

	£	£
Tax adjusted trading income		800,000
Less: trading loan relationship debits		
incidental costs of finance	4,000	
interest payable (1.7.14 – 31.3.15)		
£100,000 × 6% × 9/12	4,500	(8,500)
Trading income		791,500

(2) **Non-trading loan relationship**

	£
Non-trading loan relationship credits:	
Profit on sale of debenture stock	
(£16,000 – £14,500)	1,500
Bank interest receivable	3,750
	5,250
Less: non-trading loan relationship debit:	
interest on overdue corporation tax	(600)
Net credit taxable as non-trading loan relationship	4,650

Answer to Interactive question 2

	£
Trading income (W)	246,300
Loan relationships: bank interest	400
Chargeable gain	15,100
Taxable total profits	261,800

WORKING

Trading income

	£	£
Net profit per accounts		226,000
Less: non trading income (Note 1)		
profit on sale of investment land	23,000	
bank interest	400	
		(23,400)
		202,600
Add: disallowable expenditure (Note 2)		
depreciation		43,700
Trading income		246,300

Notes

1   The profit on the sale of the patent, and the patent royalties receivable are credits from intangible fixed assets and are therefore part of trading income. As a result, no adjustment is required for these items. Compare the treatment of the profit on the investment land.

2   The patent royalties payable (accrued amount) and the amortisation of the goodwill are debits from intangible fixed assets and are therefore allowable trading expenses. As a result, no adjustment is required for these items. Compare the treatment of depreciation.

3   It is important to remember that these rules only apply to **companies**. If you were undertaking an adjustment to profit for a sole trader or partnership, the following treatment would apply:

Item	Treatment for unincorporated business
Profit on sale of patent	Deduct. May result in capital gain on sale.
Patent royalties payable	Allowable if relating to the trade.
Amortisation of goodwill	Add back. Disallowable expense.

All other items will treated in the same way as for a company.

1 C – £13,900

Loan relationships

	£	£
Bank interest accrued income b/f	(16,000)	
Add: cash received	20,000	
closing accrual	22,000	
		26,000
Loan interest paid (accrued)	12,000	
Add cost of payment	100	(12,100)
		13,900

2 C – £275,000

	£
Profit on ordinary trading activities	240,000
Add profit on sale of goodwill (W)	35,000
Trading income	275,000

WORKING

	£	£
Sale proceeds		125,000
Less: original cost	100,000	
written off	(10,000)	(90,000)
Profit on sale		35,000

3 B – £32,000

As a small company H Ltd is entitled to an additional 125% trading income deduction.

	£
Trading income	50,000
R&D deduction (225% × £8,000)	(18,000)
Taxable total profits	32,000

4 C – £500,600

Z Ltd can claim an additional 30% R&D deduction in the accounting period.

	£
Trading income (includes R&D expense)	503,000
R&D deduction (30% × £8,000)	(2,400)
Taxable total profits	500,600

5   **Leopard Ltd**

Corporation tax computation for the year ended 31 January 2015

	£
Trading income (W1)	598,116
Loan relationships	4,000
Chargeable gains (W3)	47,495
	649,611
Less qualifying donation	(2,500)
Taxable total profits	647,111
Add FII £2,650 × 100/90	2,944
Augmented profits	650,055

Limits for marginal relief are:

Upper limit = £1,500,000
Lower limit = £300,000

Marginal relief applies

	£
FY2013: £647,111 × 2/12 × 23%	24,806
FY2014: £647,111 × 10/12 × 21%	113,244

Marginal relief

FY2013: $(£1,500,000 - £650,055) \times \dfrac{647,111}{650,055} \times \dfrac{3}{400} \times 2/12$ (1,058)

FY2014: $(£1,500,000 - £650,055) \times \dfrac{647,111}{650,055} \times \dfrac{1}{400} \times 10/12$ (1,763)

| Corporation tax liability | 135,229 |

The sale of shares in Grant Ltd is exempt under the substantial shareholding exemption.

The dividends received from UK companies are not subject to corporation tax.

WORKINGS

(1) **Trading income**

	£
Adjusted profit per question	733,943
Less: patent royalties payable	(22,500)
interest on HP agreement	(466)
interest on loan taken out to purchase factory	(1,248)
bank overdraft interest	(883)
interest on loan to purchase 5b Bay Mews	(1,192)
Adjusted trading profit	707,654
Less capital allowances (W2)	(109,538)
Trading income	598,116

(2) **Capital allowances on plant and machinery**

	Main pool £	Short life asset £	Allowances £
TWDVs b/f	384,885	11,250	
Additions (AIA)			
26.7.14 Computer	4,719		
30.7.14 Machinery	19,865		
12.12.14 Forklift truck	11,184		
	35,768		
AIA	(35,768)		35,768
Addition (no AIA)			
1.4.14 Car	23,900		
Disposals			
15.7.14 Van	(1,400)		
3.1.15 Car	(8,800)		
	398,585		
WDA @ 18%	(71,745)	(2,025)	73,770
TWDVs c/f	326,840	9,225	
Allowances			109,538

(3) **Gain on sale of 5b Bay Mews**

	£	£
Proceeds	568,880	
Less: costs of disposal	(15,875)	
Net disposal consideration		553,005
Less: cost	314,890	
costs of acquisition	8,740	
		(323,630)
Unindexed gain		229,375
Less indexation allowance		

$$\frac{258.7 - 165.6}{165.6} = 0.562 \times £323,630$$

		(181,880)
Indexed gain		47,495

6 Corporation tax computation – year ended 31 March 2015

	Trading Income UK £	Rental Income Non-UK £	Dividend Income Non-UK	Total £
Trading profits	300,500	150,000	250,000	700,500
Qualifying charitable donations	(50,500)			(50,500)
Taxable total profits	250,000	150,000	250,000	650,000
Corporation tax @ 21%				136,500

Less marginal relief (W1)

$$\frac{1}{400} \times (£750,000 - £735,000) \times \frac{£650,000}{£735,000}$$

	(33)
	136,467

Double tax relief

Lower of – UK tax (W2) £31,485 / £52,475

– Overseas tax £50,000 / £10,000

	(41,485)
Corporation tax payable	94,982

The unrelieved foreign tax of £18,515 (£50,000 - £31,485) from the rental income is lost. The DTR for the taxable foreign dividends is restricted to the £10,000 of actual foreign tax paid.

WORKINGS

(1) Augmented profits calculation

	£
Taxable total profits	650,000
Add FII: Exempt dividend received from non-associated company x 100/90	
£76,500 × 100/90	85,000
Augmented profits	735,000

The company has one associated company – Reichenbach Ltd.

Profits limits £150,000 to £750,000. The company therefore pays tax at the marginal rate.

(2) UK corporation tax suffered on foreign income

The UK corporation tax suffered on the foreign income is simply calculated at the average rate of corporation tax paid by Holmes Ltd:

$$\frac{£136,467}{£650,000} = 20.99\%$$

UK tax on foreign income is:

Rental income = £150,000 × 20.99% = £31,485

Dividends = £250,000 × 20.99% = £52,475

Note:

The calculation of the UK taxation suffered on foreign income is much simpler for corporation tax purposes than it is for income tax purposes. The rules for income tax are set out in s.36 TIOPA 2010. The income tax rules require that each source of foreign income is stripped out one by one and a full income tax computation redone with one source less of foreign income each time in order to calculate how much income tax would be payable without that source of income. The difference between the previous income tax computation and the revised computation therefore being the amount of UK income tax payable on that source of foreign income. See Chapter 14 for more details.

CHAPTER 22

Value added tax

Introduction

Examination context

Topic List

    1 Supplies

    2 Partial exemption

    3 Property transactions

    4 Capital goods scheme

    5 Overseas aspects

Summary and Self-test

Technical reference

Answers to Interactive questions

Answers to Self-test

Learning objectives

- Explain the VAT consequences of property transactions ☐

- Explain the VAT consequences of the option to tax ☐

- Explain and calculate the VAT consequences of the capital goods scheme ☐

- Calculate the VAT due to or from HMRC for both wholly taxable and partially exempt traders ☐

- Explain the VAT consequences of imports and exports of goods and services to and from VAT registered and non-VAT registered entities in the EU and overseas ☐

- Explain the classification of supplies and the distinction between goods and services ☐

- Explain the VAT treatment of single and multiple supplies ☐

Specific syllabus references for this chapter are 6a, 6b, 6c, 6d, 6e, 6f and 6g.

Syllabus links

In Chapter 11 of your Principles of Taxation study manual, you learnt about the basic principles of VAT – the scope of VAT, classification of supplies, and input and output tax.

You need to know these basic concepts in order to deal with the more advanced topics in this chapter.

Examination context

In the examination candidates may be required to:

- Explain the VAT consequences of property transactions including the option to tax

- Explain the VAT consequences for a particular transaction within the capital goods scheme

- Compute the input tax recoverable as a result of partial exemption

- Identify the VAT issues of trading with other EU states and countries outside the EU

- Explain the VAT treatment of single and multiple supplies

Candidates have historically been weak at VAT questions. It is essential that candidates take time to understand and learn VAT.

Many businesses are VAT registered and VAT issues arise in every exam.

1 Supplies

Section overview

- Taxable supplies include standard rated supplies, reduced rate and zero rated supplies. Exempt supplies are not taxable supplies.

- Determining the type of supply is a process of elimination. The legislation lists zero rated, exempt and reduced rate supplies. If the supply is not in any of the lists it is standard rated.

- A supply may be either of goods or services. Different rules may apply depending on whether the supply is one or the other.

- Where a number of items is supplied at the same time, it is essential to determine whether it is a single supply with one VAT rate, or a multiple supply, where the VAT must be apportioned between its different elements.

1.1 Classification of supplies

1.1.1 Overview

The VAT legislation lists zero rated supplies in Schedule 8, exempt supplies in Schedule 9 and reduced rate supplies in Schedule 7A. There is no list of standard rated supplies since a supply is standard rated if it does not fall within one of the other lists. A summary of the lists is available in Hardman's. [Hp236]

If a trader makes a supply you need to categorise that supply for VAT as follows:

Step 1   Look at the zero rated list to see if it is zero rated. If not:

Step 2   Look at the reduced rate list to see if the reduced rate of VAT applies. If not:

Step 3   Look at the exempt list to see if it is exempt. If not:

Step 4   The supply is standard rated.

Zero rated supplies are taxable at 0%, exempt supplies are not subject to VAT at all, reduced rated supplies are taxable at 5% and standard rated supplies are taxable at 20%.

1.1.2 Exceptions to the lists

The zero rated list, exempt list and reduced rate list outline general categories of goods or services which are either zero rated, exempt or charged at the reduced rate. The VAT legislation then goes into great detail to outline exceptions to each general rule.

For example, the zero rated list states that human food is zero rated. However, the legislation then states that food supplied in the course of catering (eg restaurant meals, hot takeaways) is not zero rated. Some snacks (eg crisps, peanuts, confectionery, chocolate covered biscuits) are also not zero rated.

The heading of Group 5 Sch 9 suggests that 'finance' is exempt. However, the detail of the legislation only includes certain specific financial services as being within the scope of the exemption (eg transferring shares and securities, and acting as an intermediary in such a transfer). Some financial services are specifically stated to be excluded from exemption and are therefore taxable (eg the management of credit unless the person supplying the service is also advancing the credit). Other financial services are not mentioned at all – this means that they are taxable, because exemption only applies to items which are explicitly included. Examples are investment advice (without intermediary services) and debt collection.

1.1.3 Zero rated or exempt?

A VAT registered trader who makes zero rated supplies (outputs) but suffers standard rate VAT on its purchases (inputs) can claim a repayment of the input VAT paid on the purchases.

A person making only exempt supplies cannot register for VAT and cannot recover VAT on inputs, so the VAT incurred is a real cost for the business. The trader could increase his prices to pass on the charge to customers, but he cannot issue a VAT invoice which would enable a VAT registered customer to obtain a credit for the VAT suffered, as no VAT is chargeable on his supplies.

1.2 Distinction between goods and services

1.2.1 Supplies of goods

Goods are broadly personal property, usually something manufactured or produced for sale.

A supply of goods includes both:

(a) The transfer of legal title to the goods (ie all the rights of ownership), and

(b) Transfer of possession of the goods under an agreement for sale of the goods or an agreement which envisages that the property in the goods will be transferred later (eg hire purchase)

The following transactions are specifically treated as supplies of goods:

- The supply of any form of power, heat, refrigeration or other cooling, ventilation, or of water

- The grant, assignment or surrender of a major interest (a freehold or a lease for over 21 years) in land

- Gifts of business assets, except:

    - Assets worth less than £50 which are gifted for business purposes
    - Samples (see below)

1.2.2 Supplies of services

A supply of services is made when a person does something or agrees to do something for a consideration, unless it is specifically treated as neither a supply of goods nor a supply of services.

Certain supplies are defined as a supply of services:

- Lease/hire of goods
- Transfer/sale of an undivided share of title in goods

The following are deemed to be a supply of services, even though there is no consideration:

- Temporary use of business assets for non-business use

- Where services, which have been supplied to a trader on which input tax has been claimed, are used for private or other non-business use. For example where building work to provide an office is treated as a business expense, but then the office is used as a bedroom instead

The European Court of Justice (ECJ) has ruled that restaurants supply services rather than goods. The food on your plate is incidental to the cooking, serving, washing up and ambience, and it loses any separate identity it might have had.

1.3 Single and multiple supplies

1.3.1 Overview

Where different goods and/or services are supplied together it is essential to determine whether the transaction is:

(a) A single supply, which is one supply with one VAT liability, or
(b) A multiple supply, which is a number of different supplies each with its own VAT liability.

This is particularly important where the supplies that make up the single or multiple supply are chargeable at different VAT rates.

1.3.2 Determining the type of supply

In order to determine whether a supply is a single or multiple supply, the following factors should be considered:

- All the circumstances in which the transaction takes place

- The nature of the supply from the viewpoint of the customer, rather than from the viewpoint of the supplier

- Each supply should usually be regarded as distinct and independent

- A single economic supply should not be artificially split

- Where one or more of the elements are merely 'ancillary' (ie simply a means for the customer to better enjoy the principal supply) it is a single supply

- The fact that a single price is charged for the supply is not decisive. If the customer intended to purchase two or more distinct services or goods, a single price will not prevent these being treated as separate supplies

1.3.3 Single (or composite) supplies

Where there are separate elements of a supply, but one is merely incidental, or 'ancillary', to the main element, or a means of better enjoying that main element, there is a single supply, to which only one VAT rate applies. The VAT rate that applies to the principal supply applies to the whole supply.

Ancillary element

In the Card Protection Plan Ltd case, the essential feature of the scheme was held to be for customers to obtain insurance cover against loss arising from the misuse of credit cards or other documents. The other features of the scheme, such as card registration and obtaining replacement cards, were found to be ancillary to the main objective of the scheme, ie the financial protection against loss of the card. Accordingly, as the provision of insurance is an exempt supply, Card Protection Plan was deemed to be making a single supply of exempt services.

Single economic supply

If the various elements supplied to the customer are so closely linked that they form, objectively, a single indivisible economic supply, which it would be artificial to split, the supply will be regarded as a single supply with only one VAT rate.

For example, the supply of the design of bespoke computer software (services) and the carrier medium on which the software is supplied (goods) is treated as a single economic supply of the design service as it would be artificial to divide them up.

Other examples

Classroom study materials are not a separate supply from the classes in which they are used. They are not 'ancillary', but simply part of a single supply of education.

The House of Lords held that when a patient visits a doctor and is given drugs, from the point of view of the customer there is only one supply: healthcare. Breaking down a visit to a doctor into two parts (1) the examination and (2) the drugs supplied would 'artificially split' the transaction.

The payment for membership of a club (Tumble Tots) which included a membership card, T-shirt, personal accident insurance, a magazine subscription, a DVD, a handbook and a gym bag was held to be a single standard rated supply of membership.

The Court of Appeal held that British Airways supplies a single zero rated service of a flight including the provision of inclusive in-flight catering. HMRC's contention that the provision of the in-flight catering was a separate standard-rated supply was dismissed by the Court of Appeal because the meal was provided regardless of whether the customer wanted it, BA was not contractually obliged to provide the meal, and customers who declined the meal could not claim a refund.

1.3.4   Multiple (or combined) supplies

A multiple supply occurs where different elements of the supply are separate and clearly identifiable but have been invoiced together at an inclusive price for both items.

A clear intention to purchase two distinct services is evidence of a multiple supply, even where only one price is paid.

Each element of a multiple supply is considered individually, so the supplier must account for VAT separately on the different elements by splitting the total amount payable in a fair and reasonable proportion between them and charging VAT on each at the appropriate rate.

The British Airways case can be contrasted with the Durham River Trips case. In the Durham case, passengers paid to enjoy a river cruise including a buffet. The buffet was optional and no refund was due if customers decided not to eat. The trader argued that it was a single zero-rated supply. However, it was held that the meal was a distinct feature of the cruise which it was not artificial to separate out into two distinct elements: one zero-rated and one standard-rated. Part of the rationale for this was that the two elements were complementary to one another rather than one being the principal and the other the ancillary supply. If there is no principal supply, there cannot be an ancillary supply.

Methods for apportioning the VAT include splitting the amount based on:

- The cost to the supplier of each element
- The open market value of each element

2   Partial exemption

Section overview

- A trader making both taxable and exempt supplies may not be able to recover all his input tax.
- Input tax directly attributable to taxable supplies is fully recoverable.
- Input tax directly attributable to exempt supplies is not usually recoverable.
- Input tax not directly attributable to taxable or exempt supplies must be apportioned.
- Input tax attributable to exempt supplies is recoverable if it falls below *de minimis* limits.

2.1   Partially exempt traders

Normally, a taxable person making wholly taxable supplies (zero-rated, reduced-rate or standard-rated) can recover input VAT on purchases and expenses relating to the taxable supply of goods.

A person who is making wholly exempt supplies cannot be a taxable person for VAT and so cannot recover input VAT.

If a taxable person makes both taxable (zero, reduced and/or standard-rated) and exempt supplies, input VAT attributable to the exempt supplies is not fully recovered unless it falls below certain limits. All of the input tax which is attributable to taxable supplies made can be reclaimed for a tax period.

2.2   Standard rate of VAT

The standard rate of VAT has fluctuated recently: [Hp227]

- From 1 April 1991 to 30 November 2008   17.5%
- From 1 December 2008 to 31 December 2009   15%
- From 1 January 2010 to 3 January 2011   17.5%
- From 4 January 2011   20%

However, for the purposes of your exam you should assume that the standard rate of VAT throughout 2014/15 and future years will remain at 20%.

2.3 Recovery of input tax

The rules for calculating the amount of input tax which is attributable to supplies are as follows:

- Input VAT directly attributable to taxable supplies is recoverable in full
- Input VAT directly attributable to exempt supplies is generally not recoverable
- Input tax not directly attributable to either type of supply needs to be apportioned between taxable and exempt supplies

The standard method of apportionment is:

$$\text{Recoverable amount} = \frac{\text{Total taxable supplies}}{\text{Total supplies}} \times \text{Non-attributable input VAT}$$

When calculating the total taxable supplies and total supplies, exclude VAT and supplies of capital items.

The ratio of supplies in the formula above is rounded up to the nearest whole percentage. The benefit of rounding up the ratio is not available to businesses whose non-attributable input VAT is £400,000 or more per month on average, where rounding should be to two decimal places.

An alternative method (special method) may be agreed with HMRC, if it produces a fairer result than using the standard method.

If the total amount of VAT relating to exempt supplies for the quarter exceeds neither of the *de minimis* limits, all input VAT can provisionally be recovered in full.

The *de minimis* limits are: [Hp239]

- £625 per month on average; and
- 50% of all input VAT for the period.

Worked example: *De minimis* limit for partial exemption

Lyra makes the following supplies in the quarter ended 31 July 2014:

	£
Standard rated taxable supplies (excluding VAT)	42,000
Exempt supplies	9,000
	51,000

Lyra's input tax for the period is:

	£
Wholly attributable to taxable supplies	2,250
Wholly attributable to exempt supplies	1,350
Non-attributable	1,800
	5,400

Requirement

Compute the input tax recoverable for the quarter.

Solution

Lyra – VAT quarter ended 31 July 2014

	Taxable Supplies £	Exempt supplies £	Total supplies £
Wholly attributable input tax:			
Taxable supplies	2,250		2,250
Exempt supplies		1,350	1,350
Non-attributable input tax:			
Recoverable amount % is			

$$\frac{42,000}{42,000 + 9,000} = 83\% \text{ (rounded up)}$$

	Taxable Supplies £	Exempt supplies £	Total supplies £
Attributable to taxable supplies:			
83% × £1,800	1,494		1,494
Attributable to exempt supplies:			
17% × £1,800		306	306
Input VAT	3,744	1,656	5,400

Tests for *de minimis* limit:

1 Is the monthly average attributable to exempt supplies £625 or less?

Monthly average $\dfrac{1,656}{3}$ = £552 per month.

Part 1 ✓

2 Is the proportion of VAT on exempt supplies no more than 50% of all input VAT for the period?

$\dfrac{1,656}{5,400}$ = 30.66%

Part 2 ✓

Both parts of the test are passed so input tax attributable to exempt supplies is below *de minimis* limits.

Conclusion

The whole of the input tax of <u>£5,400</u> for the quarter is recoverable.

2.4 Simplified partial exemption tests

The current *de minimis* rules (the standard test) require businesses to carry out detailed partial exemption calculations. Changes have been introduced to allow the vast majority of businesses to confirm their *de minimis* status using simpler calculations that rely on information that a business has readily to hand. There are two simpler tests which are available. If, in a VAT period, a business passes Test One or Test Two it may treat itself as *de minimis* and provisionally recover input tax relating to exempt supplies.

The simplified tests are:

Test One

Total input tax incurred is no more than £625 per month on average and the value of exempt supplies is no more than 50% of the value of all supplies. [Hp239]

Test Two

Total input tax incurred less input tax directly attributable to taxable supplies is no more than £625 per month on average and the value of exempt supplies is no more than 50% of the value of all supplies. [Hp239]

Total input tax excludes blocked input tax (such as VAT on the cost of business entertainment) which is irrecoverable.

A business need only pass Test One or Test Two (or the current test). If the business passes Test One or Two then there is no need to do a partial exemption calculation for the VAT period.

Worked example: Simplified Test One for partial exemption

Jessica makes the following supplies in the quarter ended 30 June 2014:

	£
Standard-rated taxable supplies (excluding VAT)	40,000
Exempt supplies	25,000
	65,000

Jessica's total input tax for the period is £1,600.

Requirement

Establish if Jessica's business passes simplified Test One for the quarter and state the input tax recoverable for the quarter.

Solution

Simplified Test One for *de minimis* limit:

1   Is the monthly average total input tax £625 or less?

Monthly average $\dfrac{1,600}{3}$ = £533 per month.

Part 1 ✓

2   Is the value of exempt supplies no more than 50% of the value of total supplies for the period?

$\dfrac{25,000}{65,000}$ = 38.46%

Part 2 ✓

Both parts of the test are passed, so Jessica's business is *de minimis* for this period as it passes Test One and she can provisionally recover all input tax.

Conclusion

The whole of the input tax of £1,600 for the quarter is recoverable.

Worked example: Simplified Test Two for partial exemption

Ciaran makes the following supplies in the quarter ended 30 June 2014:

	£
Standard-rated taxable supplies (excluding VAT)	27,000
Exempt supplies	13,000
	40,000

Ciaran's input tax for the period is £3,750 of which £2,300 is directly attributable to the making of taxable supplies.

Requirement

Establish if Ciaran's business passes simplified Test Two for the quarter and state the input tax recoverable for the quarter.

Solution

Simplified Test Two for *de minimis* limit:

1   Is the monthly average of total input tax incurred less input tax directly attributable to taxable supplies £625 or less?

Monthly average $\dfrac{3,750 - 2,300}{3}$ = £483 per month.

Part 1 ✓

2   Is the value of exempt supplies not more than 50% of the value of total supplies for the period?

$\dfrac{13,000}{40,000}$ = 32.5%

Part 2 ✓

Both parts of the test are passed, so Ciaran's business is *de minimis* for this period as it passes Test Two and he can provisionally recover all input tax.

Conclusion

The whole of the input tax of £3,750 for the quarter is recoverable.

2.5 Determining if an annual adjustment is needed using the simplified tests

At the end of each year an annual calculation is also required. The *de minimis* limits are applied to the year as a whole. As a result, an annual adjustment to the input tax recovered may be necessary.

If the amount recoverable according to the annual calculation exceeds the total of the amounts recovered each quarter, the difference will be recoverable. If the annual recoverable total falls short of the total input tax recovered each quarter, the difference is payable to HMRC.

A VAT year ends on 31 March, 30 April or 31 May depending on the trader's stagger group.

If a business passes Test One when applied to the total figures for the year, it can recover all of the input tax relating to exempt supplies and does not need to carry out any further partial exemption calculations.

When applying Test Two, a business needs to first review how much of the input tax incurred over the year is directly attributable to taxable supplies. If the business passes Test Two when applied to the total figures for the year, it can recover all of the input tax relating to exempt supplies and does not need to carry out any further partial exemption calculations.

Worked example: Determining the need for an annual adjustment for partial exemption

Arch Ltd has a partial exemption year ending on 30 April 2015. In its quarterly VAT returns, Arch Ltd has recovered all its VAT relating to both taxable and exempt supplies. During the year it makes the following supplies:

	£
Standard-rated taxable supplies (excluding VAT)	67,000
Exempt supplies	43,000
	110,000

Arch Ltd's input tax for the year is:

	£
Wholly attributable to taxable supplies	26,600
Wholly attributable to exempt supplies	6,400
Non-attributable	900
	33,900

Requirement

Establish if Arch Ltd will need to calculate an annual adjustment for its VAT year ended 30 April 2015.

Solution

If Arch Ltd passes either simplified Test One or Test Two for the year ending 30 April 2015 then no annual adjustment will be needed.

Simplified Test one:

1 Is the monthly average total input tax £625 or less?

Monthly average $\dfrac{33,900}{12}$ = £2,825 per month.

Part 1 ✗

Therefore Arch Ltd does not pass Test One for the year.

Simplified Test two:

1 Is the monthly average of total input tax incurred less input tax directly attributable to taxable supplies £625 or less?

Monthly average $\dfrac{33,900 - 26,600}{12}$ = £608 per month.

Part 1 ✓

2　Is the value of exempt supplies not more than 50% of the value of total supplies for the period?

$$\frac{43,000}{110,000} = 39.1\%$$

Part 2 ✓

Conclusion

Arch Ltd has passed Test Two for the year as a whole and therefore does not need to make a further annual adjustment calculation. The whole of the input tax of £33,900 for the year is recoverable.

___

If a business fails Test One and Test Two when applied to the total figures for the year, then it must carry out a full partial exemption calculation for the year to determine whether it passes the standard de minimis test (see Section 2.3) and account for any under/over recovery of input tax as part of the annual adjustment in the normal way.

Interactive question 1: Annual adjustment　　　　　　[Difficulty level: Exam standard]

Z plc has the following figures for the year to 31 March 2015:

	£
Standard-rated taxable supplies (excluding VAT)	1,650,000
Exempt supplies	475,000
Total supplies	2,125,000

Z plc's input tax for the year is:

	£
Wholly attributable to taxable supplies	6,600
Wholly attributable to exempt supplies	2,950
Non-attributable	19,000
	28,550

The input VAT recovered over the VAT year amounted to £24,580.

Requirement

Using the standard format below, compute the annual adjustment.

Z plc – year ended 31 March 2015

	Taxable supplies £	Exempt supplies £	Total supplies £
Wholly attributable input tax:			
Taxable supplies			
Exempt supplies			
Non-attributable input tax:			
Recoverable amount % is			
....			
.... + ...			
= ....% (rounded up)			
Attributable to taxable supplies:			
...................% × £...................			
Attributable to exempt supplies:			
...................% × £...................			
Input VAT			

Tests for standard *de minimis* limit:

1   Is the monthly average attributable to exempt supplies £625 or less?

Monthly average $\dfrac{....................}{....................}$ = £.................... per month.

Part 1....................

2   Is the proportion of VAT on exempt supplies not more than 50% of all input VAT for the period?

$\dfrac{....................}{....................}$ = ...%

Part 2 ....

Conclusion

£.................... of input tax for the year is recoverable.

Therefore the annual adjustment is:

(£.................... – £....................) = £.................... payable/recoverable.

See **Answer** at the end of this chapter.

2.6   New annual partial exemption test

The new annual partial exemption test gives most businesses the option of applying the *de minimis* test once a year. It allows a business that was *de minimis* in its previous partial exemption year to treat itself as *de minimis* in its current partial exemption year. This means it can provisionally recover input tax relating to exempt supplies in each VAT period, saving the need for partial exemption calculations.

A business must then review its *de minimis* status at year-end as outlined in Sections 2.5 and 2.6 and if it fails the *de minimis* test for the year it must repay the input tax relating to exempt supplies that was provisionally recovered.

There are three conditions which must be satisfied before the annual test may be used. The business must:

*   Pass the *de minimis* test for its previous partial exemption year

*   Consistently apply the annual test throughout any given partial exemption year

*   Have reasonable grounds for not expecting to incur more than £1 million input tax in its current partial exemption year

If any of these conditions are not met then the business is required to apply the *de minimis* test in each VAT period, which remains the default position.

Worked example: Annual test

Box Ltd has a partial exemption year ending on 30 June 2015. During the year it makes the following supplies:

	£
Standard-rated taxable supplies (excluding VAT)	99,000
Exempt supplies	51,000
	150,000

Box Ltd's input tax for the year is:

	£
Wholly attributable to taxable supplies	32,500
Wholly attributable to exempt supplies	8,200
Non-attributable	11,300
	52,000

During the year Box Ltd has recovered all £52,000 input tax suffered as it was *de minimis* in the partial exemption year ending 30 June 2014.

Requirement

Determine if Box Ltd is *de minimis* for the year ended 30 June 2015 and state the amount of any input tax that is repayable.

Solution

Check if Box Ltd has passed Test Two (as if passes Test Two must also pass Test One)

Simplified Test Two:

1   Is the monthly average of total input tax incurred less input tax directly attributable to taxable supplies £625 or less?

Monthly average $\dfrac{52,000 - 32,500}{12} = £1,625$ per month.

Part 1 ✗

2   Is the value of exempt supplies not more than 50% of the value of total supplies for the period?

$\dfrac{51,000}{150,000} = 34\%$

Part 2 ✓

Conclusion

Box Ltd does not pass Test Two. Therefore perform the standard test.

	Taxable supplies £	Exempt supplies £	Total supplies £
Wholly attributable input tax:			
Taxable supplies	32,500		32,500
Exempt supplies		8,200	8,200
Non-attributable input tax:			
Recoverable amount % is			
$\dfrac{99,000}{150,000}$ = 66% (rounded up)			
Attributable to taxable supplies:			
66% × £11,300	7,458		7,458
Attributable to exempt supplies:			
34% × £11,300		3,842	3,842
Input VAT	39,958	12,042	52,000

Tests for *de minimis* limit:

1   Is the monthly average attributable to exempt supplies £625 or less?

Monthly average $\dfrac{12,042}{12}$ = £1,003 per month.

Part 1 ✗

2   Is the proportion of VAT on exempt supplies not more than 50% of all input VAT for the period?

$\dfrac{12,042}{52,000}$ = 23.16%

Part 2 ✓

Both parts of the test are not passed so input tax attributable to exempt supplies is above *de minimis* limits.

Conclusion

£12,042 of input tax must be repaid.

3   Property transactions

Section overview

- Sales and leases of land and buildings are generally exempt. However, can opt to make the supply standard rated if it is non-residential.

- Sale and leases of new residential buildings are zero rated.

- The sale of a new (less than three years old) commercial building is standard rated.

- The supply of services relating to land or buildings is either standard rated or taxable at the reduced rate.

3.1   What is a property transaction?

A property transaction may be:

- The sale, lease or licence of land or buildings; or
- The supply of services related to land or buildings (eg conversion of existing building).

For buildings, different rules apply depending on whether the building is residential or commercial.

3.2   Land

The general rule is that the sale or lease of land is an exempt supply. [Hp237] However, the owner may opt to treat the supply as taxable. We look at the option to tax later in this section.

3.3   Residential building

The following supplies are zero-rated:

- Construction of a new residential building

- Sale of a new residential building

- Sale of new residential accommodation created by the conversion of non-residential building if sold by the person doing the conversion

As these are taxable supplies, the input tax relating to the supply can be recovered.

ICAEW

The following supplies are exempt:

- Sale of an existing residential building
- Lease of residential building

There is no option to tax in relation to residential buildings.

The following supply is standard rated:

- Work on existing residential building (but see further below)

The following supplies are taxable at the reduced rate (5%):

- Renovation of dwellings which have been empty for at least three years
- Conversion of residential building into a different number of dwellings
- Conversion of a non-residential building into a dwelling or number of dwellings

3.4 Commercial buildings

The following supplies are standard rated:

- Construction of commercial buildings
- Sale of new (less than three years old) commercial building
- Work on existing commercial building

The following supplies are exempt, but subject to the option to tax:

- Sale of old (three years old or more) commercial building
- Lease of any commercial building

3.5 The option to tax

Owners of interests in land and buildings may opt to charge VAT on supplies which would normally be exempt (except in relation to residential property). Once the option to tax is exercised, it applies to all future supplies relating to that land or building.

If the taxpayer changes his mind within six months of the effective date of the option to tax, HMRC will revoke the option provided the option to tax has not been put into practice eg by charging rent inclusive of VAT.

An option to tax in relation to a property will automatically be revoked once the person who opted to tax has held no interest in that property for six years.

Otherwise, the option to tax may be revoked after twenty years with the consent of HMRC.

The tax consequences of making an option to tax are:

- Standard rate VAT must be charged on the sale or lease (premium and rents) of the property – this may be a problem if the purchaser/tenant makes wholly or partially exempt supplies since he may be restricted in recovering this input tax

- Any inputs relating to the supply may be recovered eg heating costs, cleaning, repairs etc

The option to tax relates to individual land or buildings, not to all the land and buildings owned by the person opting to tax. However, if made, the option applies to the whole building. This may be a problem if there are a number of tenants, some of which make exempt supplies.

If a landlord purchases a new commercial building, it is a taxable transaction and the landlord will therefore pay VAT at 20% on the value of the building. Unless he opts to tax the building, renting it out would be an exempt supply, thus making the significant input tax suffered irrecoverable. Opting to tax the building converts the renting out of the building into a taxable supply and means the input tax suffered on the purchase price is recoverable.

If a VAT registered trader purchases a new commercial building for use in his taxable trade, the input VAT suffered will be recoverable. Whereas, if an exempt trader purchases a new commercial building for use in his exempt trade, the input VAT suffered is irrecoverable. It would be meaningless for the exempt trader to make an option to tax the building as it would still be used in his exempt trade and the input VAT would still be irrecoverable.

An option to tax is made by the owner of the land or building and does not transfer with the land or building on any future disposal.

Interactive question 2: Land and buildings   [Difficulty level: Exam standard]

State what type of supply is made in the following situations:

Item	Type of supply
Extension to residential building	
Lease of residential building	
Sale of factory built in 2013	
Lease of land	
Conversion of house into 3 flats	
Lease of warehouse built in 2014	
Sale of shop built in 2008	

See **Answer** at the end of this chapter.

4 Capital goods scheme

Section overview

- The capital goods scheme governs the recovery of input tax on land and buildings; ships and aircraft; and computers which may be used over a period of time to make both taxable supplies and exempt supplies.

- The scheme applies to purchases of land and buildings costing at least £250,000 or single ships and aircraft or computing items (excluding software) each costing at least £50,000.

- The initial input VAT recoverable on the item is calculated as normal.

- An adjustment is made to the recovery of input tax over

  - Ten years for land and buildings
  - Five years for ships, aircraft and computers

  This is called the adjustment period.

- Where the taxable usage of the item has increased, an additional amount of input VAT may be reclaimed.

- Where the taxable usage of the item has decreased, some of the original input VAT recovered will be clawed back.

- On sale an adjustment is made for the remaining adjustment period, assuming current usage is 100% taxable if the sale itself is taxable, and current usage is 0% taxable if the sale itself is exempt.

Normally, input tax recovery depends on the immediate use of the item purchased, ie input VAT may be recovered where it is first used to make taxable supplies and is irrecoverable where it is first used to make exempt supplies. The capital goods scheme amends this treatment for capital items which are:

- Buildings and land costing £250,000 or more; or

- Aircraft, ships, boats and other vessels that are bought after 31 December 2010 costing £50,000 or more; or

- Single computer items (excluding software) each costing £50,000 or more.

It is recognised that these items may be used for different purposes over a period of time, and therefore:

- Initial recovery on these items is calculated as normal; but

- The initial recovery is revised over an adjustment period to reflect changes in use during that time including the sale of the item.

Where a capital item within the scope of the scheme is purchased by a wholly taxable business, the capital goods scheme still applies. However, providing the items are used purely for taxable purposes throughout the adjustment period, no actual adjustments will be required. [Hp 239]

4.1 Initial recovery

Where a capital item within the scope of the scheme is purchased, initial recovery of input tax will be based on its initial use:

- Wholly taxable business – 100% of the input tax will be recoverable.

- Partially exempt business – input recovery will be based on its use in the quarter of purchase and then adjusted at the end of the VAT year. The input tax recovered for the first year as adjusted at the year end is the initial recovery.

- Wholly exempt business – no input tax may be recovered initially.

4.2 Adjustments for use

An adjustment is required for ten intervals for buildings and five intervals for aircraft, ships and computers. For each interval, the use within that VAT interval is compared to the initial recovery. Where the usage differs, that difference leads to an adjustment in respect of that interval's share of the total VAT:

$$(\frac{\text{Total input VAT}}{10 \text{ or } 5 \text{ intervals}}) \times (\text{taxable \% usage now} - \text{original taxable \% usage})$$

Where taxable usage has increased an additional amount of input tax can be recovered. Where taxable usage has reduced, some of the original input tax recovered will be clawed back.

The first interval will run from the date of acquisition to the end of that VAT return year. Subsequent intervals generally coincide with the VAT year.

A VAT year ends on 31 March, 30 April or 31 May depending on the trader's stagger group.

Worked example: Adjustments for use

Diverse plc acquired a new ten-floor office block incurring £100,000 of input tax. It uses four floors in connection with its insurance broking trade (an exempt supply) and the rest in connection with its retail trade (a taxable supply).

Five years after the acquisition it ceases its insurance broking trade and from then on it uses the whole of the building in its retail trade.

Requirement

Explain how Diverse plc will recover the input tax.

Solution

Diverse plc will initially recover £60,000 (60% × £100,000) in the first interval.

Additional input tax can be reclaimed from year 6 onwards as follows:

(£100,000/10) × (100% – 60%) = £4,000 per year

Interactive question 3: Adjustments for use

[Difficulty level: Exam standard]

A company purchases a building for £2m plus VAT on 1 July 2009. The company immediately rents it out without opting to tax the building. HMRC grants permission for the company to opt to tax the building from 1 April 2015. The company prepares VAT returns to 31 March each year.

Requirement

Calculate the initial recovery of input VAT and subsequent adjustments required in later years, if any.

See **Answer** at the end of this chapter.

4.3 Adjustments for sale

If a capital item is sold within the adjustment period, two adjustments are made:

- For the year of sale the normal adjustment is made as if the item had been used for the whole year; and

- A further adjustment for the complete intervals following the year of sale, assuming 100% taxable use if the sale itself was taxable and 0% taxable use if the sale itself was exempt. Any additional input VAT recoverable may be limited to the output VAT charged on the taxable sale where tax avoidance is in point.

Thus where a new commercial building is sold after three years it will be an exempt sale. However, if it is sold within ten intervals of acquisition, it will be subject to a claw back of input tax on the original purchase price.

Worked example: Adjustments for sale

Haddock plc purchased a new computer for £200,000 plus VAT on 15 November 2012 and used it 55% for taxable purposes each year until 31 March 2015. It then used the computer 75% for taxable purposes and finally sold it for £22,000 plus VAT on 18 June 2015. Haddock plc prepares VAT returns to 31 March.

Requirement

Calculate the initial input tax recovery and adjustments required for all subsequent years.

Solution

Haddock plc will initially recover £22,000 (55% × £40,000) in the first interval to March 2013.

In the intervals to March 2014 and March 2015 no adjustment is required as the taxable usage has remained constant.

Additional input tax can be reclaimed in interval four (to March 2016) as taxable usage has increased:

(£40,000/5) × (75% – 55%) = £1,600

As the computer is sold in the fourth interval, there is also an adjustment on disposal. This is calculated based on 100% taxable use for any remaining intervals of the adjustment period as it was a taxable sale. As this is a computer, the adjustment period is five intervals and only one interval remains to be adjusted for:

(£40,000/5) × (100% – 55%) × 1 interval = £3,600

5 Overseas aspects

Section overview

- Zero-rating applies to acquisitions of goods from another EU state where the customer is VAT registered and certain other conditions are met.

- Other acquisitions of goods from another EU state are subject to VAT in the state of origin.

- A VAT-registered trader must account for output tax on acquisitions made by him but he will also be able to recover input tax on the supply.

- Imports from outside the EU are liable to VAT on entry.

- Exports to outside the EU are zero-rated.

- VAT usually applies to supplies of services in the country of origin if the supply is to a non-business customer. If the customer is a relevant business person, VAT applies in the destination country instead and is charged using the reverse charge system. There are certain exceptions such as land related services.

5.1 Introduction to overseas aspects

VAT applies throughout the European Union (EU). However, it is not uniform so there have to be special rules which apply where supplies are made between different member states. A sale of goods within the EU is called a dispatch. The purchase of goods within the EU is called an acquisition.

In addition, VAT is relevant when goods enter or leave the EU. A sale of goods to a country outside the EU is an export. The purchase of goods from a country outside the EU is an import.

VAT may also be chargeable on a supply of services. Usually the supplier of the services will account for output tax due on the supply. In certain cases, however, there is a reverse charge to VAT where the customer must account for the output tax.

5.2 Dispatches

A dispatch is made where goods are supplied to a customer in another EU member state.

A supply of goods which are removed from the UK is treated as made in the UK and so is subject to the UK VAT rules.

The supply is zero-rated if:

- The supply is made to a registered trader; and
- The supplier quotes his customer's VAT number on the invoice; and
- The supplier holds evidence that the goods were delivered to another member state.

Because this is a taxable supply, input tax relating to the supply will also be recoverable.

If these conditions are not satisfied (for example, if the customer is not registered for VAT) the supply is subject to VAT as if the customer had been in the UK. This is called the origin system as the VAT is applied in the state of origin. For example, if the supply would be subject to the reduced rate in the UK, it will be liable to the reduced date on dispatch to a non-VAT registered customer in France.

5.3 Acquisitions

An acquisition is made when goods are acquired in the UK from a VAT registered person in another member state.

If the customer is VAT registered, he is liable to charge himself output tax in the UK at the appropriate rate for that type of supply in the UK (ie standard rated, zero-rated, reduced rate or exempt). This is called the destination system as VAT is applied in the destination state. It ensures that there is no distortion between goods bought in the UK and those acquired from other EU member states.

The VAT paid on acquisitions is also the amount of input tax. Therefore, for a trader only making taxable supplies, the effect will be tax neutral as he will charge himself an amount of output tax which can then be recovered as input tax. However, if the trader makes a mixture of taxable and exempt supplies, the partial exemption rules may restrict the recovery of input tax and therefore result in a net charge to VAT, just as it would have done if the trader had purchased the item in the UK.

If the trader makes wholly exempt supplies, he would not normally be registered for VAT and will therefore bear a VAT charge under the origin system as described in the previous section.

However, an exempt trader must register for VAT if his acquisitions from other EU member states exceed £81,000 in any calendar year or if he has reason to believe that the value of such acquisitions in the next 30 days will exceed £81,000. He must then charge himself output tax on acquisitions as described above. This moves the trader from a VAT charge under the origin system to one under the destination system. [Hp231]

If he continues to make wholly exempt supplies, there will be a net charge to VAT equal to the output tax as would be the case if the goods were acquired in the UK. If he starts to make taxable supplies, these will be liable to VAT if he is VAT registered due to the level of his acquisitions.

5.4 Imports

Imports of goods are chargeable to VAT if the same goods would be chargeable if supplied by a registered trader in the EU.

The importer calculates the VAT on the value of the imports and accounts for it at the point of entry into the EU. This amount is also deductible as input tax in the importer's next VAT return. VAT is charged on the goods in the normal way when they are sold in the EU.

5.5 Exports

Exports of goods outside the EU will be treated as supplies made in the UK. However, the supply will be zero-rated, provided that HMRC is satisfied that the goods have actually been exported.

The evidence required depends on how the export has been made (eg by sea or by air).

5.6 Supplies of services

In essence, supplies of services can be classified as business-to-business (B2B) services or business to consumer (B2C) services. It is the location of the customer that is key for B2B sales, whereas for B2C supplies it is still the location of the supplier that is the issue.

The basic rule is that most services are supplied:

- Where the customer has established his business, if supplied to a relevant business person; and
- Otherwise where the supplier has established his business.

Definition

Relevant business person:

- A person who carries out any economic activity, or
- A person who is registered for VAT in the UK, another Member State, or the Isle of Man.

Therefore, supplies of services to any business customer, even if not registered for VAT, will be taxed where the customer is established.

Therefore, the UK supplier of a service to a non-business customer accounts for any output VAT due on the supply, regardless of whether the customer is inside the EU. The origin basis therefore applies to such supplies of services.

Where services are received by a UK VAT registered trader from another country (EU or non-EU) for the purposes of his business, under the basic rule above the supply is deemed to be made in the UK. VAT is charged in the UK under the reverse charge system. This changes the basis of the VAT charge from the origin system to the destination system and is called a tax shift.

The UK customer must account for VAT on the supply to him because he is treated as making the supply. This amount will also be his input tax for the supply. The effect is tax-neutral unless the trader is making some exempt supplies.

The actual supplier of the services will not be treated as making a VAT supply where the reverse charge rules apply.

There are some exceptions to the basic place of supply rule above. For example, for land related services, the service is deemed to be supplied wherever the land is situated. There are also special rules for electronically supplied services.

Worked example: Overseas aspects

T Ltd, a manufacturing company, has the following relevant information for the quarter to 30 September 2014:

Sales

	£
Sales in the UK (standard-rated)	182,940
Sales in the UK (zero-rated)	18,450
Sales in France (VAT registered customers)	12,500
	213,890

Purchases

	£
Raw materials	37,750
Distribution expenses	9,100
Accountancy services (UK supplier)	3,750
Management consultancy services (USA supplier)	2,250
Other expenses	14,190
	67,040

All the purchases are standard-rated. The sales to France would be standard rated if sold in the UK. All figures exclude VAT.

Requirement

Compute the VAT due for the quarter.

Solution

T Ltd – VAT due quarter ended 30 September 2014

	£		£
Output tax			
Standard-rated supplies (£182,940 @ 20%)			36,588
Management consultancy services (£2,250 @ 20%)			450
			37,038
Input tax			
Purchases	37,750		
Distribution expenses	9,100		
Accountancy services	3,750		
Management consultancy services	2,250		
Other expenses	14,190		
	67,040	@ 20%	(13,408)
VAT due for the quarter			23,630

The supply of goods to the French VAT registered customers is zero-rated (assuming the other conditions have been satisfied).

The receipt of the management consultancy services from the overseas supplier is subject to the reverse charge rules and there is an output and an input on this supply for T Ltd.

Worked example: VAT treatment

Alice is a vet based in Nottingham who has a friend called Emile in Madrid. Emile is a farmer and Alice travels to Madrid to treat Emile's sick animals. Emile has a friend in Madrid called Lewis who owns a pet dog. Alice has agreed to treat his dog as a separate service when she is next in Madrid. Alice makes two trips to Madrid, one in March 2014 and the other in May 2014.

Requirement

Explain the VAT treatment of the charges by Alice to both Emile and Lewis.

Solution

The position for services for B2B supplies is the location of the customer, so the place of supply for the services supplied to Emile is Spain. Alice will not add UK VAT to the fees for treating the farm animals and Emile must account for VAT on his own return at the Spanish rate of VAT. He will then reclaim the VAT as input VAT assuming farming is a taxable activity. This is the reverse charge procedure.

However, Alice will continue to charge VAT to Lewis on the fee to treat his dog. This is because this is a B2C supply so VAT is charged based on the location of the supplier (UK) rather than the customer (Spain).

Summary and Self-test

Summary

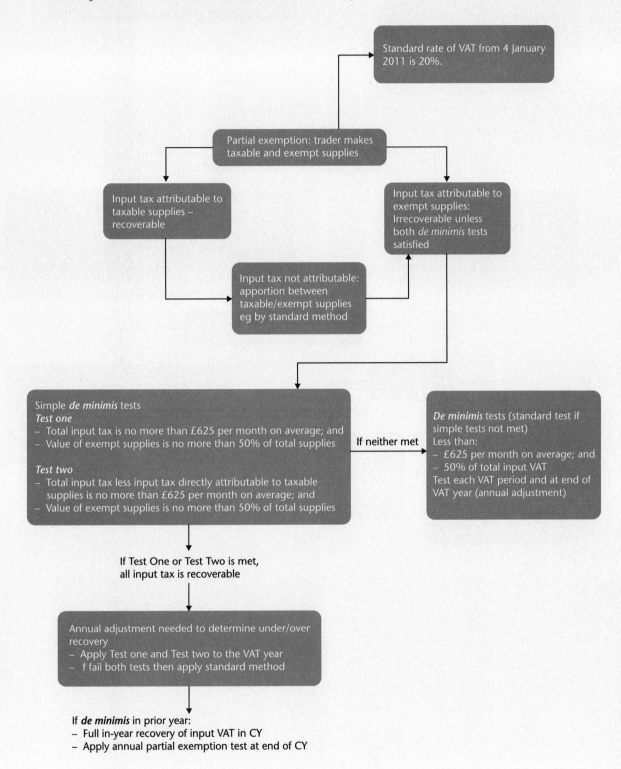

Standard rate of VAT from 4 January 2011 is 20%.

Partial exemption: trader makes taxable and exempt supplies

Input tax attributable to taxable supplies – recoverable

Input tax attributable to exempt supplies: Irrecoverable unless both *de minimis* tests satisfied

Input tax not attributable: apportion between taxable/exempt supplies eg by standard method

Simple *de minimis* tests
Test one
– Total input tax is no more than £625 per month on average; and
– Value of exempt supplies is no more than 50% of total supplies

Test two
– Total input tax less input tax directly attributable to taxable supplies is no more than £625 per month on average; and
– Value of exempt supplies is no more than 50% of total supplies

If neither met

De minimis tests (standard test if simple tests not met)
Less than:
– £625 per month on average; and
– 50% of total input VAT
Test each VAT period and at end of VAT year (annual adjustment)

If Test One or Test Two is met, all input tax is recoverable

Annual adjustment needed to determine under/over recovery
– Apply Test one and Test two to the VAT year
– f fail both tests then apply standard method

If *de minimis* in prior year:
– Full in-year recovery of input VAT in CY
– Apply annual partial exemption test at end of CY

VAT on property

Sale of a residential building
- New = zero rated
- Existing = exempt

Sale of a commercial building
- < 3 years old or opted to tax = standard rated
- > 3 years old or no option to tax = exempt (possibility of input tax clawback under capital goods scheme (CGS) on vendor)

Option to tax (OTT)
- Building by building basis
- Irrevocable outside the "cooling off" period
- Lasts 20 years
- Subsequent sale is taxable

Capital goods scheme

- Land and building ≥ £250k
- Computers ≥ £50k
- 10 year adjustment period for land and buildings
- 5 year adjustment period for computers

Recovery
- Initially based on immediate use
- Adjustment for use based on use each year Compared to original use
- Adjustment for sale – taxable sale assume remaining intervals 100% taxable
- Exempt sale assume remaining intervals 0% taxable

Overseas aspects

Goods

Within EU:
Dispatch: charged to VAT by supplier, zero rated if supply to VAT registered trader
Acquisition: output and input tax payable by VAT registered customer

Outside EU:
Import: VAT charge on importer at point of entry to EU
Export: zero-rated

Services
Supplied where:
- Supplier located if B2C (supplied to non VAT registered trader/customer
- Customer located if B2B (reverse charge then applies)

ICAEW

Self-test

Answer the following questions.

1   R Ltd makes taxable supplies of £69,400 and exempt supplies of £30,600 in a VAT quarter. In the same period, input tax is £5,500 of which £4,125 is attributable to taxable supplies and £875 to exempt supplies.

How much input tax is recoverable for the quarter using the standard method?

A   £4,125
B   £4,475
C   £4,625
D   £5,500

2   G Ltd makes taxable supplies of £48,000 and exempt supplies of £21,000 in the VAT quarter to 31 August 2014. In the same period, input tax is £5,100 of which £3,650 is attributable to taxable supplies.

G Ltd uses the simplified tests to determine if it meets the *de minimis* limit.

Which of the following statements is correct?

A   £3,650 of input tax is recoverable for the quarter and no annual adjustment is needed

B   £5,100 of input tax is recoverable for the quarter and no annual adjustment is needed

C   £3,650 of input tax is recoverable for the quarter but an annual adjustment is needed

D   £5,100 of input tax is recoverable for the quarter and an annual adjustment is needed

3   J Ltd builds a factory in 2013 and sells it to G Ltd in 2014.

What is the VAT treatment of this supply?

A   Exempt – no option to tax
B   Exempt – option to tax
C   Zero-rated
D   Standard-rated

4   Drawer Ltd, a partially exempt trader, buys a computer on 1 October 2013 incurring input VAT of £22,000. It uses it 63% of the time for taxable purchases in the quarter of purchase and 60% of the time for taxable purposes in the first year to 30 April 2014. In the following year taxable use falls to 45%.

Requirement

Calculate the input tax recovery for the first interval to 30 April 2014 and the adjustment required in the second interval to 30 April 2015.

5   Monello Ltd is a partially exempt trader. It bought a building for both taxable and exempt use on 29 July 2011. Input VAT of £445,000 was incurred on the acquisition of the building.

The building is to be sold on 2 October 2015 for £2.286m; the finance director is not sure what the effect of opting to tax the sale would be.

Under the partial exemption method agreed by Monello Ltd with the local VAT office, taxable use has been determined as follows:

Year to 31 March	Rate
2012	67%
2013	75%
2014	70%
2015	55%
2016	88%

Requirement

Calculate the input tax recoverable each year under the capital goods scheme both with and without an option to tax being made.

6   Kevin, a UK decorator who is registered for VAT, acquired £30,000 worth of tiles from Pedro, a supplier in Portugal (an EU country).

What are the VAT implications of this supply?

A   The supply is exempt so no VAT is chargeable.

B   The supply is zero-rated by Pedro; there are no VAT implications for Kevin.

C   The supply is zero-rated by Pedro; Kevin charges output tax and reclaims input tax on the supply.

D   The supply is charged at the Portuguese rate of VAT by Pedro; Kevin can recover this amount as input VAT.

7   Keira, Jonathan and Parminder

Keira and Jonathan were partners in a football academy for many years, drawing up accounts to 30 November each year until Keira left the partnership on 31 May 2014 to move to the USA. Parminder joined the partnership on 1 June 2014.

Keira and Jonathan always shared profits equally after receiving annual salaries from the business of £9,000 and £13,000 respectively. Keira has unrelieved overlap profits of £5,000.

Prior to joining the partnership, Parminder had never worked in paid employment, nor had she ever been self-employed. On joining the partnership Parminder invested £25,000 capital into the business with interest set at 4% per annum. Jonathan and Parminder agreed to split the profits 60:40 after receiving salaries of £13,000 and £10,000 per annum respectively.

Tax adjusted trading profits (after capital allowances) were £67,544 for the year ended 30 November 2014 and are estimated to be £85,352 for the year ended 30 November 2015.

The business is VAT registered and makes various different types of supply. The football academy itself makes exempt supplies; however, the academy's sportswear shop makes both standard rated and zero rated supplies. In the quarter ended 31 August 2015 the business VAT records show:

	£
Input VAT relating to standard rated supplies	4,556
Input VAT relating to zero rated supplies	2,353
Input VAT relating to exempt supplies	5,549
Non-attributable VAT	1,699
Standard rated supplies	59,654
Zero rated supplies	33,489
Exempt supplies	132,000

In addition to the VAT figures given above, during the quarter ended 31 August 2015 the business purchased a company car for the sportswear shop manager for £10,500 and a van for £4,840 for sole use at the football academy. The shop manager purchases all of his fuel and the van will always be kept at the business premises overnight.

All figures relating to supplies and purchases are VAT exclusive where appropriate.

Requirements

(1)   Calculate the trading profits assessable to income tax for each partner for all relevant tax years, identifying any overlap profits.   **(8 marks)**

(2)   Calculate the total national insurance contributions payable by Parminder for each of her first two tax years of trade.   **(3 marks)**

(3)   Calculate the net VAT payable to or repayable by HM Revenue and Customs for the quarter ended 31 August 2015.   **(9 marks)**

(20 marks)

Now go back to the Learning Objectives in the Introduction. If you are satisfied you have achieved these objectives please tick them off.

Legislation

All references are to Value Added Tax Act 1994 (*VATA 1994*) unless otherwise stated

Reduced rate supplies	Sch 7A
Zero rated supplies	Sch 8
Exempt supplies	Sch 9
Supply of goods and services	Para 1, Sch 4
Partial exemption	SI 1995/2518
	paras 99 – 111
Zero-rating of residential property transactions	Sch 8 Group 5
Reduced rate on certain residential property transactions	Sch 7A, Group 6
Exempt supply of land	Sch 9 Group 1
Option to tax	Sch 10 para 2
Capital goods scheme	Regs 112-116, SI 1995/2518
Place of supply	s.7
Reverse charge	s.8
Acquisitions from other member states	ss.10 – 14
Importation of goods from other member states	s.15

HMRC manual references

To find out more practical information about VAT, access the relevant section of the HMRC website through the main home page (http://www.hmrc.gov.uk/) and then following the link, or access it direct at http://www.hmrc.gov.uk/vat/index.htm

A series of information and guides is available by clicking on the various links.

For example, Introduction to VAT (Found at http://www.hmrc.gov.uk/vat/start/introduction.htm) is a summary of the most common VAT issues and a good place to start finding out how it affects you and your business.

In addition, the VAT manuals may be found at http://www.hmrc.gov.uk/thelibrary/vatmanuals-a-z.htm.

> This technical reference section is designed to assist you. It should help you to know where to look for further information on the topics covered in this chapter.

Answer to Interactive question 1

Z plc – year ended 31 March 2015

	Taxable supplies £	Exempt supplies £	Total supplies £
Wholly attributable input tax:			
Taxable supplies	6,600		6,600
Exempt supplies		2,950	2,950
Non-attributable input tax:			
Recoverable amount % is			
$\dfrac{1,650,000}{1,650,000 + 475,000}$ = 78% (rounded up)			
Attributable to taxable supplies:			
78% × £19,000	14,820		14,820
Attributable to exempt supplies:			
22% × £19,000		4,180	4,180
Input VAT	21,420	7,130	28,550

Tests for *de minimis* limit:

1 Is the monthly average attributable to exempt supplies £625 or less?

Monthly average $\dfrac{7,130}{12}$ = £594 per month.

Part 1 ✓

2 Is the proportion of VAT on exempt supplies not more than 50% of all input VAT for the period?

$\dfrac{7,130}{28,550}$ = 24.97%

Part 2 ✓

Both parts of the test are passed so input tax attributable to exempt supplies is below *de minimis* limits.

Conclusion

£28,550 of input tax for the year is recoverable.

Therefore the annual adjustment is:

(£28,550 – £24,580) = £3,970 ~~payable~~/recoverable.

Answer to Interactive question 2

Item	Type of supply
Extension to residential building	Standard rate
Lease of residential building	Exempt (no option to tax)
Sale of factory built in 2013	Standard rate
Lease of land	Exempt (option to tax)
Conversion of house into 3 flats	Reduced rate
Lease of warehouse built in 2014	Exempt (option to tax)
Sale of shop built in 2008	Exempt (option to tax)

Answer to Interactive question 3

The input VAT on the building is £300,000 (VAT rate was 15% in July 2009). The building cost at least £250,000 and is therefore within the scope of the capital goods scheme. Annual adjustments are required for 10 intervals.

From 1 July 2009 to 31 March 2015, the building is rented out as an exempt supply. Thus, initially, no input VAT can be recovered. The initial interval is to 31 March 2010. No adjustment is required for March 2011, March 2012, March 2013, March 2014 or March 2015 as taxable use is still 0%.

From 1 April 2015 onwards the rental has become a taxable supply and each year an additional amount of input VAT can therefore be recovered:

$$£300,000/10 \times (100\% - 0\%) = £30,000$$

In total four intervals of adjustments will be required totalling £120,000 (March 2016, March 2017, March 2018, March 2019).

Answers to Self-test

1 D – £5,500

	Taxable supplies £	Exempt supplies £	Total supplies £
Wholly attributable input tax:			
Taxable supplies	4,125		4,125
Exempt supplies		875	875
Non-attributable input tax:			
Recoverable amount % is			
Attributable to taxable supplies:			
70% × £500	350		350
Attributable to exempt supplies:			
30% × £500		150	150
Input VAT	4,475	1,025	5,500

Recoverable amount % is

$$\frac{69,400}{69,400+30,600} = 70\% \text{ (rounded up)}$$

Tests for *de minimis* limit:

1 Is the monthly average attributable to exempt supplies £625 or less?

Monthly average $\frac{1,025}{3} = £342$ per month.

Part 1 ✓

2 Is the proportion of VAT on exempt supplies not more than 50% of all input VAT for the period?

$$\frac{1,025}{5,500} = 18.64\%$$

Part 2 ✓

Both parts of the test are passed so input tax attributable to exempt supplies is below *de minimis* limits.

Conclusion: The whole of the input tax of £5,500 for the quarter is recoverable.

2 D Test Two for *de minimis* limit:

1 Is the monthly average of total input tax incurred less input tax directly attributable to taxable supplies £625 or less?

Monthly average $\frac{5,100-3,650}{3} = £483$ per month.

Part 1 ✓

2 Is the value of exempt supplies not more than 50% of the value of total supplies for the period?

$$\frac{21,000}{69,000} = 30.43\%$$

Part 2 ✓

Conclusion

Both parts of the test are passed so the whole of the input tax of £5,100 for the quarter is recoverable. An annual adjustment will be needed at the end of the partial exemption year.

3   D – Standard rated

The sale of a new (less than 3 years old) commercial building is standard rated.

4   As the input VAT equates to a purchase price of £132,000, the acquisition is within the scope of the capital goods scheme. For the first interval, the recovery (after the annual partial exemption adjustment) is:

£22,000 × 60% = £13,200.

For the second year, the capital goods scheme adjustment is:

£22,000/5 × (45% – 60%) = (£660) payable to HMRC.

5

Year	To	Adjustment calculation	Amount
1	March 2012	£445,000 × 67%	£298,150
2	March 2013	£445,000/10 × (75% – 67%)	£3,560
3	March 2014	£445,000/10 × (70% – 67%)	£1,335
4	March 2015	£445,000/10 × (55% – 67%)	(£5,340)
5 use	March 2016	£445,000/10 × (88% – 67%)	£9,345
5 sale	Opt	£445,000/10 × (100% – 67%) × 5	£73,425
	Do not opt	£445,000/10 × (0% – 67%) × 5	(£149,075)

The total difference between opting to tax and not opting to tax is £222,500 or 5/10 × £445,000. However, the output tax charge on a sale price of £2.286m is £457,200 (or £2.286m × 1/6 = £381,000 if the purchaser is exempt and will not accept the addition of VAT to the purchase price). The loss of input tax may be less of a problem than the charging of output tax.

6   C – The supply is zero-rated by Pedro; Kevin charges output tax and reclaims input tax on the supply.

The supply is a dispatch by Pedro and so is zero-rated. However, it is also an acquisition by Kevin who must account for output tax on the supply at the UK standard-rate of VAT (but can also reclaim this amount as input tax).

7   **Keira, Jonathan and Parminder**

(1)   **Trading profits assessable 2014/15 and 2015/16**

Allocation of profits

	Total £	Keira £	Jonathan £	Parminder £
y/e 30.11.14				
1.12.13 – 31.5.14				
Salaries × 6/12	11,000	4,500	6,500	
PSR 1:1	22,772	11,386	11,386	
	33,772			
1.6.14 – 30.11.14				
Salaries × 6/12	11,500		6,500	5,000
Interest	500			500
PSR 6:4	21,772		13,063	8,709
	67,544	15,886	37,449	14,209
y/e 30.11.15				
Salaries	23,000		13,000	10,000
Interest	1,000			1,000
PSR 6:4	61,352		36,811	24,541
	85,352		49,811	35,541

Assessable profits

	£	£	£
2014/15			
Keira			
Cessation	15,886		
Less overlap relief	(5,000)		
	10,886		
Jonathan			
CYB		37,449	
Parminder			
Opening year rules, commencement to next 5 April			
1.6.14 – 5.4.15			
£14,209 + (4/12 × £35,541)			26,056
2015/16			
Jonathan and Parminder			
CYB		49,811	35,541
Parminder's overlap profits			
1.12.14 – 5.4.15			
4/12 × £35,541			11,847

(2) **National insurance contributions – Parminder 2014/15 and 2015/16**

2014/15

	£
Self-employed 1.6.14 – 5.4.15 = 44 weeks	
Class 2 = 44 weeks @ £2.75	121
Class 4 = (£26,056 – £7,956) @ 9%	1,629
	1,750

2015/16

	£
Class 2 = 52 weeks × @ £2.75	143
Class 4	
(£35,541 – £7,956) @ 9%	2,483
	2,626

(3) **Net VAT payable/recoverable for quarter ended 31 August 2015**

Simplified Test Two for *de minimis* limit:

1 Is the monthly average of total input tax incurred less input tax directly attributable to taxable supplies £625 or less?

Monthly average $\dfrac{15,125 - 6,909}{3}$ = £2,739 per month.

Part 1 ✗

2 Is the value of exempt supplies not more than 50% of the value of total supplies for the period?

$\dfrac{132,000}{225,143}$ = 58.6%

Part 2 ✗

Conclusion

The simplified Test Two (and therefore also the simplified Test One) is not met. Therefore the standard test must be used.

	Taxable supplies £	Exempt supplies £	Total supplies £
Wholly attributable input tax:			
Standard-rated taxable supplies	4,556		4,556
Zero-rated taxable supplies	2,353		2,353
Exempt supplies		5,549	5,549
Car – irrecoverable			
Van £4,840 × 20%		968	968
Non-attributable input tax:			
Recoverable amount % is			
$\dfrac{(59,654+33,489)}{(59,654+33,489+132,000)}$ = 42% (rounded up)			
Attributable to taxable supplies:			
42% × £1,699	714		714
Attributable to exempt supplies:			
58% × £1,699		985	985
Input VAT	7,623	7,502	15,125

Tests for *de minimis* limit:

1. Is the monthly average attributable to exempt supplies £625 or less?

   Monthly average $\dfrac{7,502}{3}$ = £2,501 per month.

   Part 1 ✗

2. Is the proportion of VAT on exempt supplies not more than 50% of all input VAT for the period?

   $\dfrac{7,502}{15,125}$ = 49. 6%

   Part 2 ✓

Both parts of the test must be passed for *de minimis* rules to apply.

Conclusion

Only the input tax of £7,623 relating to taxable supplies for the quarter is recoverable.

VAT payable to HMRC

	£
Output VAT collected £59,654 × 20%	11,931
Less recoverable input VAT	(7,623)
Payable to HMRC	4,308

Tax Compliance

CHAPTER 23

Stamp taxes

Introduction

Examination context

Topic List

Summary and Self-test

Technical reference

Answers to Interactive questions

Answers to Self-test

Learning objectives

- Identify common situations in which a liability to Stamp Duty Land Tax, Stamp Duty Reserve Tax and Stamp Duty arises

- Identify situations where there is an exemption from stamp taxes

- Calculate the amount of stamp taxes due in straightforward transactions

Specific syllabus references for this chapter are 6h, 6i and 6j.

Syllabus links

Stamp taxes were not covered in your Principles of Taxation study manual.

Examination context

In the examination a candidate may be required to:

- Compute the stamp duty/stamp duty land tax payable on a transaction

1 Stamp duty

Section overview

- Stamp duty is payable on stock transfer forms used to transfer shares and securities.
- The rate of duty is usually 0.5%.
- There are exemptions for transfers for no consideration such as gifts.
- Stamp duty is payable within 30 days on presentation of the transfer form.
- Interest is charged for late payment of duty.
- A penalty may be charged for late presentation of the transfer form.

1.1 Charge to stamp duty

Stamp duty is payable on the transfer of shares and securities where the transfer is made using a stock transfer form. Stamp duty can only be charged where an instrument, in this case a stock transfer form, is used to execute the transfer. For paperless transactions, Stamp Duty Reserve Tax applies instead (see below).

The rate of stamp duty is 0.5% of the consideration. This is called **ad valorem** duty as it is imposed on the value of the consideration. [Hp221]

The duty is payable by the person acquiring the shares and is rounded up to the nearest £5.

However, stamp duty is not chargeable if the value of the consideration is £1,000 or less, as the duty payable would only be £5. In this case, the stock transfer form does not need to be presented to HMRC and can be sent directly to the company registrar.

Worked example: Stamp Duty

Julie sells her shares in R Ltd to Colin for £72,480 on 10 July 2014.

Requirement

Compute the stamp duty payable by Colin.

Solution

£72,480 × 0.5% = £362 rounded up to   £365

1.2 Exemptions from stamp duty

There are exemptions from stamp duty for certain transactions where there is no consideration for the transfer such as:

- Gifts
- Divorce arrangements
- Variations of Wills

The transfer must state which exemption is being claimed. The categories are usually printed on the back of the stock transfer form.

Securities dealt on 'recognised growth markets' are also exempt from stamp duty from 28 April 2014, in order to promote investment in such markets and help growing companies raise finance. Such markets have to be on HMRC's list of approved recognised stock exchanges and meet one of two conditions. The first is that the majority of companies trading on that market must have market capitalisations of less than £170m. Alternatively, the market's rules must require that companies seeking admission demonstrate at least 20% compounded annual growth in revenue or employment over the three years preceding admission.

1.3 Bearer shares

A company may issue share warrants transferable by delivery, so that there is no written transfer on which stamp duty is paid. To prevent avoidance by this means a share warrant is subject to stamp duty (or stamp duty reserve tax, in the case of on-exchange transactions – see below) at three times the rate applied to a share transfer, ie 1.5% at the present time. This is paid at the time of issue of the warrant and recovered from the shareholder to whom the warrant is originally issued. There is an obligation to file the appropriate forms with HMRC before the issue of the warrant. Penalties are imposed for dealing in unstamped bearer instruments.

1.4 Administration of stamp duty

Stamp duty is administered by HMRC Stamp Taxes.

The stock transfer form must be presented to HMRC within thirty days of execution and the duty paid at that time.

Interest may be charged if the duty is paid late. Interest runs from the end of the thirty day period to the day before the duty is paid. Interest is rounded down to the nearest multiple of £5 and is not charged if the amount is less than £25.

In addition, a penalty may be imposed if the transfer is presented late for stamping.

If the transfer is presented up to one year late, the maximum penalty is the **lower** of: [Hp221]

- £300; and
- The amount of the unpaid duty.

If the transfer is presented more than one year late, the maximum penalty is the **greater** of:

- £300; and
- The amount of the unpaid duty.

The penalty can be reduced, for example if there is a reasonable excuse for the delay.

Interactive question 1: Stamp duty payment, interest and penalties

[Difficulty level: Exam standard]

K Ltd sold its shares in A Ltd to Z plc for £882,800 on 12 December 2014 and executes a stock transfer form on that day.

Z plc presented the form for stamping on 15 February 2015 and paid the duty at that time.

Requirement

Using the standard format below, compute the stamp duty, the interest and maximum penalty payable.

Assume the interest rate on overdue stamp duty is 3%

Stamp duty

£................. × ....% = £................. rounded to   £_____

Interest
Due date: ....
Paid: ....
Days overdue: ....
.... × £................. × ....% = £................. as less than £................there is   £_____
no interest due

Maximum penalty

Transfer presented .... late, so maximum penalty is .... of:
£.................; and
£................. ie   £_____
See **Answer** at the end of this chapter.

2 Stamp duty reserve tax

Section overview

- Stamp duty reserve tax is payable on the paperless electronic transfer of shares and securities.

- The rate of duty is usually 0.5%. Unlike stamp duty, there is no rounding.

- There are few exemptions.

- SDRT is payable on the 7th day of the month following the month of sale if not made through CREST.

- SDRT is payable 14 days after the trade date if via CREST.

2.1 Charge to stamp duty reserve tax

Stamp duty depends on there being a document which can be stamped. It is not able to cope with paperless transactions. For that reason, Stamp Duty Reserve Tax (SDRT) was introduced in 1986. SDRT is now the largest source of stamp duty revenue on share transfers. SDRT is payable on the paperless ie electronic transfer of shares and securities. Most such transfers are executed via the CREST system.

The principal charge to SDRT is **on agreements** to transfer 'chargeable securities' (most stocks and shares) for consideration in money or money's worth. SDRT applies instead of stamp duty where the transfer is not completed by an instrument of transfer (ie by a stock transfer form stamped with ad valorem duty).

The rate of stamp duty reserve tax is 0.5% of the consideration. Unlike stamp duty, there is no rounding. [Hp225]

2.2 Exemptions from stamp duty reserve tax

If there is no consideration in money or money's worth there is usually no SDRT charge.

As with stamp duty, securities dealt on a recognised growth market are exempt from SDRT.

2.3 Cancellation of stamp duty reserve tax

To prevent a double charge to both stamp duty and SDRT, any SDRT paid on an agreement to transfer shares will be repaid if the transaction is subsequently completed by a stamped stock transfer form. Normally, if the subsequent stock transfer form is exempt from stamp duty it will also be exempt from SDRT and any SDRT paid will still be repaid.

2.4 Administration of stamp duty reserve tax

Stamp duty reserve tax is administered by HMRC Stamp Taxes but is actually collected automatically via stock brokers.

SDRT is payable on the seventh day of the month following the month in which the agreement was made or became unconditional. If however, the payment is capable of being made via CREST, it should be paid over by 14 calendar days after the trade date. The charge is unrelated to settlement or completion. It is, therefore, possible that Stamp Duty Reserve Tax will be payable before the transaction is carried out.

In practice penalties may not be imposed if the stamp duty is paid within 60 days after the contract date. The time is not extended because there may be delays in paying or depositing the stamp duty. The SDRT has to be deposited and reclaimed when the stamp duty is paid even when there is an adjudication for a stamp duty exemption which will cancel the charge.

3 Stamp duty land tax

Section overview

- Stamp duty land tax (SDLT) is chargeable on land transactions, including sales of land and grants of leases.

- Where there is chargeable consideration, SDLT is charged as a percentage of the consideration.

- The rate of SDLT depends on whether the land is residential or non-residential.

- There is also a charge to SDLT on a grant of a lease based on the Net Present Value of the rents receivable over the term of the lease.

- There are a number of exemptions from SDLT.

- A land transaction form must usually be delivered to HMRC within 30 days of the transaction and the SDLT paid at that time.

- Interest is payable on late paid SDLT.

- There are penalties for late delivery of a land transaction form.

3.1 Charge to SDLT

Stamp duty land tax (SDLT) is chargeable on land transactions. Examples include the transfer of freehold land, the assignment of a lease and the grant of a lease.

Where a land transaction is made for chargeable consideration (payment in money or money's worth), there is a charge to SDLT based on the amount of that consideration. It is based on the VAT inclusive amount.

SDLT is payable by the purchaser.

The rate of SDLT depends on whether the land is used for residential purposes or non-residential purposes: [Hp217]

%	Residential	Non-residential
0	Up to £125,000	Up to £150,000[1]
1	£125,001-£250,000	£150,001-£250,000
3	£250,001-£500,000	£250,001-£500,000
4	£500,001-£1,000,000[2]	£500,001 or more
5	£1,000,001-£2,000,000[2]	N/A
7	£2,000,001 or more[2]	N/A

Notes:

1. For non-residential property, where the transaction involves a grant of a lease, the zero rate band is not available if annual rent exceeds £1,000.

2. For acquisitions by a company, a partnership with a corporate member and a collective investment scheme the rate is 15%.

For transactions where the effective date is on or after 19 July 2011, there is relief for purchasers of residential property who acquire more than one dwelling via linked transactions. Where the relief is claimed, the rate of SDLT on the consideration attributable to the dwellings is determined not by the aggregate consideration but instead is determined by the mean consideration (ie by the aggregate consideration divided by the number of dwellings), subject to a minimum rate of 1%.

Where there are a number of linked transactions, the relevant consideration is the total of the chargeable considerations for each transaction.

Once the rate of SDLT has been determined, this rate is then applied to the **whole** of the consideration, not just the amount over the relevant threshold.

Worked example: SDLT on sale of freehold land

Harold sells his house to Lily for £375,000 on 10 April 2014.

Requirement

Compute the SDLT payable by Lily.

Solution

The rate of SDLT for transactions between £250,001 and £500,000 is 3%.

SDLT is therefore £375,000 × 3%

£11,250

3.2 Leases

Stamp duty land tax is chargeable on the grant of leases, both on the lease premium and on the net present value of the rental. The net present value of the rental is basically the rent payable over the term of the lease.

The lease premium is charged under the normal rules as if the lease premium were the chargeable consideration. However, if the rent is £1,000 or more and the land is non-residential property the zero rate band is not available. Consideration in that band is treated as if it were in the 1% band.

Interactive question 2: SDLT on lease premium [Difficulty level: Interactive]

G plc is granted a lease of a factory by T plc. The lease is for seven years. The premium payable by G plc is £45,000 and the annual rent is £3,000.

Requirement

Using the standard format below, compute the SDLT payable by G plc in respect of the premium.

The rate of SDLT on the premium on the grant of a non-residential lease between £................... and £............................ is ....% where the annual rent exceeds £............................ .

SDLT on the premium is therefore £............................ × ....%

£ _____

See **Answer** at the end of this chapter.

On the grant of a lease, in addition to any SDLT payable on the premium, SDLT is also chargeable on chargeable consideration consisting of rent. The charge is based on the Net Present Value (NPV) of the rent payable to the landlord over the term of the lease. This is the total rent payable, discounted by 3.5% each year.

For examination purposes, you may take the NPV to be the total rents payable over the term of the lease.

Again, the rate of SDLT depends on whether the land is residential or non-residential. [Hp219]

%	Residential	Non-residential
0	Up to £125,000	Up to £150,000
1	Excess over £125,000	Excess over £150,000

Note the difference in how the thresholds work for lease premiums and lease rentals. For lease premiums, the whole of the premium is charged if it is above the relevant threshold. For lease rentals, only the excess over the threshold is chargeable at 1%.

Worked example: SDLT on rental

Donald is granted a 25 year lease of a factory by Simon on 1 August 2014. He pays an annual rental of £9,000 per year for the term of the lease.

Requirement

Compute the SDLT payable by Donald.

Solution

	£
Rental payable over term of lease	
£9,000 × 25	225,000
Less non-residential threshold	(150,000)
Amount chargeable	75,000
SDLT £75,000 × 1%	£750

Note the difference between this calculation (on the excess consideration over the threshold) and the main SDLT calculation (on the whole consideration).

3.3 Exemptions from SDLT

There are a number of exemptions from SDLT including transfers:

- For no chargeable consideration (eg gifts)
- On divorce
- Effecting a variation of a Will

In these cases, no land transaction form needs to be submitted to HMRC (see further in the next section).

If land is transferred to a company which is connected with the transferor in exchange for shares, the transaction is not exempt. It is deemed to be made for chargeable consideration at least equal to the market value of the land. This situation could occur on the incorporation of a business.

Note that where responsibility for a debt is assumed by the purchaser, the value of the debt is treated as consideration and not an outright gift eg an intra spouse transfer where the property transferred is subject to a mortgage.

3.4 Higher rate for transfers to companies

Where an interest in a single dwelling is sold for consideration of more than £500,000 (between 21 March 2012 and 20 March 2014 the limit was £2,000,000) the rate of SDLT is 15% (rather than the usual 4%, 5% or 7%) if the buyer is:

- A company,
- A partnership where at least one partner is a company; or
- A collective investment scheme.

3.5 Administration of SDLT

SDLT is administered by HMRC Stamp Taxes.

A land transaction form must be submitted to HMRC by the purchaser within thirty days of a land transaction and the SDLT paid within the same time limit. The purchaser will self-assess the SDLT due on the land transaction form.

Note that a land transaction form must be submitted even if there is no SDLT payable, for example because the 0% rate applies or the group transfer exemption is being claimed.

Interest may be charged if SDLT is paid late. Interest runs from the end of the thirty day period to the day before SDLT is paid.

In addition, a penalty may be imposed if the land transaction form is submitted late. [Hp219]

- If the form is filed up to three months late, a fixed penalty of £100 is automatically imposed.
- If the form is submitted over three months late, a fixed penalty of £200 is automatically imposed.

This penalty is imposed regardless of whether SDLT is actually payable on the transaction.

In addition, if the form is submitted over one year late, a tax geared penalty up to the amount of SDLT due may be imposed.

Penalties can be reduced, for example if there is a reasonable excuse for the delay.

Finance Act 2009 creates a new penalty regime for the late filing and late payment of SDLT. However, this has yet to be implemented.

From April 2010 SDLT is, however, within the FA 2007 harmonised penalty rules for incorrect returns. Penalties will therefore apply where deliberate or careless errors are made in SDLT returns, which result in either an underpayment or an excessive repayment. The maximum penalties range from 30% to 100% of the tax lost, depending on whether the error was careless, deliberate but not concealed or deliberate and concealed. The penalties can be reduced for disclosure on the part of the taxpayer, with the level of reduction depending on whether the disclosure was prompted or unprompted.

Worked example: SDLT payment, interest and penalties

Y Ltd sold a freehold warehouse to O plc for £195,500 on 9 October 2014 and executed a transfer on that day. Y Ltd and O plc are not associated in any way. Due to an oversight, O plc did not submit a land transaction form to HMRC until 12 December 2015 and paid the SDLT at that time.

Requirement

Compute the SDLT, the interest and maximum penalties payable. Assume the interest rate on overdue SDLT is 3%.

Solution

SDLT

The rate of SDLT on non-residential land for transactions between £150,001 and £250,000 is 1%.

SDLT is therefore £195,500 × 1%   £1,955

Interest

Due date: 7 November 2014   Paid: 12 December 2015

Days overdue: 399

$\frac{399}{365} \times £1,955 \times 3\%$ £64

Maximum penalties

Fixed penalty (over three months late)   £200

Tax-geared penalty (over twelve months late)   £1,955

Summary

```
                              ┌─────────────────┐
                              │   Stamp duty    │
                              └─────────────────┘
        ┌──────────────────────────┼──────────────────────────┐
        ▼                          ▼                          ▼
┌────────────────────┐  ┌────────────────────┐  ┌────────────────────┐
│ Charge: 0.5% on    │  │ Exemptions: eg     │  │ Administration:    │
│ transfer of shares │  │  – Gifts           │  │ submit stock       │
│ by stock transfer  │  │  – Divorce         │  │ transfer form for  │
│ form               │  │  – Variations      │  │ stamping and pay   │
│                    │  │                    │  │ duty within 30     │
│                    │  │                    │  │ days, interest and │
│                    │  │                    │  │ penalties if late  │
└────────────────────┘  └────────────────────┘  └────────────────────┘
```

```
                        ┌──────────────────────────────┐
                        │ Stamp duty reserve tax (SDRT) │
                        └──────────────────────────────┘
        ┌──────────────────────────┼──────────────────────────┐
        ▼                          ▼                          ▼
┌────────────────────┐  ┌────────────────────┐  ┌────────────────────┐
│ Charge: 0.5% on    │  │ Exempt if no       │  │ Payable on 7th day │
│ paperless          │  │ consideration.     │  │ of month following │
│ electronic         │  │ Repaid if later    │  │ month of transfer  │
│ transfer of shares │  │ execute with       │  │ (or 14th day after │
│                    │  │ stamped transfer   │  │ the trade if via   │
│                    │  │ form.              │  │ CREST)             │
└────────────────────┘  └────────────────────┘  └────────────────────┘
```

```
                        ┌──────────────────────────────┐
                        │  Stamp duty land tax (SDLT)   │
                        └──────────────────────────────┘
        ┌──────────────────────────┼──────────────────────────┐
        ▼                          ▼                          ▼
┌────────────────────┐  ┌────────────────────┐  ┌────────────────────┐
│ Charge payable on  │  │ Exemptions:        │  │ Administration:    │
│ all transfers of   │  │  – Gifts           │  │ submit land        │
│ an interest in     │  │  – Divorce         │  │ transaction form   │
│ land (eg sales of  │  │  – Variations      │  │ and pay SDLT       │
│ freehold land,     │  │                    │  │ within 30 days,    │
│ assignment of      │  │                    │  │ interest and       │
│ leases, grant of   │  │                    │  │ penalties if late  │
│ leases) at between │  │                    │  │                    │
│ 0% and 7% of       │  │                    │  │                    │
│ chargeable         │  │                    │  │                    │
│ consideration, or  │  │                    │  │                    │
│ max 15% if         │  │                    │  │                    │
│ purchaser is a     │  │                    │  │                    │
│ company            │  │                    │  │                    │
└────────────────────┘  └────────────────────┘  └────────────────────┘
```

Self-test

Answer the following questions.

1. Harriet gives her shares in P Ltd to her husband on 1 December 2014 when they are worth £30,000.

   What stamp duty is payable?

   A   NIL – the transfer is between spouses
   B   NIL – if the transfer is certified on the stock transfer form as a gift.
   C   NIL – the transfer is for less than £125,000
   D   £30,000 × 0.5% = £150

2. H Ltd sells some shares in B Ltd to Q plc for £65,000 on 1 September 2014.

   The stock transfer form is not presented for stamping until 15 September 2015.

   What is the maximum interest and penalty which will be charged?

   Assume the rate of interest on late paid stamp duty is 3%.

   A   £300
   B   £309
   C   £325
   D   £350

3. Oliver sells his house to Emily in July 2014 for £140,000.

   What is the SDLT payable?

   A   NIL
   B   £150
   C   £1,400
   D   £4,200

4. Rodney grants a 10 year lease over a shop to Clarissa on 10 January 2014. The premium payable is £30,000 and the annual rental is £7,000.

   What is the SDLT payable?

   A   NIL
   B   £70
   C   £300
   D   £370

5. Kevin sells his house to Larry for £100,000 on 10 August 2014. It is now 12 December 2014.

   Which **two** of the following statements are **true**?

   A   Larry does not have to submit a land transaction form to HMRC.
   B   Larry does have to submit a land transaction form to HMRC.
   C   No fixed penalty will apply on the late submission of the land transaction form.
   D   A fixed penalty will apply on the late submission of the land transaction form.

6. **Hawks Ltd and Huxley House**

   Leopard Ltd prepares accounts to 31 January each year. Leopard Ltd is considering the following transactions, both of which would occur on 1 February 2015.

   (1) The purchase of shares in Hawks Ltd, a small UK trading company, for £53,000. Leopard Ltd would purchase 5% of the shares in this company, the remainder being held by individuals.

   (2) Entering into a five year lease on Huxley House. Leopard Ltd would use Huxley House as office premises. The terms of the lease involve Leopard Ltd paying a premium of £72,500 on 1 February 2015 and rent of £29,600 pa quarterly in advance. The landlord, Hepburn Ltd, has owned Huxley House for many years and also prepares accounts to 31 January each year.

   Requirements

   Describe the corporation tax and any stamp taxes consequences of the proposed transactions, using calculations to illustrate your answer.   **(7 marks)**

7   Rectangle Ltd needs to raise cash. It has decided to dispose of a factory to an unconnected property investment company, House Ltd, for £4.5m on 31 March 2015. House Ltd will then immediately lease the factory back to Rectangle Ltd on a 22 year lease. The annual rental will be £241,500 plus a lease premium of £432,000.

If House Ltd were to sell the factory with the tenants still in occupation it would be worth £4.3m.

The factory has a historic cost in Rectangle Ltd's financial statements of £945,000 (including land of £535,000); and its net book value is £725,000 as at 31 March 2015. The factory was originally purchased on 1 April 2008 as a newly constructed building.

Both Rectangle Ltd and House Ltd prepare their accounts and their annual VAT returns to 31 March. Rectangle Ltd pays corporation tax at the main rate and is VAT registered making wholly standard rated supplies.

Requirements

(i)   Calculate the net cash generated by Rectangle Ltd as a result of the sale of the freehold factory (ie deduct the tax due on the gain on disposal from the proceeds of sale).

(ii)   Explain, with supporting calculations, the implications of the capital goods scheme on the disposal of the freehold factory by Rectangle Ltd. You should include a discussion of the difference it would make depending on whether Rectangle Ltd makes an election to opt to tax the factory prior to its disposal.

(iii) Explain, with supporting calculations, the VAT and stamp taxes implications of the purchase of the freehold factory by House Ltd.

(iv)   Explain, with supporting calculations, the tax implications of the purchase of the lease by Rectangle Ltd.

(v)   Explain, with supporting calculations, the tax implications of the grant of the lease by House Ltd.

Assume an RPI for March 2015 of 262.3.   **(20 marks)**

Now go back to the Learning Objectives in the Introduction. If you are satisfied you have achieved these objectives please tick them off.

Technical reference

Legislation

Stamp Duty

Ad valorem duty on shares	Finance Act 1999 Sch 13 para 3
Exempt Instruments Regulations	SI 1987/516
Interest on late stamping	Stamp Act 1891 s.15A
Penalties on late stamping	Stamp Act 1891 s.15B

Stamp Duty Reserve Tax

References are to Finance Act 1986 (*FA 1986*)

The principal charge	s.87
Exceptions	s.90
Repayment or cancellation of tax	s.92
Definition of chargeable securities	s.99

Stamp Duty Land Tax

References are to Finance Act 2003 (*FA 2003*) unless otherwise stated

Land transactions	s.43
Rates of SDLT	s.55
Leases – amount of tax chargeable on rent	Sch 5 para 2
Exemptions:	
• No chargeable consideration	Sch 3 para 1
• Divorce	Sch 3 para 3A
• Variations	Sch 3 para 4
Filing of land transaction form	s.76
Payment of SDLT	s.86
Interest on late payment	s.87
Penalties on failure to deliver return	Sch 10 paras 3, 4

HMRC manual references

Stamp Duty Land Tax (Found at http://www.hmrc.gov.uk/manuals/sdltmanual/SDLTM00010.htm)

SDLTM00010 – Introduction to stamp duty land tax

SDLTM00050 – Introduction to stamp duty land tax – rates of tax

SDLTM10000 – Leases

See also Stamp Taxes guidance (Found at http://www.hmrc.gov.uk/so/index.htm)

See also Stamp Taxes: Stamp Duty Reserve Tax (Found at http://www.hmrc.gov.uk/sdrt/index.htm)

> This technical reference section is designed to assist you. It should help you to know where to look for further information on the topics covered in this chapter.

Answers to Interactive questions

Answer to Interactive question 1

Stamp duty

£882,800 × 0.5% = £4,414 rounded up to   £4,415

Interest

Due date: 10 January 2015
Paid: 15 February 2015
Days overdue: 35

$\frac{35}{365}$ × £4,415 × 3% = £13, as less than £25 there is no interest due   £NIL

Maximum penalty

Transfer presented up to one year late, so maximum penalty is lower of:

£300; and

£4,415 ie   £300

Answer to Interactive question 2

The rate of SDLT on the premium on the grant of a non-residential lease between £0 and £150,000 is 1% where the annual rent exceeds £1,000.

SDLT is therefore £45,000 × 1%   £450

1 B – NIL – if the transfer is certified on the stock transfer form as a gift.

2 A – £300

   Stamp duty is £65,000 × 0.5% = £325

   Interest

   Due date: 30 September 2014
   Paid: 15 September 2015
   Days overdue: 349

   $\dfrac{349}{365}$ × £325 × 3% = £9.32

   Less than £25 so not charged.

   Maximum penalty

   Transfer presented up to one year late, so maximum penalty is lower of:

   £300; and

   £325

   ie   £300

3 C – £1,400

   The rate of SDLT is 1% on the whole consideration, not just the excess above £125,000.

4 C – £300

   The rate of SDLT on the premium on the grant of a lease between £0 and £150,000 is 1% where the annual rent exceeds £1,000.

   SDLT on the premium is therefore £30,000 × 1%   £300

   No SDLT on rental as NPV is less than £150,000.

5 B and D

   A land transaction form must be submitted to HMRC even if the chargeable consideration falls within the 0% band.

   A fixed penalty will be charged if the form is submitted more than 30 days after the transaction, even if no SDLT is payable.

6 **Hawks Ltd and Huxley House**

   (1) **Purchase of shares in Hawks Ltd**

        Corporation tax

        The purchase represents an acquisition of a chargeable asset, upon which corporation tax will be payable on sale, unless the shareholding is sold in circumstances where the substantial shareholding exemption applies.

        Stamp duty

        Stamp duty of 0.5% on the consideration for the purchase of shares in Hawkes Ltd is payable ie £53,000 × 0.5% = £265

   (2) **Five year lease on Huxley House**

        Hepburn Ltd – Landlord

        Corporation tax

        The rent receivable for the year ended 31 January 2016 of £29,600 will be subject to corporation tax as Property Income for Hepburn Ltd.

The income element of the premium received will also be subject to tax as Property Income for Hepburn Ltd in the year ended 31 January 2016 as follows:

$$\frac{50-(5-1)}{50} \times £72{,}500 = £66{,}700$$

A chargeable gain will also arise on the grant of the lease in the year ended 31 January 2016.

The proceeds used in the gains calculation will be the capital element of the premium, ie £5,800 (£72,500 – £66,700). A part disposal calculation is then required using the premium, the capital element of the premium, and the market value of the reversionary interest, to determine how much of Hepburn Ltd's original cost of Huxley House can be deducted.

Indexation from the date Hepburn Ltd purchased the property to the date the lease was granted, will further reduce the chargeable gain.

Leopard Ltd – Tenant

Corporation tax

The rent payable of £29,600 will be deductible as an allowable trading expense for Leopard Ltd for the year ended 31 January 2016.

Leopard Ltd will also be entitled to a deduction against its trading profits for part of the lease premium paid. The trading profits deduction is calculated as the income element to the landlord/life of lease = £66,700/5 years = £13,340 pa.

Stamp duty land tax

Stamp duty land tax (SDLT) is payable on leases at the rate of 1% of the NPV of rent charged.

There is no charge where the NPV is less than £150,000.

In this case, no SDLT is payable on the rental.

However, SDLT is payable on the premium @ 1% × £72,500 = £725 as the annual rental exceeds £1,000 and so the zero rate band is not available.

7 Cash generated by disposal

The disposal of the factory will give rise to a chargeable gain of £3,341,430 (Working 1). This will give rise to additional corporation tax of £701,700 meaning that the sale will only generate cash of £3,798,300.

Capital goods scheme/option to tax

As the factory is more than three years old and assuming the option to tax was not exercised, there is no VAT to be charged on the sale. However, as the building is only seven years old and originally cost more than £250,000 it falls within the capital goods scheme. Therefore on an exempt disposal before 1 April 2018 there will be a claw back of some of the initial input VAT recovered:

Original input VAT recovered = £945,000 × 17.5% = £165,375

The sale adjustment under the capital goods scheme will be:

(£165,375/10) × (0% – 100%) × 3 intervals = £49,613 repayable to HMRC

Rectangle Ltd could opt to tax the building prior to its disposal. This would make the sale a standard rated supply. There would then be no sale adjustment under the capital goods scheme.

However, this may affect the purchase price payable by House Ltd, depending on whether House Ltd is prepared to opt to tax the building in order to recover the input tax paid. As House Ltd will be renting out the property it will be an exempt supply and the input tax would be irrecoverable unless House Ltd also opted to tax the building.

Stamp taxes and VAT implications of purchase for House Ltd

If both companies opt to tax the building, the VAT payable will simply be a timing difference for House Ltd. However, stamp duty land tax is payable on the VAT inclusive price. This is a permanent increase in price.

Opting to tax would enable House Ltd to recover any input VAT incurred on the expenses of the business. House Ltd would need to charge VAT on the lease premium and the annual rental. As Rectangle Ltd is VAT registered, this will simply represent a cash flow timing difference.

Stamp duty land tax will be payable on the purchase price of the factory at 4% ie £180,000 if a VAT exclusive sale or £216,000 if the purchase price is £4.5m plus VAT.

Tax implications of purchase of lease by Rectangle Ltd

SDLT at 3% will be payable on the lease premium inclusive of VAT. In addition, SDLT will also be payable at 1% on the net present value of the total lease rentals inclusive of VAT in excess of £150,000. Assuming there is no VAT on the lease, this will give total SDLT payable on the lease of £64,590 (Working 2).

Some of the lease premium will be treated as rental income for House Ltd and will therefore be allowed as additional deemed rent for Rectangle Ltd. The additional annual rent allowable as an expense for corporation tax purposes will be £250,560 / 22 = £11,389 (Working 3).

The lease rentals will be a tax deductible expense.

Tax implications of grant of lease by House Ltd

The grant of the lease is a chargeable transaction and will give rise to an allowable chargeable gain of £1,994 (Working 4). In addition, £250,560 of the lease premium would be chargeable as rent in the first year giving total property income in the first year of £492,060.

The lease rentals will be taxable income.

WORKINGS

(1) **Chargeable gain on sale of factory**

	£
Proceeds	4,500,000
Less cost	(945,000)
Less IA April 2008 to March 2015	
$\dfrac{262.3-214.0}{214.0} = 0.226 \times £945,000$	(213,570)
Chargeable gain	3,341,430

(2) **SDLT on lease**

	£
SDLT on lease premium at 3%	12,960
SDLT on NPV of lease premiums	
22 × £241,500 = £5,313,000 – £150,000 = £5,163,000 @ 1%	51,630
Total SDLT	64,590

(3) **Deemed additional rent**

	£
Deemed rent = £432,000 × [(50 – 21) / 50]	250,560

(4) **Chargeable gain on grant of lease**

	£
Capital proceeds (£432,000 × (22 – 1) × 2%)	181,440
Less deemed cost $\dfrac{£181,440}{£432,000 + £4,300,000} \times £4,680,000$ (ie incl SDLT)	(179,446)
Chargeable gain	1,994

Note. This style of question in the exam would be very challenging and there would therefore be more marks available than the maximum possible. It would therefore be possible to achieve full marks even if a few parts had been omitted. As the question contains some of the more complex parts of the syllabus, the style of the question is likely to be broken down with very specific requirements to help you answer the question as was given here.

Index

1982 pool, 407

Expense relief, 435
Exports, 470

U

Underlying tax (ULT), 435, 438
Unilateral relief, 434
Unit trusts, 345
Unrelieved foreign tax, 438

V

Valuation, 343

W

Wear and tear allowance, 52
Will trusts, 199
Withholding tax (WHT), 435
Writing down allowances, 146

Z

Zero rated supplies, 453

Notes

Notes

Notes

REVIEW FORM – TAX COMPLIANCE STUDY MANUAL

Your ratings, comments and suggestions would be appreciated on the following areas of this Study Manual.

	Very useful	Useful	Not useful
Chapter Introductions	☐	☐	☐
Examination context	☐	☐	☐
Worked examples	☐	☐	☐
Interactive questions	☐	☐	☐
Quality of explanations	☐	☐	☐
Technical references (where relevant)	☐	☐	☐
Self-test questions	☐	☐	☐
Self-test answers	☐	☐	☐
Index	☐	☐	☐

	Excellent	Good	Adequate	Poor
Overall opinion of this Study Manual	☐	☐	☐	☐

Please add further comments below:

Please return completed form to:

The Learning Team
Learning and Professional Department
ICAEW
Metropolitan House
321 Avebury Boulevard
Milton Keynes
MK9 2FZ
E learning@icaew.com